The
Continent
Steam   Tram

Frontispiece: Milan-Magenta No. 16 in Corso Vercelli yard, Milan, with coaches
which had wartime "utility" bodies on secondhand underframes, on
28th May 1951.   Photo: G. E. Baddeley 4045.

Cover Photo: Milan-Magenta No. 110 at Vercellese, just beyond the electric tram
terminus.   Colour Photo: F. W. Hunt.

The Continental Steam Tram

by

Geoffrey E. Baddeley, B.Com., M.C.I.T.

Published in London by

THE LIGHT RAIL TRANSIT ASSOCIATION

in association with

THE TRAMWAY AND LIGHT RAILWAY SOCIETY

1980

Printed by **NEMO PRODUCTIONS**, Hartley, Dartford, Kent.

Made in England.   Design by E.R.Oakley.

CONTENTS

Note – In the tables which appear at the end of each chapter, undertakings are listed in alphabetical order of the names of the principal places or districts served.

4

THE CONTINENTAL STEAM TRAM
by
G.E.BADDELEY

AUTHOR'S NOTE

In 1937, the late Dr. H. A. Whitcombe read a paper before the Institution of Locomotive Engineers, entitled "The History of the Steam Tram" and in 1954, Charles E. Lee used the material contained therein to produce a most interesting and readable book. In addition, Dr. Whitcombe left a large collection of notes and photographs to the Science Museum at South Kensington, London.

It is fair to say that this book sets out to provide an account of tramway locomotives, with particular emphasis on those constructed and used in Great Britain. Mr. Lee draws attention to this limitation and quotes from an appendix to the original paper, giving figures for the output of certain continental manufacturers and mentioning the countries to which they were exported. There is some reference to developments in Holland, Australia and New Zealand, with one illustration of a tramway engine in Australia, but little else about overseas tramways. On the other hand, the Science Museum collection does include a number of very interesting photographs of continental steam tramway locomotives and stock, particularly in Holland and Germany, together with a number of British and German manufacturers' photographs of locomotives built for a variety of overseas destinations.

It may seem a piece of impertinence of the present writer to attempt to follow in the footsteps of two so eminent authorities, but since seeing steam tramways in operation on the Continent of Europe during the 1939-45 war, it had been the writer's ambition to give a fuller account of the part that the steam tram played on the Continent of Europe, as a sequal and complementary to Dr. Whitcombe's work. As Dr. Whitcombe makes clear, British steam tramways were nearly all urban in character and enjoyed a very short life, in comparison with other forms of public transport. On the other hand, the majority of continental steam tramways were inter-urban and some were extremely long-lived, nevertheless, urban steam tramways on the whole fared little better than their British counterparts, being replaced by electric cars at an early date, except in a few cases where there were special reasons for their retention (i.e. Paris).

Since Mr. Lee's publication appeared, Ir. S. Overbosch, a correspondent of Dr. Whitcombe's has produced a fully detailed book about Dutch steam tramway locomotives; he called on the present writer when visiting England and has made much of his correspondence with Dr. Whitcombe available to him. In the book, "Les Tramways Français" Monsieur J. Arrivetz has made ample reference to those tramways in France which were worked by steam and the quarterly publication "Chemins de Fer Secondaires"* from time to time contains detailed articles on individual systems. Likewise, Mr. W. J. K. Davies has produced a general book on Light Railways and one about Minor Railways in France, both of which make numerous references to steam tramways and define the accepted differences between railways and steam tramways. There are numerous references to enclosed locomotives and steam operation on tramways in contemporary tech-

---

* now called "Chemins de Fer Régionaux et Urbains".

nical books, particularly in German ones. It is interesting to note, however, that Italy which was one of the best served, had the least written about its steam tramways. Dr. Whitcombe stated that while he was aware that it had many, he knew nothing about them. This is rather surprising, since official statistics show that sixteen undertakings were still operating steam at the time of his writing. In this respect, the present writer has been rather more fortunate, in being able to make a number of visits to Italy in the early 1950's, while a few were still working, obtain first hand information and contact the small but growing band of railway and tramway enthusiasts in that country. It is also very fortunate, that in spite of the absence of other written information, the Italian Ministry of Transport maintained very detailed statistics of all tramways and light railways and the writer has been shown their Annual Reports covering several widely separated years (1885, 1901, 1907, 1930 and 1956).

This book deals only with steam tramways which existed on the continent of Europe, but they are known to have existed in other parts of the world as well, notably, in the United States of America, Australia, New Zealand, India, a few in South America, North and South Africa and a very large concentration in the then Dutch East Indies, particularly Java, where at least two are still running at the time of writing. Many of these were of considerable interest, but the present writer must leave to others, the task of describing them. *

Naturally, in a work of this nature, it has been found necessary to invoke the assistance of a very large number of people, both at home and abroad and in fact, each chapter has been sent abroad for checking, in most cases several times. The writer would like to offer particular thanks to John H. Price, without whose suggestions and encouragement, this book would never have been attempted, his considerable knowledge of European geography and political history, together with various translations from German, have been invaluable. Special thanks also go to P. M. Kalla-Bishop, the well-known authority on Italian locomotives, whose advice and assistance has extended well beyond that sphere. Many others have assisted with advice and the loan of books, catalogues and works lists, in particular, G. S. Moore who has put up patiently with the writer's numerous enquiries over the past ten or more years. Experts in almost every country concerned, have come forward with information and checked material; many of them have recommended other experts, previously unknown to the writer, who have been equally helpful. Several of these experts have given useful information about steam tramways in countries other than their own, but owing to the numbers involved, the writer hopes they will excuse him if their names are mentioned only once in the list of acknowledgements below, under the country for which they gave the most important information. Sincere thanks

* Works describing steam tramways outside Europe:-
   (1). "Steam Tramways in New South Wales" W. Shellshear, Institute of Civil Engineers Journal, London, 1885.
   (2). "Lagos Steam Tramways", N. Miller, LRTL Booklet, London 1958.
   (3). "P. N. K. A. Power Parade" (Indonesia), A. E. Durrant, Harrow 1972.
   (4). "Steam Tramways in Surinam" Article in "Modern Tramway" May 1968. J. G. Todd & J. H. Price.
   (5). "Modern Tramway" August 1977 "Transport in Calcutta", T. V. Runacles.
   (6). "Modern Tramway" December 1970 "The Surabaja Steam Tram", J. G. Todd.

are extended to all of the following, for :-

General Information. - The late F. Merton Atkins, D. J. W. Brough, J. R. Day, A. E. Durrant, K. W. Clingan, G. L. Gundry, B. J. Hawkesworth, W. G. S. Hyde, F. Jones, H. Luff, J. H. Meredith, the late Dr. Hugh Nicol, W. Nicholls, R. T. Russell, D. J. Sibley, E. K. Stretch, W. J. Wyse.

France. - J. Chapuis, A. A. Jackson, J. H. Renaud, B. Rozé and S. Zalkind.

Germany. - P. Boehm, H. Bombe, R. Copson, H. Hinze, late F. Kemper, E. Konrad, S. Lossberger, P. J. Walker, G. Wandel, late E. J. Wolff and his son Gerd Wolff.

Luxembourg. - R. C. Riley.

Belgium. - F. van de Gragt, W. J. K. Davies, B. Y. Williams.

Netherlands. - Prof. Dr. H. J. A. Duparc, Ir. S. Overbosch, Prof. Dr. A. D. de Pater, B. H. Steinkamp, Dr. H. A. Vreedenberg.

Italy. - P. M. Kalla Bishop, G. Cornolò, G. Croci, M. Grillo, C. Marzorati, late Dr. G. Masino, G. Spaventa-Filippi, G. de Grisantis, G & M Sartori, Dr. E. Tascheri, E. Tonerelli.

Switzerland. - W. Hefti, J. Wiseman.

Austro-Hungarian Empire. - O. Bamer, Ing. M. Dvorak, F. Kraus, J. O. Slezak, H. Stern-hart, W. Vreedenberg, Dr. D. Szabo, N. N. Forbes.

Spain & Portugal. - R. Fraser, J. Ibanez, J. Morley, K. P. Plant, D. Trevor Rowe, G. Reder, J. A. Tartajo and F. Zurita.

Scandinavia. - N. Bonnesen, D. Cole, U. Diehl.

Eastern Europe. - R. F. Makewell, M. Murray.

Greece. - L. A. Constantinides, D. Dixon.

In addition the management of several operating undertakings have searched their files for historical information, particularly at Augsburg in Germany and at Ostrava in Czechoslovakia, while the following archives, musea and libraries have been consulted :-

The Archivist, Tramway & Light Railway Society, London.
Patent Office Library, Chancery Lane, London.
Science Museum, South Kensington, London (in particular the Whitcombe Collection).
British Museum Library, Holborn & Colindale, London.
British Railways' Archives, London (Now part of the Public Record Office).

Deutsches Museum, Munich, Germany.
Narodni Technicke Museum, Prague (Prague Technical Museum), Czechoslovakia.
Spoorwegsmuseum, Utrecht, Netherlands. (Dutch Railway Museum).
Eisenbahn Museum, Vienna, Austria. (Austrian Railway Museum).
Verkehrsmuseum Dresden, East Germany. (German Transport Museum).
Institute of Transport Library, London.

Several preserved railways which have tramway locomotives in stock have been visited and many of the above have been at great pains to check information for the writer. It should be put on record that at the Vienna Railway Museum, J. O. Slezak was able to arrange an introduction to the Director himself, who went to considerable trouble to meet the writer's request to see a preserved locomotive, then in store.

Although every effort has been made to achieve factual accuracy in the information presented and particularly in giving proper acknowledgment where it is due, in view of the length of time which has elapsed, since this work was started, the writer could have missed someone who gave important information in the early days and offers his sincere apologies to any whom he has failed to acknowledge. Sincere thanks are also due to E. R. Oakley, Mrs. J. Tribe for typing manuscript, D. W. Willoughby and the binders for all the trouble they have gone to in the exacting task of preparing this book, with all its unfamiliar languages and symbols and to all members of the L. R. T.A. Publications Committee and to the L. R. T.A. & T. & L.R.S. Joint Publications Committee for their help and advice.

London, June 1980.

CARMAGNOLA · Borgo Vecchio.   Pellazza edit.

"Passenger carriages were drawn by horses and farm carts by mules or oxen". Standard Henschel tram-engine and ox cart at Carmagnola between Turin and Saluzzo.
Commercial Postcard.   Courtesy: late Dr. G. Masino.

INTRODUCTION EN LANGUE FRANCAISE

En 1937 le docteur Whitcombe prononça un discours devant l'Institution of Locomotive Engineers à Londres, au sujet de l'histoire des tramways à vapeur et en 1954, Charles E. Lee transforma l'information contenue dans les fiches du docteur Whitcombe dans un livre "The History of the Steam Tram".

Naturellement ce livre traitait principalement les tramways à vapeur en Grande-Bretagne avec quelques mentions des tramways sur le continent d'Europe et dans les colonies britanniques. La collection des photos du docteur Whitcombe est déposée actuellement dans le Science Museum, South Kensington, Londres. Ils comprennent les locomotives carrossées construites en Allemagne et aux Pays Bas, pour les tramways dans les pays du monde entier.

Pendant et immediatement après la guerre de 1939-45, j'ai vu en exploitation, les tramways à vapeur qui existaient en France, en Belgique, aux Pays Bas et en Italie et j'ai cru qu'il faudrait les décrire dans un livre complémentaire à celui de Charles E. Lee, pendant que les renseignements restent encore disponibles.

J'ai reçu beaucoup d'aide de la part des experts dans les pays divers (une liste de leurs noms se trouve dans l'introduction en anglais et bien que quelquesuns m'aient donné des informations sur plus d'un pays, je m'excuse de n'avoir mentionné leurs noms qu'une seule fois). Je les remercie tous vivement.

Dans quelques pays, il existe une distinction juridique entre les chemins de fer secondaires et les tramways à vapeur (en particulier en Grande-Bretagne, en Allemagne et en Italie) mais dans la plupart des pays cette distinction n'est pas clairment définie; dans le cas de la France j'ai eu beaucoup de difficulte à decider lesquels étaient les vrais "tramways", mais par contraire, aux Pays Bas tous les tramways et les secondaires étaient denommés "Stoomtram".

Dans les tableaux qu'on trouvera à la fin de chaque chapitre, j'ai utilisé des initiales et des symboles pour indiquer les informations :-

(a). Chaque ligne est indiquée par sa longueur maximum (pendant l'exploitation par vapeur).

(b). Les dates indiquent seulement l'année de commencement et de termination d'exploitation et traitent au réseau entier (sauf indication contraire).

H. (Horse) année ou commença l'exploitation par traction hippermobile.

S. (Steam) "   "   "   "   à vapeur.

A. (Accumulator) " " "   "   par locomotives ou auto - motrices à accumulateurs.

P. (Petrol) "   "   "   "   "   "   à essence.

D. (Diesel) annee ou commenca l'exploitation par traction diesel

E. (Electric) "   "   "   "   électrique.

GS. (Goods) date ou la traction à vapeur pour les circulations ordinaires fut supprimée, mais la vapeur subsista pour les circulations à marchandises.

WS. (Workmen) date ou la traction à vapeur pour les circulations ordinaires fut supprimée, mais la traction à vapeur subsista pour les ouvriers.

GD & WD. Idem-mais traction diesel, pour les marchandises ou les ouvriers.

R. (Railway) date de transformation en vrai chemin de fer.

C. (Closed) date de suppression de chaque ligne autrefois exploitée par vapeur, même si elle était exploitée par une autre méthode à la date de suppression.

Aussi dans les tableaux, j'ai donné le nom du constructeur de chaque groupe de locomotives et la disposition d'essieux (ou roues :) dans la notation anglaise "Whyte", parce qu'il existe quelques systèmes divers au continent. J'ai donné aussi le numero et la date de construction et un symbole pour indiquer si la locomotive était completement carrossée, bicabine, à mécanisme couvert ou locomotive du type industriel sans couverture :-

Locomotive carrossée avec tôlage de protection et un toit sur toute sa longueur.

Locomotive "bicabine" carrossée, mais avec deux cabines separées.

Locomotive carrossée, mais avec boîte à fumée et cylindres exposés.

Locomotive à une cabine, mais avec mécanisme couvert par des jupes en tôle.

Locomotive carrossée à chaudière verticale.

Locomotive industrielle sans tôlage de protection.

Automotrice à vapeur à un étage du type "Rowan" etc.

Automotrice à vapeur avec impériale.

Z Locomotive equipée pour la circulation sur cremaillere.

(II)2 La deuxième locomotive du parc du réseau à porter le numero 2.

*: Locomotive achetée d'occasion, si originaire d'un autre réseau décrit dans ce livre, je donne le numero de renvoi. p. ex. Ex-No. 26 = rachetée au 26e tramway de ce même pays.

ZUSAMMENFASSUNG IN DEUTSCHER SPRACHE

Im Jahre 1937 hielt Dr. Whitcombe eine Vorlesung vor dem "Institute of Locomotive Engineers" in London über die Geschichte der Dampfstrassenbahnen, und 1954 wurde dieser Stoff von Charles E. Lee umgearbeitet und in einem Heft "The History of the Steam Tram" veroffentlicht.

Selbstverständlich berichtet dieses Heft hauptsächlich von den Dampfstrassenbahnen in Grossbritannien doch würden äuch einige Strassenbahnen auf dem Festland Europas und in den britischen Kolonien vorübergehend erwähnt. Das Archiv des Herrn Dr. Whitcombe ist jetzt im Naturwissenschaftlichen Museum in South Kensington (London) hinterlegt: darunter befinden sich mehrere Fotos von in Deutschland und den Niederlanden gebauten Dampfstrassenbahnloks für Länder in der ganzen Welt.

Während des Krieges 1939-45 und unmittelbar danach habe ich die damals noch überlebenden Dampfstrassenbahnen in Frankreich, Belgien, Italien und den Niederlanden in Betrieb gesehen, und ich dachte, solche Bahnen sollten in einem Buch beschrieben werden, dass das Heft von Charles E. Lee ergänzen wurde, während die nötigen Unterlagen noch vorhanden sind.

Fachleute aus verschiedenen Ländern haben mir viel Hilfe geleistet, (eine Liste von ihren Namen befindet sich in der Einführung in englischer Sprache; obgleich einige mir Auskünfte über mehr als ein Land gegeben haben, entschuldige ich mich, dass ich ihre Namen nur einmal erwähnt habe). Ich danke ihnen allen herzlich.

In einigen Ländern unterscheiden sich gesetzlich Dampfstrassenbahnen und Kleinbahnen (insbesondere in Grossbritannien, Deutschland, und Italien), aber in den meisten Ländern wird dieser Unterschied nicht anerkannt. In Frankreich ist es schwer gewesen zu unterscheiden, welche die echten „Strassenbahnen" waren, da im gegenteil in den Niederlanden sämtliche Strassen-und Kleinbahnen „Stoomtram" genannt würden.

In den Tabellen am Ende jedes Kapitels habe ich folgende Abkürzungen und Zeichen verwendet, um die gewunschten Angaben zu erklären:

(a) Für jede Strecke ist die Gesamtlänge zur Zeit des Dampfbetriebes angegeben.

(b) Die Daten beziehen sich auf die Eröffnung und endgültige Einstellung der ersten bzw letzten Strecke des ganzen Netzes (wenn nicht anders vermerkt)

(H) (horse): Jahr der Eröffnung des Pferdebetriebes.

(S) (steam): " " " " Dampfbetriebes.

(A) (accumulator): " " " " Betriebes mit Akkumulatorloks oder Triebwagen.

(P) (petrol): " " " " Betriebes mit Benzinloks oder Triebwagen.

11

(D) (diesel): " " " " Betriebes mit Dieselloks oder Triebwagen.

(E) (electric): " " " " elektrischen Betriebes.

(GS) (Goods): Datum woran der Dampfbetrieb für den gewöhnlichen Verkehr aufgegeben wurde, jedoch fur den Güterverkehr erhalten blieb.

(WS) (Workmen): Datum woran der Dampfbetrieb für den gewöhnlichen Verkehr aufgegeben wurde, jedoch für Arbeiterverkehr erhalten blieb.

(GD & WD): Dasselbe, aber bezieht sich auf Dieselbetrieb für Güter - bzw Arbeiterverkehr.

(R) (Railway): Datum des Umbaus auf „echte" Eisenbahn.

(C) (Closure): Datum der Einstellung von jeder früher mit Dampf betriebenen Strecke, auch wenn andere Betriebsmittel zur Zeit der Einstellung verwendet wurden.

Auch habe ich in den Tabellen die Baufirma und Bauart jeder Lokreihe angegeben. Bauarten sind nach dem englischen System „Whyte", worin nicht Achsen sondern Räder gezählt werden angegeben, weil auf dem Festland Europas verschiedene Bauartbezeichnungssysteme verwendet werden. Ich habe auch Baunummer und Baujahr angegeben, und die folgenden Zeichen verwendet, um Karosserie bzw Aussehen der Loks anzuzeigen:

„Kasten"- lokomotive mit Blechverkleidung und mit Dach uber ihrer Gesamtlänge.

Lokomotive mit zwei getrennten Führerhäusern und Verkleidung über den Rädern. („Zweikabinenlok").

Lokomotive mit Blechverkleidung und Dach aber ungeschützten Rauchkammer und Zylindern.

Lokomotive mit einem einzelnen Führerhaus und mit Blechverkleidung nur über dem Triebwerk und den Rädern.

„Kasten" - lokomotive mit Stehkessel.

Industriebahnlokomotive ohne Verkleidung.

Einstockiger Dampftriebwagen (Bauart „Rowan" u. dgl.).

Doppeldeck- Dampftriebwagen

Z   Fur Zahnradbetrieb ausgerustete Lokomotive.

Zweite Lokomotive eines einzigen Netzes mit der Nummer 2.

∵ „Aus zweiter Hand" gekaufte Lokomotive; wenn ursprünglich von einem anderen in diesem Buch beschriebenen Netz, wird die Hinweisnummer dieses Netzes angegeben; z.B Ex-No.26 = von dem Netz Nr 26 desselben Landes gekauft.

"In the Netherlands, Some tramway locomotives looked rather like mobile chests of drawers". No.9 of the "S.A.Vicinaux Hollandais" a Belgian-owned tramway at 's Hertogenbosch.
Tubize Catalogue.   Courtesy: Prof.A.D.De Pater.

The earliest type of Krauss tram engine, their class XXXVIa (36a), supplied widely in the early days to tramways in Germany, Bohemia, Italy, Spain and even South America. This particular example is thought to have been for Naples.
Photo: Science Museum London - Whitcombe Collection 9650.

INTRODUZIONE IN LINGUA ITALIA

Nell'anno 1937 il Dr. Whitcombe pronunciava un discorso davanti alla "Institution of locomotive engineers" a Londra, sulla storia delle tranvie a vapore, e nel 1954 Charles E. Lee integrava le informazioni contenute nella relazione del Dr. Whitcombe con un libro, dal titolo "The history of the steam tram". (La Storia del Tram a Vapore).

Naturalmente questo volume trattava principalmente delle tranvie del Regno Unito, con qualche nota sulla tranvie delle Colonie e del Commonwealth e su quelle di altri paesi europei. La stessa raccolta di fotografie, consegnata dal Dr. Whitcombe al Science Museum di South Kensington, a Londra, contiene poche fotografie di locomotive tranviarie costruite in Germania e in Olanda per altri paesi.

Durante e subito dopo la II^a Guerra mondiale ho visto personalmente in esercizio tranvie a vapore in Francia, Belgio, Olanda e Italia, e ho quindi ritenuto utile trattare la storia di queste Amministrazioni, integrando in un libero che possa completare l'opera del Dr. Whitcombe, e di Charles E. Lee.

Ho ricevuto notevole aiuto da parte di esperti ed appassionati della materia di vari paesi - un elenco degli stessi appare in calce all'introduzione in lingua inglese - e voglio qui tutti ringraziare per aver reso possibile il completamento di questa opera. Ogni nome e dita una volta solo.

In alcuni dei paesi considerati esisteva una distinzione giuridica tra ferrovie secondarie e tranvie, particolarmente in Inghilterra, Germania e Italia, ma nella maggiorparte degli altri paesi non è ben chiara la distinzione tra i due tipi di strada ferrata.

In Francia ad esempio era molto difficile discernere tra le vere tranvie e le ferrovie secondarie, ed in Olanda poi venivano chiamate tutte allo stesso modo: "Stoom Trams".

Nelle tavole che si trovano al termine di ogni capitolo ho utilizzato una opportuna simbologia al fine di sintetizzare meglio i dati salienti di ciascuna amministrazione:

(a). Di ogni linea è indicata la massima estensione al tempo della trazione a vapore (non sono considerate eventuali estensioni delle linee doppo l'elettrificazione).

(b). Le date indicano rispettivamente l'anno di attivazione e di soppressione dell'esercizio a vapore. Le estensioni attivate sin dall'origine con altro sistema di trazione non sono menzionate.

(c). H (Horse)   - Anno di attivazione della trazione a cavalli (animale)

S (Steam)   - Anno di attivazione della trazione a vapore

A (Accumulator) - Anno di attivazione della trazione a accumulatori

P (Petrol)   - Anno di attivazione della trazione con locomotive o automotrici a benzina

D (Diesel)   - Anno di attivazione della trazione con locomotive o automotrici a nafta

E (Electric)   - Anno di attivazione della trazione elettrica

GS(Goods Steam) - Anno di soppressione della trazione a vapore per
i treni viaggiatori, ma suo mantenimento per i
treni merci

WS(Workmen Steam) - Come sopra, ma mantenimento della trazione
a vapore per i soli treni-cantiere(per lavoranti)

GD & WD   - Come sopra, ma trazione con motori termici
per treni merci e cantiere

R (Railway)   - Anno di conversione della tranvia in ferrovia.

C (Closed)   - Anno di soppressione della tranvia, anche se
esercitate con sistema diverso da quello originario
all'epoca della soppressione.

In aggiunta, nelle tavole ho indicato anche il nome del costruttore delle singole locomotive, il rodiggio, secondo lo schema inglese "Whyte", (perche sono sistemi diversi nei altri paesi) nonche il numero di costruzione di ogni locomotiva, cosi come appare dai cataloghi delle case costruttrici, ed infine un simbolo per indicare lo stile della locomotiva, se completamente o parzial-mente cabinata, a meccanismo coperto o scoperto, disposizione della caldaia, ecc.

Locomotiva cabinata con tetto su tutta la lunghezza

Locomotiva con due cabine separate

Locomotiva parzialmente cabinata, con camera fumo e gruppo cilindri non protetti

Locomotiva non cabinata, ma con ruote e meccanismo di distribuzione coperti da grambiulatura

Locomotiva cabinata, ma con caldaia verticale

Locomotiva industriale non cabinata

Automotrice a vapore, senza imperiale, tipo Rowan, ecc.

Automotrice a vapore con imperiale

z   Locomotiva per tranvia o ferrovia a dentiera

(II)   La seconda locomotiva della stessa amministrazione a recare lo stesso numero n° 2)

∵   Locomotiva acquistata d'occasione. Se proviene da un'altra amministrazione menzionata in questo libro, appare apposita menzione. Es.: ex n° 26. Significa che la locomotiva citata proviene dall'amministrazione n° 26 dello stesso paese.

15

"The skirting was hinged at the top and could be lifted up for maintenance of the motion". SNCV No.494 (Class 4) of 1908 in a yard off the Chaussée de Haecht, Brussels. This loco had just brought in a double headed goods train from Antwerp and a short section in the middle at Haecht was not electrified. The electric loco which it had piloted carried on to the City centre. June 1945.

Photo: G.E.Baddeley 287.

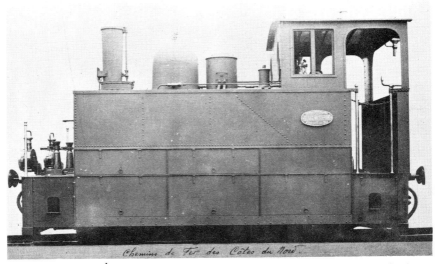

Some tramways permitted the use of locomotives which had only the wheels and motion covered and an ordinary cab at the rear. Chemins de Fer des Côtes du Nord, France, Nos.1-17.

Tubize Catalogue.   Courtesy: Prof.A.D.De Pater.

1. INTRODUCTION & GENERALITIES

The object of this book has already been defined in the "Author's Notes", which precede this chapter. The main difficulty encountered in preparing this work, was one of definition or deciding how much to include and how much to leave out. The terms "Steam Tramway" and "Light Railway" must in many cases be regarded as a distinction without a difference; so far only in the cases of Great Britain, Germany and Italy has the writer been able to find a clearly stated legal difference between the two. He has therefore, limited the scope of this book to descriptions of those undertakings which used enclosed locomotives and those regarded by title or legal status as tramways. This must inevitably lead to the exclusion of many interesting lines, but most of those excluded were really light railways, a subject on which, by comparison, there already exists an abundant supply of literature. Lines which were definitely railways, but for some special reason used enclosed locomotives and those which were railways when steam operated, but subsequently converted to electric tramways are mentioned, but not necessarily described in full detail.

Development of Steam Tramways

Although there were numerous experiments with steam traction on street tramways in the early 1870's, their serious operation on the Continent of Europe may be said to have begun with the services worked by Mr. Palmer Harding in Paris in 1876. These were followed by the introduction of regular services in Germany and Spain in 1877 and in Holland (The Netherlands) and Italy in 1878. Within a few years, many tram routes, both urban and inter-urban, were being worked by steam in a number of European countries. It can be said that, generally urban working was short-lived, as traffic soon built up sufficiently to justify electrification, which before long became an attractive alternative. On the other hand, steam operation on many inter-urban lines, where by comparison the amount of fixed equipment required made electrification more costly, lingered until quite recent times. There were still some tramways in the Netherlands and Italy, working some passenger journeys by steam until the late 1950's, while others continued as long with goods operation and one, the Chiemseebahn, in South Germany survives as a tourist attraction to this day. It is the long-lived inter-urban lines which form the principal point of distinction from British experience.

Perusal of contemporary literature, shows that the main distinction between a tramway and a light railway, which existed in the minds of those who legislated and constructed, was that while a railway ran on its own right of way, a tramway ran on or beside public roads. Nevertheless, many continental light railways had long stretches of roadside track and as many tramways had deviations and "short cuts" on private track. In the Netherlands, all steam tramways and light railways were known by the general term "Stoom Tram" and included some down-graded main line railway branches.

In the days when steam tramways were first developed, the only other forms of transport common on public roads were animal drawn; passenger carriages were pulled by horses and farm carts by mules or oxen. Small wonder then, that the authorities should be concerned about the effect of a locomotive, with its clouds of steam and shrieking whistle, would have on domestic animals. One contemporary writer maintained that if a frightened horse were led up to a locomotive and made to smell it, its fear would disappear. The outcome in most cases was an insistance by the authorities that all working parts should be concealed from view. The additional British requirement that locomotives should consume their own smoke, does not appear to have been insisted upon by continental operators, except in the very early days. Hence, the condensers which looked like spring matresses on the roofs of British tram engines were not often seen on their continental counterparts except in the case of some early Winterthur machines from Switzerland.

The Enclosed Locomotive

Dr. Whitcombe points out in his book, that the first steam trams were self-propelled cars with the engine and passenger accommodation mounted together on one underframe; this, however led to a number of technical difficulties, because of the lack of space available for the boiler and moving parts and it was difficult to make them controllable from either end. Although the "Rowan" car enjoyed a period of success in a number of European cities, self-propelled cars were only developed extensively in Paris. The separate locomotive, often referred to as the "Dummy" was the answer to this problem. The enclosure of its wheels and motion was a legal requirement in most countries, but the insistence by some Italian local authorities that the engine must "resemble the passenger carriages" does not appear to have been taken seriously. Some efforts in this direction were made by early British manufacturers, who fitted drop windows and waist rails to the side covering of their locomotives, but only the American "Baldwin" tram engines were enclosed in a really saloon-like body and none of these ever saw service in Europe.

The orthodox tramway locomotive was enclosed in an all-over cab, at first made of timber by some British manufacturers, but normally of sheet steel. The chimney, safety-valve and whistle protruded through holes in the roof and doorways were usually provided in the side panelling for the use of the crew. For some reason some early machines built by Henschel in Germany and some early British manufacturers put them in the end sheet (presumably to give through access to the carriages).

It is interesting to observe how the "enclosure" regulations were interpreted in different countries and by different manufacturers. In the wet and windy Netherlands, some locomotives were so much closed in with a collection of folding and sliding plates that they looked rather like a mobile chest of drawers. On the other hand, in warm and sunny Italy, covering over the wheels and motion was soon found to cause overheating and these plates had a habit of "getting lost". From the earliest days, the firm of Krauss of Germany provided this covering in the form of a row of plates hinged at the top which could be turned up to expose the motion for maintenance, and for this purpose, a row of catches was fixed high up on the side sheeting, to retain them in the upturned position while the fitter was at work. In fact the engines of the Turin-Giaveno tramway in Italy appear to have always run with their "skirts hitched up" thus. The Krauss arrangement was certainly most practicable and their example, was

18

soon followed by other manufacturers. However, the early Henschel machines had a fixed skirting only covering the upper half of the wheels (it had to be supplemented locally where the authorities insisted on full covering); it was omitted altogether on some of their later models. At the same time, some Belgian inside-cylinder tram-engines had a solid fixed skirting, in which were cut two large apertures for oiling and maintaining the coupling rod bearings. The covering normally came to within a few inches of the rails.

A feature not always appreciated, is that the majority of tramway engines had well tanks, since in most cases, the external sheeting gave the appearance of side tanks. A few early British machines had saddle tanks. Side tanks were to be found on the Belgian locomotives of the "Tubize" design, but practically all other types had the tanks below the footplate. In the case of outside cylinder machines, such as the Krauss design, the frames were closed in top and bottom and at the ends to form a box, through which the axles passed in tubes and this box formed the water tank. On inside cylinder engines, the tanks were usually shaped to occupy the space ahead of the smokebox and behind the firebox, the frames being shortened to make room for them. Either arrangement gave a low centre of gravity and permitted the crew to walk from end to end unobstructed.

Although the introduction of the Wilkinson Patent tram engine popularised vertical boilers in Great Britain, they were little used on the continent, except in self-propelled cars. Basically, a tramway locomotive was a normal steam engine with a horizontal boiler and other fitments of normal design, but of small proportions. In general, it was the simplest and most robust machines which gave the best service. Since tram engines were only smaller versions of railway locomotives, we have not gone into detail here about performance and other such technical matters.

Control of the Locomotive

Most supervising authorities stipulated that "the driver must have a good view ahead at all times and be able to control his machine when travelling in either direction" or words to that effect. The means by which this was achieved, tended to follow two schools of thought; some engines, such as the Belgian "Tubize" type, had the essential controls (regulator handle, brake and reversing lever) duplicated, so that they could be driven from either the smokebox or firebox end and they usually had wide glass windscreens, which gave excellent visibility when travelling in either direction. However, as they had side tanks, it was impossible for the crew to pass from end to end and the fireman had to always remain at the firebox end. The only way that these locomotives could be worked by one man, was to arrange the route so that the engine could be turned at either end and always run firebox leading (after the style of Kitson engines in Britain).[1] This practice was adopted by one Dutch tramway and possibly one in France. A derivitive of the "Tubize" design, probably only found in France and Ireland, was the side tank locomotive with two separate cabs, one at each end of the tanks. In France there were also some unenclosed locomotives, designed to always run cab leading.

Although the Swiss "Winterthur" tram-engines were of quite distinctive design, they also had two driving positions and duplicated controls, often with the regulator on top of the dome worked by a rod running along inside the roof and a suspended handle at each end just above the driver's head. They had well tanks, but as the cylinders were invariably above the footplate, it was necessary to climb over them to get from end to end, a practice not to be recommended while the engine was in motion.

By contrast, most German tram engines and some others, had only one driving position, usually on the left-hand side of the boiler, where the driver had an excellent view to his left, a reasonable view to the front, but a rather restricted view to the right, an embarrassment which increased as boilers grew larger and the number of domes, sand boxes and other accessories multiplied. On these engines, the regulator handle issued from the side of the dome and the other controls, such as the reversing lever and the brake handle, were located as near to it as possible; many manufacturers even located the firebox door to the left hand side of the box, so that the locomotive could be driven by one man and fired without moving out of reach of his controls. With this layout, it was no longer necessary to leave a space between the smokebox and the front sheeting, although most builders left sufficient for doors (usually the double-opening "oven door" type) to be opened; Krauss and some other German manufacturers actually incorporated the smokebox door in the front sheet, and this gave a rather pleasing appearance.

As the regulations about enclosure came to be interpreted less strictly in later years, many authorities were prepared to accept locomotives of ordinary outline, with only the wheels and motion covered. These of course, had the controls in a rear cab like a railway locomotive. Later still, authorities in some countries (particularly France and Italy) ceased to object to completely unenclosed industrial type machines working on street tramways. Even rack locomotives were to be found on five European steam tramways. They adopted the Riggenbach system [2] as it was the only one suitable for use on a paved steet. A number of tramways in France were worked successfully with fireless loco-motives, but there were unsuccessful experiments with them in the Netherlands and Great Britain (Croydon). We might almost include Mekarski compressed air locomotives and cars, used extensively in France and elsewhere, as they were driven through cylinders and conventional valve gear, but had containers of compressed air instead of boilers. We have excluded experiments with loco-motives deriving heat from the combination of certain chemicals, eg., ammonia, soda, etc., as they appear to have had no practical impact on future dev-elopment.

Braking

Tram engines were commonly fitted with screw handbrakes operated by a vertical column and handle. In fact the bulbous windscreens of standard Belgian engines were so designed to allow for the sweep of the handle. However, Krauss fitted their engines with weighted lever handbrakes. After various experiments with chain and other semi-automatic braking systems, at the end of the 19th century, most steam tramways turned to continuous braking, which was made compulsory in France in 1937. Austrian and some French tramways chose vacuum brakes, but most other preferred the Westinghouse compressed air brake, complete with pump and reservoirs. The latter were often mounted along the cab roof. The only large operator not to widely adopt continuous brakes was the Belgian S.N.C.V., who, on their narrow gauge lines, relied on the steam brakes of the locomotive to stop the train. Even they had to fit their standard gauge engines with Westinghouse brakes, so that they could work with main line stock.

Buffer and Coupling Arrangements

Some form of combined centre buffer and coupling was normally accepted tramway practice and the earlier steam tramways usually had a kind of link and pin on the end of a fairly long coupling bar. Numerous other types were subsequently in use. Most tramways equipped with rolling stock from Belgian manufacturers, were supplied with vehicles fitted with a square centre buffer and a screw coupling beneath, where it appears to have been difficult to get at when coupling up. The Grondana coupling invented and common in Italy, looked similar, but had a curved face and the screw-coupling above, the buffer being pushed outwards and the coupling held back by a volute spring between them. This appears to have been a very satisfactory arrangement. Some standard gauge tramways anticipated a considerable interchange of goods traffic with main line railways and consequently fitted all their stock with screw couplings and side buffers; among these were the Bologna-Malalbergo tramway in Italy and the Westland tramway in the Netherlands.[3] Others compromised and fitted only centre buffer tramway couplings to their passenger stock, but dual-equipped their locomotives with both side and centre buffers, etc. These included the Grande Banlieue system of Paris, both Verona and Vicenza and also the Giaveno line at Turin in Italy and Brünn (now Brno in Czechoslovakia). Even the metre gauge Plettenburger tramway in Germany fitted side buffers slightly offset to one side to some of its locomotives, so that they could pull standard wagons on three rail, mixed gauge track. The Belgian Vicinal system which had both three and four rail sections of mixed gauge, had some dual-equipped locomotives and some match trucks to interpose between metre gauge locomotives and standard gauge wagons.

Visible and Audible Warning

Rather unexpectedly, the steam tramway locomotive was one of the quietest forms of road transport. The late Dr.Hugh Nicol, a friend of Dr.Whitcombe, once said that the noise was so soft that it sounded as if the locomotive was running on methylated spirit on the drawing room floor.[4] The present writer can vouch that they were quiet from his own experience in Belgium, the Netherlands and even Italy, during and just after the 1939-45 war. This led controlling authorities to pay considerable attention to the form of visible or audible warning to be adopted on steam tramways. Some interesting light is thrown on this subject in an Italian booklet published in 1885,[5] in which the undertakings in the Province of Lombardy were listed according to whether they used flags, bells, whistles or trumpets for warning. Presumably the "trumpets" were those squeaky little horns so popular among continental railway guards. The tables also show whether a man with a red flag was required to walk in front of or beside the train when proceeding through a built-up area and whether the locomotives were fitted with "Parascintile" (Spark-arresters) or "Scaracapietri" which were small brushes fixed low down on the buffer beam to remove stones and other objects from the track. These little brushes were most common in the Netherlands, as one might expect from the Dutch tidy habits, but for the same purpose, some German and Italian tramways had bunches of willow twigs pushed through a ring just above each rail. Often above this there was a fitting that looked like an inverted step; it was in fact a socket into which a lifting jack could be inserted in the event of a derailment.

Not unnaturally, the steam whistle was the most common form of audible warning; those on the Belgian-built locomotives of the Bari-Barletta tramway in Italy, gave out a high pitched shriek like a French main-line railway engine, but on the other hand, the later-built engines delivered to the Rotterdam steam tramway carried a deep-tones hooter, more akin to a ship's siren and perhaps this was not out of place as the first few miles of the line ran in close proximity to the docks. Early Krauss tram engines carried a gong on the roof as a standard fitment and many others, particularly in the Netherlands, had large brass bells. It is reported that the original locomotives of the Tramways Bretons, at St.Malo in France, had no means of audible warning and therefore the drivers were equipped with trumpets. With their later machines, this company went to the opposite extreme, fitting whistles and bells which tolled continuously while the engine was in motion. 6 Many German-built engines had steam-operated bells, which sounded like banging a tin plate with a wooden spoon. French "Fireless" locomotives had hand operated klaxons, as presumably the steam in the reservoir was too precious to use for a whistle.

Very few steam tramway trains carried any indication of their destination. The Paris-Arpajon and the Milan-Magenta both carried small boards on the front of the locomotive as both had branches and operated short workings. Some of the Belgian "Vicinal" locomotives in the Ostend area, for a time carried three boards along the side above the tanks. Some other lines had small boards on the sides of the carriages and in the early days a few steam tramways had a title including the names of the places served displayed on their carriage sides.

Names, Numbers and Liveries

Those readers who know of the writer's interest in colour schemes may be surprised to find very little reference to that subject in this book. In fact, very little information is available on that aspect of steam tramway operation and it would appear that a large number of undertakings, particularly in France, adopted an uninteresting shade of dark green for both locomotives and carriages, However, certain manufacturers appear to have had standard liveries in which they delivered locomotives, if not instructed to the contrary (see German Chapter). There were a few more enterprising operators who adopted distinctive liveries and where details are known, they will be mentioned in the text.

One of the more pleasant features of steam tramway operation, was the custom of naming locomotives. Germany and Belgium were the two principal exporters of tram engines and the supply of locomotives with names was noticably more prevalent among the former. Evidently the German manufacturers realised the advertising value of a nice polished brass name plate. Names were usually taken from places served, including "Gorgonzola", where one of the Milan steam tramways had a depot, but occasionally locomotives were named after famous people or even directors of the company.

Many tramways which bought second-hand locomotives did not bother to remove name plates from them, and they are shown in brackets in the tables.

22

Some others transferred name places from their own old locomotives about to be scrapped.

Generally tramway locomotives were numbered in the conventional way, with brass numbers on the side of the locomotive, often painted as well on the buffer-beam. Some tramways under the control of a railway undertaking numbered their tramway locomotives and carriages in the same series as the railway stock, while others used Roman figures to distinguish them and Cherbourg, in France, lettered their engines A to H. A few tramways used the French railway system of making the first figure of the number denote the number of axles or class of locomotive and several smaller Italian tramways, which acquired engines second-hand from a larger neighbour, left the old number on them, especially if it looked impressive and was much higher than anything they were likely to acquire new. Just a few tramways did not number their locomotives at all and knew them only by their names, or builder's works numbers.

Many continental authors go to great trouble to quote the initials by which each undertaking was known, as well as giving its title in full. The present writer finds this rather tedious and has only given initials separately, when those displayed conspicuously on locomotives and stock, were not immediately obvious from the official title. e.g., Verona & Vicenza Provincial trams used the monogram "vTv".

Although a few tramways were in a position to return engines to the manufacturer or to a main line railway workshop for major repairs, the majority had to be self-sufficient and undertake quite formidable tasks in small workshops tucked away at the backs of their depots. Although most British tramways burned coke to prevent the emission of black smoke, coal "briquettes" were preferred on the Continent and some tramways with depots in urban surroundings took water direct from the town mains with a hosepipe. The scale on which depots and stations were provided varied very considerably from one system and country to another. Some examples are mentioned in chapters dealing with individual countries.

Passenger and Goods Stock

The pioneer builder of passenger stock for European tramways was George Starbuck of Birkenhead.[7] He built single and double deck cars suitable for either animal or steam traction. They usually had seven or more side windows, with fancy shaped coloured glass lights above each. Although British tramways formed Starbuck's principal market, he did build cars for Continental tramways, several of which used them as trailers with steam locomotives; among these may be mentioned Cassel in Germany, Copenhagen in Denmark, Geneva in Switzerland and Oporto in Portugal, all of which were using Starbuck cars with steam traction in the late 1870's.

In the late 1880's, the Falcon Works at Loughborough (which later became The Brush Electrical Engineering Co. Ltd.), became well known not only as a builder of locomotives, but also the very large double-deck bogie trailer cars, favoured by British steam tramways; these enormous vehicles were forced upon the British operators by the refusal of the authorities to permit an engine to pull more than one car, therefore it had to be as large as possible to get the most economical use out of the locomotive. Such regulations did not obtain in other countries and in most, one tended to find little trains of several small cars and baggage vans. Those cars exported, although sometimes on bogies, were almost invariably single deckers. In fact, there were very few double deck trailers at all on continental steam tramways. Such as did exist included, the original cars at Hamburg, one or two at Valencia in Spain (built by G. F. Milnes, Starbuck's successor) and a few at St. Petersburg and Odessa in Russia. The only place where double deckers, both in the form of trailers and self-propelled cars, were common, was Paris.

Before long, continental coach builders were also constructing stock for tramways and among the earliest was F. Grondana of Milan, Italy, who built light-weight passenger and goods stock for many of the earlier Italian steam tramways. The most prolific builder and exporter of tramway stock was the Nivelles works in Belgium, which was part of the "Métallurgique" organisation, who equipped a large number of Belgian, French, Italian and Spanish tramways. Their earlier carriages were usually four wheelers with plain elliptic roofs, six or more drop windows either side and open end platforms closed by fancy gates. Similar vehicles, including matching luggage vans, were turned out at the same group's works at Blanc Misseron in France and by builders in other countries. Most of the earlier vehicles were adapted from horse tramcar designs and were very light, with perhaps the underframe strengthened to take account of the drawbar pull of the locomotive. It was soon found that steam traction required something more substantial and locomotives of increasing power, tended to be matched by heavier passenger stock, the tendency being away from the traditional horse-car designs towards the light railway pattern, particularly in those countries where the distinction between light railways and tramways was very lightly drawn. Although frowned upon in Belgium and Italy, heavy bogie stock became common in some other countries, particularly the Netherlands.

There is little to say about goods stock on continental steam tramways, as although extensively used, it was almost entirely of ordinary light railway design. As mentioned below, several tramways were laid out to accept mainline goods stock and this did present some difficulties over the type of rail to be used. The wheel-flanges of main-line stock are too deep to run in ordinary grooved tram rails and unless the expedient of Glasgow, Huddersfield and Portsmouth were employed, ie., tightening the gauge to 4ft. 7$\frac{3}{4}$ins. trucks would derail. This does not appear to have been done anywhere on the continent, but some towns in the former Austro-Hungarian Empire used very heavy rails with an extra deep groove which would accept main-line flanges, while some French systems used ordinary flat-bottomed railway rails with a continuous check rail for all sections laid on the streets. This was an effective but rather cumbersome solution to the problem. Some narrow gauge tramways carried main-line stock on transporters (see German Chapter).

Sources of Information

The greater part of detailed information quoted in this book, is obtained from old technical books and periodicals or from Maker's Catalogues and Works Lists. (See appendix for list). The majority of European works lists were extracted by the late Dr. Schmeiser of Vienna or by G. S. Moore of Beckenham. When extracting information from works lists, there are certain pitfalls of which the reader should be warned. The lists give the names (in abreviated form) of the undertakings who placed the orders for the locomotives; in some cases there were large financial groups who owned a number of separate tramways and distributed their purchases at random among the systems which they controlled. (In such cases where it has proved impossible to say to which they went, or where they were moved around from time to time - locomotives are shown under the heading of the owning group). In other cases locomotives never reached the destination for which they were intended, but finished up on some other line. On the other hand, some manufacturers claimed credit for loco- motives which they had only assembled from a set of parts supplied by a larger manufacturer in another country. Such machines usually received numbers on the lists of both manufacturers. (ie., Henschel and Hohenzollern machines built in Germany and assembled by Cerimedo in Italy). While on this subject, it should be noted that there were two separate manufacturers trading under the name "Breda". The above mentioned Cerimedo, later became S.A.Ernesto Breda, of Milan, while the Dutch firm of Backer en Rueb, of the town of Breda, took the name "Machinefabriek Breda" in later years. Fortunately neither exported engines into the territory of the other. On the other hand, the Krauss establishments at Sendling in the suburbs of Munich, Germany and at Linz in Austria were two branches of one firm, using a common works list.

There were even notes and catalogue "photographs" of locomotives for tramways which never opened. Sometimes the locomotives were completed, photographed and then sold off elsewhere, but sometimes existing photos of similar locomotives were "doctored" and engines occasionally appeared wearing the name and number plates of another of the same class, presumably because the particular locomotive of which the customer wanted a photo, was not ready when the photographer called at the works.[8] In later years in some countries, there was a healthy trade in secondhand or reconditioned tram engines, and unless an enthusiast happened to spot them and note the works number, it was very difficult to establish their former ownership.

This chapter would appear to be the only suitable place to mention collectively, those British tramway locomotives that were exported to the continent. Some of the earliest were built in London by Merryweather and ran in Paris, Barcelona, the Hague, Cassel, Oporto and Vienna. They were followed by a few Hughes and Fox Walker machines in France. These early engines were light machines, in fact often too light to stand up to continental working conditions and the only place where British tram-engines gained a foothold, was Spain. Continental engines were even less popular in Britain, where one Winterthur for Sunderland (162 of 1879, Brown's Patent) was followed by two similar machines built locally by Hawthorns when Brown returned to England. Reports that another was supplied to Guernsey are not confirmed,[9] although a Lewin engine incorporating some of Brown's features did work there for a time. It is also recorded that two German Krauss tramway engines worked on the Wolverton & Stony Stratford tramway[10] but Krauss records account for four (Works Numbers 1861-1864 of 1887) and it is stated that they were built narrower than their standard model with the boiler slightly offset to one side, to comply with British regulations, and still leave room for the driver to stand beside the boiler. The fireless locomotives for Croydon, mentioned elsewhere, were Hohenzollern 0-4-0's, 319-324 of 1884 (apparently imported but not used).

Nomenclature

One difficulty which cannot be lightly dismissed, was that of place names and national frontiers. Two major wars have taken place since steam trams began to operate in Europe and each has been followed by numerous changes in national boundaries, accompanied in almost all cases by changes in the names of towns, which have been unfortunate enough to find themselves on a different side of the frontier. Even where names have not changed completely, there have often been irritating changes in spelling and the reader of tables in this book must not be surprised if he finds the name of a place spelt differently in the heading and in the list of routes, either for the above reason or because the tramway was owned by a holding group with its head office in another country who preferred their spelling of the name. In Germany C was replaced by K in many place names in the early 1920's and the Dutch language was officially simplified in 1946, and Flemish which differed in a few aspects was brought into line at the same time. In order to present a picture most in keeping with the epoch when steam tramways were developed, the writer has decided, not without much heart-searching, to keep to names and nationalities which were in vogue before the 1914-18 war, with suitable notes where necessary.

In some countries, Switzerland and Belgium for example, more than one language was (and is) in use in different regions of the country. As far as possible, we have given names in the language correct for the region in which the tramway operated, with the alternative name in brackets.

Tables

In the tables of undertakings to be found at the end of each chapter, considerable pains have been taken, involving several years of research, to list all known steam tramways in Europe, but it would be too much to claim that the lists are 100% complete. Although the Ministries of Transport in some countries, (particularly Italy) issued detailed statistics of tramway undertakings under their jurisdiction, indicating motive power and other features of each in turn, no similar information with official backing is available from other countries. Undertakings are listed by Countries, in alphabetical order of the names of the principal places served on each system, cross referenced as necessary. The numbers given before the titles of undertakings are there for reference purposes only and should not be taken as an indication of the number of tramways in each country. Names of undertakings are given with some reserve, as in some cases they have been noted from works of reference in languages other than that of the country concerned. In other cases (particularly Italy) changes in ownership and title were so frequent that the writer could not hope to give all variations and generally titles of owners who took over on or immediately prior to electrification, are not included.

Although for some time considered impracticable, works numbers are given in all cases where they are available, as they add the ring of authority, but a few of the smaller French manufacturers do not appear to have allocated them and those for the Merryweather and Falcon companies are given with some reserve, being obtained only from some hand-written notes in Dr. Whitcombe's folios. (There has been some recent research by G. Toms of Loughborough). (See overleaf).

Table 1

In order to condense the information given in the tables, within the limits of a reasonable sized book, the lists of undertakings are tabulated as follows:

(a). Lines are indicated by their furthest terminals and lengths given in kilometres, as at their maximum length as used for steam working. Extensions made on or after electrification are not included.

(b). Dates indicate only the year of first and last operation and relate to the undertaking as a whole unless otherwise stated.

(c). Locomotives are described by the generally accepted abbreviation of the title of the manufacturer, followed by the wheel formation, using the British "Whyte" notation, as there were three different notations in vogue on the Continent, ie., the French, German and Swiss. This is followed by the works number and date.

(d). The following symbols are used in the tables :-

H - (Horse) The year in which animal traction started on lines subsequently worked by steam, or date of reversion to animal working after steam working had been given up.

S - (Steam) First date of steam operation on any line of the undertaking.

A - (Accumulator) Date when all or part of the operation of a steam tramway was taken over by electric battery railcars or locomotives.

P - (Petrol) Date when operation was taken over as above with petrol cars or locomotives.

D - (Diesel) As above but diesel cars or locomotives.

E - (Electric) Date when all or part of a steam tramway is converted to electric traction. If steam is retained for certain services only, that is noted in brackets or as below.

GS - Date from which ordinary operation with steam is replaced, but there is still a steam goods service on the line.

WS - Date from which ordinary operation with steam is replaced, but there are still workmen's journeys operated with steam.

GD-WD As above but diesel goods and workmen's services.

R - Date when upgraded to a proper railway. (Details are generally not furnished for locomotives supplied after that date).

C - Date of final closure of a line formerly worked by steam, even if worked by some other form of traction at the time of closure. Lines still providing a railed service at the time of publication are shown as "Still Operating", irrespective or whether steam, diesel or electric at the time.

Z - Locomotives equipped to work on the rack.

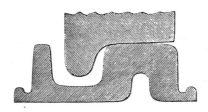

Cassel Tramway-Section of rail and wheel-tyre

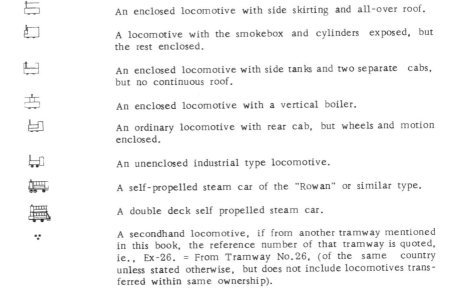

An enclosed locomotive with side skirting and all-over roof.

A locomotive with the smokebox and cylinders exposed, but the rest enclosed.

An enclosed locomotive with side tanks and two separate cabs, but no continuous roof.

An enclosed locomotive with a vertical boiler.

An ordinary locomotive with rear cab, but wheels and motion enclosed.

An unenclosed industrial type locomotive.

A self-propelled steam car of the "Rowan" or similar type.

A double deck self propelled steam car.

A secondhand locomotive, if from another tramway mentioned in this book, the reference number of that tramway is quoted, ie., Ex-26. = From Tramway No.26, (of the same country unless stated otherwise, but does not include locomotives transferred within same ownership).

These symbols should not be taken as giving an impression of the actual appearance of the locomotives.

Passenger and Goods Stock

Unfortunately, it has not been found possible to give details of passenger and goods stock in the tables, since apart from Italy, comprehensive information about their type and numbers does not appear to have been consistently available in a form suitable for tabulation.

For similar reasons we have not been able to quote scrapping dates of individual locomotives.

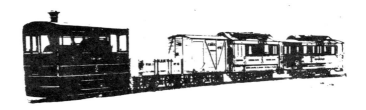

Continental Measures, Distances and Gauges

Because this book deals with European tramways and all available data was quoted in the metric system, the writer has left them thus and not attempted to convert them to feet and inches. For the benefit of British readers who may not be familiar with the metric notation, some equivalents in British measures are given below :-

1 Yard = 0-915 Metres.   1 Metre = 1.094 Yards.
1 Mile = 1.609 Kilometres.   1 Kilometre = 0.621 Miles.
1 Pound = 0.453 Kilogrammes.   1 Kilogramme = 2.205 Pounds.

Gauges :-

	British	Metric
Spanish & Portuguese	5'6"	1672mm
Irish Main Line	5'3"	1596mm
Russian	5'0"	1524mm
European Standard	4'8½"	1435mm
	(or 4'9")	(or 1440)
Glasgow, Huddersfield, etc.	4'7¾"	1416mm
North Lancashire, Reading, etc.	4'0"	1219mm
Italian minor railways	3'7½"	1100mm
Cape Gauge (Kaapspoor)	3'6"	1067mm
Metre Gauge	3'3"	1000mm
Italian Light Railways	3'1"	950mm
Three Foot (Ireland, Isle of Man, etc.)	3'0"	915mm
German contractors' railways	2'11¾"	900mm
Swedish Light Railways	2'11"	891mm
Austrian Light Railways	2'6"	760mm
Russian Light Railways	2'5½"	750mm
British Military Railways	2'0"	610mm
Decauville Light Railways, (France, etc.).	1'11½"	600mm

A few European tramways were constructed to other gauges not shown above, but from those given it should be easy to estimate the British equivalents of any others.

STEAM TRAMWAYS ON COUNTRY ROADS IN ITALY—ENGINE AND TRAIN, VERCELLI TRINO LINE

Notes

1. "Whitcombe" page 26.

2. The Riggenbach system could be built as a steel ladder embedded in the road surface, and the teeth on the locomotive's sprocket engaged in the spaces between the rungs and the ladder.

The tramways were at Appenzell, Neuchâtel (Switzerland), Naples (Italy), Filderbahn (Germany) and Wilanow (Poland).

3. The Bologna - Malalbergo Tramway served the Casaralta Carriage Works in the outskirts of Bologna and the Westland Co. served an intensive agricultural area around the Hoek van Holland.

4. See "Railways", April 1940, article on steam trams in Belguim by Dr. Hugh Nicol.

5. See "La Costruzione e l'Esercizio delle Tranvie" by A. Viappiani, Turin, Italy, 1893.

6. See "Chemins de Fer Secondaires" No. 33, September 1959, page 17. See also "La Vie du Rail" for 26th August 1963. Articles by J. Chapuis.

7. See "The Story of G. F. Milnes" by J. H. Price in "Modern Tramway", July 1964, page 239.

8. Overbosch, "De Stoomlocomotiven der Nederlandse Tramwegen" page 135.

9. "Locomotive Magazine" 15th April 1914, page 105, "Railways of the Channel Islands" by A. R. Bennett.

10. "Railway Magazine" August 1952, page 547. Article by Charles E. Lee on the Wolverton & Stony Stratford Tramway.

Manufacturers did not always put the right name plates onto locomotives if the official photographer called unexpectedly. This is one of the Westland Tramway's "Verhoop" locos in the Netherlands, but none of this class bore the name "Westland" in service.

Hohenzollern Catalogue.   **30**   Courtesy: Helmuth Hinze.

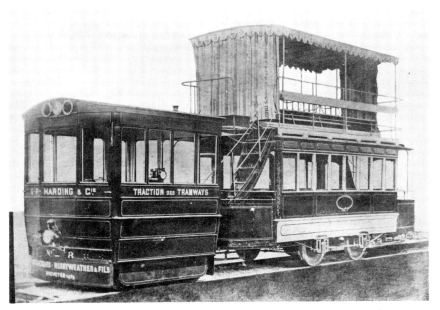

The first steam tramways to provide a regular service on the Continent of Europe were those in Paris worked by G. Palmer Harding, using small Merryweather and Fox-Walker machines. Some of each were later used at Rouen.
Both photos: Science Museum London - Whitcombe Collection 1169 & 1188

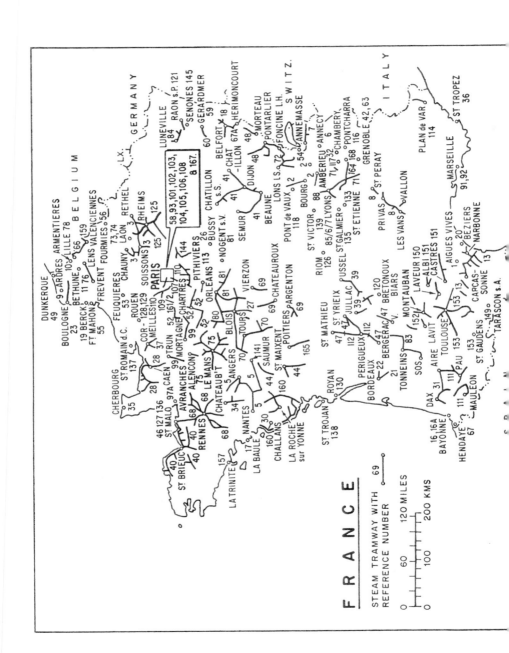

2. FRANCE

Paris had the honour of being the first city in Europe to introduce public passenger transport in 1662 and was also the first city on the mainland of Europe to operate a regular service with steam tramways. An Englishman named Palmer Harding brought to Paris, two very small enclosed locomotives with vertical boilers, built by Merryweather & Co., the London manufacturer of fire appliances. They underwent trials on the Porte de Chatillon-Saint Germain des Prés line of the Paris Southern tramways in November 1875. Slightly larger Merryweather locomotives with horizontal boilers were put into service on the Gare Montparnasse -Place Valhubert line in August 1876. However, it was soon shown that even these were too light for the job they were called upon to do, but too heavy for the lightly laid horse tram track on which they ran. Moreover, the streets of Paris were very muddy at that time and as these engines had inside cylinders, set below the footplate, their motion was very susceptible to damage from mud and flying stones. Harding persevered and next brought over some "Falcon" locomotives designed by Henry Hughes of Loughborough and some Fox Walker locomotives from Bristol, which were put to work on other routes of the Paris Southern tramways, but they were found to suffer from the same defects as the earlier machines. Such was the lack of reliability of these early engines, that about 70 of them were required to work a handful of short routes.[1] They were all withdrawn in February 1878 and these routes reverted to horse traction.

Undaunted, Harding removed the best of his engines to Rouen, where the track was said to be better laid and the streets less muddy.[2] Here, after some stronger rails had been laid, he was more fortunate and the steam engines ran successfully for seven years. One of the routes was on the opposite side of the River Seine from the others and the authorities were not prepared to let the locomotive cross the bridge under its own power, so it had to be dragged across daily by horses.[3]

There followed a short period when there were no steam trams on the streets of Paris, but later in 1878, a concession was granted to another under-taking, to use steam traction on the Arc de Triomphe-Courbevoie line of the "Tramways Nord" and the sponsors were greatly impressed by a Brown's Patent tram engine built at Winterthur in Switzerland, which was on show at the Paris International Exhibition of that year.[4] As mentioned elsewhere, the "Brown" design incorporated cylinders and motion above the footplate, driving the wheels through a rocking shaft, so that they were unaffected by mud. Seventeen loco-motives were ordered for this line, not from Winterthur (as previously stated), but built under licence to Brown's design by L. Corpet in Paris. In the meantime, urban steam tramway lines, using Hughes' machines were opened at Lille in 1880 and at St. Etienne with Winterthur machines in 1881.

The second phase began in Paris at about the turn of the century, when most other capital cities in Europe had already electrified their tramways; the Parisian authorities refused to permit the erection of overhead wires within the city area and in consequence a large variety of alternative methods of propulsion were employed by the several undertakings that provided tram services in the city. These included, as well as the costly slot conduit and less expensive but less reliable stud system, accumulator cars with electric traction, also compressed air cars and steam trams. Of all these, steam was probably the most reliable and Paris was the only place to make really extensive use of self-propelled steam cars. Some "Rowan" cars which were single decked and single ended were introduced in the first place to serve the 1889 exhibition and subsequently ran on a lengthy surburban route. Later, two of the companies built up quite large fleets of double-deck "Serpollet" cars. Later still there were some similar but lighter "Purrey" cars as well. Like the Rowan cars, these were also single ended and had to be turned at each terminus. Steam operation continued in Paris until 1910, when pressure from the authorities forced the companies into more widespread electrification, mainly on the conduit system. The change was accelerated by the serious flooding which occurred in that year and destroyed much of the existing equipment.

Two lengthy interurban lines entered Paris, from St.Germain en Laye and Arpajon respectively. The former was electrified in 1911, but although part of the Arpajon line from the Porte d'Orleans to Antony was electrified in 1901, the rest subsisted with steam until finally closed in 1936. (Trials with an internal combustion car resulted in a fatal accident).

Apart from Lille, Rouen and St.Etienne,[5] there were urban steam trams at several other French towns, including Lyon, St.Malo, Marseille (part in tunnel), Cherbourg and Saumur. For the mostpart these used locomotives, but there were self-propelled steam cars as well.

France was best known however, for the vast quantity of interurban steam tramways and light railways with which the whole country was liberally covered. They ran through the streets of small towns and for mile after mile along the grass verges of country roads. In fact their tracks half covered with vegetation were as typical of the French countryside as were the straight roads lined with tall pollarded trees. (The main line of the Tramways de l'Isère was so long that the journey could not be completed in one day.'). In this book, France is the country for which it has been found most difficult to draw a clear line of distinction between a tramway and a light railway. Legally, the position was not absolutely clear but it would appear that if over 70% of the line was on or beside a road, then it was classified as a tramway. Owing to the large amount of material offered by his French advisors the writer may have tended to be over-liberal in coverage in this chapter. As an example of the difficulty of definition, we mention the Chemins de Fer du Périgord, which used only enclosed locomotives, but in later years this company amalgamated with the Tramways de la Dordogne, none of whose locomotives was enclosed. Over the years, many other systems replaced enclosed locomotives by unenclosed ones, a change which was accelerated by the destruction of the 1914-18 war, in which French tramways suffered considerably. The Banlieue de Riems and neighbouring systems were used for military purposes by both the French and German armies at different phases in the war and the tramway serving the famous town of Armentières got "knocked about a bit".

Although the little tramway at Villiers le Bel was built at an early date to a peculiar gauge, the authorities soon stepped in and decreed that all tramways and light railways should be laid to standard, metre or 750mm gauges. However, after Decauville had demonstrated the practicability of the 600mm gauge, this was accepted instead of 750. The majority of tramways were constructed to the metre gauge and although there was an almost continuous network all over the country, a lack of uniformity in loading gauge, coupling arrangements and braking systems prevented much through running between the various undertakings in France or over the border on to the Belgian "Vicinal" system (as was attempted during the 1914-1918 war). Consent to use the 600mm gauge was largely brought about by the efforts of the Decauville company, who specialised in the construction of agricultural equipment including material for 600mm light railways originally for agricultural and constructional use. In fact, if one chose that gauge, the task of equipping a line was made comparatively easy, as from their works at Corbeil near Paris, Decauville could supply locomotives, carriages, wagons and even track already mounted on metal sleepers. Thus a complete tramway or light railway could be built up from a Decauville set of "kits" ordered from a catalogue. To demonstrate the advantages of that gauge and system, three steam tramways were actually built and equipped and then operated by Decauville in their early years. One was the Calvados, a straggling system in Normandy which was at first worked by unenclosed Decauville/Mallet articulated locomotives, but later used Belgian enclosed machines. The original section of this line, as laid by Decauville continued to operate until its career was abruptly cut short by the allied landings in the summer of 1944. (The writer saw some of the original metal sleepered track still in situ at that time). The seaside tramway at Royan suffered a similar fate and the third was Pithiviers à Toury, which more happily survived as an agricultural light railway until 1964 and part has more recently been reopened as a museum line, with various appropriate steam locomotives.

In France, in order to construct and operate a tramway or light railway, one had to obtain a "Concession" from the regional authority. These tended to be very specific and detailed in their requirements, often laying down which locomotives were to be used on a particular section of line, but in later years these edicts tended to go by default. Before the 1914 war, a number of French tramways were in the hands of holding companies, such as the "Compagnie Française des Voies Ferrées Economiques", "Chemins de Fer Economiques du Nord" etc., (not all of whose lines were in the North). Some of these were in turn owned by a group controlled by Baron Empain in Belgium. The rolling stock builders Carel et Fouché also owned two or three tramway systems. eg. Sarthe Loir et Cher, etc.

The story of France is something like that of Ireland, as outside the large towns, development was slow and did not follow the construction of tramways as had been expected.[6]   Even so a few lines managed to just survive the 1939-45 war; the Tramways Bretons at St.Malo continued to   use steam for through journeys until 1947, albeit with borrowed unenclosed locomotives, as their own had worn out before the war. On most of the other tramways the service had been decidedly thin for years (possibly worked by a variety of quaint railcars) and they were often eventually replaced by an even thinner bus service, without appearing to cause undue hardship. Several which served large factories, maintained a diesel goods service on a small part of. their line, long after the rest had closed. Two were even upgraded to standard gauge and became in effect main line sidings.

Locomotives

It has already been recorded how Palmer Harding introduced Merryweather, Hughes and Fox Walker locomotives to Paris and the reasons why they were not a conspicuous success have been recounted. In fact Merryweather locomotives were usually known in France as "Machines Harding". At about the same time in 1876, a Bollée self-propelled steam car, built at Le Mans was tried at several places and he subsequently built a small number of enclosed locomotives (used at Poitiers).

Following the demonstration of a Swiss "Winterthur" four coupled locomotive at a Paris Exhibition in 1877, the next tramway locomotives to appear on Paris streets were a batch built by L. Corpet to the Winterthur design, with tall fireboxes and the cylinders mounted above the footplate, driving the wheels through a rocking shaft. These were evidently reasonably successful, but were shortly followed by some Belgian Saint Léonard 0-4-2 tram engines, with the cylinders towards the rear and fitted with Vaessens' patent condensing equipment.[7]

Other urban steam tramways opened at an early date had a variety of locomotives supplied by several builders, including some more Hughes locos at Lille, Winterthur at Saint Etienne, Marseille and Lyon and Tubize machines at Valenciennes. These latter are of particular interest, since they preceeded the general introduction of the Tubize design in Belgium itself and may be said to have formed a testing ground for them.

Although it is rather difficult to describe a typical French tramway engine, the most interesting and perhaps the greatest break with tradition was afforded by the Lamm & Francq fireless locomotive. Based on the standard industrial fireless machine, a design suitable for tramways was produced in America by Dr. Lamm and was perfected in France by Monsieur Francq of the Cail engineering works in 1876. This design had several special features and incorporated instead of a boiler, a heavily lagged cylindrical reservoir of water, into which steam from a static boiler at the depot was forced under pressure, through a perforated pipe near the bottom and bubbled up through the water. By this means it was found possible to conserve a greater volume of steam than by the conventional method. These engines had ordinary cylinders and valve gear, were enclosed and could be driven from either end. Thus, provided that they did not have to operate too far from the static supply of steam, the design was particularly attractive to the tramway operator, as they were silent and gave off no offensive steam or smoke. The first Lamm & Francq locomotives were put on the road in 1878 on the Rueil-Port Marly tramway near Paris and soon followed on other tramways in the Paris area. They were also used at Lille, Lyon and on a line with an underground terminus in Marseille. The history and details of construction of these interesting machines are somewhat obscured by the fact that Francq set up a works of his own for the production of fireless locomotives, but the majority of them appear in fact to have been rebuilds of existing steam locomotives, while the later ones turned out to be rebuilds of the earlier fireless models. The final model produced was strictly not fireless, as it incorporated a small coke stove for superheating the steam. These latter, operated on the Saint Germain-Poissy tramway.

Some Lamm & Francq type fireless locomotives were built in Germany by

Hohenzollern, presumably under licence and were used in Java [8] where they lasted to the 1930s and for the unsuccessful experiments at Croydon in England.

Several of the earlier interurban lines had Belgian six-coupled locomotives, supplied by Tubize or St.Léonard, but after difficulty was experienced with import licences, the Métallurgique organisation which owned the Tubize works, set up a subsidiary assembly works on the French side of the frontier at Blanc Misseron, near Valenciennes. From here, over three hundred locomotives were turned out between 1885 and 1911, the earlier ones, although closely similar to the standard Belgian model, did not have windscreens nor a duplicate set of controls at the front end, later ones were identical to their Belgian counterparts, with works plates inscribed, "Ateliers de Construction du Nord de la France - Blanc Misseron" and carrying works numbers in their own list, but numbers for them were also allocated in the Tubize list. These machines are therefore shown in the lists that follow as, for example "Tubize(BM) 0-6-0, 679(17) of 1885". 679 being Tubize Works Number and 17 the Blanc Misseron number. Later some other locomotives were built to closely similar design by several French firms, such as Corpet, Pinguély, Decauville, Weidknecht and Buffaud et Robatel, [9] only a few in each case. At the same time the Franco-Belge organisation set up a workshop at Raismes, like Blanc Misseron, on the French side of the border, and they built a few enclosed locomotives there.

The standard gauge locomotives of the Paris-St.Germain tramway, were of the usual Tubize design but lacked windscreens, and had large spark arrester chimneys. Those of the Paris-Arpajon were similar, but had inside cylinders and peculiar divided windscreens, because the Paris police refused to allow glass directly in front of the driver. This line had a batch of three almost identical but slightly smaller machines for working goods trains of perishables at night over the Paris horse tram lines, whose track was lighter than their own. In the daytime, passenger trains were pulled over part of the same section by compressed air locomotives, later replaced by accumulator tractor cars. A late arrival in the Paris area was the Chemins de Fer de Grande Banlieue, which commenced operation in 1911 on some lengthy roadside lines in the countryside to the west and south of Paris. They absorbed two existing steam tramways and were physically connected to the Arpajon and Saint Germain tramways, so that they could run through goods trains at night to the vegetable markets (Les Halles) in the centre of Paris, (another proposed connection at Versailles was not completed). All the G.B. locomotives had inside cylinders because of tight clearances and the original stock were railway type 2-6-0 and 0-8-0 tank engines, but in 1926, eight enclosed 0-6-0 locomotives were acquired for the through perishable traffic. In France an enclosed locomotive is known as a "locomotive bicabine" and these latter were literally bicabine with two separate cabs, not connected by a continuous roof. The Pinguély locomotives for the Isère tramway and some Blanc Misseron machines for the Jura system also had this feature (as did certain tramway locomotives in Ireland).

The French authorities never appear to have been particularly strict about the total enclosure of tram-engines and machines with only the wheels and motion enclosed were fairly common from quite an early date. In later years many enclosed locomotives were replaced by ordinary light railway type 0-6-0 tank engines, the majority of which were built by L.Corpet (later Veuve Corpet et L.Louvet) or by Pinguély, each of which supplied over 100 locomotives to

French tramways, a figure no doubt swelled by post-war replacement of enclosed machines destroyed during the fighting. However the very last "Tubize" type locomotives built were for the Artois tramway, who in 1928, when their claim for "reparations" was at last recognised, still insisted on like for like and received three La Meuse enclosed machines. (One is now preserved at Hoorn in the Netherlands).

Several other firms in France supplied unenclosed 0-6-0, 2-6-0 and 0-6-2 tank engines to tramways and these included Weidknecht, Fives Lille, Batignolles and Piguet, but only a small number from each. The Weidknecht works list is not well documented and we only know the works numbers of a proportion of their locomotives. Piguet, Buffaud et Robatel and Aulnoye et Berlaimont were small firms which do not appear to have gone to the trouble of allocating works numbers to their products (except that one batch of Piguet machines was known by their official boiler numbers).

Paris was notable for the large number of self-propelled steam cars which worked on its tramways. "Rowan" cars first appeared in 1889 and were single deckers, which like the other types described below, could be driven from one end only and had to be turned at each end of the journey. They had a vertical boilered power unit mounted on a bogie at the front end and most had only a single axle at the rear. (The "Rowan" car is described in greater detail in Chapter 11, as it was first used in Scandinavia). The "Serpollet" car which appeared in 1895, was used extensively by two Parisian tram companies and in this case a double deck body was mounted on a massive plate underframe, with a short wheelbase, slightly towards the front of the body. The boiler, of the flash watertube type, was carried just behind the driver where the front stairs would have been and the roofed upper deck was open at the sides, but protected by a very solid bulkhead in front, behind which the chimney was concealed. One of these companies followed the Serpollet cars with some Purrey cars,[10] which were of similar appearance but more lightly constructed and capable of a better performance. A second batch of Purrey cars for the same company were single decked and pulled trailers. There were no single deck Serpollet cars in Paris, but they were to be found in Lille, Marseille, Saint Etienne and Cherbourg, while la Vallée de Celles, le Loiret, Reims and Saumur had single deck Purrey cars on urban services. There were also a few Rowan cars and some Pinguély cars with "Field" vertical boilers in the provinces. The Versailles-Maule line had two cars with a bogie at the rear, but permanently articulated at the front onto a very small vertical boilered Pinguély locomotive.[11]

Really outside the scope of this book, were the Mekarski and Popp Conti compressed air cars used in Paris and a number of other cities. The Mekarski cars used in Paris were of similar appearance to the Purrey cars and Mekarski locomotives were used on the Versailles line (from Paris, Louvre to Porte de Saint Cloud) and for Paris-Arpajon trains working over the Luxembourg-Porte d'Orleans section of the urban tramways. In 1907, those of the Versailles line underwent a very peculiar transformation and were converted to Purrey steam locomotives. In their compressed air guise they were six-coupled, but for steam operation the centre axle was removed and they became 0-4-0s. There was a central cab, from the roof of which, there protruded a tall smoke stack of square section and turned over at the top like a factory ventilator shaft; they pulled electric cars from the Porte de Saint Cloud to the Louvre until 1913, when the section within the city walls was electrified on the centre slot conduit system.

French tramways had little need to import motive power and after the very early years, most tramway locomotives were at least assembled on French soil. However, during the 1914-1918 war, a few captured enemy locomotives found their way as "reparations" onto French tramways and some built for American military light railways were acquired second-hand.

Rolling Stock, Stations, etc.

In the earliest days, ordinary horse tramway stock was hauled by steam locomotives and some of the cars were double decked. Later many of the urban tramway systems had long single deck vehicles mounted on bogies, often with centre entrances. Others had open sided crossbench cars; these were in regular use at Cherbourg and Saumur had some with a side corridor and wrought iron railings. However, most of the rural lines had small four wheeled vehicles with a single saloon and open end platforms. A large proportion of these came from the Nivelles works in Belgium and others of similar design from the Blanc Misseron works in France (both belonged to the "Métallurgique" Group). The output of the latter included the double deck cars used on the Paris-Arpajon tramway. Strange to relate, these were replaced in the late 1920s by other double deckers, but larger and mounted on bogies; they were in fact former Paris electric cars, gutted of all their electrical equipment.

For the narrower gauges, especially the 600mm gauge, Decauville produced a standard multi-windowed bogie car with open end platforms. They also supplied a bogie crossbench car with lattice underframes, a model which was popular with seaside tramways which carried holiday traffic.[12] The most popular livery for French steam tramways was a very dark green, lined in the early days and displaying the class in Roman numerals. Some lines brightened their trains by painting first class carriages red and the Côtes du Nord system painted their newer locomotives in a dark red colour. The Calvados locomotives were a rather lighter green, but the coaches were the usual dark green or red. In Paris, the Arpajon and St. Germain stock were the usual dark green, as were the Serpollet cars, but the Purrey cars were painted in a chocolate colour.

A few of the steam tramway lines had quite elaborate stations, for example, the terminal of the Tramways de la Sarthe at Le Mans was worthy of a main line railway[13] and that of the Côtes de Nord at St. Brieuc was hardly less imposing. On the other hand, nearby, the little tramway Dinard-Saint Briac ended with a turntable laid on the surface of a narrow street.[14] Like many others, this tramway ran through the town as a single track laid close to the kerb on one side of the road, so that trains running in one direction, inevitably had to proceed against the general flow of traffic, a situation which would have been quite unacceptable under present day conditions.

Intermediate stations on rural lines were often in the form of two storey houses, at the roadside, with the ticket office and waiting room on the ground floor and the station master's residence above. The name of the station would appear high up on the end walls, almost invariably painted in white letters on bright blue. Many of the intermediate stations on the Sarthe system were extremely simple with no points or passing loop, only a small turntable giving access to a siding. This system did not have a telephone network and experiments were carried out in later years, to keep in touch with radio telephones.

In French, they have unusual names for the different types of rail. Grooved tram rail is known as "Rail Broca", ordinary flat bottomed railway type is "Rail Vignoles", Bullhead rail is "Rail Double Champignon" (double mushroom) and track laid with a continuous check rail, so that it can be used by trams and main line railway stock, as on the Arpajon line, is "Rail Marsillon".

Notes

1. See "Les Tramways Parisiens" by J. Robert, Paris 1959.

2. See "Proceedings of the Institution of Civil Engineers", Vol. LXXIX, 1885, "Correspondence on Steam Tramways" describing replacement of bridge rails at Rouen in 1883.

3. See "Chemins de Fer Secondaires" No. 71, 1965, article "Les Transports Urbain de l'Agglomeration Rouennais" by J. Chapuis (also as booklet).

4. See "The Engineer" 24th May 1878, pages 361-361, for note on Winterthur locomotive at Paris Exhibition. See also "Engineering" 16th January 1850, pages 46-47.
See "Engineering" 28th July 1878, page 76, for Hughes' loco. in Paris.
See "Engineering" 9th March 1883, page 220, for Merryweather locos in Paris.

5. See "Proceedings of the Institution of Civil Engineers", Vol. LXXIX, 1885, for description of St. Etienne system.

6. See "French Minor Railways & Light Railways" by W. J. K. Davies.

7. See "The Engineer" of 16th August 1878, page 108, for illustrations and note on St. Léonard tram engines in Paris.

8. See "Engineering" for 1st September 1872, page 208.

9. The Buffaud et Robetal locos for the Pontarlier-Mouthe tramway had only driving controls at the front end and the fireman's position at the rear, so that they required a two-man crew and had to be turned at each end of the route. Otherwise they were of standard "Tubize" layout and appearance.

10. See France No. 105 in the tables.

11. As in Great Britain, many urban continental steam tramways had triangular layouts at terminals to avoid uncoupling locomotives. A few had turntables, laid on the surface of the street.

12. See "Light Railways" by W. J. K. Davies, page 222 and plate facing page 248.

13. See "Chemins de Fer Secondaires" article "Les Tramway de la Sarthe" by J. Chapuis.

14. See "Railway Magazine" photo and paragraph December 1929, page 397.

Notes on Tables

In accordance with the custom in France, accents are not shown on capital letters.
Mileages are based on information supplied by Messrs. B. Rozé and J. H. Renaud.

Table 2, FRANCE

1. AIGUES VIVES. (Compagnie Nationale des Chemins de Fer à Voie Etroite).
   Aigues Vives-Gare d'Aigues, 2.0 km.
   S.1892, C.1901. Gauge. 600.
   <u>Locomotives.</u> - Nos. 1-2, ? ?

2. AIN. (Compagnie des Tramways de l'Ain).
   From 1919 (Régie Départementale des Tramways de l'Ain).
   (Operated tramways and light railways, took over two existing steam tramways in 1919,
   at Ferney and Pont de Vaux). See Nos. 54 & 118.
   Ars-Amberieu, 50.0 km. (Not directly connected with other lines).
   Preau-St. Martin du Fresne, 14.0 km.
   Nantua-St. Martin du Fresne-Hauteville, 37.0 km. (E.1926).
   Bourg-La Madeleine, 72.0 km. (Not directly connected with other Lines).
   S.1911/20, part E.1926, D.1933, C.1937/54. Gauge. 1000.

<u>Locomotives.</u> -	Nos.	31-34,	Buffaud & Robatel	0-6-0	- - of 1904/05.	
		61-70,	Buffaud & Robatel	0-6-0	- - of 1910 ?.	"
		91-96,	Decauville	0-6-0	? - ? of 1913.	"
		1-16,	Corpet Louvet	0-6-0	639-654 of 1895/97.	"
		17-18,	Corpet Louvet	0-6-0	693-694 of 1898.	"
		51-53,	Corpet Louvet	0-6-0	781-783 of 1899.	"
		54,	Corpet Louvet	0-6-0	818 of 1900.	"
	(II)	1-2,	Schneider	0-4-0	1969-1970 of 1879.	"
	(II)	3,	Corpet Louvet	0-4-0	? of ?.	"
	(III)	1-2,	Buffaud et Robatel	0-6-0	- - of 1901 ex-No. 118	
	(III)	3,	Sornin ?	0-6-0	- of 1908. ex No.118.	"
	(IV)	1-2,	Winterthur	0-6-0	866&868 of 1894. ex No.54.	
	(IV)	3,	Winterthur	0-6-0	620 of 1890. ex No.54	
		103,	Corpet Louvet	0-6-0	1411 of 1913. ex ?	
	(II)	17-18,	Corpet Louvet	0-6-0	966-967 of 1904.	"
<u>Standard gauge.</u> -		1-4,	Buffaud et Robatel	0-6-0	- - of 1910.	"
(Haute Rhône line)		5.	Pinguély	0-6-0	371 of 1930.	"

   Names. - (II) 1-Chatillon, (II) 2-Marlieu, (IV) 3-Voirons.

3. AISNE. (Chemins de Fer Départementaux de l'Aisne).
   From 1922 (Compagnie des Chemins de Fer du Nord Est.)
   From 1952 (Régie des Transports de l'Aisne).
   (Light railways with some roadside running. Took over No.73 and lines of the Banlieue de
   Reims system in the Soissons area in 1919. See No.125. Converted the Soissons-Beaurieux
   and Guigniceur-Evergnicourt sections to standard gauge in 1921).
   Soissons-Oulchy Breny, 31.0 km.
   Soissons-Montécouvé-Vic sur l'Aisne, 38.0 km.
   Montécouvé-Guny, 9.0 km.
   Chauny-Blérancourt-Guny-Coucy le Château, 30.0 km. (mixed gauge).
   Soissons-Beaurieux-Guignicourt-Evergnicourt-Asfeld-Rethel. 71.0 km. ex No.125.
   Taken over 1919, Part p, - ? C.1959. Gauge. 1000. Part later 1435.

<u>Locomotives.</u> -	Nos.	1-3,	Corpet Louvet	2-6-0	1097-1099 of 1906.	
		4,	Corpet Louvet	2-6-0	1152 of 1908.	"
		5-6,	Corpet Louvet	2-6-0	1161-1162 of 1909.	"
		7-10,	Corpet Louvet	2-6-0	1179-1182 of 1910.	"
		11,	Corpet Louvet	2-6-0	1279 of 1910.	"
		12,	Corpet Louvet	2-6-0	1304 of 1911.	"
		13-15,	Corpet Louvet	2-6-0	1396-1398 of 1912.	"
		21,	Corpet Louvet	2-6-0	1469 of 1913.	"
		201-202,	Borsig	0-4-4-0	5465-5466 of 1905.	"
		31-34,	SACM	0-6-2	3950, 3958, 4051, 4053 of 1886/8.	"

   (Acquired secondhand in 1943 but not used).

   Names. - 31-St. Pourçain, 32-Chantelle. 33-St. Menoux, 34-Cosne.

4. ALPES MARITIMES. See Plan de Var. No.114

5. ANJOU. (Compagnie des Chemins de Fer d'Interêt Local de l'Anjou).
    Light railways with much roadside running).
    Angers-Noyant, 66.0 km.
    Saumur-Cholet, 81.0 km. (Connecting with No.141).
    Cholet-Beaupréau-Nantes,)
    Beaupreau-La Possonière,) 114.0 km.
    La Possonère-St.Jean de Linières, 12.0 km.
    Condé-St.Jean de Linières-Angers, 42.0 km.
    S.1893, P.1924, D.1934, C.1947/55. Gauge. 1000.
    Locomotives. -   Nos. 21-24, SACM   0-6-0   4239-4242 of 1892.   ⌴⌿
                             25-26, SACM   0-6-0   4443-4444 of 1893.   "
                             51-70, Tubize(BM) 0-6-0   955-974(114-133) of 1895.   "
                           101-104, Weidknecht 0-6-0   ? - ? of 1908.   "
                       3809, 3811, Decauville 2-6-0   670 & 672 of 1914.   "

6. ANNECY. (Compagnie du Tramway d'Annecy à Thones).
    Annecy-Thones, 21.5 km.
    S.1898, C.1930. Gauge. 1000.
    Locomotives. -   Nos. 1-3, Buffaud et Robatel 0-6-0   - - of 1898. °(Tubize type). ⊏⊐
                             4. Buffaud et Robatel 0-6-0   - of 1899.   "   "   "
                       ° Buffaud et Robatel are not known to have used works numbers.

7. ANNEMASSE. (Compagnie des Chemins de Fer Economiques du Nord).
    Known as (Réseau de Haute Savoie).
    Annemasse-Samoëns, 43.2 km. (Connecting with Switzerland No.6).
    St.Jeoire-Marignier, 7.0 km.
    Bonne sur Menage-Bonneville, 12.0 km.
    S.1891, E.1932, (GS to 1948), C.1959. Gauge. 1000.
    Locomotives. -   No.   26, Franco Belge 0-6-0 952 or 956 of 1894. ex No.63. ⋎   ⊏⊐
                             40, Weidknecht 0-6-0   ? of ?.   ⋎
                             51, Tubize(BM) 0-6-0   ? of ? ex-Valenciennes ?.   "
                       (II) 40,   ?   ?   0-6-0   ? of 1894.   "
                              6,   ?   ?   0-6-0   ? of ? ex-Valenciennes ?.   "
                             50,   ?   ?   0-6-0   ? of ?   "
                       35-39, Tubize(BM) 0-6-0 807-811(39-43) of 1891.   "
                          -. Serpollet Steam Car, 1895.   ⛟

8. ARDECHE. (Société des Tramways de l'Ardèche).
    Privas-Le Pouzin,   16.0 km.
    Privas-Aubenas,   33.0 km.
    Aubenas-Uzer,   14.0 km.
    Uzer-La Croizette-Les Vans,   23.0 km.
    Les Vans-St.Paul le Jeune,   13.0 km.
    La Croizette-Largentière,   4.0 km.
    Ruoms-Vallon,   9.0 km (Isolated line).
    Saint Peray-Vernoux,   31.0 km.   "   "
    S.1910, Part P. 1925, C.1914/1929. Gauge. 1000.
    Locomotives. -   Nos. 1-12, Piguet, 2-6-0   - - of 1910/1911. °   ⌴⌿
                         - -   Orenstein & Koppel 0-6-0   4801 of 1912 & 6005 of 1913. "
                       (II)   1, Orenstein & Koppel 0-6-0   4055 of 1910. ⋎   "
                          -, Borsig 0-6-0   7435 of 1910. Hired in 1913.   "
                       81-82, Pinguély 0-6-0   112-113 of 1902.   "
    Railcars. -   VAB.544-555, Purrey steam cars   - 544-555 of 1912.   ⛟
                       ° - Piguet are not known to have issued works numbers. (but see No.125).

42

9. ARDRES. (Compagnie du Tramway à Vapeur d'Ardres à Pont d'Ardres).
   Later worked by (Compagnie Générale des Voies Ferrées d'Interêt Local).
   as a branch of their Anvin-Calais line.
   Ardres-Pont d'Ardres, 6.0 km.
   S.1902, GS.1949, C.1955. Gauge. 1000.
   Locomotives. -

Nos.	1-2,	Corpet Louvet	0-6-0	- - of ?		
(II)	1,	Corpet Louvet	0-6-2	547 of 1892		
(II)	2,	Jung.	0-6-0	277 of 1897	(Formerly "11").	
	3,	Henschel	0-6-0	11393 of 1912.		

10. ARMENTIERES. (Compagnie des Chemins de Fer Economiques du Nord).
    From 1928 (Société Générale des Transports Départementaux).
    Armentières-Halluin, 24.8 km.
    S.1895, C.1930. Gauge. 1000.
    Locomotives. -

Nos.	15-16,	Tubize/BM	0-6-0	996-997(138-139) of 1896.	
	19,	Tubize/BM	0-6-0	1000(142) of 1896.	
	21,	Tubize/BM	0-6-0	1002(144) of 1896.	

Note. - CFEN was a large holding group and these locomotives were numbered in their general list.

11. ARTOIS. (Compagnie des Tramways de l'Artois).
    From 1919 (Compagnie des Chemins de Fer d'Interêt Local de l'Artois).
    Worked over by British and German armies during 1914-1918 war.
    Bethune-Estaires, 17.9 km.
    Bethune-Houdain, (Not constructed, but some locomotives officially allocated).
    S.1899, C.1932. Gauge. 1000.
    Locomotives. -

Nos.	A1-A3,	Weidknecht	0-6-2	? - ? of 1899.	
	B1,	Weidknecht	0-6-0	? of 1897 ex-Contractor.	
	BM1,	Tubize	0-6-0	462 of 1884 ex-No.66.	
	BM2,	Tubize	0-6-0	601 of 1885 ex-No.63.	
	BM3,	Tubize/BM	0-6-0	1001 (143) of 1896 ex-No.63.	
	BM5,	Tubize/BM	0-6-0	910 (80) of 1894 ex-No.42.	
	BM7,	Tubize/BM	0-6-0	912 (82) of 1894 ex-No.42.	

Name. - BM2-Maria, (BM1-2, originally came from the Bruxelles-Ixelles tramway).

Replacements. -

1,4,5,6,	SACM	2-6-0 7383-7386 of 1924.
11-13.	La Meuse	0-6-0 3337-3339 of 1928. (Tubize SNCV type).

Most of the locomotives were destroyed or requisitioned during the 1914-1918 war and some Schneider locomotives were then borrowed from the Côte d'Or Tramway to maintain the service until new machines could be acquired. Three Corpet Louvet locos (1618-1620) were ordered but the order was cancelled before they were completed.

12. AUBE. See LUNEVILLE, No.84.

13. AUDE. (Compagnie des Tramways à Vapeur de l'Aude).

Ouveillan-Narbonne-Fleury,	30.0 km.
Narbonne-Thézan,	27.0 km.
Lézignan-Fabrezan-Les Palais-Thezan-Ripaud-La Nouville.	54.0 km.
Ripaud-Tuchan,	25.0 km.
Fabrezan-Saint Pierre des Camps,	14.0 km.
Les Palais-Mouthoumet,	28.0 km.
Olonzac-Lézignan(Gare Midi),	15.0 km.
Carcassonne-Conques-Olonzac,	52.0 km.
Conques-Lastours,	11.0 km.
Castelnaudary-Belpech,	37.9 km. (Isolated line).
Fanjeaux-Bram-Saint Denis,	39.0 km.

S.1901/06. P.1926. C.1933. Gauge. 1000.

```
Locomotives. -   Nos.   1-3,   Corpet Louvet   0-6-0   776-778 of 1899.              ⊔⊓
                        4-8,   Corpet Louvet   0-6-0   785-786 & 789-791 of 1899/1900. "
                          9,   Corpet Louvet   0-6-0       751 of 1900.                "
                      10-12,   Corpet Louvet   0-6-0   792-794 of 1901.                "
                         13,   Corpet Louvet   0-6-0       755 of 1901.                "
                      14-23,   Corpet Louvet   0-6-0   795-804 of 1901.                "
                      24-26,   Corpet Louvet   0-6-0   805-807 of 1902.                "
                      28-35,   Corpet Louvet   0-6-0   809-816 of 1903.                "
                         27,   Corpet Louvet   0-6-0       932 of 1902.                "
                      36-37,   Corpet Louvet   0-6-0   1164-1165 of 1908.              "
                         38,   Corpet Louvet   0-6-0      1229 of 1909.                "
                      39-41,   Corpet Louvet   0-6-0   1370-1372 of 1912.              "
                      42-43,   Corpet Louvet   0-6-0   1495-1496 of 1914.              "
                       Two,   Unknown          0-6-0       ?      ? ex-Germany  ∵    "
```

14.   AULT.   See FEUQUIERES FRESSENVILLE, No.53.

15.   AVRACHES.   See 97A, NORMANDIE.

16.   BAYONNE. (Société Anonyme des Chemins de Fer à Voie Etroite du Midi). Before
      opening, then (Compagnie des Chemins de Fer de Pau-Oloron-Mauléon et du Tramway de
      Bayonne à Biarritz). (Baron Empain group).
      Bayonne-Allées Paulmy-Biarritz,   8.5 km.
      Allées Paulmy-Lycée de Marracq,   1.4 km.
      S.1888, E.1914, C.1948. Gauge. 1000.
      Locomotives. -   Nos.   1-6,   Tubize/BM   0-6-0   691-696(33-38) of 1887.   ⊏

16A. BAYONNE. (S.A. du Chemin de Fer de Bayonne à Anglet et Biarritz).
      A standard gauge railway with double deck stock, electrified as a tramway.
      Bayonne-Anglet-Biarritz, 8.0 km.
      S.1877, E.1922, C.1952. Gauge. 1435 (1000 on electrification).
      Locomotives. -   Nos.   1-3,   Schneider 0-4-2   1824-1826 of 1876. (Compound).   ⊔⊓
                              4-5,   Passy   0-6-0   -   - of 1878.   "   "
                              6-8,   Corpet Louvet 0-6-0   669-670 & 685 of 1896. (Simple). "
                             9-10,   Couillet   0-6-0   1564-1565 of 1910.   "

      Names. -   1-Bayonne, 2-Anglet, 3-Biarritz, 4- ?, 5-Dax, 6-Paris, 7-Biarritz,
                 8-La Négresse, 9-Bayonne, 10-Anglet.

17.   LA BAULE (formerly La Bôle). (Originally owned by Monsieur Aubry in 1887).
      became - (S.A. "Le Trait d'Union") in 1888.
      From 1904 (Société de la Tramway de la Baule au Pouliguen).
      A steam tramway constructed largely on private beaches from le Pouliguen to la Baule,
      extended in 1891 to le Vieux Pornichet. Abandoned in 1903, but rebuilt largely on the road
      from Pouliguen to la Baule only, in 1904, for use with petrol cars. These proved unreliable
      and steam working was restored.
      Le Pouliguen-la Baule-Pornichet, 7.6 km.   Gauge. 600.
      S.1887, C.1903. Rebuilt P.1904, H.1904, S.1907, C.1914 (requisitioned).
      Locomotives. -   Unnumbered Decauville 0-4-0   50 of 1887.   ⊔⊓
                                  Decauville 0-4-0   97 of 1891.   "
                                  Decauville 0-4-0   134 & 148 of 1892.   "

      Names. -   Francillon, Pornichette, Le Pouliguen & Pornichet.

      Replacements. -   1-2,   La Buire   0-4-0   -   - of 1909. (underpowered).   ⊥
                    (II) 1-2,   Decauville 0-4-0   Acquired in 1910, secondhand ? ∵   ⊔⊓

      Names. -   1-2 & (II) 1 unnamed.   (II) 2 "La Seine".

                                           44

18. BELFORT. (Compagnie des Chemins de Fer d'Interêt Local du Territoire de Belfort).
Electric tramways worked by steam 1922/23 after war damage.
Belfort-Chatenios-Sochaux,   16.3 km.
Belfort-Rechésy,   28.9 km.
Belfort-Les Errues-Etueffont le Haut,   16.0 km.
Les Errues-Rougement le Château,   6.0 km.
Les Errues-La Chapelle sous Rougemont,   5.0 km.
La Chapelle sous Rougemont-Sentheim,   9.0 km. (Military line).
E.1913, S.1922, E again 1923, D.1936, C.1932/48. Gauge. 1000.
Locomotives. -   Nos. 11-18, Baldwin   0-6-2   ? - ? of 1916 *(ex American Army).
                           37, Baldwin   0-6-2   44168 of 1916.
                          ?,   Orenstein & Koppel 0-8-0   ? of ?   "
                         Ten, Pinguély   0-6-0 of ?.   *   "
                      Twelve, Corpet Louvet 0-6-0   ? of ? *   "
                 Twenty eight, Baldwin   0-6-0   - ? of 1916. (ex American Army).* "

19. BERCK PLAGE. (Compagnie du Chemin de Fer de Berck Plage à Paris Plage).
Berck Plage-Paris Plage, 17.2 km.
S.1909/1912, C.1914, Reopened 1920, C.1927. Gauge. 1000.
Locomotives. -   No.   1, Decauville 0-6-0   512 of 1908.
                            2, Borsig   0-6-0   7434 of 1910.
                          3-4, La Meuse   2-6-0   2858-2859 of 1912. (Requisitioned 1914).
Replacements. -   (II) 3-4,   S.A.C.M.   2-6-0   7381-7382 of 1924.

20. BEZIERS. (Compagnie Régional des Tramways du Midi).
Later (Compagnie du Chemin de Fer sur la route de Béziers à la Mer).
Béziers-Serignan, 5.0 km.
H.1878, S.1879, E.1901, C.1948. Gauge. 1435 (1000 on electrification).
Locomotives. -   Unnumbered Corpet   0-4-0 246-248 of 1877. (not delivered).
                        "   Corpet   0-4-0 288-289 of 1879. (Brown's type).

Names. -   288-L'Hirondelle, 289-La Renaissance.

21. BORDEAUX. (Compagnie du Tramway de Bordeaux à Cadillac).
Bordeaux(Bastide)-Cadillac, 32.4 km.
S.1897, C.1935. Gauge. 1000 (part running alongside town tramways).
Locomotives. -   Nos.   1-3, Tubize/BM   0-6-0   975-977 (111-113) of 1895.
                            4-5, Tubize/BM   0-6-0   1234-1235(247-248) of 1900.   "
                            6-7, Tubize/BM   0-6-0   1617-1618(343-344) of 1909.   "
                            8-9, Tubize   0-6-0 - 1783-1784 of 1913.   "

Names. -   1-La Garonne, 2-La Pimpine, 3-L'Oeuille, 4-La Gaillardon,
                   5-L'Artoli, 6-L'Aubes, 7-La Jaugue, 8-Bordeaux, 9-Cadillac.

22. BORDEAUX. (Tramway à Vapeur de Bordeaux à Camarsac).
Owned by (Société Générale des Chemins de Fer Economiques).
Taken over by Departement in 1910, and by Bordeaux Tramways in 1921.
Bordeaux(Benauge)-Carmasac, 15.7 km. (On far side of level crossing
                                      from town tramways).
S.1900, E.1923, C.1953. Gauge. 1435.
Locomotives. -   Nos.3041-43, Corpet Louvet 0-6-0   702-704 of 1898.

Names. -   3041-La Benauge, 3042-Floriac, * 3043-Camarsac.
                   * 3042 may have been named Salleboeuf.

23. BOULOGNE. (Compagnie des Chemins de Fer Economiques du Nord).
Boulogne sur Mer-Colembert-Bonningues, 44.0 km.
Boulogne sur Mer-Le Portel, 4.0 km. (Worked by urban electric trams).
S.1899/1903, GS.1937, C.1947. Gauge. 1000.
From 1937 to 1947, the Colembert-Bonningues section was worked for freight as an extension
of an adjoining light railway .

Locomotives. -   Nos. 47-49, Tubize/BM   0-6-0   1161-1163(227-229), 1899.
                        51, Tubize/BM   0-6-0   1253 (261) of 1900.
                 (II)   23, Piguet 0-6-0   - of 1924, ex- ?
                 (II)   1? Corpet Louvet 0-6-0   1635 of 1925.

24. BRETENOUX BIARS. See Quercy, No.120.

25. BRETONS. See St.Malo, No.136.

26. BUSSY. (S.A. du Chemin de Fer de Bussy à Ercheu).
     Leased to (Société Générale des Chemins de Fer Economiques).
     Bussy-Ercheu, 13.0 km.
     S.1897, C.1954. Gauge. 1000.
     Locomotives. -   Nos. 3571
                             -3572, Nord 0-6-2   3601-3602 of 1897.
                       (Built in La Chapelle workshops of C.F. du Nord).

     Names. -   3571-Bussy, 3572-Beaulieu.

27. BLOIS. (Compagnie du Chemin de Fer de Paris à Orleans).
     Worked by Tramways à vapeur de Loir et Cher. See No.80.
     Blois(Vienne)-Cellettes-Saint Aignan-Noyers, 38.0 km.
     S.1899, C.1937. Gauge. 1000.
     Locomotives. -   Nos. Po1-Po4,
                             Weidknecht 0-6-0   - - of 1899. (Tubize Type).

28. CAEN. (Société Decauville ainé. Worked as "Tramway du Calvados").
     From 1895 (S.A. du Chemin de Fer de Caen à Dives et Luc sur Mer).
     Later (S.A. des Chemins de Fer du Calvados).
     from 1937 (Société des Courriers Normands).
     Really a light railway with street running in towns and on the roadside between them. All
     but one of the Tubize locomotives were enclosed. Mixed gauge with a standard gauge light
     railway between Luc sur Mer and Courseulles. *
     Caen-Benouville-Luc sur Mer-Courseulles-Ryes-Bayeux, 57.0 km.
     Benouville-Cabourg-Dives, 15.0 km.
     Ryes(Embranchement)-Arromanches, 2.5 km.
     Caen-Vaucelles-Falaise, 46.0 km.
     Bayeux-Port en Bessin, 10.6 km.
     Bayeux-Balleroy le Bourg-Saint Martin des Bésaces, 40.5 km.
     Balleroy le Bourg-Littry les Mines-Grandcamp-Isigny, 52.0 km.
     S.1892, Part P.1925, C.1944 (War destruction), Gauge. 600.
     (intermittent use of petrol railcars 1925-1939).
     Locomotives. -   Nos. 1-3, Decauville 0-4-4-0   74-75 & 109 of 1891.ex-No.130,
                             4, Decauville 0-4-4-0   173 of 1892.
                             5, Decauville 0-4-4-0   87 of 1891.
                             6, Decauville 0-4-4-0   72 of 1891. **(Tubize 736).
                             7, Decauville 0-4-4-0   110 of 1891. **(Tubize 806).
                     (II)   7, Weidknecht 0-6-2   ? of 1908. (Later 0-6-4).
                             8, Decauville 0-6-2   158 of 1892.   "   "
                      or (Weidknecht 0-6-2   542 of 1893. ?)**
                             9, Tubize/BM   0-6-0   986(135) of 1895. (Later unnumbered)
                      222-225, Tubize/BM   0-6-0   1146-1149(222-225) of 1899.
                      231-232, Tubize/BM   0-6-0   1207-1208(231-232) of 1900.
                      233-234, Tubize/BM   0-6-4   1209,1212(233-234) of 1900.
                      100-103, Tubize/BM   4-6-0   1307-1310(278-281) of 1903.
                      104-108, Tubize/BM   4-6-0   1340-1344(289-293) of 1903.
                          109, Tubize/BM   4-6-0   1620(349) of 1909.
                      301-303, Tubize/BM   0-6-2   1753-1755(379-381) of 1912.
                     (II) 101, Guillaume 0-4-0   - of 1896. ex-Contractor.
                     (II)   9, Weidknecht 0-4-2   558 of 1900.   "   "

                                   46

Replacements. -   9-11, Weidknecht 4-6-0   689-691 of 1902.   ⊔⊓
                     12-13, Weidknecht 4-6-0   751-752 of 1906.   "
                       14, Weidknecht 4-6-0   ? of 1908.   "

Names. -   1-Cabourg, 2-Sallenelles, 3-Ouistreham, 4-Falaise, 5-Benouville,
               6-Varaville, 7-Luc sur Mer (later Grandcamp), (II) 7-Unnamed,
               8-Ville de Caen, 9-La Brêche d'Hermanville (later "Isigny"),
               222-Bayeux, 223-Port en Bessin, 224-Arromanches, 225-Courseulles,
               231-Ryes, 232-Saint Laurent sur Mer, 233-Formigny, 234-Trevières.
               Others not named.

Notes.-   1.° See "Light Railways" by W.K.J.Davies, plate facing page 104.
               2.°° It would appear that Nos.6,7 & 8 were assembled by Decauville from parts
               supplied by Tubize and Weidknecht respectively.
               (II) 7 & 8 ran as 0-6-4s for a time.

29.   CELLES, Vallée de. See Raon l'Etape. No.121.

30.   CHALLANS. (Tramway à Vapeur de Challans à Fromentine).
      Taken over by Tramways de la Vendée in 1914. See No.160.
      Challans-Beauvoir-La Barre de Monts-Fromentine, 24.4 km.
      S.1896, P.1923, D.1933, C.1949. Gauge. 1000.
      Locomotives. -   Nos. 1-3, Corpet Louvet 0-6-0 614-616 of 1895   ⊔⊓

      Names. -   1-Challans, 2-Beauvoir, 3-Fromentine.

31.   CHALOSSE. (Tramways à Vapeur de la Chalosse et du Béarn).
      Dax(St.Pierre)-Péyrehorade, 31.0 km.
      Dax(Midi)-Dax(St.Pierre)-Amou-Orthez, 53.0 km.
      Amou-Aire(Midi), 51.0 km. (Connecting with No.111).
      S.1902/24, GS.1937, C.1938. Gauge. 1000.
      Locomotives. -   Nos. 1-2, Corpet Louvet 0-6-0   1032-1033 of 1908.   ⊑
                              3-4, Corpet Louvet 0-6-0   1102 & 1135 of 1908.   "
                              5-7, Corpet Louvet 0-6-0   1196-1198 of 1909.   "
                              8-9, La Meuse   2-6-0   2619-2620 of 1913.   ⊔⊓

32.   CHAMBERY. (Chemin de fer de Challes les Eaux à Chambéry).
      From 1898 (Société Anonyme des Tramways de la Savoie).
      From 1913 (Chemins de Fer Départementaux de la Savoie).
      Chambéry-Challes les Eaux-Chignin les Marches, 11.0 km.
      Chambéry-Bissy-La Motte Servolex, 4.8 km.
      Chambéry-Chambéry le Vieux-LeBourget du Lac, 10.6 km.
      Chambéry-Cognin-St.Cassin-Pont St.Charles, 4.3 km.
      S.1892, Part P.1924, C.1932. Gauge. 600.
      Locomotives. -   Nos. 552
                            -555, Weidknecht   0-4-0   552-555 of 1892/93.   ⊔⊓
                               1, Corpet Louvet   0-4-2   673 of 1896.   ⊑
                               3, Corpet Louvet   0-6-0   623 of 1894.   ⊔⊓
                         2 & 4, Buffaud & Robatel 0-6-0   - - of 1898.   ⊑
                             5-6, Buffaud & Robatel 0-6-0 - - of 1905/06.   "
                     (II)   4, Pinguély,   0-6-0 326 of 1912.   "
                     (II)   2, Orenstein & Koppel 0-4-0 4101 of 1910.   ⊔⊓
                               8, Orenstein & Koppel 0-4-0 4025 of ?.   "
                              -., Orenstein & Koppel 0-8-0 ? of ?.   "

Names. -   552-555 not named, 1-Challes les Eaux, 2-La Motte Servolex,
               3-La Motte Servolex, (II) 4-La Savoie. Others not named.

Note. -   There was a very short branch line to the Cassino at Challes. Decauville
               had laid down an exhibition line in 1889, from Chambéry to Mont Lepine,
               3.0 km, on the Le Bourget line.

33.   CHARTRES. See Eure et Loire, No.52.

34. CHATEAUBRIANT. (Compagnie des Chemins de Fer à Voie Etroite de Châteaubriant à Erbray et Extensions).
Châteaubriant-Erbray-La Chapelle Glain, 19.0 km.
Erbray-Ancenis (and River Port branch), 43.0 km.
Châteaubriant(La Greyouillère)-La Place des Terrasses, 1.0 km.
S.1888/1913, P.1923, C.1936/47. Gauge. 1000.
Locomotives. -   Nos.   1-3, Tubize/BM   0-6-0   714-716(30-32) of 1888.
                          4, Tubize/BM   0-6-0   1306/277) of 1902.
                        5-9, Corpet Louvet 0-6-0   1319-1323 of 1911.

Note. -   No.8 was loaned to Tramways de la Vendée 1920-1928.

35. CHERBOURG. (Compagnie des Tramways de Cherbourg).
Cherbourg-Equeurdreville-Querqueville-Urville,)
) 11.0 km.
Cherbourg-Tourlaville,   )
Place du Château-Gare-Octroi, 5.5 km. (Urban Line).
S.1897, C.1914, Reopened E.1919, C.1944. Gauge. 1000.
(Urban section E.1910, C.1944 War destruction).
Locomotives. -   A-B, Winterthur 0-6-0   1017-1018 of 1897.
                   C-D, Winterthur 0-4-0   1044-1045 of 1897.
                     E, Winterthur 0-4-0   1062 of 1897.
                   F-G, Winterthur 0-4-0   1104-1105 of 1898.
                     H, Winterthur 0-6-0   ?   of 1890 ex- Geneva ? *

Serpollet Cars. - 1-3 Tubize/BM, 1074-1076(188-190) of 1896.

36. COGOLIN. (Tramway de Cogolin à Saint Tropez).
Owned by (Cie. des Chemins de Fer du Sud de la France).
Cogolin-La Foux-Saint Tropez, 9.2 km.
S.1894 ?, D.1935, C.1948. Gauge. 1000.
Locomotives. -   Nos. 70-72, Corpet Louvet 0-6-0   591-593 of 1894. (Small type).

Names. -   70-Hyères, 71-Meyrargues, 72-Saint Tropez.

37. CORMEILLES. (Compagnie du Chemin de Fer d'Interêt Local de Cormeilles à Glos Montfort et Extensions).
Cormeilles-Glos Montfort, 30.3 km.
Cormeilles-Pont l'Evêque, 17.0 km.
Cormeilles-Bernay Boucheville 29.0 km.
S.1902, P.1921, C.1933/44 (war destruction). Gauge. 1000.
Locomotives. -   Nos.   1-3, Buffaud et Robatel 0-6-0   - - of 1902.
                         21-23, Corpet Louvet 2-6-0   943-945 of 1904.
                   (II)   21, Corpet Louvet 2-6-0   ? of ?. ex No. ? *
                         11-12, Corpet Louvet 0-8-0   1716-1717 of 1926.

Names. -   1-Cormeilles, 2-St.Georges, 3-Lieury, 21-Bonneville, 22-Tiberville,
                   23-Bernay. Others not named.

38. COLMAR. See Kolmar, Alsace Lorraine, Chapter 4.

39. CORREZE. (Compagnie des Tramways de la Corrèze).
From 1925, (Société d'Exploitation de Chemins de Fer en Correze).
Later worked by P.O.Railway, with other light railways as "P.O.C."
Ussel-Neuvic-Le Mortier-St.Bonnet,   90.8 km. (Through running to Tule over)
Le Mortier-Laroche Camillac,   4.5 km. (C.1939).   P.O.C.)
Aubazine-Le Moulin du Faure-Le Bosplos-Beaulieu, 39.8 km.
Le Bosplos-Turenne,   19.0 km.
Le Moulin du Faure-Beynat,   2.0 km.
La Rivière de Mansac-Ayen Jullac-Jullac,   27.0 km. (C.1931).
S.1912, P.1923, C.1932/1959. Gauge. 1000
Locomotives. -   Nos. 1-12, Piguet 0-6-0   - - of 1911. (Large type).
                         13-18, Piguet 0-6-0   - - of 1912. (Small type).

40. COTES DU NORD. (Compagnie Centrale de Chemins de Fer, de Tramways et d'Electricité).
From 1904 (Compagnie des Chemins de Fer des Côtes du Nord).
From 1921 (Régie départementale des Chemins de Fer des Côtes du Nord).
Light railways with some street running and first locomotives with enclosed wheels and motion.

Guingamp-Plouha-Saint Brieuc-Le Légué(Phare),	56.4 km.	
Brelidy Plouec-Tréguier-Petit Camp-Lannion,	47.0 km.	
Petit Camp-Perros Guirec,	5.0 km.	?
Saint Brieuc-Yffiniac-Plemy-Collinée,	43.1 km.	
Plancoet-Matignon-Saint Cast,	18.7 km.	
Yffiniac-Saint Alban-Matignon,,	47.0 km.	
Quintin-Saint Nicolas du Pelem-Rostrenen,	45.8 km.	
Lannion(Gare de l'Etat)-Plestin,	16.6 km.	
Lamballe-Saint Alban,	11.0 km.	
Dinan-Plenée Jugon-Collinée,	46.2 km.	
Plouha-Paimpol-Pleumeur-Tréguier,	39.0 km.	
Guingamp-Saint Nicolas du Pelem,	41.2 km.	
Plémy-Loudéac,	21.8 km.	
Le Guildo (near Matignon)-Lancieux-St.Briac,	11.0 km.	(Goods only) S.1929.

(was to have connected with No.46).

S.1904, Part P.1923, D.1938, C.1937/1956.   Gauge. 1000

Locomotives. -

	Nos.				
	1-17,	Tubize/BM	0-6-0	1370-1386 (298-314) of 1904.	
	18-22,	Tubize/BM	0-6-0	1387-1391 (315-319) of 1904.	
	23-25,	Tubize/BM	0-6-0	1420-1422 (326-328) of 1905.	"
	26-28,	Corpet Louvet	0-6-0	1142-1144 of 1907.	"
	29,	Corpet Louvet	0-6-0	1159 of 1908.	"
	30-34,	Corpet Louvet	0-6-0	1608-1612 of 1923.	"
	35-42,	Corpet Louvet	0-6-0	1678-1685 of 1925.	* "
	201,	Corpet Louvet	0-6-0	1358 of 1912 (for Finistere Ry).	"
	202-203,	Corpet Louvet	0-6-0	1489-1490 of 1914 " " " "	"
	Cdn. 1,	Pinguély ?	0-6-0	? in 1921 for extension work.	"
	Cdn. 2,	Cail	0-6-0	? " " " " "	"
	RB.203,	S.A.C.M.	2-6-0	4261 of 1892 (Hired).	"
	"La Bretagne" German ? ?		0-4-4-0	? of ? for experiments in 1924.	"

Note. -   Loco No.42 said to be renumbered 40 after the former was damaged in an accident Nos.1-3, were delivered in advance of opening in 1904 for construction work and scrapped in 1922, when 201-203 took the numbers 1-3.   * No.36 is preserved at Longueville.

41. COTE D'OR. (Tramways de la Côte d'Or).
Owned by (Chemins de Fer du Sud de la France).
From 1910 (Régie des Chemins de Fer Départementaux de la Côte d'Or).
From 1934 (Société Générale des Transports Départementaux).
Dijon-Fontaine Française-Champlitte, 58.0 km.
Chatillon sur Seine-Vaurois-Dijon, 107.0 km.
Vaurois-Baigneux les Juifs, 23.0 km.
Dijon(Porte Neuve)-Gevrey-Meuilley-Beaune, 56.0 km.**
Meuilley-Nuits Saint Georges, 7.0 km.
Beaune-Saulieu-Semur, 98.0 km.
S.1891/1922, P.1924, Part E.1910**, D.1935, C.1933/1953.   Gauge. 1000.

Locomotives. -

	Nos.				
	1-12,	Schneider	0-6-2	2456-2467 of 1890.	
	13-15,	Corpet Louvet	0-6-2	582-584 of 1893.	"
	16,	Pinguély	0-6-2b	306 of 1911.	"
	20-21,	Corpet Louvet	0-6-0	674-675 of 1896.	"
	30-31,	Belfort	2-6-0	4698-4699 of 1898.	"
	32-33,	Pinguély	2-6-0	169-170 of 1903.	"
	34-36,	Pinguély	2-6-0	171-173 of 1904.	"
	37-39,	Piguet	2-6-0	- - of 1913/14.	"
	50-51,	Orenstein & Koppel	0-10-0	10926-10927 of 1926.	"

Steam Cars. -   -   Petolat "Scotté" steam car 1909.
                AT.1-AT.2,   Purrey steam cars 1912.   "

Note. -   ** The section Dijon-Gevrey was electrified by the town tramways in 1910 and handed back to the Côte d'Or Co. in 1920 but remained electric.

42. DAUPHINE. (Compagnie Française de Voies Ferrées Economiques).
Later (Société des Voies Ferrées du Dauphiné).
From 1920 (Régie Départementale des Voies Ferrées du Dauphiné).
Grenoble-Gières-Vizelle-Bourg d'Oisans, 55.0 km.
Gières-Froges, 13.3 km.
Vizelle-Jarrie, 2.0 km. (Three rail mixed gauge with 1435 gauge).
S.1893, Part E.1902, DG.1951, C.1964. Gauge. 1000 (see above).

Locomotives. -   Nos.   1-4,   Tubize/BM   0-6-0   893-896 (71-74) of 1892.
                          5-16,   Tubize/BM   0-6-0   910-921 (80-91) of 1893.
                          17-19, Pinguély   0-8-0   365-367 of 1922.
                          20,   Pinguély   0-8-0   198 of 1905.
                   (II)   17,   Tubize/BM   0-6-0   1024 (166) of 1897 ex-No.44
                   (II)   12,   Pinguély   2-6-0   ? of 1914. ex-C.F. Rhône.
                          21-24, Pinguély   2-6-0   ? - ? of 1914. ex-C.F. Rhône.
                          25-27, Corpet Louvet 0-6-0   1143-1146 of 1913.
                          30-32, Piguet   2-6-0   - of 1920/21.
                          41-42, Pinguély   2-6-0   298 & 336 of 1910.
                          51-52, Pinguély   0-6-0   240-241 of 1908 (Twin Cab).
                   (II)   6,   Winterthur   2-6-0   2416 of 1914.
                   (II)   7,   Winterthur   2-6-0   2417 of 1914. ex-Furka-Oberalp.
                   (II)   8,   Winterthur   0-6-0   883 of 1894. ex-B.A.M.

Names. -   25-Senlis, 26-Plailly, 27-Chamant ?, Others not named.

Note. -   Most of the remaining locomotives were destroyed by the Resistance in
                  1943, but replaced by some from Swiss minor railways).

43. DAX. See CHALOSSE et Béarn, No.31.

44. DEUX SEVRES. (Compagnie des Tramways Départementaux des Deux Sevres).
Owned by (Compagnie des Voies Ferrées Economiques).
Saint Maixent-Melle,   49.0 km.
Saint Maixent-Parthenay,   43.0 km.
Parthenay-Saint Laure,   43.0 km.
Bressuire-Montreuil Bellay, 62.0 km. (Separate line).
S.1897, P.1923, C.1947 (Short section at Melle remained DG). Gauge. 1000.
Locomotives. -   Nos.   1-20,   Tubize/BM   0-6-0   1008-1027 (150-169) of 1896.
                         (Nos.17-20, possibly delivered to No.42 before coming to No.44).

45. DIJON. See COTE D'OR, No.41.

46. DINARD. (S.A. du Tramway de Dinard à Saint Briac et Extensions).
This line closed while an extension of No.40 to meet it at St.Briac was still under construction.
Street running in Dinard.
Dinard-Saint Briac, 9.2 km. (Connected by ferry with No.136).
S.1901, P.1911, C.1929. Gauge. 1000.
Locomotives. -   Nos.   1-3,   Weidknecht   0-6-0   676-678 of 1901. (Found unsuitable).
                   (II) 1-4,   Weidknecht   0-6-0   ? - ? of 1905. (Compound).
                         10,   Turgan-Foy   0-6-0   - of 1904. (with brake-van
                                                                   attached).
Motive Power. -   T1-T2, Turgan Steam Cars,   1903.
                  S1,   Solignac Steam Car.   1902. ex-No.59
                                                          (rebuilt from "Serpollet" car)

47. DORDOGNE. (Société des Tramways de la Dordogne).
Really extensions of the C.F. du Périgord (see No.112, with which it amalgamated in 1921
as (Régie Départementale des Tramways de la Dordogne).
Vergt-Bergerac,   32.0 km.
Thiviers-Saint Yrieix,   33.0 km.
Saint Pardoux-Saint Mathieu, 39.0 km.
Sarlat-Villefranche,   54.0 km. (Isolated line).
GS.1911, S.1912, D.1937, C.1934/1949. Gauge. -1000.

Locomotives. -   Nos.   1-16, Pinguély, 0-6-0   245-260 of 1909.
                            81-82, Pinguély, 0-6-0   112-113 of 1902, (after 1921 ∵).

Note. -   In the combined fleet after 1921, the Périgord locomotives retained
                     their old numbers 1-10 and 1-16 above became 11-26.

48.   DOUBS. (Compagnie des Chemins de Fer du Doubs).
      From 1945 (Régie Départementale des Chemins de Fer du Doubs).
      A group of light railways amalgamated in 1927 which included one tramway with enclosed
      locomotives.
      Besançon-Amathay Vésigneux-Entreporte,   ?   km.
      Pontarlier-Entreporte-Andelot,   39. 0 km.
      Andelot-Levier,   21.4 km. (formerly independent light rly.).
      Pontarlier-Mouthe-Foncine le Haut,   41.9 km. (Tramway, See No.115).
      Morteau-Maîche-Trévillers,   45.0 km. (Isolated Light Railway).
      S.1900/1930, P.1925, D.1947, C.1952.   Gauge. 1000.
      Locomotives. -   Nos.   1, ? Corpet Louvet 2-6-0   1209 of 1909. (Besancon).
                                       2-4, ? Corpet Louvet 2-6-0   1276-1278 of 1910. "
                                         5, ? Corpet Louvet 2-6-0   1303 of 1911.
                                         6, ? Corpet Louvet 0-6-0   946 of 1903. (Pontarlier).
                                         7, ? Pinguély 2-6-0 . 325 of 1911.   "
                                      8-10, Buffaud & Robatel 0-6-0   - - of 1900.   "
                                     11-12, Buffaud & Robatel 0-6-0   - - of 1900. (Andelot).
                                         ?, Baldwin 0-6-2   ? of 1917. ?
                                 3615-3616, Buffaud & Robatel 2-6-0   - - of 1912.
                                         ?, Schneider 2-6-0   ? of 1905.
                                   (II)11-12, Corpet Louvet 0-8-0   1716-1717 of 1926. ex-No.37. ∵
                                   (III)11, ? Corpet Louvet 0-6-0   946 of 1903. (Pontarlier).
                                     12-14, Corpet Louvet 0-6-0   947-949 of 1904. (Morteau).
                                 (IV)11,15, Corpet Louvet 0-6-0   1034-1035 of 1906.   "
                                        16, Pinguély 2-6-0   335 of 1911.   "
                                        17, Corpet Louvet 0-6-0   ? of ?.   "
                                        50, Decauville 2-6-0   ? of 1910.
                                     52-53, Decauville 2-6-0   648-649 of 1912.
                                         - Winterthur 0-6-0   552 of 1888. ∵

49.   DUNKERQUE. (Société Anonyme des Tramways de Dunkerque et Extensions).
      Trials with steam on urban horse tramways.
      H.1880, S.1880, E.1902, C.1952. Gauge. 1435.
      Locomotives. -   Nos.   1-2, Aulnoye & Berlaimont 0-4-0   - of 1880. ?

50.   EPERNAY. (Société du Tramway de Epernay-Ay-Mareuil).
      A horse tramway acquired by the Banlieue de Reims tramways, See No.125.
      and adapted for steam traction in 1905, as through route.
      H.1893, S.1905, (C1914-1918), P.1923, C.1937. Gauge. 1000.
      Locomotives. -   Provided by No.125.

51.   ETEL. See Trinité, No.157.

52.   EURE ET LOIR. (Compagnie des Tramways d'Eure et Loir).
      Léves-Chartres-Bonneval,   33.0 km. (Including Chartres urban service).
      Chartres-Sours-Angerville,   50.0 km.
      Sours-Prunay le Gillon,   5.5 km.
      Bonneval-Brou-Nogent le Rotrou,   59.0 km.
      Dreux-Brezolles-Senonches,   41.0 km. (Isolated Line).
      St.Sauveur-Châteauneuf-Digny la Loupe,   25.6 km.
      S.1899, P.1925, C.1935. Gauge. 1000.
      Locomotives. -   Nos.   1-6,   Corpet Louvet 0-6-0   716-721 of 1899.
                                   7-8,   Corpet Louvet 0-4-0   732-733 of 1899.
                                  9-10,   Corpet Louvet 0-6-0   850-851 of 1900.
                                    11,   Corpet Louvet 0-6-0   856 of 1901.
                                 12-14,   Corpet Louvet 0-6-0   1077, 1079-1080 of 1906.

	(II)	7-8,	Corpet Louvet	0-6-0	1076 & 1078 of 1906.	⊔⊐
		10-18,	Corpet Louvet	0-6-0	1081, 1083-1085 of 1907.	"
		19-21,	Corpet Louvet	0-6-0	1158, 1174-1175 of 1908.	"
		22-24,	Corpet Louvet	0-6-0	1472-1474 of 1914.	"
	(II)	?,	Corpet Louvet	0-6-0	789 of 1900. ∵ (ex-No.13)	"
		?,	Corpet Louvet	0-6-0	809 of 1903. ∵	"

Names. -   1-Dreux, 2-Brezolles, 3-St.Sauveur, 4-Châteauneuf, 5-Chartres,
6-Bonneval, 7-Leves, 8-Luisant, 9-Laons, 10-Thivars, 11-Mignières,
12-Sours, 13-Prunay le Gillon, 14-Santeuil, 15-Francourville,
16-Angerville, 17-Brou, 18-Dangeau, 19-Yevres, 20-Unverre,
21-Nogent le Rotrou, 22-La Loupe, 23-Digny, 24-Belhomert, (II)7-Senoches,
(II)8-Louvilliers.

53.   FEUQUIERES.   (Tramway de Feuquières-Fressenville à Ault).
Later (Compagnie des Chemins de Fer Industriels et Balnèaires de la Somme).
Short lived steam tramway partly covered by a railway in 1921.
Feuquières Fressenville-Ault Onival, 13.0 km.
S.1904, C.1906.   Gauge. 1435.

Locomotives. -	Nos.	1-2, ? ?		0-4-0	? of ? (Saddle tank).	⊔⊐
		3, ?	Tubize/BM	0-6-0	929 or 930(93 or 94) of 1894. ex-No.107.	
	AB.3.	Serpollet steam car.				∵⊏⊐ ⊞

54.   FERNEY VOLTAIRE.   (Société du Tramway de Gex à Ferney).
Later part of (Tramways de l'Ain). from 1920. See No.2.
Ferney Voltaire-Gex, 10.0 km.   (Connecting with Switzerland No.6).
S.1900, C.1938.   Gauge. 1000.

Locomotives. -	Nos.	11,	Winterthur	0-6-0	620 of 1890. (Hired from Switzerland	⊏⊐
					No.7).	
		14,	Winterthur	0-6-0	623 of 1890. " " "	"
		22,	Winterthur	0-6-0	643 of 1891. " " "	"
Replaced by. -		15,	Winterthur	0-6-0	866 of 1894. (ex-Switzerland No.2). ∵	"
		17,	Winterthur	0-6-0	868 of 1894. (" ").	"

Names. -   11-Voirons, 14-Savoie, 22-Crépy.   (These locos returned in 1904).

55.   FORT MAHON.   (Société de Quend Plage & Société de Fort Mahon).
From 1913 (Tramways à Vapeur de Marquenterre).
Quend(Gare du Nord)-Monchaux-Quend Plage, 8.4 km.
Monchaux-Fort Mahon Plage,   4.6 km. (Horse worked at first).
S.1903, Part H.1905, Part P.1911, C.1931.   Gauge. 600.

Locomotives. -	Nos.	4, ?	Decauville	0-4-0	230 of 1900. ?	⊔⊐
		-	Decauville	0-4-2	279 of 1899.	"
		2	Decauville	0-4-0	? of ?	"
		-	German?	0-4-0	? of ? (Acquired 1905).	∵ ⊔⊐
		-	Decauville	0-6-2	? of ? (Acquired 1911).	∵ "
	After 1914 war, Two German?		0-4-0	? of ?	"

Names.-   4-Jeanette, (279)-Bienvenue, 2-Minus (German)-Marie Antoinette.

56.   FOURMIES.   (S.A. du Tramway de Fourmies à Wignehies).
Fourmies-Wignehies, 6.0 km.
S.1883, C.1914.   Gauge. 1000.

Locomotives. -	Nos.	1-2,	Tubize	0-6-0	457-458 of 1883.	⊏⊐
		3,	Tubize	0-6-0	504 of 1882.	"
		4.	Tubize	0-6-0	597 of 1885.	"
		-.	Purrey Steam car on trial.			⊞

Names. -   1-Wignehies, 2-Fourmies, 3- ?, 4-lettered "Fourmies-Wignehies".

57. FRANCHE COMTE. (Chemins de Fer Régionaux de Franche Comte).
     A light railway taken over by No.48 in 1947, which see for details.
     Morteau-Maîche-Trévillers, 45.0 km.

58. GARGAN. (Tramway à Vapeur de Gargan-Livry à Livry Ville).
     Owned by (Société d'Etude et Entreprises de Chemins de Fer).
     Built and worked by (Compagnie des Chemins de Fer de l'Est).
     Gargan-Livry, 3.0 km. (Outer suburbs of Paris).
     S.1890, C.1930. Gauge. 1435.
     Locomotives. -   Nos. 0203-4, Mulhouse 0-6-0   24-25 of 1857. *
                                0208-9, Mulhouse 0-6-0   29-30 of 1857. *

     Names. -   0204-La Liepvrette, 0203-L'Ill, 0208-La Thurr, 0209-La Zorn.

     Note. - *   Built in Railway Coy's workshops and modified there for tramway
                         use, 0204 & 0208 in 1890 and 0203 & 0209 in 1891.
                         (See "Railway Magazine" July 1928, page 120. Note by O.J.Morris).

59. GERARDMER. (Société Anonyme des Tramways de Gérardmer).
     From 1925 (Société Générale des Chemins de Fer Economiques).
     Gérardmer-Retournemer, 11.0 km.
     S.1897, E.1929, C.1935 (Used 1939 for war defences ?) Gauge. 1000.
     Locomotives. -   No.   1,   Winterthur   0-6-0 ? of ?.
                               2-3, Weidknecht   0-6-0 ? - ? of 1898.
                        (II)   1,   ?   0-6-0 ? of ? in 1908.
                        (II)   3-4, Corpet Louvet   0-6-0 719-720 of 1899 hired from No.52.
                                 -   Serpollet Steam car 1897 (Trials).

     Names. -   1-La Forgette, 2-La Vologne, 3-La Jamagne, (II)1-La Forgette.
                         Under S.E. 3151-La Jamagne, 3152-La Vologne.

60. GERARDMER. (S.A. des Tramways des Vosges).
     Gérardmer(Gare de l'Est)-Remiremont, 27.7 km.
     S.1900, C.1934. Gauge. 1000.
     Locomotives. -   Nos.   1-3, Batignolles 0-6-0   1411-1413 of 1899.
                                4.   ?   0-6-0   ?   of 1900.

61. GRAULHET. (Chemins de Fer à Voie Etroite et Tramways à Vapeur du Tarn).
     See Tarn, No.150.

62. GRENOBLE. (Voies Ferrées du Dauphiné). See No.42.

63. GRENOBLE. (Compagnie des Chemins de Fer Economiques du Nord).
     Taken over by Grenoble Electric Tramways in 1901/02.
     Grenoble(Square des Postes)-Veurey, 15.8 km.
     S.1894, E.1901/05, C.1939/54. Gauge. 1000.
     Locomotives. -   Nos. 26-27, Franco Belge 0-6-0 952-953 ? of 1894.
                               ?, Tubize   0-6-0 601 of 1885 ex-Bruxelles-Ixelles.
                               ?, Tubize   0-6-0 ? of ?   "
                               20, Tubize/BM 0-6-0 1001(143) of 1896.

     Name. -   Tubize 601-Maria.

64. HALLUIN. See Armentières No.10.

65. HAUTE RHONE. (Compagnie du Chemin de Fer du Haute Rhône).
     A light railway acquired by No.2 in 1920.

66. HELLEMMES. . (Compagnie des Chemins de Fer Economiques du Nord).
Hellemmes-Saint Amand les Eaux, 32.0 km.   (See Nos.78 & 159).
S.1897, C.1932. Gauge. 1000.
Locomotives. -   No.   14, Tubize/BM 0-6-0   937(97) of 1895 from No.159
                            15, Tubize/BM 0-6-0   996(138) of 1896 from No.10.
                         17-18, Tubize/BM 0-6-0   998-999(140-141) of 1896.
Later. -   30, Tubize   0-6-0   462 of 1884, ex-Belgium No.5. **
             (II)   30. Piguet   0-6-0   - of 1924.

Note. -   Locomtives numbered in CFEN general stock.

66A. Le HAVRE. (Funiculaire de la Côte).
In 1895, this funicular was worked by two Serpollet steam cars fixed to
the opposite ends of a cable.

67. HENDAYE. (S.A. du Tramway d'Hendaye). (M.Martinet).
Hendaye Ville-Hendaye Plage, 3.0 km.
S.1901, P. ?, E.1908, C.1935. Gauge. 600 (1000 on electrification).
Locomotives. -   ?   ?   ? Decauville ?.

67A. HERIMONCOURT. (S.A. du Tramway de la Vallée d'Herimoncourt).
Herimoncourt-Audincourt-Montbéliard, 11.0 km. (Connecting with No.18).
Audincourt-Valentigny-Mandeure,   14.0 km.
S.1886, C.1932. Gauge. 1000.

Note. -   Part subsequently replaced by a standard gauge freight line.

Locomotives. -   Nos.   1-3, Tubize/BM 0-6-0 643-645(6-8) of 1886.
                             4, Tubize/BM 0-6-0 711(29) of 1888.
                           5-6, Tubize/BM 0-6-0 1413-1414(324-325) of 1905.
                             7, Unknown German 0-6-0
                           8-9, Tubize   0-6-0 1779-1780 of 1913.
                         ?-18, Baldwin   0-6-2   ? & 44073 of 1917 in 1923.

68. ILLE ET VILAINE. (Compagnie des Tramways a Vapeur de l'Ille et Vilaine).
Rennes-La Meziere-St.Malo,   79.0 km.
La Mezière-Becherel,   24.0 km.
Rennes-Mi Fôret-Liffré-Fougères,   50.0 km.
Liffré-Sautoger-Sens-Antrain,   35.0 km.
Mi Fôret-Sautoger,   20.0 km.
Sens-Pleine Fougères,   27.0 km.
Rennes-Bréal-Guer-La Porte-Redon,   88.0 km.
Bréal-Pipriac-La Porte,   67.0 km.
Rennes-Le Grand Fougeray,   64.0 km.
Rennes-Moulins-La Guerche,   50.0 km.
S.1897, P.1927, D.1938, C.1937/50. Gauge. 1000.
Locomotives. -   Nos.   1-3, Tubize/BM   0-6-0 1056-1058(182-184) of 1896.
                           4-9, Tubize/BM   0-6-0 1093-1098(206-211) of 1896.
                         10-12, Tubize/BM   0-6-0 1102-1104(215-217) of 1896.
                         51-56, Corpet Louvet 0-6-0 862-867 of 1902.
                            57, Corpet Louvet 0-6-0 935 of 1903.
                         58-69, Corpet Louvet 0-6-0 869-880 of 1902/04.
                         70-72, Corpet Louvet 0-6-0 1190-1192 of 1908. *
                         73-87, Corpet Louvet 0-6-0 1232-1246 of 1909/12. *
                         88-91, Corpet Louvet 0-6-0 1465-1468 of 1914.
                       101-104, Corpet Louvet 0-4-4-0   676-679 of 1897.
                       201-202, Corpet Louvet 0-8-0 1804-1805 of 1931.

Note. -*   Locos Nos. 70, 71, 76, 79, 80-85 & 87 were rebuilt as 0-6-2

Names. -   1-Liffré, 2-Gosné, 3-St.Aubin du Cormier, 4-Romagné, 5-Thorigné,
                 6-St.Marc Sur Couësnon, 7-St.Jean sur Couësnon, 8-Treffendel,
                 9-St.Thurial, 10-Bréal, 11-Mordelles. 12-Chantepie.

Nos. 51-81 not named.
101-Rennes, 102-Fougères, 103-Plélan, 104-Châteaugiron.

69. INDRE. (Compagnie des Tramways de l'Indre).
     Châteauroux-Valencay,   50.0 km. (Separate line).
     Argenton-St.Benoît-Le Blanc,   64.0 km.
     St.Benoît-Chaillac,   12.0 km.
     Issoudun-Vierzon,   57.0 km. (Separate line).
     S.1902, P.1924, C.1938. Gauge. 1000.
     Locomotives. -   Nos.   1-4, Pinguély 0-6-0   110-111 & 115-116 of 1901.
                              5-10, Pinguély 0-6-0   120-122 & 136-137 of 1902.
                             11-12, Pinguély 0-6-0   ?   ? of 1902.
                             50-53, Pinguély 0-6-0   117-119 & 149 of 1902.
                                81, Pinguély 0-4-0   327 of 1912. (No.104 rebuilt).

     Steam Cars. -   101-103, Pinguély "Rowan" cars, 180-182 of 1904.
                             104, Pinguély "Rowan" car, 327 of 1912.

70. INDRE ET LOIR. (Compagnie de Chemins de Fer Départemantaux, - Réseau d'Indre et Loir).
     Roadside light railways with street running over electric tramways from Fondettes to Tours
     (Place Anatoile France), 1.1, km.   See No.155.
     Rillé Hommes-Fondettes(for Tours),   26.0 km.)
     Port Boulet-Rillé Hommes-Châteaurenault,   104.0 km.) Reseau Nord.
     Lesves-Ligueil-Le Grand Pressigny,   55.0 km.)
     Ligueil-Loches-Ecueillé,   28.5 km.) Reseau Sud.
     S.1884, P.1924, (Part E.1930), D.1947, C.1949. Gauge. 1000.
     Locomotives. - (Réseau Nord):-
                     Nos.   1-3, St.Léonard 0-6-0   643-645 of 1884.
                            4-6, Couillet   0-6-0   693-695 of 1883.
                            7-8, Couillet   0-6-0   818-819 of 1885.
                             10, Couillet   0-6-2   841 of 1888.
                          85-86, St.Léonard 2-6-0   1646-1647 of 1910.
                    (Réseau Sud):-
                     No.   12,   Couillet   0-6-2   843 of 1888.
                            13,   Couillet   0-6-2   825 of 1886.
                         15-16,   Couillet   0-6-2   827-828 of 1886.
                         20-21,   St.Léonard 0-6-2   723-724 of 1886.
                            42,   S.A.C.M.   0-4-4-0   ? of 1888.
                            49,   S.A.C.M.   2-6-0   4951 of 1900.

     Note. -   Locomotives were numbered in C.F.Départementaux general list with
                   several other light railways, and sometimes changed around.
                   S.A.C.M. Locomotives would have carried "Graffenstaden" works plates
                   until 1919. (See chapter 4 page 3).

71. ISERE. (S.A. des Tramways de l'Isère). Bankrupt in 1908.
     Then (Compagnie des Chemins de Fer du Sud de la France, Réseau de l'Isère).
     From 1914 (Tramways Départementaux de l'Isère).
     To No.42 in 1921, worked as (Tramways de l'Ouest du Dauphiné).
     Lyon(Monplaisir)-St.Jean de Bournay-La Côte St.André-St.Marcellin, 116.5 km.
     La Côte St.André-Le Grand Lemps, 13.5 km. (Connecting with No.164).
     La Tour de Pin-Les Avenières, 17.5 km. (Separate Line).
     Bonpertuis-Le Pont de Beauvoisin, 26.2 km. (Separate Line).
     S.1899, P.1922, C.1937. Gauge. 1000.
     Locomotives. -   Nos.   1-5, Pinguély 0-6-0   59-63 of 1898 (Twin Cab).
                               6-7, Pinguély 0-6-0   65-66 of 1898   "   "
                                 8, Pinguély 0-6-0   92 ? of 1900 "   "
                              9-14, Pinguély 0-6-0   234-239 of 1908   "   "
                             15-16, Pinguély 0-6-0   307-308 of 1910   "   "
                             17-18, Pinguély 0-6-0   328-329 of 1915 ?"   "
                             19-20, Pinguély 0-6-0   283-284 of 1909   "   "
                                21, Pinguély 0-6-0   330 of 1915 ?   "
                             41-42, Pinguély 2-6-0   ? - ? of 1913/14.
                            M1-M2.   Serpollet Steam Cars, 1925.

55

72. JURA. (S.A. des Tramways à Vapeur du Jura) ?.
     Later(Compagnie Générale des Chemins de Fer Vicinaux).
     Lons le Saunier-Bifurcation St.Maur-Clairvaux-St.Claude, 68.0 km.
     Bifurcation St.Maur-Orgelet-Arinthod, 28.0 km.
     Clairvaux-Foncine le Bas-Foncine le Haut, 45.0 km. (Connecting with No.115).
     S.1898, P.1923, C.1936/48. Gauge. 1000.
     Locomotives. -   Nos. 11-15, Franco Belge 0-6-0 1169-1173 of 1897.
                              16-17, Franco Belge 0-6-0 1277-1278 of 1899.
                            320-323, Tubize/BM,   0-6-0 1409-1412(320-323) of 1905. (Twin
                                                                                         Cab).
                            101-102, Tubize   0-6-0 742 & 744 of 1889. (Ex-Bruxelles-
                                                                             Ixelles).

73. LAON. (S.A. du Chemin de Fer de la Banlieue de Laon).
     From 1907 (Chemins de Fer Départementaux de l'Aisne). See No.3.
     From 1918 (Chemins de Fer Secondaires du Nord Est.).
     La Neuville-Laon(Gare)-Nouvion le Vineux, 14.0 km.
     S.1907, (C.1914-1918), C.1932. Gauge. 1000.
     Locomotives. -   No.   151, Boussu 0-6-0 190 of 1907.
                                152, Tubize/BM 0-4-0 1631(350) of 1909.
                         101-103, Pinguély Steam Cars, 211-213 of 1906.

74. LAON. (Tramway de la Ville de Laon).
     (Following approximately the course of the present electric tramway).
     Laon(Gare)-Laon Ville, 2.0 km.
     S.1888, C. ?, (Possibly only trials). Gauge. 600.
     Locomotive. -   Tubize(Decauville) 0-4-4-0   697(61) of 1887.

     Name. -   "L'Intrepide".

75. LE MANS. (Compagnie des Tramways de la Sarthe) Owned by Carel et Fourché group.
     Le Mans-Loué-Saint Denis d'Orques-Saint Jean sur Erve, 51.2 km.
     Le Mans-Bonnétable-La Détourbe-Mamers. *   56.0 km.
     La Detourbe-La Ferté Bernard-Montmirail,   37.8 km.
     Le Mans-Saint Jean d'Assé-Ségrie,   37.2 km.
     Saint Jean d'Assé-Antoigne-Ballon, **   10.5 km.
     Le Mans-Cérans-La Flèche,   49.4 km.
     Cérans-Foulletourte-Le Mayet,   25.1 km.
     Le Mans-Changé-Le Grand Lucé-La Chartre sur Loir, 52.0 km.
     Changé-Jupilles-Château sur Loir,   62.0 km.
     Le Grand Lucé-Saint Calais,   26.5 km.
     Fresnay sur Sarthe-Alençon, (Isolated Line).   32.4 km.

     Notes. -   * Saint Remy-Mamers was mixed gauge with Mamers-Saint Calais Railway.
                       ** Industrial service retained Antoigne-Montbizot.

     S.1882, Part P.1922, D.1933, C.1947 (See ** above). Gauge, 1000.
     Locomotives. -   Nos.   1-4, Corpet 0-4-0   341-344 of 1881.
                                5-10, Numbers not occupied.
                                  11, Tubize 0-6-0 533 of 1882. (intended for St.Etienne ?).
                                  12, Tubize 0-6-0 513 of 1882.
                               13-14, Tubize 0-6-0 537 & 540 of 1883.
                                  15, Tubize/BM 0-6-0 626(1) of 1885.
                               16-19, Tubize/BM 0-6-0 687-690(25-28) of 1887.
                                  21, Dubois   0-6-0   - of 1885. (Experimental).
                               50-56, Tubize/BM 0-6-0 1049-1055(175-181) of 1896. (51 Preserved).
                               60-62, Tubize/BM 0-6-0 1059-1061(185-187) of 1897.
                             101-104, Tubize/BM 0-6-0   1636-1639(351-354) of 1910.
                             105-106, Tubize/BM 0-6-0   1737-1738(377-378) of 1913.
                             107-122, Tubize/BM 0-6-0   1642-1647(357-362) of 1911.
                             113-116, Tubize/BM 0-6-0   1648-1652(363-366) of 1913.
                             117-119, Tubize/BM 0-6-0   1653-1655(367-369) of 1913.
     Note. -   Ille et Vilaine Nos.1-3, 5-8 & 10 were borrowed 1939-1945. (See No.68).

1-Le Mans, 2-Le Grand Lucé, 3-Ballon, 4-Montbizot, 11-not named,
12-Parigné l'Evêque, 13-Challes, 14-Volnay, 15-Loué, 16-Saint Denis
d'Orques, 17-Coulans, 18-Crannes, 19-Vallon, 21-La Chartre; 50-Bonnetable,
51-Foulletourte, 52-Mayet, 53-Pont Vallin, 54-Masigné, 55-Allonnes,
56-Coulaines, 57-Savigne l'Evêque, 58-Beaufay, 59-Mamers, 60-La Ferté
Bernard, 61-Saint Cosme de Vair, 62-Nogent le Bernard, 101-119-not named.

76. LENS. (Compagnie des Chemins de Fer Economiques du Nord).
Lens-Frèvent, 53.5 km.
S.1894, C.1947. Gauge. 1000.

Locomotives. -		Nos.	21-25,	Franco Belge	0-6-0	947-951 of 1894 (Belgian	
						Vicinal type).	⊏
			28-29,	Franco Belge	0-6-0	955 & 954 of 1894 " "	"
			46,	Tubize/BM	0-6-0	1160(226) of 1899. " "	"
		(II)	23,	Piguet	0-6-0	- of 1924.	⊌⊐
			14,	Tubize/BM	0-6-0	937(97) of 1895. (from No.159).	⊏

Note. -   These locomotives were numbered in the CFEN general series.

77. LE RAINCY. See PARIS No.108.

78. LILLE. (Compagnie des Tramways du Département du Nord).
Lille-Hellemmes-Roubaix,   11.2 km.
Lille-Tourcoing,   13.0 km.
Lille-Haubourdin,   7.0 km.
S.1880/89, E.1900, C.1966. Gauge. 1435.

Locomotives. -	Nos.	1-6,	Falcon (Hughes)	0-4-0	31-36 of 1880.	⊏
		7-12,	Falcon (Hughes)	0-4-0	37-42 of 1881.	"
		15,	Carels	0-4-0	112 of 1880 (Brown's type) (later re-No.19).	"
		16-18,	Carels	0-4-0	115-157 of 1881. (later rebuilt as Fireless).	"
		19,	No.15 renumbered.			"
		20-21,	Carels	0-4-0	? - ? of 1885.	"

Fireless Locos. -		-,	Bédé	0-4-0	? Trials in 1879.	
		1-2,	Cail	0-4-0	? - ? of 1878.	"
		3-15,	Cail	0-4-0	? - ? of 1881.	"
	(II)	13-14,	Nos. 4 & 7 renumbered.			"
		20-29,	Cail	0-4-0	? - ? ?	"

Railcars. -   51-54,   Serpollet Tubize (BM) 1028-1031(170-173) of 1896.   ⇑⇑

79. LIVRY. See Gargan, No.58.

80. LOIR ET CHER. (Compagnie des Tramways à Vapeur du Loir et Cher).
From 1927 (Régie Départementale des Tramways du Loir et Cher).
Blois(Vienne)-Neung sur Beuvron-Lamotte,   60.0 km. (Connecting with No.81).
Blois(St.Lazare)-Oucques,   27.0 km.
Vendôme-Oucques-Ouzouer le Marché,   42.0 km.
Vendôme-Gué du Loir-Mondoubleau,   36.0 km.
Ouzouer le Marché-Orleans(Moulin de l'Hôpital),   32.0 km. (Worked by No.81 from 1931).
Gué du Loir-Drove,   33.0 km.
Neung sur Beuvron-Romorantin,   28.0 km.
Blois(Les Lices)-Châteaurenault,   44.0 km.
Blois(Vienne)-Cellettes-Contres-St.Aignan,   38.0 km. (See No.27).
Cellettes-Les Motils-Montrichard,   31.0 km.
S.1888/1908, Part P.1924, C.1934. Gauge. 1000.   ⊏

Locomotives. -	Nos.	1-3,	Tubize(BM)	0-6-0	628-630(3-5) of 1887. (Intended for No.75)
		4,	Tubize(BM)	0-6-0	627(2) of 1887. (" " ")
		5,	Tubize(BM)	0-6-0	683(21) of 1888.	"
		6-7,	Tubize(BM)	0-6-0	679-680(17-18) of 1888.	"
		8,	Tubize(BM)	0-6-0	685(23) of 1888.	"

9,	Tubize(BM)	0-6-0	681(19) of 1888.		⊟
10,	Tubize(BM)	0-6-0	684(22) of 1888.		"
11,	Tubize(BM)	0-6-0	682(20) of 1888.		"
12,	Tubize(BM)	0-6-0	686(24) of 1888.		"
TL.1-2,	Tubize(BM)	0-6-0	933-934(95-96) of 1894. (on Orleans line)		"
TL. 3,	Tubize(BM)	0-6-0	1366(297) of 1903.	" "	"
TL. 4,	Tubize(BM)	0-6-0	1104(217) of 1898 ∵	" "	"
			(ex-No. 68).		
Nos. 21-24,	Weidknecht	0-6-0	662-666 of 1899/1900. (Tubize type).		⊟
31-38,	Tubize(BM)	0-6-0	1433-1450(329-336) of 1905/06.		🗄
39-40,	Tubize(BM)	0-6-0	1640-1641(355-356) of 1910.		"
			(Orleans line).		
51-55,	Corpet Louvet	0-6-0	1066-1070 of 1906.		🔟
56,	Corpet Louvet	0-6-0	1228 of 1909. (On Orleans line).		"

Names. -   1-Blois, 2-Oucques, 3-Bracieux. 4-Neung sur Beuvron, 5-Binas, 6-Ouzouer le Marché, 7-Mont, 8-Pontijou Maves, 9-Dhuizon, 10-Marchenoir, 11-Chaumont sur Tharonne, 12-Lamotte sur Beuvron, TL.1-Orleans, TL.2-Coumiers, TL.3-**Epieds**, TL.4-Ingre. Other locomotives not named.

80A. LOIR ET CHER. (Société des Tramways Electriques du Loir et Cher).
An electric interurban tramway system connecting with Nos.80 and 81.
which kept four steam locomotives in reserve. Gauge. 1000. 🔟
Locomotives. -   Nos. 1-4, Pinguély 0-8-0 (or 2-4-2) flexible wheelbase 309-312 of 1911.

81. LOIRET. (Compagnie des Tramways du Loiret).
Orléans(Saint Marceau)-Cléry-Neung sur Beuvron, 48.4 km. (Connecting with No.80).
Orléans(Saint Marceau)-Orléans(Moulin de l'Hôpital) 1.3 km.   " " "
Orléans-Tigy-Brinon,   67.4 km.
Tigy-Châteauneuf sur Loire,   7.5 km.
Orléans(Moulin de l'Hôpital)-Ouzouer le Marché, 12.0 km. (worked for No.80 from 1931).
Nogent sur Vernisson-Chatillon Coligny,   10.4 km. (separate line).
S.1905, P.1922, C.1934. Gauge. 1000.
Locomotives. -   Nos. 1-5, Corpet Louvet 0-6-0 989-993 of 1905.   🔟
	6-8,	Corpet Louvet	0-6-0	995-997 of 1905.		"
	9,	Corpet Louvet	0-6-0	999 of 1905.		"
	10,	Corpet Louvet	0-6-0	1207 of 1910.		"
	TLC.51,	Corpet Louvet	0-6-0	1074 of 1905. (for Neung line)		"
	TLC.52,	Corpet Louvet	0-6-0	1064 of 1906. (" " ")		"
	TL.1-2,	Tubize(BM)	0-6-0	933-934(95-96) of 1894. (Orleans line		⊟
				ex-No. 80).		
	TL. 3,	Tubize(BM)	0-6-0	1366(297) of 1903.	" "	"
	TL. 4,	Tubize(BM)	0-6-0	1104(217) of 1898.	" "	🗄
	TL.39-40,	Tubize(BM)	0-6-0	(355-356) of 1910.	" "	🗄

Railcar. -   181, Purrey steam railcar of 1905.   🚃

Names. -.   1-Orléans, 2-Ligny, 3-Cléry, 4-Sandillon, 5-Jargeau, 6-Tigy, 7-Châteauneuf, 8-Nogent sur Vernisson, 9-Chatillon Coligny, 10-Souvigny, TLC.51-Villeny, TLC.52-La Marolle, TL.1-TL.4-as with No.80. Others not named.

82. LONS LE SAUNIER. See Jura, No.72.

83. LOT ET GARONNE. (Compagnie des Chemins de Fer et Tramways Départementaux du Midi de la France). Purchased by the Département in 1914.
From 1923 (S.A. des Voies Ferrées Départementales).
Villeneuve-Beauregard-Villereal, 36.8 km.
Beauregard-Tonneins,   42.9 km.
Tonneins-Sos,   49.1 km.
S.1911, P.1924, C.1933. (Temporarily closed 1918-1922). Gauge. 1000.
Locomotives. -   "Mina", Corpet Louvet 0-6-0 874 of 1901. (Left by 🔟
| | Nos. | 1-5, | Piguet | 2-6-0 | _ - of 1911. | Contractors). | " |

```
        60-61,   Corpet Louvet   0-6-0   1258-1259 of 1910.   ⁙           ⊡
           65,   Corpet Louvet   0-6-0         1263 of 1910.   ⁙  in 1927.  „
          .69,   Corpet Louvet   0-6-0         1280 of 1910.   ⁙    "    "  „
        74-75,   Corpet Louvet   0-6-0   1285-1286 of 1911.   ⁙    "    "  „
           82.   Corpet Louvet   0-6-0         1293 of 1913.   ⁙           „
          Two,   Orenstein & Koppel  0-6-0    ?         ?                  „
```

84.   LUNEVILLE.   (Compagnie du Tramway de Lunèville à Einville).
       From 1921 (Compagnie des Chemins de Fer Départmentaux de l'Aube).
       including C.F.Lunèville-Blamont-Badonviller.
       (a). Lunèville-Einville,   10.0 km.
            Lunèville Jolivet-Jolivet, 1.5 km.
       (b). Lunèville-Herbéviller-Blamont,)
            Herbeviller-Badonviller,   ) 46.0 km.
       S.1902/11, P.1927, C.1936/42.   Gauge. 1000.
       Locomotives. - (a)Nos.   ?   ? 0-4-0   1902.
                                   ?   Corpet Louvet 0-4-0   853-854 of 1902.
                                   ?   Corpet Louvet 0-6-0   1104 of 1907.
                      (b)   1-5, Corpet Louvet 2-6-0   1271-1275 of 1910/11.
                                  12, Schneider 2-6-0   ? (Trials only).
       War time. -   30,40,47,49, Baldwin 0-6-2   44084, 44171, 44219 & 44221
                                   ?   and one other of 1916.

85.   LYON.   (Compagnie des Omnibus et Tramways de Lyon).
       La Charité-Oullins, 5.0 km. (trials in 1884).
       Bellecour-Bon Coin, 5.6 km. in 1887) (Mekarski cars).
       Bellecour-St.Fons-Vénissieux, 9.2 km.
       H.1881, S.1888, E.1895, C.1937. (Reopened 1939-1949).   Gauge. 1435.
       Locomotives. -
                        No.   1500, Winterthur 0-6-0   ? of ? (for construction).
                              1-5,   Fives Lille 0-4-0 Fireless, 2683-2687 of 1888.
                               6,   Not completed.
                              7-10, Fives Lille 0-4-0 Fireless, 2765-2768 of 1889.

86.   LYON.   (Compagnie Lyonnaise de Tramways et de Chemins de Fer).
       From 1901 (Nouvelle Lyonnaise de Tramways).
       From 1906 as No.85.
       Pont Lafayette(Les Cordeliers)-Cimetière de la Guillotière,   5.0 km.
       Pont Lafayette(Les Cordeliers)-Asile de Bron,   6.0 km.
       Pont Lafayette(Les Cordeliers)-Monchat,   5.5 km.
       S.1889, A.1896, E.1902, C.1948/52.   Gauge. 1000.
       Locomotives. -   Nos.   1-2? Pinguély 0-4-0 Fireless, 1-2 of 1889.
                              3-13? Lamm & Francq 0-4-0 Fireless, ? of ?. (Tubize?).

87.   LYON.   (Compagnie Fourvière-Ouest Lyonnais).   From 1911 as No.85.
       Started in 1878 with funiculars to Fourvière and St.Just, and built a lengthy
       light railway starting from the latter, which was subsequently converted to an
       electric tramway.
       Lyon(St.Just)-Fourvière-Le Turpinier-Vaugneray, 14.8 km.
       Le Turpinier-Mournant,   18.0 km.
       S.1886, E.1899/1911, C.1935/54.   Gauge. 1000.
       Locomotives. -   Nos.   1-3, Fives Lille 0-6-2   2637-2639 of 1886.
                               4-5, Fives Lille 0-6-2   2661-2662 of 1888.
                                6,   Fives Lille 0-6-2   2866 of 1892.
                             16-17? Tubize(BM) 0-6-0   ? - ? of 1894 ex No.? ⁙

       Names. -   1-Vaugneray, 2-Mornant, 3-Craponne, 4-Loire, 5- ?, 6- ?,
                     (Later No.1 named Loire).

88.   LYON.   (Compagnie des Tramways de Lyon à Neuville et Extensions).
       From 1902 worked by (Compagnie des Omnibus et Tramways de Lyon).
       on behalf of the Department.   See over.

                                   59

Lyon(Quai de la Pecherie)-Fontaines-Neuville. 15.0 km.
S.1890. E.1932. C.1957. Gauge. 1435 (to 1000 on electrification).
Locomotives. -   No.   11.   Winterthur 0-6-0 918 of 1895.
                         12-14.   Winterthur 0-6-0 973-975 of 1896.
                         15-18.   Winterthur 0-6-0 1019-1022 of 1897.
                         19-21.   Winterthur 0-6-0 1203-1205 of 1899.
                         22.   Winterthur 0-6-0 1286 of 1900.

Motive Power   AB.1-AB.4.   Buffaud & Robatel "Rowan" Cars of 1890.
                     ? - ?   Franco Belge "Rowan" Cars 829-830 of 1891.

89. LYON. (S.A. des Tramways de l'Isère). See ISERE No.71.

90. MARQUENTERRE. See FORT MAHON. No.55.

91. MARSEILLE. (Compagnie Générale Française de Tramways).
     Place Castelaine-Avenue du Prado-Plage du Prado. 5.0 km.
     Place Joliette-L'Estaque.   11.0 km.
     H.1876 ?. S.1890, E.1900. C.1957. Gauge. 1430.
     Locomotives. -   Nos.   1-4,   Winterthur 0-6-0 790-793 of 1893.
                         5,   Winterthur 0-6-0 794 of 1895.
                         ?-?.   Carels   0-4-0   ? - ? of 1890.

     Motive Power. -   ?-?. ?   "Rowan" cars 1890 (Sold to Paris or rebuilt
                                         as Compressed air cars).

92. MARSEILLE. (Compagnie des Tramways à Voie Etroite de l'Est Marseille).
     Bankrupt 1903. Taken over by No.91.
     Marseille(Noailles)-Cimitière Saint Pierre, 2.9 km. (Part in Tunnel).
     S.1893. E.1905. Still Operating. Gauge. 1000 (1430 on electrification).
     Motive Power. -   Nos. ?-?. Lamm & Francq fireless 0-4-0 1893.

93. MEAUX. (Compagnie des Chemins de Fer d'Interêt Local de l'Yonne - Tramway de
     Meaux à Dammartin).
     From 1931 (Compagnie des Chemins de Fer Départementaux - Réseau de Seine et Marne).
     Worked from 1938 by (Sucrerie S.I.A.M.N.A.).
     Meaux Est-Dammartin (Saint Jean), 29.3 km.
     S.1910, GS.1936, C.1958. Gauge. 1000.
     Locomotives. -   Nos. 01-04.   Corpet Louvet 0-6-2 1211-1214 of 1910.
                         05.   Piguet   2-6-0   - of 1912.
                         5,   St.Léonard   0-6-0   811 of 1889 ♥ in 1934.
                         79,   St.Léonard   0-6-2   1278 of 1901 ♥ in 1934.

94. MONT BLANC. (Compagnie du Tramway de Mont Blanc).
     A tramway in name only, built as a metre gauge mountain rack railway.

95. MORBIHAN. (S.A. des Chemins de Fer d'Interêt Local du Morbihan).
     A metre gauge light railway undertaking which took over and rebuilt the tramway
     ETEL à TRINITE. See No.157.

96. MOUSSEY. (Tramway de Senones à Moussey). See SENONES, No.145.

97. MULHOUSE. See Chapter 4 - Alsace Lorraine, Nos. 4 & 6.

97A. NORMANDIE. (Compagnie des Tramways Normands).
      Avraches-Saint James, 21.1 km.
      S.1901, P.1923, C.1937. Gauge. 1000.

Locomotives. -   Nos.   1-2,   Corpet Louvet 0-6-0   833-834 of 1901.
                          3,   Corpet Louvet 0-6-0   1193 of 1908.

Names. -   1-Avraches, 2-St.James.

98.   ORLEANS.   See No.80 LOIR ET CHER and 81. LOIRET.

99.   ORNE.   (Compagnie des Voies Ferrées Economiques de l'Orne).
       Mortagne-La Loupe, 54.0 km.   (Connecting with No.52).
       Carrouges-Argentan-Trun, 44.0 km.   (Separate line).
       S.1913, P.1923, C.1934. Gauge. 1000.
       Locomotives. -   Nos.   1-8,   Piguet 0-6-0   - - of 1913.

100.   OUEST DAUPHINE.   See (S.A.Tramways de l'Isère).   No.71.

101.   PARIS.   (Compagnie des Tramways de Paris - Réseau Sud).   Bankrupt 1894.
       From 1894 (Compagnie Générale Parisienne des Tramways).
       Porte de Châtillon-Saint Germain des Prés,   ? km. (Trials only).
       Gare de Montparnasse-Place Valhubert,   ? km. (Trials only).
       Place de la Bastille-Gare de Montparnesse, 5.3 km.
       Place de la Bastille-Saint Mandé,   ? km.
       Gare d'Orleans-Ville Juif,   8.7 km.
       H.1875, S.1877, H(again) 1878, E.1898/1905, C.1936.   Gauge. 1435.
       Locomotives. -   Nos.   1-2,   Merryweather 0-4-0   3-4 of 1875/76.
                                3-6,   Merryweather 0-4-0   5-8 of 1876.
                                7-28,   Merryweather 0-4-0   10-31 of 1876.   "
                                29-36, Merryweather 0-4-0   38-45 of 1876.   "
                                37-46, Merryweather 0-4-0   51-60 of 1877.   "
                                47-52, Fox Walker   2-4-0   362-367 of 1877.   "
                                53-58, Fox Walker   2-4-0   412, 420 & ? of 1878. (probably   "
                                                                              412-420).
                                59-70, Falcon 0-4-0, 19-30 of 1879.   "

102.   PARIS.   (Société de Traction de l'Etoile).
       Later (Compagnie des Tramways du Nord).   Bankrupt 1894.
       From 1894.   (Compagnie des Tramways de Paris et du Departement de la Seine)
       See also No.104.
       Place de l'Etoile-Courbevoie-Suresnes, 3.5 km.   (Corpet locos).
       Clichy-Saint Denis,   ? km.   (St.Léonard locos).
       H.1874, S.1878, H(again) 1882, S.1900, E.1892/1911, C.1936.   Gauge. 1435.
       Locomotives. -   Nos.   1-14,   Corpet 0-4-0   260-273 of 1878. (Brown type).
                                15-16,   Corpet 0-4-0   276-277 of 1878/79.   "
                                17,   Corpet 0-4-0   256 of 1878.   "
                                18-24?   St.Léonard 0-4-2   475-481 of 1877/79. (Vaessen's type).   "

Note. -   A Winterthur 0-4-0 111 of 1877 built for the Paris Exhibition ran on
           trials and the Corpet locos were copies of its design.
           (See "Engineer" 16th August 1878).

103.   PARIS.   (S.A. du Tramway de Rueil à Marly le Roi).   Owned by Sieur Tarbré des Sablons.
       Later taken over by No.106 by No.104 in 1910.
       Marly le Roi-Port Marly-Rueil, 8.2 km.
       H.1865, S.1878, E.1911, C.1935.   Gauge. 1520 as horse then 1435.
       Locomotives (Trials).
                          No.   1,   Cail (Lamm & Francq) 0-4-0, fireless - of 1877.(Retained).
                                 2-3, Corpet 0-4-0   228-229 of 1876. (Stored and used by 106)
                                 4-5, Tilkin-Mention 0-4-0   (Aulnoye et Berlaimont 301-302 of 1876).
              (for service).   2-5,   Cail (Lamm & Francq) 0-4-0 Fireless 1878. (intended for
                                                                              Versailles).
                                 6-8, Lamm & Francq 0-4-0 Fireless 1886.   "

Names. -   1-Rueil, 2-Malmaison, 3-Bougival, 4-Port Marly, 5-Marly le Roi.
                     6-?, 7-Louveciennes, 8-?.

104. PARIS. (Compagnie des Tramways de Paris et du De'partement de la Seine).
Took over No.102 in 1894 and 106 (including 103) in 1910. From 1921 as No.107.

Place de l'Etoile-Courbevoie,	km.)	3.5 km.	Ex-102 Fireless locos.
Courbevoie-Suresnes,	km.)		Ex-102 Steam locos.
La Madeleine-Genevilliers	8.4 km.)		Serpollet steam cars.
La Madeleine-Asnie`res-Colombes,	9.0 km.)		

H.1874, S.1895, E.1902/1912, C.1936. Gauge. 1435.

Locomotives. - Nos. 1-14, Corpet (Lamm & Francq) 0-4-0 Fireless. ⊟
(rebuilt by Cail from 14 of those of No.102 in 1888).
15-19, Cail (Lamm & Francq) 0-4-0 Fireless. "
(rebuilt from those of No.103).
20, Lamm & Francq 0-4-0 Fireless, (formerly No.6 of No.103).
21-23, Corpet (Brown's type) 0-4-0 (ex No.102 not rebuilt).

Steam Cars. - Nos. 1-23, Pierson "Serpollet" cars (rebuilt from compressed air 1895). 🚃

105. PARIS. (Compagnie Ge'ne'rale des Omnibus) Tramways department.
Trocade'ro-Exposition ? km.)
Autreuil-Bois de Boulogne ? km.) Trials with "Rowan" cars 1889-1902.
Trocade'ro-Place Pigale, ? km.)
Louvre-Charenton-Creteil, 13.6 km. Regular service with "Rowan" cars 1903-1913.
La Bastille-Cimitie`re Saint Ouen, 7.5 km.)
Les Halles-Porte d'Ivry, 4.0 km.) "Serpollet" cars 1897-1913.
Clichy-La Madeleine, 2.0 km.)
La Bastille-Porte Rapp, 6.0 km.)
Place de l'Etoile-La Villette ? km.)
Trocadero-La Villette,) 12.4 km.) "Purrey" cars 1900-1914.
Place de la Nation-La Villette)
Gare de Lyon-Avenue Henri Martin, 9.0 km.)
Louvre-Se'vres (Versailles line) ? km.) "Purrey" Locomotives 1907-1913.
H.1874, S.1889, E.1914, C.1935. Gauge. 1435.
Steam Cars. - Nos. 1-14, (Franco-Belge "Rowan" cars 690-693 of 1889. (Kitson type).🚃
(Buffaud et Robatel "Rowan" cars of ? " " 🚃
401-415, Tubize/BM "Serpollet" cars 1078-1092/191-205 of 1896. "
416-460, ? "Serpollet" cars ? 1895/1896 "
701-750, "Purrey" cars 1900/1904 "
751-786, "Purrey" cars 1904 🚃
801, "Serpollet" car 1900. "

Locomotives. - 1-12, "Purrey" 0-4-0 1907 (rebuilt from "Mekarski" 0-6-0s). 🚂

Note. - Some of the "Rowan" and "Serpollet" cars had boilers and mechanical parts
supplied by Buffaud et Robatel.
See "La Vie du Rail" 23rd November, 1975, which says that 62 "Purrey"
cars were rebuilt from "Serpollet" cars by Valentin Purrey of 231 Rue
d'Ornano, Bordeaux and could carry coke and water for $\frac{3}{4}$ hours running.

106. PARIS. (S.A. des Voies Ferre'es Economiques, Paris-Saint Germain).
Took over No.102 and obtained through running over No.103.
Was taken over by No.104 in 1910.
Paris(Etoile)-Courbevoie-Port Marly-Saint Germain en Laye, 15.0 km.
Port Marly-Marly le Roi, 2.3 km. (Ex No.103).
Rueil(Gare)-Rueil(Ville)-Le Pecq (Saint Germain), ? km.
(New part)S.1891, E.1910, C.1935. Gauge. 1435.
Locomotives. - Nos. 1-6, Cail (Lamm & Francq) 0-4-0, (Fireless) - - of 1877/1886. ⊟
7-15, Fives Lille (Lamm & Francq) 0-4-0, (Fireless) - - of 1890. "
16-17, Corpet 0-4-0 228-229 of 1876 ex-No.103. ⊟
21-22, Tubize (BM) 0-6-0 819-820(44-45) of 1891. ⊟
23-26, Tubize (BM) 0-6-0 826-829(46-49) of 1891. "
27-37, Tubize (BM) 0-6-0 856-866(60-70) of 1892. "
(II)3,5,6,7,8, Winterthur 0-4-0 425, 338, 588 &.717-718 of 1885/92. "
ex-Geneva in 1902. ⁖

107. PARIS. (Compagnie du Chemin de Fer sur la Route de Paris à Arpajon).
From 1921 (Société des Transports en Commun de la Région Parisienne).
Paris(Porte d'Orleans)*-Antony-Montlhéry-Arpajon, 32.1 km.
Montlhéry-Marcoussis, 3.0 km.
S.1893, Part E.(Paris-Antony) 1901, Part D.1925, C.1936. Gauge. 1435.

Locomotives. -	Nos.	1-10,	Tubize(BM) 0-6-0	838-847(50-59) of 1891.	
		11-15,	Tubize(BM) 0-6-0	904-908(75-79) of 1893.	"
		16-18,	Tubize(BM) 0-6-0	949-951(108-110) of 1894.	"
		101-103,	Tubize(BM) 0-6-0	928-930(92-94) of 1894 (Smaller type).	"

Mekarski Compressed air locos. -

| | ? - ? | Cail | 0-6-0 | 2439-2443 of 1895. | |

Note:-   * Night vegetable trains extended to Les Halles.

108. PARIS. (S.A. du Tramway du Raincy à Montfermeil).
Later (Société des Tramways de l'Est Parisien). From 1921 as No.107.
(Scene of Larmanjat monorail experiments in 1868).
Le Raincy-Montfermeil, 5.5 km.
S.1890, E.1895, C.1938 (Last tram route in Paris area). Gauge. 1000 (later 1435).

Locomotives. -	Nos.	1-2,	Pinguély 0-4-0	7-8 of 1890.	
		3-4,	Pinguély 0-4-0	3-4 of 1890.	"
		5,	Weidknecht 0-4-0?	557 of 1891.	"

109. PARIS. (S.A. du Tramway Mécanique, Saint Germain-Poissy).
Later (Compagnie des Tramways Mécaniques des Environs de Paris).
Taken over by No.110 in 1911.
Saint Germain en Laye-Poissy 5.5 km. (not connected with No.106).
S.1896, P.1911, C.1933. Gauge. 1435.

Locomotives. -	Nos.	1-5,	Cail	0-4-0 (Fireless) ? - ? 1896.	
				(Rebuilt by Fives-Lille from five of those of No.106).	

110. PARIS. (Compagnie des Chemins de Fer de Grande Banlieue).
A company constituted in 1911 to take over Nos.109 and 162. It also built some lengthy
roadside light railways to the North-West and South of Paris. These connected with Nos.
106 and 107, permitting through working of goods trains worked by enclosed locomotives to
the markets in the centre of Paris.
Worked by (Société des Transports en Commun de la Région Parisienne),
from 1923 to 1933 then by (Société des Chemins de Fer Economiques),
less No.109 which was then closed.
Saint Germain en Laye-Bouafle-Meulan-Sagy, 30.9 km. (Connecting with No.106).
Saint Germain en Laye-Poissy-Gency, 21.3 km. (including No.109).
Pontoise-Gency-Sagy-Magny, 35.7 km.
Versailles(Clagny)-Noisy le Roi-Maule-Bouafle, 30.? km. (including No.162).
Arpajon-Etampes-Saint Martin d'Etampes, 32.0 km. (through running over No.107).
Etampes-Bouville-Maisse, 21.2 km.
Maisse-Milly-Corbeil, 32.6 km. (not connecting with No.143).
Bouville-La Ferté Alais, 8.9 km.
S.1911, Part P.1924, GS.1948, C.1953. Gauge. 1435.

Locomotives. -	Nos.	1-16,	Pinguély 2-6-0	263-278 of 1911.	
		51-53,	Energie 0-8-0	301-303 of 1912.	"
		54,	Energie 0-8-0	332 of 1923.	"
		101-108,	Schneider 0-6-0	4319-4326 of 1925/26. (Twin cab).	
			(No.103 preserved).		

111. PAU. (Compagnie des Chemins de Fer de Pau-Oloron-Mauléon).
Pau-Pontacq, 27.0 km.
Pau-Saint Laurent-Aire, 65.0 km. (Connecting with No.31).
Saint Laurent-Lembeye, 19.0 km.
Pau-Monein, 27.0 km.
Sauveterre-Oloron-Mauléon, 84.0 km. (Isolated line).
S.1900, C.1938 ? Gauge. 1000.

Locomotives. -	Nos.	1-4,	Tubize(BM) 0-6-0	1222-1225(235-237 & 246) of 1900.	⊟
		5-8,	Tubize(BM) 0-6-0	1249-1252(249-252) of 1900.	"
		9-11,	Tubize(BM) 0-6-0	1284-1286(274-276) of 1901.	"
		12-14,	Tubize(BM) 0-6-0	1352-1354(294-296) of 1902.	"
		15-16,	? ? ?		"
		17,	Tubize(BM) 0-6-0	1582(336) of 1908.	"
		18,	Tubize(BM) 0-6-0	1660 of 1909.	"
	(II)	2-5,	Tubize(BM) 0-6-0	692-695(34-37) of 1888. ex No.16 in 1914.	
	(II)	1 & 6,	Tubize(BM) 0-6-0	691 & 696(33 & 38 of 1888. ex No.16 in 1919.	

112. PERIGUEUX. (Chemins de Fer du Périgord). See also No.47.
From 1921 (Réseau Départemental de la Dordogne).
Périgueux-Saint Pardoux-La Rivière   54.0 km.
Périgueux-La Juvenie-Saint Yrieix,   70.0 km.
Périgueux-Vergy,   24.0 km.
S.1889, D.1937, C.1949. Gauge. 1000.

Locomotives. -	Nos.	-	Weidknecht 0-6-0	528 of 1889. (for construction ?).	⊔⊓
		1-8,	Tubize(BM) 0-6-0	653-660(9-16) of 1889.	⊟
		9-10,	Tubize(BM) 0-6-0	1142-1143(218-219) of 1898.	"
		11-26,	Pinguély 0-6-0	245-260 of 1909. Ex No.47.	⊔⊐
		81-82,	Pinguély 0-6-0	112-113 of 1902. Ex No.47 & ?	∵

113. PITHIVIERS. (Société d'Exploitation des Etablissements Decauville Ainé) until 1899.
Known as (Le Tramway de Pithiviers à Toury).
Later (Régie Départementale du Chemin de Fer d'Interêt local de Pithiviers à Toury).
A roadside line at first worked as a tramway, but latterly as an agricultural light railway,
using heavy industrial and ex-military locomotives.
A section of 4.0 km re-opened in 1966 as a museum line.
Pithiviers-Ormes-Toury, 32.0 km (+ about 49 km of agricultural branches).
S.1892, Part P.1922, GS.1952, C.1965 (see above). Gauge. 600. ⊔⊐

Locomotives. -	Nos.	-	Tubize	0-4-4-0	767 of 1889. (Decauville 87)for con-
		-	Decauville	0-4-2	158 of 1892. ⊔⊐)struction.
		2.1,	Decauville	0-4-2	189 of 1894. ⊟
		2.2,	Decauville	0-4-2	184 of 1894. "
		2.3,	Decauville	0-4-2	176 of 1894. "
		3.1,	Decauville	0-6-0	393 of 1903. ⊔⊐
		3.2,	Decauville	0-6-0	476 of 1905. "
		3.3,	Decauville	0-6-0	592 of 1908. (and all below)
		3.4,	Decauville	0-6-0	394 of 1904 *.* in 1925 (at first 732).
		3.5,	Tubize(BM)	0-6-0	1317/282 of 1902.Ex-No.127 (" 706).
		3.6,	Orenstein & Koppel 0-6-0		8083 of 1915. (Renumbered 3.7).
		3.8,	A.L.C.O.	2-6-2	57148 of 1916. Ex-American Army.
		3.9,	A.L.C.O.	2-6-2	57092 of 1916. " "
		3.10,	Hunslet	4-6-0	1238 of 1916. Ex-British Army.
		3.11,	Hunslet	4-6-0	1274 of 1917. " " (first 362).
		3.20 & 3.21 = 3.8 & 3.9 renumbered.			
		3.22,	A.L.C.O.	2-6-2	57131 of 1916. Ex-US Army in 1934.
		3.23,	A.L.C.O.	2-6-2	57156 of 1916 " " " 1935.
		4.1,	Humboldt	0-8-0	1250 of 1916. Ex-German Army.
		4.2,	Schwartzkopff	0-8-0	6724 of 1918. " "
		4.3,	Henschel	0-8-0	15545 of 1917. " "
		4.4,	Krauss	0-8-0	7463 of 1918. " "
		4.5,	Henschel	0-8-0	15270 of 1917. " "
		4.10,	Franco Belge	0-8-0	2839 of 1945 meant for German Army.
		4.11,	Franco Belge	0-8-0	2838 of 1945 " " " "
		4.12,	Franco Belge	0-8-0	2843 of 1945 " " " "
		4.13,	Franco Belge	0-8-0	2844 of 1945 " " " "
		4.14,	Franco Belge	0-8-0	2836 of 1944. Ex-German Army
		4.15,	Franco Belge	0-8-0	2825 of 1944 " "
		5.1,	Borsig	0-10-0	10235 of 1917 " "
		5.2,	Schwartzkopff	0-10-0	6744 of 1917. Ex-German Army.
		5.3,	Orenstein & Koppel 0-10-0		8285 of 1917 " "
		22.1,	Orenstein & Koppel 0-4-4-0		1752 of 1905 ∵ in 1917.
		22.2,	Decauville	0-4-4-0	110 of 1892 ∵ ex. No.28 in 1929.

22.3,	Decauville	0-4-4-0	135 of 1892.	All
22.4,	Decauville	0-4-4-0	136 of 1892.	
22.5,	Orenstein & Koppel	0-4-4-0	1769 of 1905	·.·
22.6,	Orenstein & Koppel	0-4-4-0	1825 of 1906	·.·
22.7,	Orenstein & Koppel	0-4-4-0	1772 of 1905	·.·
33.1,	Decauville	0-6-6-0	6009 of 1915	
			(originally with tender).	

Names. - Construction Locos - Dumbarton, Outarville; 2.1-Ormes, 2.2-Outarville (II)
2.3-Bazoches, 3.1-Torville, 3.2-Izy, 3.3-Brandélon, 3.4-Decauville,
3.5-Couthon (Le Minhic), 3.6 to 3.23 not named, 4.1-Humboldt,
4.2-Schwartzkopff, 4.3 to 4.15 not named, 5.1-Borsig, 22.1-Belfort,
22.2-(Grandcamp), 22.5-Koppel, 33.1-Marocaine.

Note. - Axle formation numbering was adopted in 1930, formerly a few locos retained
numbers given by previous owners, others not numbered.
Names and details of locomotives brought in after 1964 for museum purposes are
not included here.

114.   PLAN DE VAR. (S.A. des Tramways des Alpes Maritimes).
Constructed as a group of interurban electric tramways, but one line was worked by steam pending
delivery of electrical equipment.
Plan de Var-Saint Martin-Vesubie, ? km.
S.1909, E.1910, C.1928. Gauge. 1000.
Locomotives. -   Three Orenstein & Koppel 0-6-0   3528-3630 of 1909.?
                                                              (hired from contractor).

114A.   POITIERS. - See No.165, La Vienne.

115.   PONTARLIER. (Compagnie du Tramway de Pontarlier à Mouthe). (Intended for No.48 Morteau-Maiche).
From 1913 (Compagnie du Chemin de Fer de Pontarlier à Mouthe et Extension),
from 1930 part of No.48.
Pontarlier-Mouthe-Foncine le Haut, 41.9 km. (Connecting with No.72).
S.1901, C.1952. Gauge. 1000.
Locomotives. -   Nos.   1-3,   Buffaud et Robatel 0-6-0   - - of 1901. (Tubize type *)
                         4,   Corpet Louvet   0-6-0   946 of 1903.
                                                           (intended for No.48 Morteau-Maiche).
                         5,   Pinguély   2-6-0   325 of 1913.

* These locomotives had driving controls only at the front and fire doors only at the rear
and had to be turned at termini. Buffaud et Robatel did not allocate works numbers.

116.   PONTCHARRA. (S.A. du Tramway de Pontcharra à la Rochette et à l'Allevard).
Pontcharra-Detrier-La Rochette, 10.0 km.
Detrier-Allévard,   7.0 km.
S.1895, GS.1932, (S again 1941-1947), DG.1947 (still DG). Gauge. 1000 (1435 for DG).
Locomotives. -   Nos.   1-4,   Buffaud et Robatel 0-6-0   - - of 1895 (Tubize type).
                         5.   Buffaud et Robatel 0-6-0   - of 1910 ("   ").

Note. - Passenger service restored 1941-1947. Now standard gauge goods branch,
Pontcharra-Detrier-Allevard, worked by state railway diesel locos.

117.   PONT DE BEAUVOISIN. (S.A. du Tramway du Pont de Beauvoisin).
Saint Béron-Pont de Beauvoisin-Saint Genix sur Guiers, 16.0 km.
S.1897, D.1924, C.1933. Gauge. 1000.
Locomotives. -   Nos.   1-3,   Pinguély 0-6-0   25-27 of 1896.
                         4,   Pinguély 0-6-0   58 of 1898.

Note. - A compressed air car was borrowed from Aix les Bains in 1913.

118. PONT DE VAUX. (Compagnie du Tramway de Pont de Vaux à Fleurville).
Worked by (Chemins de Fer Economiques du Sud Est) from 1909.
Taken over by No.2 in 1919.
Pont de Vaux-Fleurville, 5.1 km.
S.1901, C.1908, Reopened 1909, P.1924, C.193?. Gauge. 1000.
Locomotives. -   Nos.   1-2,   Buffaud et Robatel 0-6-0 - - of 1901. (Tubize type).
                        3.   Sornin ?   0-6-0   - of 1908. (Transverse firebox). "

Name. -   No.3-Marie Louise.

119. QUEND. See FORT MAHON, No.55.

120. QUERCY. (Compagnie des Tramways du Quercy).
From 1922 (Chemin de Fer Départemental de Bretonoux Biars à Saint Céré).
Bretonoux Biars-Saint Céré, 10.0 km.
S.1907, P.1912 & 1924, C.1934. Gauge. 1000.
Locomotives. -   Nos.   1-2,   Corpet Louvet 0-6-0   1065 of 1906 & 1153 of 1907.
                        3,   Corpet Louvet 0-4-4-0   one of 676-679 of 1897. from No.68.
                      5009,   Carels,   2-4-0   ? of 1887. (loaned from industry)

121. RAON. (Société du Chemin de Fer de la Vallée de Celles).
From 1936 (Compagnie de Chemins de Fer Secondaires).
Raon Est-Raon sur Plaine, 24.1 km.
S.1907, P.1936, D.1937, C.1950 (Closed 1944/45). Gauge. -1000. (sidings 1435).
Locomotives. -   Nos.   1-2,   Corpet Louvet 2-6-0   1088-1089 of 1906.
                        3,   Corpet Louvet 0-6-0   1160 of 1908.   "
                        4,   Hanomag   0-4-0   5886 of 1911.   "
                        0.   Cockerill   0-4-0   2520 of 1906 (1435 gauge).
Four Purrey steam cars acquired secondhand. ∵

122. LE RAINCY. See PARIS No.108.

123. RENNES. See ILLE ET VILAINE, No.68.

124. RIBEAUVILLE. See Chapter 4, Alsace Lorraine. (German name is RAPPOLTSWEILER).

125. REIMS. (S.A. du Chemin de Fer de la Banlieue de Reims).
Lines in the SOISSONS area passed to the (Régie des Transports de l'Aisne)
after the 1914-1918 war, see No.3. The rest was then controlled by the (Société
Générale des Transports Départementaux).
Reims-Beine,   19.0 km.
Reims-Asfeld,   30.0 km.
Reims-Cormicy-Roucy-Soissons,   57.0 km. (See No.3).
Roucy-Corbeny,   ?   km.
Cormicy-Guignancourt-Asfeld-Rethel,   ?   (See also Nos. 3 & 146).
Reims-Bouleuse-Fismes,   42.0 km.
Bouleuse-Dormans,   26.0 km.
Reims-Ambonnay-Chalons sur Marne,   57.0 km.
Ambonnay-Ay-Epernay-Montmirail,   84.0 km. (See also No.50).
S.1896, Part P.1923, GS.1940, C.1953. Gauge. 1000.
Locomotives. -   Nos.   1-5,   Tubize(BM) 0-6-0 1003-1007(147-149) of 1896. ∵
                         6,   Tubize   0-6-0 743 of 1889, Ex-Belgium No.5. ∵
                      7-18,   Tubize(BM) 0-6-0 1263-1274(262-273) of 1903.
                        19,   Hagans   0-4-0   ? of ? . Ex-Contractor.   ∵
                     20-26,   Decauville 0-6-0 652-631 of 1912/13.(Tubize design).
                     30-32,   Corpet Louvet 0-6-0 982-984 of 1904. ("   ").
                     33-34,   Corpet Louvet 0-6-0 987-988 of 1905. ("   ").
                     40-43,   Piguet   2-6-0   - - of 1922.*
    Note. - °   + Nos.40-43 had Piguet boiler numbers 6421, 6425, 6428 & 6429.

66

	50-57,	Corpet Louvet 0-6-0	957-964 of 1903.
	58-59,	Corpet Louvet 0-6-0	1063, 1073 of 1905.
	60,	Corpet Louvet 0-6-0	1378 of 1911.

Railcars. -   1-2,   Purrey Steam Cars,   118-119 of 1896.

Name. -   No.19-La Maselotte.   Others not named.

126.   RIOM. (Société de Construction des Batignolles).
From 1903 (Société des Chemins de Fer de la Limagne).
Riom-Volvic, 17.5 km.
S.1890, P.1925, C.1936. Gauge. 1000.
Locomotives. -   Nos.   11-12,   Batignolles 0-6-0   1197-1198 of 1888.
                         69,   Batignolles 2-4-0   1479 of 1904. ∵

127.   ROTHENEUF. (Société du Tramway de Rothéneuf).
Paramé(Rochebonne)-Rothéneuf, 4.0 km. (See also No.136).
S.1896, C.1914 (Stock requisitioned). Gauge. 600.
Locomotives. -   Nos.   1-2,   Decauville   0-4-2   215-216 of 1896.
                        3,   Decauville   0-6-2   244 of 1898.
                        4,   Tubize(BM)   0-6-0   1317(282) of 1902. (Preserved).
                        5,   Decauville ? 0-6-0   ? of 1912.

Names. -   1-Paramé, 2-Rothéneuf, 3-Rochebonne, 4-Le Minihic, 5-Paramé (II).

128.   ROUEN. (Tramways Company of France). - Concession to Mr.Palmer Harding.
Later (Compagnie des Tramways de Rouen).
Hotel de Ville-Darnétal,   3.5 km.
Hotel de Ville-Mont Riboudet, 1.5 km.
Pont de Pierre-Maromme,   6.6 km.
Pont de Pierre-Saint Hilaire, 1.5 km.
Saint Sever-Quevilly,   3.3 km. (opposite side of River Seine).
H.1876, S.1878, H again 1884, E.1896, C.1953. Gauge. 1435.
Locomotives. -   Nos. 34-38,
                    & 42,   Merryweather 0-4-0   43-45, 51-52 & 56 of 1876/77) ∵
                   four   Merryweather 0-4-0   from 51-60 of 1877 ex-No.101) ∵
                   seven   Fox Walker   2-4-0   362-367, 412 & 420 of 1877 " ∵
                   six   Fives Lille 0-4-0   (between 2174 & 2185 of 1878.
                   one   Kitson   0-4-0   T.3 (2377) of 1878.

129.   ROUEN. (Compagnie du Tramway de Rouen-Trianon à la Forêt de Rouvray).
Trianon-Rond Point du Madrillet, 2.2 km.
(Part of the route was later covered by a Rouen electric tram route).
S.1906, P.1907, C.1908. Gauge. 600.
Locomotives. -   Possibly   Jung 0-4-0   1035 & 1061 of 1906/07. ?

130.   ROYAN. (Société Générale des Tramways de Royan).
Saint Georges de Didonne-Royan-Pontaillac, 7.2 km.
Royan(Casino)-Royan depôt,   0.3 km.
Saint ·Georges Port-Le Paradou, 2.0 km.
Pontaillac-La Grande Côte,   6.0 km. (Connecting with horse tramway).
H.1868, S.1890, C.1945 (War destruction). Gauge. 600.
Locomotives. -   Unnumbered   Decauville 0-4-0   56 of 1887 (for construction).
                    four   Decauville 0-4-0-0   59, 72-74 & 75 of 1889.
                 Nos.   1-8, Decauville 0-4-2   137-144 of 1891.
                        9-10, Decauville 0-6-2   234 & 237 of 1897.
                        11,   Decauville 0-6-2   267 of 1898.
                        12-13, Decauville 0-4-2   ? of ?
                   (II) 10,   Decauville 0-4-2   ? of ?
Names. -   1-Royan, 2-Le Chay, 3-St.Georges ?, 4-Pontaillac, 5-St.Palais, 6-Foncillon,
7-Valliers, 8-Le Parc, 9-Fernande, 10-Marie, 11-Eléna, 12-Alsacienne,
13-Italienne. Original Locos :- Ma Camarade, Ville de Laon, Kairouan,
(All ex-Paris Exhibition). Australie, Dumbarton, (II) 10 La Coubre.

131. RUEIL. See Paris, No.103.

132. SAINT AMAND. (Société des Chemins de Fer Economiques du Nord).
      See Hellemmes, No.66 and Valenciennes, No.159).

133. SAINT ETIENNE. (Compagnie des Chemins de Fer à Voie Etroite de Saint Etienne,
      Firminy, Rive de Gier et Extensions).
      Octroi de la Terrasse-Saint Etienne(Hotel de Ville)-Bellevue, 5.5 km.
      Bellevue-Croix de l'Orme-Firminy,   9.6 km.
      Bellevue-Octroi de la Digonnière   0.6 km.
      Hotel de Ville-Terrenoire-Rive de Gier,   24.0 km.
      Terrenoire-La Fouillouse,   7.3 km.
      S.1881, E.1907/1914, Part still working. Gauge. 1000.

Locomotives. -	Nos.	1-5,	Winterthur	0-4-0	238-242 of 1881.	
		6-10,	Winterthur	0-4-0	243-247 of 1882.	"
		11-22,	Winterthur	0-4-0	273-284 of 1882.	"
	?	23-25,	Tubize	0-6-0	501-503 of 1882.	"
	?	26,	Couffinhal	0-4-0?	experimental ? 1882.	"
		27-30,	Tubize	0-6-0	509-512 of 1882.	"
		31-37,	Carels	0-6-0	278 etc. of 1884/87.	"
		38-39,	Own works	0-4-0	- - of 1892.	"
	?	40,	Winterthur	0-4-0	231 of 1881, ex-Luxembourg. ⚡	"

Names. -   1-St.Etienne, 2-Chambon, one of 11-20-La Digonnière. 21-St. Etienne, 22-?.
              36-Valfleury, 37-Archiac. 40-Luxembourg.

134. SAINT CLAUDE. See Jura, No.72.

135. SAINT GALMIER. (Compagnie du Tramway à Vapeur de Saint Galmier Ville a Saint
      Galmier Gare).
      Saint Galmier Véauche (Gare)-Saint Galmier Ville, 3.4 km. (branches to Sources 1.6)
      S.1911, GS.1914-1920, C.1954. Gauge. 1000.

Locomotives. -	One or two	Decauville	0-6-0	?	?
	One	Orenstein & Koppel	0-6-0	5860 of 1912.	"
	One	Winterthur	0-4-0	?	?

                                        ex-St. Etienne(See No.133).

136. SAINT MALO. (Société des Tramways Bretons).
      Saint Malo-Rocabey-Paramé,   5.0 km.)
      Rocabey-Saint Servan,   3.0 km.) Urban routes. Connecting with No.68
      Paramé-La Langottière-Cançale(Ville),   13.0 km.)   & No.127.
      La Langottière-Terlabouët-Cançale(La Houle), 3.6 km.) Interurban routes.
      S.1889, E.1927 (Urban services only), Rest P.1925, D.1934, C.1947/49. Gauge. 1000.

Locomotives. -	Nos.	1-6,	Carels	0-4-0	? - ? of 1889.	
		10-11,	Tubize(BM)	0-6-0	1144-1145(220-221) of 1898.	"
		12,	Tubize(BM)	0-6-0	1206(234) of 1900.	"
		13,	Franco Belge	0-6-0	1871 of 1909. (Tubize type).	"
		14,	Franco Belge	0-6-0	1957 of 1910. " "	"
		15,	Franco Belge	0-6-0	2087 of 1913. " "	"
	(II)	9,	Tubize(BM)	0-6-0	1098(211) of 1896 (Hired from No.68)	"
		56,	Corpet Louvet	0-6-0	867 of 1902 " " "	
		67-68,	Corpet Louvet	0-6-0	878-879 of 1904 " " " "	

Names. -   1-Saint Malo, 2-Saint Servan, 3-Paramé, 4-Cancale, 5-Dinard, 6-Ille et Vilaine,
              10-Saint Melior, 11-Saint Coulomb, 12-La Houle, 13-La Langottière, 14-Terlabouët
              15-La Beuglais, (II)9-Saint Thurial.

137. SAINT ROMAIN DE COLBOSC. (Compagnie du Tramway de Saint Romain de Colbosc).
      Saint Romain(Ville)-Saint Romain(Gare Etainhus). 4.3 km.
      S.1897, C.1929. Gauge. 1000.

Locomotives. -	Nos.	1-3,	Corpet Louvet	0-4-0	680-682 of 1897.
		Three	Serpollet steam cars, (Trials, 1896).		

138. SAINT TROJAN. (Société du Tramway Touristique de Saint Trojan).
A tramway with a preserved locomotive serving pleasure beaches
on the Ile d'Oléron.
Saint Trojan-Gatseau, 4.2 km.
Gatseau-Maumusson, 2.0 km.
D.1965, S.1966, Still operating. Gauge. 600.
Locomotives. -   Couillet 0-6-0   1576 of 1910. ex-industry ⁛

139. SAINT VICTOR. (Compagnie du Chemin de Fer de Saint Victor à Thizy).
Saint Victor-Thizy, 6.8 km.
S.1882, GS.1932, C.1934. Gauge. 1000.
Locomotives. -   Nos.   1-2,   Cail   0-6-0   2131-2132 of 1881.
                        3,   Pinguély   0-6-0   17 of 1892. (? enclosed).
                        4-6, Corpet Louvet 0-6-0 739, 858 & 1365 of 1898, 1901 & 1911.

140. SARTHE. See Le MANS, No.75.

141. SAUMUR. (Compagnie Française des Voies Ferrées Economiques-Réseau de Saumur
et sa Banlieue) owned by (Compagnie des Tramways à Vapeur de l'Ouest).
From 1901 (Compagnie des Tramways de Saumur et Extensions).
From 1926 (Compagnie Nouvelle des Voies Ferrées d'Interêt Local de
Saumur et des Environs).
Saumur-Saint Florent-Saint Hilaire, 7.5 km. (Urban line).
Saumur-Fontevrault,   15.5 km. (Interurban line).
S.1896, C.1916-1918, Reopened 1918, P.1925 ?, C.1930 ?, Gauge. 1000.
Locomotives. -   Nos.   1-4,   Pinguély 0-6-0 28-31 of 1896.
                        5,   Pinguély 0-6-0 148 ? of 1901.
                 Three   "Purrey" Steam cars 1907.

142. SAVOIE. See Chambery No.32.

143. SEINE ET MARNE. (Société des Tramways du Sud de Seine et Marne).
Melun-Chailly en Bière-Barbizon, 11.0 km.
Chailly en Bière-Milly Ville,   22.0 km (Not connecting with No.110 at Milly).
S.1899, P.1923/28, C.1938. Gauge. 1000.
Locomotives. -   Nos.   1-3,   Corpet Louvet 0-6-0   713-715 of 1898.
                        4-5,   Corpet Louvet 0-6-0   1177-1178 of 1908.
                        6?   Corpet Louvet 0-6-0   ? 1195 of 1908 ?

Names. -   1-Melun, 2-Barbizon, 3-Milly, 4-Chailly, 5-Arbonne.

144. SEINE ET MARNE. (Société Générale des Chemins de Fer Economiques - "Tramways
de Seine et Marne").
Meulan-Verneuil l'Etang,   18.4 km. (Isolated line).
Jouy le Châtel-Marles en Brie, 23.6 km.
Jouy le Châtel-Nangis-Bray,   ) 87.7 km. (Connecting with light railway).
Jouy le Châtel-St.Simeon-Sablonnieres,)
S.1901, P.1927 to 1934, GS.1934 (parts S again 1940) C.1965. Gauge. 1000.
Locomotives. -   4501-4503, Graffenstaden 0-4-4-0 4440-4442 of 1893. ⁛
                 3701-3711, Cail *   0-6-2   2545-2555 of 1900.
                 3712,   Cail   0-6-2   2580 of 1902.
                 3713,   Cail   0-6-2   2557 of 1900.
                 3714,   Buffaud & Robatel 0-6-2   - of 1910.
                 3756,   Corpet Louvet 0-6-2   1122 of 1907.
                 Eight   Baldwin   0-6-2   used by Military authorities 1914-1918.
Note. - *   The Cail and Buffaud et Robatel 0-6-2s were designed to run with
                 the cab always leading, but were not enclosed. Other locos on loan.

Names. -   4501-Orcenais, 4502-Tortezais, 4503-St.Janvrin, 3701-Melun, 3702-Vernueil,
                 3703-Guignes, 3704-Nangis, 3705-Sablonnières, 3706-Marles, 3707-St.Siméon,

3708-Jouy, 3709-Rozoy, 3710-Rebais, 3711-Donnemaire, 3712-Vimpelles, 3713-Bray, 3714-Béton Bazoches (This loco preserved). 3756-not named.

145. SENONES. (Société Anonyme du Tramway de Senones à Moussey).
Senones-Moussey, 5.6 km. (Connecting with C.F. Senones à Etival).
S.1914, C.1914 (War destruction), Reopened 1928, D.1928, C. ?. Gauge. 1435.
Locomotives. - No. 0.165, Est (Epernay Works) 0-6-0 (rebuilt from SACM 419 of 1867).
6123, Graffenstaden (SACM) 0-6-0 4827 of 1898 (ex-A.L.Rly.).∵ ..
6141, Graffenstaden (SACM) 0-6-0 5026 of 1899 ("   ).∵ "

146. . SOISSONS. See BANLIEUE DE REIMS, No.125 and AISNE, No.3.
No.125 operated a local service in Soissons with Purrey steam cars.
Soissons(Gare du Nord)-Faubourg Saint Waast, 2.0 km.
S.1896, C.1914. Gauge. 1000.
Motive Power. - Nos. 1-2, "Purrey" steam cars, 118-119 of 1896.

147. SOMME. See FEUQUIERES, No.53.

148. STRASBOURG. See STRASSBURG, Chapter 4, (Alsace Lorraine).

149. TARASCON. (Compagnie du Tramway de Tarascon sur Ariège à Auzat).
Tarascon sur Ariége-Auzat, 16.2 km.
S.1911, C.1932. Gauge. 1000.
Locomotives. - Nos. 1-4, Corpet Louvet 0-6-0 1222-1225 of 1909. (later numbered 34-37).
?, Pinguély 0-6-0 107 of 1910. "
Three Piguet 0-6-0 - - of 1909. "
38. Corpet Louvet 0-6-0 1300 of 1911. "

150. TARN. (Compagnie des Chemins de Fer à Voie Etroite et Tramways à Vapeur du Tarn).
Laboutarie-Graulhet-La Ramière-Laveur, 34-0 km. (Laboutarie-Réalmont, horse worked).
La Ramière-Saint Sulpice, 14.0 km. (Not completed to Salvagnac).
S.1895, P.1925 ?, C.1936. Gauge. 600.
Locomotives. - Nos. 1-3, Decauville 0-6-2 203-205 of 1895.
4-5, Weidknecht 4-6-0 698-699 of 1902. "
6. Weidknecht 4-6-0 ? of 1913. "

Names. - 1-Graulhetoise, 2-Réalmontoise, 3-Montdragonne. Others not named.

151. TARN. (Compagnie des Chemins de Fer Départementaux du Tarn). Owned by No.40.
From 1933 (Voies Ferrées Départementales du Midi).
From 1954 (Société Auxiliare pour les Chemins de Fer Secondaires).
Castres-Le Bouissas-Lacaune-Murat, 75.0 km.
Le Bouissas-Brassac, 12.2 km.
Albi-Valence d'Albigeois, 30.3 km. (Separate line).
Albi-Saint Juery-Alban, 33.2 km.
S.1905, P.1925, D.1934, C.1962. Gauge. 1000.
Locomotives. - Nos. 1-7, Graffenstaden (SACM), 2-6-0 5441-5447 of 1904. (small)
11-17, Graffenstaden (SACM), 2-6-0 5448-5454 of 1904. (larger) "
21, Pinguély 0-6-0 (one of 94-99) of 1900 ∵ (ex-No.153). "
30-31, Carels 0-4-0 Tram, ? - ? of ?

152. TARN ET GARONNE. (Compagnie des Tramways de Tarn et Garonne).
From 1932 (Société des Transports Auxiliaires des Chemins de Fer du Midi).
Montauban-Gasseras-Molières, 35.0 km.
Gasseras-Verdun sur Garonne, 29.5 km.
Montauban-Monclar de Quercy, 24.6 km.
Coussadd-Caylus, 22.3 km.
Castelsarrasin-Lavit de Lomage, 27.2 km.

Valence d'Agen-Montaigu de Quercy, 43.5 km.
S.1913, C.1914-1916, P.1924, C.1933. Gauge. 1000.

Locomotives. - Nos. 1-7, Buffaud et Robatel 0-6-0 - - of 1913 ?
              8-11, Corpet Louvet 0-6-0 1366-1369 of 1911. "
          15,12-14,16, Corpet Louvet 0-6-0 1373-1377 of 1913. "
           18-19, Corpet Louvet 0-6-0 1449-1450 of 1914. "
            17, Corpet Louvet 0-6-0 1494 of 1914. "
           20-21, Corpet Louvet 0-6-0 1544-1545 of 1915. "
      "Marie Louise"- Weidknecht 0-6-0 529 of 1889. (ex-Contractor 1928). "

153. TOULOUSE. (Compagnie du Chemin de Fer d'Interêt Local de Toulouse à Boulogne sur Gesse).
From 1902 (Compagnie des Chemins de Fer du Sud Ouest), which also ran light railways
around Toulouse.

Toulouse(Roguet)-Fonsorbes-Boulogne sur Gesse, 97.5 km.
Fonsorbes-Saint Foix de Péyrolières, 7.2 km.
S.1900, A.1934, C.1949. Gauge. 1000.

Locomotives. - two unnumbered Weidknecht 0-6-0 ? ? - ? of ? (ex-Constructor).
             Nos. 1-6, Pinguély 0-6-0 94-99 of 1900. "
             101-102, Decauville 0-6-0 272-273 of 1901. "

Names. - Weidknechts = La Madeleine & La Meuse.

154. TOURS. (Compagnie Générale Française de Tramways).
From 1901 (Compagnie des Tramways de Tours).
Depôt St.Symphorien-Grammont, 4.4 km.
H.1877, S.1895, E.1900, C.1949. Gauge. 1435 (1000 on electrification).

Motive Power. - Nos. 1-2, Cail "Serpollet" cars, 1895.
             3-6, Decauville "Serpollet" cars, 1896. "
            7-10, Bonnefond "Serpollet" cars, 1896. "

155. TOURS. (Société du Tramway à Vapeur de Tours à Vouray).
From 1943, as No.154.
Tours(Place des Arts)-Vouray, 7.6 km. (1.8 common track with No.154 above).
S.1889, E.1911, C.1932. Gauge. 1435 until 1901, then 1000.

Locomotives. - Nos. 11-13, St.Léonard 0-4-0 1242-1244 of 1900 (1435 gauge).

Motive Power. - Nos. 1-2, Franco Belge "Rowan" cars, 697-698 of 1889. (1000 gauge)
            3-4, Franco Belge "Rowan" cars, 753-754 of 1890. " " "
             5, Franco Belge "Rowan" car, ? ?

156. TOURS. (Compagnie Générale Française de Tramways). As No.154.
Tours(Place Choiseul)-Mareuil-Luynes, 10.3 km. (and depôt working over No.154).
Mareuil-Fondettes, 1.4 km. (connecting with No.70).
S.1899, E.1912, C.1935. Gauge. 1000.

Locomotives. - Nos. 1-3, St.Léonard 0-4-0 1170-1172 of 1898.
             4, Corpet Louvet 0-4-0? ? of 1902. "
             5, St.Léonard 0-6-0 1521 of 1908.

157. TRINITE. (Société Anonyme du Chemin de Fer Economique de la Trinité sur Mer à Etel).
La Trinite-Plouharnel-Etel, 19.9 km.
S.1901, C.1914 (Requisitioned), Reopened 1923, C.1935. Gauge. 600 (1000 in 1923).

Locomotives. - Nos. 1-3, Decauville 0-4-2 321, 323 & 322 of 1900.
             4 Orenstein & Koppel 0-6-0 1070 of 1903.
            5-6? Orenstein & Koppel 0-6-0 ? - ? of 1911. "

Names. - 1-Etel, 2-Carnac, 3-La Trinité. (600 gauge). 4-6 not named.
          (No.5 possibly Orenstein & Koppel 0-4-0 1676 of 1905).

Note. - Taken over by C.F. du Morbihan (No.95) in 1923 and reconstructed to
metre gauge. Then worked by the following locomotives.

Locomotives. - Nos. 1-3, Corpet Louvet 0-6-0 1605-1607 of 1922.
             4, Corpet Louvet 0-6-0 1633 of 1923. "
            38, Pinguély 0-6-0 317 of 1911 ex-No.95 in 1928. "

157A. VALENCE. (?).
    Note.-   SLM Winterthur Works list indicates that their No.166, a standard
                    gauge tramway locomotive was built in 1880 for "Valence". It is
                    not known whether this was Valence in France, Valenza in Italy or
                    Valencia in Spain, all three of which are known as "Valence" in
                    French.

158.   VALLEE DE CELLES. See RAON, No.121.

159.   VALENCIENNES. (S.A. du Tramway de Valenciennes à Anzin et Extensions).
       Later (Compagnie des Chemins de Fer Economiques du Nord).
       Valenciennes-Anzin-Raismes-Saint Amand, 13.1 km. (Connecting with No.66).
       Croix d'Anzin-Condé-Bonsecours,   18.3 km. (Belgian Frontier).
       Condé-Hergnies,   8.0 km.
       Valenciennes-Blanc Misseron,   12.0 km. (Connecting with Belgian SNCV).
       Valenciennes-Denain-Lourches,   14.6 km.
       S.1881, E.1914/23, C.1966. Gauge. 1000.   (Full steam working in 1914 war).

Locomotives.-	Nos.	1-6,	Tubize	0-6-0	413-418 of 1880.	"
		7,	Tubize	0-6-0	514 of 1882.	"
		8,	Tubize	0-6-0	456 of 1882.	"
		9-10,	Tubize	0-6-0	515-516 of 1882.	"
		11-13,	Tubize	0-6-0	541-543 of 1884.	"
		14,	Tubize(BM)	0-6-0	937(97) of 1895. (like Belgian SNCV Class 13).
		31-37,	Tubize	0-6-0	443-449 of 1881.	"

       Note.-   Loco No.14 was soon transferred to the Lens-Frévent line of the same company
                but was back at Valenciennes in 1944, renumbered 30!

160.   VENDEE. (Compagnie des Tramways de la Vendée). Took over No.30 in 1914.
       Later (Chemins de Fer de l'Etat - Réseau de la Vendée).
       From 1939 (Compagnie des Chemins de Fer Départementaux).
       La Roche sur Yonne-Les 4 Chemins de l'Oie-Les Herbiers, 41.9 km.
       Les 4 Chemins de l'Oie-Montaigu,   25.0 km.
       Les 4 Chemins de l'Oie-Chantonnay,   17.0 km.
       Les Sables d'Olonne-Talmont-Le Champ Saint Père, 38.3 km.
       L'Aiguillon sur Mer-Lucon-Chantonnay,   53.7 km.
       La Roche sur Yonne-Legé,   35.1 km.
       Bourgneuf-Beauvoir sur Mer,   18.0 km.
       La Barre de Monts-Les Sables d'Olonne,   64.2 km.
       Branch to the Harbour at Les Sables d'Olonne, 1.5 km.
       Challans-Beauvoir-La Barre de Monts-Fromentine, 25.0 km. (ex-No.30).
       Talmont-Luçon,   46.9 km.
       S.1900, Part D.1923, GS.1933, C.1959. Gauge. 1000.

Locomotives.-	Nos.	1-18,	Decauville	0-6-0	- - of 1900/01 (two sizes).	
		101-104,	Corpet Louvet	0-6-0	898-901 of 1902.	"
		201-203,	Corpet Louvet	0-6-0	1400-1402 of 1911/12.	"
		251-253,	Corpet Louvet	0-6-0	? - ? of ? ex-C.F.Charentes.	"
		301-303,	Corpet Louvet	0-6-0	1283, 1292 & 1322 of 1910/11	"
		401-407,	Piguet	2-6-0	- - of 1907.	"
		408-411,	Corpet Louvet	2-6-0	1654-1656 & 1742 of 1910/1911.	"
		501-505,	Corpet Louvet	2-6-0	1757-1761 of 1930.	"
	(II)	1-3,	Corpet Louvet	0-6-0	614-616 of 1895. ex-No.30 in 1914.	"
	(II)	4,	Pinguély	0-6-0	64 of 1898	" " "	"
	(II)	101,	?	0-6-0	?	ex-? in 1943.	"
	(II)	8,	?	0-6-0	?	ex-? in 1946.	"

161.   VERSAILLES. (Société du Tramway de St.Cyr l'Ecole à Versailles). *
       Later owned by "Economique" Group. See No.22.
       Saint Cyr-Versailles(Orangerie), 3.9 km. (Through running to Gare Rive Gauche).
       S.1891, E.1897, C.1937. Gauge. 1435.

Locomotives.-	Nos. 9-12,	Pinguély	0-4-2	9-12 of 1890

                         (Intended for No.108. Regauged).

       Note.-   *See "Chemins de Fer Régionaux et Urbains" No.144, 1977 page 52.

162. VERSAILLES. (Société Française du Tramway de Versailles à Maule).
Taken over by No.110 in 1911 and converted to standard gauge.
Versailles(Clagny)-Le Chesnay-Maule-Meulan, 37.5 km.
S.1899, (C.1912-1913 for gauge change), C.1944.   Gauge. 1000 to 1913 then 1435.

Locomotives. -   Nos.   1-2,   Pinguély 0-4-0   32-33 of 1896/97. (articulated onto carriage).

(Metre gauge).   3-4,   Pinguély 0-6-0   56-57 of 1898.
    5,   Corpet Louvet 0-6-0   ? of ?   •:• ?
    6,   Not delivered.
    7-8,   Corpet Louvet 0-6-0   1133-1134 of 1907.   "

Note. -   When converted to standard gauge, used general stock of No.110.

163. VEUREY. See Grenoble, No.63.

164. VIENNE (Isère). (Compagnie des Chemins de Fer Economiques du Nord).
Worked by No.42 from 1930.
Vienne-Le Grand Lemps-La Ravinghouse-Charavines, 68.0 km. (Connecting with No.71).
La Ravinghouse-Voiron,   12.0 km. (Connecting with No.168).
Vienne-Faubourg d'Estressin-Pont l'Evêque,   ? km. (Urban line).
S.1891. (Urban line H.1895), P.1925, C.1937. Gauge. 1000.

Locomotives. -   Nos.   41-45,   Franco Belge 0-6-0 785-789 of 1890. (Tubize type).
    51,   Pinguély   0-6-0   77 of 1889.
    ?,   Pinguély   0-6-0   106 of 1901.   "

165. VIENNE (La Vienne). (Compagnie des Tramways de la Vienne).
Poitiers-Saint Martin d'Ars,   48.0 km.
Poitiers(Ligne des Boulevards),   4.0 km.
S.1895, P.192?, C.1933. Gauge. 1000.

Locomotives. -   Nos.   1-7,   Bollée 0-4-0 2-8 of 1895.
    (II)   1-14.   Corpet Louvet 0-6-0   1330-1343 of 1910/13.

Names. -   1-Poitiers, 2-St.Martin d'Ars, 3-St.Benôit, 4-Gençay, 5-St.Secondin,
    6- ?, 7- ?, (Scrapped in 1898/99 and names not recorded).
    (II)-1-Châtellerault, 2-Verneuil, 3-Chauvigny, 4-Llomaise, 5-Verrières,
    6-Bouresse, 7-Lencloître, 8-Neuville, 9-Voille, 10-Latille, 11-Lavausseau,
    12-Sanxay, 13-Jazeneuil, 14-Luzignan.

166. VICINAUX. See JURA, No.72. (This company also controlled a number of light railways).

167. VILLIERS LE BEL. (Société des Chemins de Fer sur Route à Traction de Locomotives).
Villiers le Bel-Gare de Gonesse, 3.2 km.
S.1878, C.1914 Reopened E.1928, C.1949.   Gauge. 1060 steam. 1000 electric.

Locomotives. -   Nos.   1-2,   Crespin et Marteau 0-4-0 ? - of 1878.
    3,   Tilkin-Mention   0-4-0   ? of ?
    4.   Anjoubalt   0-4-0   ? of ?   •:•
    (II)   1,   Corpet   0-4-0 452 of 1886.   "
    (II)   3,   Corpet Louvet   0-6-0   ? of ?   •:• "

168. VOIRON. (Société du Chemin de Fer de Voiron à Saint Béron).
From 1928, worked by (Chemin de fer de l'Est de Lyon). Département from 1932.
Voiron-Saint Laurent du Pont-Saint Béron, 34.1 km.   (Connecting with No.164).
Saint Laurent du Pont-Fourvoire,   1.8 km.
S.1894, P.1926, GS.1936, C.1938. (Sidings GD to 1955). Gauge. 1000.

Locomotives. -   Nos.   1-7,   Pinguély 0-6-0 18-24 of 1894.

Names. -   1-Grande Chartreuse, 2-Fourvoire, 3-Le Trou, 4-La Perelle, 5-Chailles,
    6-Le Crossey, 7-Le Grand Som.

169. VOSGES. See GERARDMER, No.60.

(Upper). Paris was the only city to make extensive use of self-propelled steam cars. A "Serpollet" double-deck car receiving attention at La Bastille.
(Lower). A rather "clapped-out" "Rowan" car in its final days in front of the Louvre.

Photos: RATP. R 201 & 205.

Tramways Haute Saône et Jura.

France and Ireland each had a few twin-cab locomotives on tramways. This one is No. 323 for "Les Tramways du Jura". Note that they used the Blanc Misseron works number as a fleet number.
Tubize Catalogue.   Courtesy: Prof. A. D. De Pater.

St ETIENNE   21

Most of the later Winterthur tram-engines were six-coupled, but those for St. Etienne were four-coupled. No. 21, "St. Etienne".
Winterthur Catalogue.   Courtesy: Deutsches Museum, Munich.

The Arpajon Station of the Paris-Arpajon tramway, with loco No.15. Note the braking system being recharged from compressed air cylinders on a wheelbarrow. Commercial Postcard.

Plettenburger Strassenbahn, Henschel loco No.4 (II) with standard gauge trucks on transporters. Note that the locomotive has offset side buffers and dual coupling arrangements for shunting on three-rail mixed gauge track.

Photo: Lawrence Marshall.

This photograph of "Königsberg" is rather a mystery. It is not captioned but is thought to be one of the very narrow gauge Hohenzollern locomotives for Kattowitz.
Hohenzollern Catalogue?   Courtesy: Helmuth Hinze.

Hagans 339 of 1896 for the short Rees-Empel tramway.
Hagans Catalogue.   Courtesy: late Friederich Kemper.

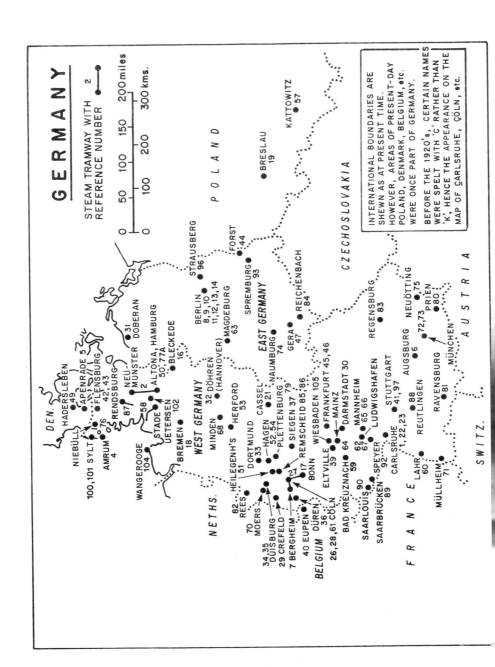

GERMANY

STEAM TRAMWAY WITH
REFERENCE NUMBER ●——● 2

0   50   100 150 200 miles
0   100   200   300 kms.

INTERNATIONAL BOUNDARIES ARE
SHEWN AS AT PRESENT TIME.
HOWEVER, AREAS OF PRESENT-DAY
POLAND, DENMARK, BELGIUM, etc.
WERE ONCE PART OF GERMANY.

BEFORE THE 1920's, CERTAIN NAMES
WERE SPELT WITH 'C' RATHER THAN
'K', HENCE THE APPEARANCE ON THE
MAP OF CARLSRUHE, CÖLN, etc.

POLAND

CZECHOSLOVAKIA

AUSTRIA

SWITZ.

DEN.

NETHS.

BELGIUM

FRANCE

WEST GERMANY

EAST GERMANY

KATTOWITZ 57

BRESLAU 19

FORST 44

STRAUSBERG 96

BERLIN 8,9,10 11,12,13,14

MAGDEBURG 63

SPREMBURG 93

REICHENBACH 84

GERA 47

NAUMBURG 74

REGENSBURG 83

NEUÖTTING 75

PRIEN 80

MÜNCHEN 72,73

AUGSBURG 6

RAVENSBURG 81

REUTLINGEN 88

STUTTGART 1,22,23

CARLSRUHE 41,97

LAHR 60

MÜLLHEIM 71

SPEYER 92

MANNHEIM 65 66

LUDWIGSHAFEN 67

DARMSTADT 30

MAINZ 64

FRANKFURT 45,46

ELTVILLE 39

WIESBADEN 105

SIEGEN 37

REMSCHEID 85,86

PLETTENBURG 52,54

HAGEN 21

CASSEL 79

HERFORD 53

DÖHREN (HANNOVER) 32

MINDEN 68

DORTMUND 33

HEILEGENH'S 51

DÜSSELDORF 34,35

CREFELD 29

BERGHEIM 7

EUPEN 40

DÜREN 36

CÖLN 26,28,61

BONN 17

BAD KREUZNACH 27

SAARLOUIS 59

SAARBRÜCKEN 89

MOERS 70

REES 82

BREMEN 18

UETERSEN 102

STADE 58

WANGEROOGE 104

AMRUM 4

NIEBÜLL 100,101 SYLT

HADERSLEBEN 49

APENRADE 5

FLENSBURG 42,43

RENDSBURG 76

NEÜ-MÜNSTER 2

ALTONA,HAMBURG 50,77A

BLECKEDE 16

DOBERAN 31

WANGEROOGE 104

3.GERMANY

Prior to the 1914-1918 war, the German Empire consisted of a number of loosely united sovereign states, owing some allegience to a central government in Berlin. Within this Empire, there were both urban and interurban steam tramways. The urban tramways which were few in number adopted steam traction at a very early date, but electrification also followed at an early date. On the other hand, most of the interurban and rural lines were built fairly late and because of the difficulties occasioned by the war and subsequent depression, several escaped replacement until quite recent times (in fact one is still operated as a tourist attraction at Chiemsee). Many were of a rural character, but the feature which contributed to the long survival of some of them, was that they served a chain of small semi-industrialized towns and provided a large number of industrial sidings, connecting factories with the main line railways. Even if the tramway were laid to a narrow gauge, thanks to the availability of transporter trucks, they were still able to bring main line wagons right into the factory premises for loading with their products. Several tramways, although equipped with enclosed locomotives for working on public roads, were built entirely for goods transporter traffic and never carried passengers. On others, goods traffic continued long after passenger traffic had been given up.

The methodical Germans, not unexpectedly, have a legal distinction between tramways and railways, but such railways as are known to have used enclosed locomotives at any time, receive a mention in the tables that follow. Mention is also made of any undertaking that changed its status and although built as a steam railway, was subsequently electrified as a tramway. (e.g. Eisern-Siegen, Moers-Homburg & Herford). Moreover, it should not be forgotten that under the strain of war, between 1939 and 1945, a number of electric tramways, whose overhead wires had been brought down by bombing, or power stations destroyed, hired steam engines from local industrial establishments to pull trains of "dead" electric tramcars. This is known to have happened in Essen, Bochum, Dortmund, Mullheim on Ruhr, Saarbrucken and no doubt other places. (Unfortunately full details do not appear to have been recorded).

Returning to the beginning, there were trials with steam tramway locomotives at Hamburg as early as 1875, but the first line to provide a regular service, opened at Cassel on the 9th July 1877 and it belonged to a British company entitled "The Cassel Tramways Company Limited". Appropriately enough the first locomotives came from Merryweather & Co., London and Starbuck of Birkenhead provided the coaches. The track was laid on the streets in the town and on private right of way in the outskirts. Ten days later, a regular service commenced at Hamburg, to the suburb of Wandsbek, using Winterthur locomotives, similar to the one exhibited in Paris. They hauled double deck carriages. Because of the pointed fenders with which these locomotives were fitted, at the front, they soon became known as "Flat Irons" and like many British models, they had tall chimneys so that the smoke should clear the upper decks of the carriages. Like London and Paris, Berlin was served by a number of tramway companies, which between them tried various methods of propulsion, including some early experiments with steam; one made extensive use of "Rowan" cars. Other urban steam tramways existed at Carlsruhe, Crefeld, Frankfurt, Darmstadt, Dortmund, Duisburg, Magdeburg, Munich and Wiesbaden. The latter line was also British owned at first.

In spite of the fact that Germany has been at the forefront of modern technical development for many years, the last remaining enclosed locomotive in public service in Europe, (apart from those officially "Preserved") is that on the Chiemsee line in South Germany. It is a standard Krauss model, overhauled in the 1960s by Jung, and is used in the summer months to carry holiday-makers from the main line railway station to a jetty whence a paddle steamer takes them to an island on the lake, topped by one of King Ludwig's castles. The Forst line (now in East Germany) was the last goods tramway to survive with transporter trucks pulled by steam and the few others that remain use diesel motive power. Some German steam tramways used diesel railcars in their later years, but less than in other countries.

Locomotives

Germany is best known, not for the steam tramways which operated within its boundaries, but for its prodigious output of tramway locomotives, exported to all parts of the world. In his book, Dr. Whitcombe points out [1] that the firm of Henschel und Sohn of Cassel [2], started building tram engines in 1877 and eventually supplied some 500 of them. This is confirmed by an examination of their Works list, which shows that they built 140 for Italy, 129 for the Netherlands, about 100 for Germany, 7 for Portugal and a few for Austria, Hungary, Argentina and Java. Their earliest products were known as "Square [3] engines" because of their angular outline and robust proportions, most had disc wheels and inside cylinders. The second largest builder and exporter of tram engines was Lokomotivfabrik Krauss A. G. of Sendling in the suburbs of Munich with a second factory at Linz in Austria. To quote Dr. Whitcombe again, he attributes 300 tram engines to this firm, again confirmed by the Works list [4] which gives 140 for Italy, 60 for Germany, about 40 for Austria (including towns now in Czechoslovakia), 21 for Russia, 17 for Greece, 6 for Belgium, only 3 for the Netherlands, about 20 for Spain and a few for Java and Venezuela. Their records also show four for Great Britain (Wolverton & Stony Stratford tramway). Krauss tram engines invariably had outside cylinders and Stephenson's valve gear with outside eccentrics; they were among the most elegant of enclosed locomotives, with a very neat outline and a turtle-back roof, which someone who had seen one of their catalogues, with a portrait of the founder of the firm, likened to the curve of his sweeping moustache.

The two firms, Henschel and Krauss are noteworthy in that they were the first to realize that all that was required of an enclosed tramway engine, was a conventional steam locomotive, built to small dimensions but robust and suitably enclosed. Most of their predecessors had built machines that were complicated and often underpowered for the job they had to do. Moreover, Henschel and Krauss each concentrated on the production of a small number of standard models, suitable for various conditions, but which soon came to be known as reliable and therefore could be ordered direct from a catalogue specification, without the risk of being let down. It is mainly for this reason that the two firms were able to go into the wholesale market with the success indicated in the paragraph above. The various types of locomotive available from Krauss were distinguished in their catalogues by Roman numerals and the three standard tram engine models were their types XXXVI, LXIII and LVIII, These numbers evidently referred to the general layout of the locomotive and not to its wheel arrangement, since all three classes were available as 0-4-0s and 0-6-0s. Type XXXVI (36) was the most common in the early days and had the cylinders set just ahead of the smokebox and a small footplate over them, between the smokebox and the front sheet, by which the crew gained access to the engine. Over the years, type LXIII (63) became the most widely used and this had the cylinders and smokebox front set flush with the end-sheet, with the smokebox door set visibly therein. The doorway for the crew was towards the rear. Type LVIII (58) was similar, but some of them had the whole of the cylinders and smokebox exposed, with the covering starting behind them.

Although Henschel and Krauss were the largest producers of tram engines, several other German manufacturers were not far behind them. One which did much pioneer work in the early days was Hohenzollern of Dusseldorf, which between 1879 and 1925 produced at least 200 enclosed engines, largely for the Netherlands, Italy and Germany, but quite a large number for Java, of which several are still in use (in 1978). Some of their earliest products were very small and some did not have the wheels coupled; they had small carrying wheels at the front and larger driving wheels at the back. Hohenzollern appears to have specialized in building tram engines for very narrow gauge lines (Geldersche and Kattowitz), and as a side line they built a batch of Lamm & Francq fireless tram engines for Java, plus half a dozen similar machines for the abortive steam line in Croydon, England. In Germany itself there were experiments with a Honigmann fireless loco, using a soda solution to generate heat.[5] Hagans of Erfurt built a small number of tramway engines in the early days, for Germany, Italy, the Netherlands and Spain, about 40 in all; those for Brescia in Italy were of particularly primitive appearance. Several other firms started building tram engines in the 1880s and at first at least they based their machines on the Henschel design, these included Emil Kessler, lately moved from Karlsruhe to Esslingen, who supplied about 50 locomotives mainly for Italy, where they had an assembly works at Saronno. Kessler built the locos for the Filderbahn at Stuttgart, including those for the rack section, and a few tram engines for Sumatra.

The Hannoversche Maschinenfabrik, which traded under the name of "Hanomag" built about 70 tram engines for Germany, the Netherlands, Java and one for Italy. This firm ceased building locomotives and turned to other work in 1931, while a large Garratt enclosed locomotive for a Dutch tramway was on the drawing board; it was completed by Henschel. (The late Friedrich Kemper, who assisted the author with this chapter, was a draughtsman with Hanomag and claimed to have been involved in this drawing).

When Kessler moved from Karlsruhe, their former works there was taken over by the Badische Maschinenbau Gesellschaft Karlsruhe who built about a dozen engines for local tramways and one for Strassburg. They resembled Henschel machines but had outside cylinders. Maffei of Munich built ten enclosed locomotives for Mantua in Italy; they resembled the Krauss design but had outside frames.[6] Later they built some partly enclosed locomotives for Dutch tramways in the 1920s. One of the more important builders of tramway engines was E. Borsig of Berlin-Tegel, who started off, however by building 50 "Rowan" steam cars, for Germany, Sweden, Denmark and Russia, before turning their hands to enclosed locomotives, of which they also built about 50. While they tended to build machines resembling the Henschel design, their products were if anything more robust, particularly some superheated six coupled locomotives for Italy which was their principal market, but they also supplied engines to Spain, Alsace Lorraine, Luxembourg, French Indo-China and Surinam, where four were still in use in the 1960 s.[7]

Another large constructor of tram engines was Orenstein & Koppel, who really specialized in the manufacture of small contractors' locomotives, which were mechanically similar to tram engines and in later years some found their way onto tramways. They did however build at least 40 enclosed locomotives for tramways in Germany, the Netherlands, Italy, Poland and Spain. In 1886, Arthur Koppel broke away from the firm and set up as a free-lance selling and constructional agent. He was responsible for the construction of several tramways in Spain, for which he arranged the provision of locomotives and rolling stock. However, he did not always order locomotives from his parent firm, but sometimes had contractor's locomotives from Krauss and enclosed tram engines from Arnold Jung, who also supplied about 40 tram engines direct, for Germany, the Netherlands and surprisingly enough for the SNCV in Belgium. This accounts for the regular builders of tram engines in Germany, but in the early days a few were built by Schwartzkoppf [8], Humboldt and Wohlert for various German tramways, while later Heilbronn built some with enclosed wheels and motion for lines at Darmstadt and Reutlingen.

We cannot conclude without mention of three double boiler Fairlee locomotives built by Hartmann of Chemnitz, for a tramway at Reichenbach (now in East Germany).[9] They were enclosed at first, but the all-over roofs were later removed. The line closed in the 1960s, but one of them is preserved. Orenstein & Koppel built three Mallet 0-4-4-0 tram engines for Flensburg and on a few other lines, Mallet unenclosed locomotives were used in later years to replace tram engines.

It would be very difficult to describe a typical German tram engine. One characteristic feature was that nearly all had a single set of controls and a driving position on the left hand side of the boiler. German designers were versatile and their products varied considerably in size and appearance, ranging from the little narrow gauge Hohenzollerns to the massive superheated Borsig and Henschel 0-6-0s supplied to Italy. Moreover, most German manufacturers were quite accomodating and prepared to build engines to someone else's design if given a special order to do so; i.e. the Jung locomotives mentioned above for the Belgian SNCV, were to that undertaking's standard Tubize design.

The last manufacturer to start building tram engines in Germany and indeed in Europe, was Linke Hofmann, who built a few for the Netherlands in 1922 and possibly two for Spain (some doubt as to whether they were enclosed).

German manufacturers were extraordinarily prolific in supplying industrial locomotives to all parts of the world and it is not surprising, therefore, that in later days, when the regulations requiring enclosure came to be interpreted more liberally, some industrial locomotives found their way onto those tramways still operating and these included a few from manufacturers not known to have supplied tram engines, such as Vulkan, Schichau, etc.

Passenger Stock

The original passenger stock at Cassel like the locomotives came from Great Britain and was supplied by Starbuck of Birkenhead. These cars were typical single deck products of that firm, with ornamental glass lights above narrow side windows; one car at least was mounted on six wheels. Wiesbaden at first had some ornate four-wheeled cars with centre entrances, but later had some rather rakish bogie cars. However, just as solid looking end-platform four wheeled carriages enjoyed a long and widespread life on German main line railways, so did similar vehicles on German tramways. Double deck cars were very rare indeed and the only examples known to the writer were those at Hamburg, already mentioned and a very large car built by Kessler of Esslingen for Mullhausen. Kessler also built some more conventional four wheeled cars, some of which had centre entrances for the Pisa-Pontedera tramway in Italy. Another locomotive builder who included passenger stock in their range of products was Orenstein & Koppel, who are known to have supplied saloon and open cross-bench cars to Spanish steam tramways.

Although it was the original intention of the Munich-Nymphenburg tramway to paint their passenger stock yellow, in fact their stock appeared in a light blue livery, including the locomotives! Evidently it was the same shade of blue as is still favoured by public transport in that city. There are reports that unless otherwise instructed, Messrs. Henschel delivered locomotives painted in a dark brown colour, while Krauss painted theirs dark green with red wheels and skirting. (This style survived to the end on the Milan-Magenta tramway and on the preserved loco at Vienna). It is more than likely that a number of tramways took their standard livery from an initial delivery of Henschel or Krauss locomotives. Passenger carriages were generally designated "Second" or "Third" class, but the Vorgebirgsbahn at Cologne provided some "Farmers' Carriages" designated "Fourth Class". They were in fact goods trucks fitted with roofs and remained in the goods stock livery, while second class cars were green and third class cars brown. The Bad Doberan line has black engines and wine red and ivory coaches.[10]

Operating Methods and Sundry Items

Like most other European countries, steam tramways in Germany were laid in towns with grooved rails set in the paved roadway and in the countryside, with vignoles rails on a roadside reservation. It is reported, however, that the first steam tramway at Cassel was laid with bridge rails. Some of the steam tramways had elaborate terminal layouts and workshop facilities and many had numerous sidings laid into factory yards. The little Plettenburger Strassenbahn whose goods traffic survived with enclosed locomotives until 1962, had at one time as many as 65 such sidings. Some of their locomotives had side buffers and screw couplings, slightly offset towards one side, so that they could pull standard gauge trucks on three-rail mixed gauge track, the locomotive running on the metre gauge.

As mentioned earlier, standard gauge main line goods wagons were often carried over narrow gauge tramways and light railways on transporter trucks. These were of two basic types; some comprised two separate bogies, each of which could be clipped under the axle of a standard gauge wagon and hold it with its wheels just above the track. The other type comprised a narrow gauge bogie flat truck with a very low outside framework, the outer edges of which were made up from rails set at the standard gauge distance apart, so that a wagon could be run onto them and its wheels clipped firmly when in position. Both types required a special pit or transfer siding where the standard gauge trucks could be run onto the transporter. Some had transfer sidings at intermediate points, where the trucks were parked for unloading, other loaded and unloaded them while still on the transporter. When fully loaded these trucks would tower above the rest of the train and they needed very high and wide clearances, but in this respect a tramway on the road is better than a railway.

It is reported that the Munich-Nymphenburg tramway originally shared the main avenue between the city centre and the royal palace with a horse tramway service, but on one occasion an engine drawing a train frightened the horses pulling the Prince Regent of Bavaria's carriage, causing them to bolt and the carriage to overturn. As there was more than one occasion when this tramway was in trouble with the horses of nobility, it was eventually banished to a side street.

The Germans are great lovers of order and uniformity; it is not surprising, therefore, that most of their steam tramways were laid to standard or metre gauge, but there was one noteable exception; the large network based on Kattowitz in the Upper Silesian coalfield, was constructed to the very narrow gauge of 785 mm. to enable it to connect with the local mining railways. It was electrified early, still to that gauge, but over the years, as the various limitations made themselves felt, it has been gradually reconstructed to standard gauge. Part of the area was ceded to Poland in 1919 and the rest in 1945, but the gauge conversion continued and was completed under their auspices. One or two rural tramways were constructed to 750mm gauge.

A number of tramways in Germany were under the control of large holding companies. The two most important of which, also controlling a number of light railway, were the "Suddeutsche Eisenbahn Gesellschaft", originally owned by Herman Bachstein, with a fleet of enclosed tramway engines numbered between 50 and 104 in its combined locomotive list. It is not known for certain on which of the company's lines some of these operated, so in the tables which follow, they are all shown under the heading of the parent company, with a note against those whose actual place of operation is known. The second large company was the "Lokal Eisenbahn Gesellschaft, Munchen", who also had a combined fleet of Locomotives for tramways and light railways, numbering them all in one series. The location of all the tramway engines is known, so they are shown under the separate headings. As the Krauss locomotive manufacturing company held a controlling interest in this group, not unexpectedly nearly all their engines were of Krauss manufacture.

Although most of the urban steam tramways were electrified at a very early date, Germany being one of the pioneers of electric traction, most of the rural lines were replaced by motor buses in the early 1930s, but a few did survive long enough to acquire diesel railcars or locomotives and there was a limited use of accumulator cars. Steam working survived longest on those lines that had a heavy goods interchange traffic into rail connected factories.

Note. - It is hardly necessary to remind readers, that the present division into East and West Germany did not occur until after nearly all steam tramways had disappeared and is not, therefore, referred to in the text. Of those known to have survived the 1939-45 war with steam, Doberan, Forst and Reichenbach are now in East Germany, while Eiseren, Hohenlimburg, Plettenburg, Prien (Chiemsee) and Uetersen are in West Germany.

Notes

1. See "The History of the Steam Tram" by Dr. H. A. Whitcombe, London, 1954.

2. The spelling Cassel, Crefeld, etc. was altered to Kassel, Krefeld, etc. in the early 1920 s.

3. These were known officially as the "OVADA" class, as Novi-Ovada in Italy was one of the first lines to purchase them.

4. See "Krauss Lokomotiven" by B. Schmeister edited by J. O. Slezak, Vienna 1977.

5. The Honigmann experiment was carried out on a line 6km. long between Wurschen and Solberg near Aachen.

6. Krauss and Maffei amalgamated in 1931 under the title "Krauss-Maffei".

7. See article by G. Todd in "Modern Tramway" May 1968, page 157, "Steam Tramways in Surinam".

8. See "Tramway & Railway World" page 122, 1894. Articles by H. Conradi.

9. See "Locomotive Magazine" page 309, November 1903.

10. The light railway at Bad Doberan still carries heavy summer traffic with street running, but heavy 2-8-2 and 0-8-0 locomotives. See "Railway Scene" No. 2, 1968, article by K. Kieper.

Hagans prototype tram-engine, which does not appear to have appealed to any operator and ended up in a sawmill.

Hagans Catalogue.   **85**   Courtesy: J. H. Price.

Table3, GERMANY

1. ALBTALBAHN. (Alb Thalbahn A.G.). Worked by Badische Lokal Eisenbahn A.G.).
   Later (Deutsche Eisenbahn Betriebs Gesellschaft). Now Karlsruhe Tramways.
   Carlsruhe-Busenbach-Herrenalb, 26.4 km.
   Busenbach-Pforzheim, 23.8 km.
   A steam light railway with some enclosed locomotives, later electrified, but part
   reverted to steam during the 1914-1918 war. Converted to standard gauge from
   1958 and part of branch abandoned.
   S.1897, E.1898/1910 (GS to 1960). Still Operating. Gauge. 1000. (Now 1435).

Locomotives. -	Nos.				
	1-4,	Carlsruhe	0-4-0	1455-1457 & 1477 of 1897.	
	5,	Carlsruhe	0-4-4-0(Mallet)	1458 of 1897.	
	6,	Carlsruhe	0-4-4-0(Mallet)	1459 of 1897.	"
	7,	Carlsruhe	0-4-4-0(Mallet)	1478 of 1897.	"
	8,	Carlsruhe	0-4-4-0(Mallet)	1572 of 1900.	"
	9,	Humboldt	0-4-4-0(Mallet)	1913 of 1898.	"
	10-11,	Tubize	0-6-0,	1188-1189 of 1899 (SNCV type).	
	12,	Hanomag	0-6-6-0(Mallet)	10570 of 1928.	
	14,	Hohenzollern	0-4-0	1109 of 1898 (later reno.16).	
	15-16,	Hohenzollern	0-4-0	1108-1109 of 1898.	"
(II)	6,	Carlsruhe	0-4-4-0(Mallet)	2056 of 1918.	
(II)	11,	Krauss	0-8-0	7561 of 1919.	
	99.7203.	Borsig	0-6-0	5326 of 1924 ∵ For gauge conversion.	"

2. ALTONA. (Eisenbahn Gesellschaft Altona-Kaltenkirchen-Neümunster).
   Altona(Hamburg)-Kaltenkirchen-Neümunster, 67.5 km.
   Built as a roadside light railway with enclosed locomotives. Later resited as a
   proper railway, with heavier unenclosed locomotives (not described below).
   S.1884, R.1898, D.1930 Still Operating. Gauge. 1435.

Locomotives. -	Nos.			
	1-2,	Henschel 0-4-0	1513-1514 of 1884.	
	3-4,	Henschel 0-4-0	1702-1703 of 1884.	"
	5,	Henschel 0-4-0	2062 of 1884.	"
	6,	Henschel 0-4-0	2598 of 1889.	"
	7,	Henschel 0-6-0	3328 of 1890 (Side & Centre buffers).	"
	8-9,	Henschel 0-6-0	4645-4646 of 1898.	
	10,	Henschel 0-6-0	5273 of 1899.	"
	11,	Henschel 0-6-0	6022 of 1902.	"

   (Subsequent locomotives not of tramway type).

3. ALTONA. (Ottensener Industriebahn). See OTTENSEN No.77A.

4. AMRUM. (Amrumer Inselbahn) from 1902 (A.G. Wittdün-Amrum Konkurs). A Friesian Island.
   Wittdün-Kniepsand, 14.3 km.
   S.1894, E.1909, S again 1921. C.1939. Gauge. 900. (Originally 600?).

Locomotives. -	Nos.				
	1-2,	Jung ? 0-4-2	- - of 1894. (A.Koppel order).		
	3.	? 0-4-0?	? ? ?		

   Names. - 1-Wittdun, 2-Amrum, 3- ?.

5. APENRADE. (Kreis Apenrade Lokalbahn ?).
   Ceded to Denmark in 1919 and became (Aabenraa Amstbaner).
   Apenrade-Lugumkloster, 31.4 km.
   Apenrade-Gravenstein, ? km.
   S.1898, C.1926 ? Gauge. 1000.

Locomotives. -	Nos.	1-4,	Hagans	0-4-0	365-368 of 1898.	
		5-6,	Hagans	0-4-0	374-375 of 1898.	"
		7-10,	Hagans	0-4-0	381-384 of 1899.	"
	(II)	1-4,	Orenstein & Koppel	0-4-0	586-589 of 1900.	"
					(intended for No.42).	

6. AUGSBURG. (Augsburger Trambahn).
    Experiments with steam using locomotives hired from the manufacturer on an
    existing horse tramway line.
    Augsburg-Göggingen, 2.5 km. (approx).
    H.1881, S.1886 only, E.1895, Still operating.   Gauge. 1435 (1000 on electrification).
    Locomotives. -   Krauss 0-4-0   1678 of 1885 (intended for Vienna).
                                Krauss 0-4-0   1800 of 1886 ("   "   "   ).
                                Krauss 0-4-0   1674 of 1885 (intended for Munich, No.72).

7. BERGHEIM. (Kreis Bergheim Nebeneisenbahn).
    Later (Westdeutsche Eisenbahn Gesellschaft).
    A light railway with some enclosed locomotives. Converted to a standard gauge
    railway and later taken over by the Prussian State Railway.
    Ameln-Bedburg-Bergheim-Horrem-Modrath,   31.0 km.
    Elsdorf-Bergheim-Romerskirchen,   19.0 km.
    Blatzheim-Modrath-Benzelrath,   14.1 km. (Connecting with No.28).
    S.1896, R.1914, Still operating as Railway.   Gauge. 1000 (1435 as railway).
    Locomotives. -   Nos. 41-42, Vulkan   0-4-0   1439 & 1441 of 1896 ex-contractor.
                            1-4, Hohenzollern 0-4-4-0 1472,1474 & 1304-1305 of 1900/01.
                               5, ?
                               6, Hohenzollern 0-4-4-0 1498 of 1902.
                               7, Couillet   0-6-0   1024 of 1891. (ex-Belgian SNCV 429).
                               8, Tubize   0-6-0   835 of 1891. ("   "   "   427). "
                               9, Meuse   0-6-0   1208 of 1891. ("   "   "   438). "
                           10-11, Humboldt   0-4-4-0   236-237 of 1904.

    Note. -   Nos.1-4 renumbered 81-84, 7-9 as 51-53 and 11 as 85, by W.E.G.

8. BERLIN. (Berliner Pferdeeisenbahn).
    Experiments with steam on an existing horse tramway.
    Charlottenburg-Küpfergarten, 8.0 km.
    H.1865, S.1878 only, E.1902, Still Operating.   Gauge. 1435.
    Locomotives. -   Krauss   0-4-0   574 of 1877.
                                Wohlert 0-4-0   695-696 of 1878.

9. BERLIN. (Grosse Berliner Pferdeeisenbahn A.G.).
    Experiments with steam on an existing horse tramway.
    Schönhauser Tor-Pankow, 3.5 km.
    H.1871, S.1876 to 1880, E.1897, Still Operating.   Gauge. 1435.
    Locomotives. -   One   Smith & Myginds 0-4-0   -   of 1875 (from Copenhagen ?).
                      Two   Wohlert   0-4-0   695-696 of 1878, ex-No.8.
                      Six   Schwartzkopff   0-4-0   992-997 of 1878 intended for Magdeburg.

10. BERLIN. (Wilmersdorf-Schmargensdorfer Dampfstrassenbahn). Later part of No.11.
    Apostelkirche-Wilmersdorf-Grünewald, 3.8 km.
    S.1888, E.1899, C.1954. Gauge. 1435.
    Locomotives. -   Nos.   1-6   Hohenzollern 2-2-0   450-455 of 1888.

11. BERLIN. (Kurfürstendamm Gesellschaft).   Took over No.10.
    Later (Berliner Dampfstrassenbahn Konsortium).
    From 1898 (Westliche Berlinger Vorortbahn).
    Nollendorferplatz-Kurfürstendamm-Grünewald, 6.5 km.
    Zooligischer Garten-Nollendorferplatz-Steglitz, 7.5 km.
    Zooligischer Garten-Kaiserallee-Steglitz, 7.5 km.
    S.1886, E.1899, C.1954. Gauge. 1435.
    Rowan Cars. -   Nos.   1,   Borsig   3780 of 1882.
                            2-5, Borsig   4132,4125,4131 & 4156 of 1885.
                              6, Borsig   4234 of 1887.
                           7-10, Borsig   4257-4260 of 1888.
                          11-15, Borsig   4219-4223 of 1887.
                             16, Borsig   4212 of 1887.

87

Nos.	17-18,	Borsig	4261-4262 of 1888.

	Nos.	17-18,	Borsig	4261-4262 of 1888.
		19-24,	Borsig	4269-4274 of 1889.
		25-30,	Schwartzkopff	1957-1962 of 1890.

Note. -   Nos.7-10, 17-24 & 25-30 were on two bogies, the others had a powered bogie in front and a single radial axle at the rear.

Locomotives. -	Nos.	1-6,	Hohenzollern	2-2-0	450-455	of 1888 ex-No.10.
		7-8,	Wohlert	0-4-0	695-696	of 1878 ex-Nos.8 & 9.
		9,	Winterthur	0-4-0	339	of 1883.
		10-13,	Schwartzkopff	0-4-0	1728-1731	of 1890.

12.   BERLIN. (Stadtische Strassenbahn Cöpenick).
Formerly (Friedrichschagener Strassenbahn).
Friedrichshagen-Muggelsee, 1.5 km. (Summer operation only).
S.1892, H.1894, E.1903, Still Operating. Gauge. 1000 (1435 on electrification).

Locomotives. -	"Helene"	Hohenzollern	2-2-0	635 of 1892.
	"Auguste"	Hohenzollern	2-2-0	636 of 1892.
	"Georg"	Hohenzollern	2-2-0	639 of 1891.

13.   BERLIN. (Dampfstrassenbahn Grosslichterfeld-Stahnsdorf).
Later (Berliner Dampfstrassenbahn Konsortium) as No.11.
Finally (Teltower Kreisbahn A.G.).
Lichterfeld Ost-Stahnsdorf, 8.6 km.
S.1888, E.1907 (GS). C.1960. Gauge. 1435.

Locomotives. -	Nos.	1-2,	Unknown 0-4-0	- - of 1888.
		3-4,	" 0-4-0	- - of ?

Rowan Cars. -	Nos.	1-2,	Borsig, 4235-4236 of 1887.

14.   BERLIN. (Berlin-Görlitzer Eisenbahn).
A suburban railway branch line worked at first with enclosed locomotives and double deck carriages.
Berlin-Grünau, 13.6 km.
S.1877, E. ? Still Operating as railway. Gauge. 1435.

Locomotives. -	Nos.	1-2,	Krauss 0-4-0	570 & 572 of 1877,
		3-4,	Krauss 0-4-0	993-994 of 1881.

Names. -   1-Aldershof, 2-Grünau, 3-Görlitz, 4-Zittau.

15.   BERGISCHE KLEINBAHN. See HEILIGENHAUS No.51.

16.   BLECKEDE. (Bleckeder Kleinbahn GmbH.) from 1917 (Bleckeder Kreisbahn).
A light railway with some street running and one enclosed locomotive.
It was converted to a standard gauge railway in 1919.
Bleckede-Lüneburg,   23.8 km.
Dahlenburg-Bleckede-Echem, 47.0 km. Closed 1919.
S.1895, R.1919, Still Operating as railway. Gauge. 750 (to 1435 in 1919).

Locomotives. -	Nos.	1-4,	Vulkan	0-4-0	1484-1487 of 1895.
(Narrow Gauge)		5,	Vulkan		1519 of 1896.
		6,	Orenstein & Koppel	0-4-4-0	2066 of 1906.
		7,	Jung	2-6-0	2835 of 1919.
	(II)	4,	Esslingen	0-4-0	3633 of 1912. (Kittel boiler).
	(II)	5,	Maffei	0-8-0	3745 of 1912.

Steam Cars.	1-3,	Esslingen	?	3558-3560 of 1910. (Kittel boiler).

Locomotives. -	6,	Jung	0-6-0	559 of 1902
(Standard Gauge)	7,	Hagans	0-6-0	487 of 1903.
	8,	Borsig	0-4-0	6947 of 1908.
	9,	Borsig	0-6-0	10816 of 1920.

17. BONN. (Firma Haverstedt & Contag A.G. "Dampf Strassenbahn Bonn-Godesberg-Mehlem").
    Later (Bonner Strassenbahn A.G.).
    Bonn-Godesberg-Mehlem, 10.5 ? (Connecting with No.27).
    S.1892, E.1911, Still Operating (Part R.1974). Gauge. 1000 (1435 on electrification).
    Locomotives. -   Unnumbered   Hohenzollern 2-2-0   675-676 of 1892.
                                    Hagans   0-4-0   252 of 1892.   "
                                    Hohenzollern 2-2-0   712 of 1893.   "
                                    Hohenzollern 0-4-0   757 of 1893.   "
                                    Hagans   0-4-0   289 of 1894.   "
                                    Hohenzollern 0-4-0   1122 of 1898.   "
    Names. -   675-Bonn, 676-Godesberg, 252- ?, 712-Möllenhof, 757-Hoppertz, 289- ?
                      1122-Roswandis. (Names of Hagans locomotives not known).

18. BREMEN. (Bremer Strassenbahn ?).
    Experiments with steam on an existing horse tramway.
    Route ?.
    H. ?, S.1880 only, E.1897, Still Operating. Gauge. 1435.
    Locomotive. -   Krauss 0-4-0 775 of 1880. (Later used at Brünn,
                                                               Czechoslovakia).

19. BRESLAU. (Breslau-Trebnitz-Pausnitzer Kleinbahn).
    Owned by (Allgemeine Deutsche Kleinbahn A.G.) Ceded to Poland in 1945.
    Breslau(Benderplatz)-Trebnitz-Pausnitz, 37.1 km.
    S.1898, D. ?, Part Still Operating. Gauge. 750. (0.9 km mixed gauge with 1435 trams).
    Locomotives. -   Nos.   1-2,   Krauss 0-6-0   3768-3769 of 1898.
                              3-9   Krauss 0-6-2   3761-3767 of 1898.   "
                              10.   Krauss 0-6-2   4376 of 1901.   "

20. BRIESEN. (Stadtbahn Briesen, Westpruessen).
    An electric tramway ceded to Poland in 1919, then called Wabzrezno.
    Worked by Steam during 1939-45 war. See POLAND No.7.

21. CASSEL. (Cassel Tramways Co. Ltd., London).
    from 1881 (Casseler Strassenbahn Gesellschaft).
    from 1898 (Grosse Casseler Strassenbahn A.G.).
    Cassel(Königsplatz)-Wilhelmshöhe Park, 5.6 km.
    S.1877, C.1884, S again 1885, E.1899, Still Operating. Gauge. 1435.
    Locomotives. -   Nos.   1-5,   Merryweather 0-4-0   33-37 of 1877.
                              6,   Merryweather 0-4-0   81 of 1878.   "
                              7-8,   Henschel   0-4-0   996-999 of 1878.   "
                              9-12,   Henschel   0-4-0 1857-1860 of 1884/85.   "
                              13-16. Winterthur   0-4-0 304,310,318 & 329 of 1882, ex-No.50. "

22. CARLSRUHE. (Vereinigte Carlsruher, Mühlburger und Durlacher Pferde und Dampfbahn A.G.).
    Later (Carlsruher Strassenbahn A.G.).
    Carlsruhe(Durlacher Tor)-Durlach(Turmburg Funicular), 3.7 km.
    S.1881, E.1900, Still Operating. Gauge. 1435.
    Locomotives. -   Nos.   1,   Henschel 0-4-0   1066 of 1880.
                              2,   Carlsruhe 0-4-0   1022 of 1881.   "
                              3-4.   Carlsruhe 0-4-0   -   -   of ?

23. CARLSRUHE. (Carlsruher Lokalbahn). (Owned by Herman Bachstein, Later S.E.G. No.99).
    Taken over by No.22 in 1915.
    Spock-Carlsruhe(Durlacher Tor)-Grünwinkel-Morsch-Durmersheim 30.8km.
    Grünwinkel-Daxlanden,   1.7 km.
    S.1890, E.1919/1936, C.1923/55. Gauge. 1000.
    Locomotives. -   Nos.65 & 68,   Henschel 0-4-0   2835 & 2838 of 1889.
                      72,   Henschel 0-4-0   2883 of 1889.   "
                      89-95,   Carlsruhe 0-4-0   1278-1284 of 1890.   "

    Note. -   Locomotives numbered in S.E.G. general series. See No.99.
                      Lines 22 & 23 crossed at right angles.

89

24. CARLSRUHE. See ALBTALBAHN No.1.

25. CHIEMSEE. See PRIEN No.80.

26. CÖLN. (Cölner Strassenbahn ?).
Experiments with steam on existing horse tramway.
Route - Unknown.
H. ?, S.1878 only, E. ?, Still Operating. Gauge. 1435.
Locomotive. -   Falcon (Hughes) 0-4-0 11 of 1878.

27. CÖLN. (A.G. der Vorgebirgsbahn Cöln-Bonn). Later (Cöln-Bonner Kreisbahn) in 1901.
Later (Köln-Bonner Eisenbahn).
A metre gauge steam tramway owning some important standard gauge goods lines,
converted to a standard gauge electric railway, retaining steam for goods.
Cöln-Brühl-Bonn, 32.4 km.
Brühl-Wesseling, 4.7 km. (Mixed gauge).
Cöln-Berrenrath 12.3 km. (Standard gauge railway).
S.1898, Part P.1926, E.1929/51, Still Operating. Gauge. 1000 (1435 on electrification).
Locomotives. -   Nos.   1-5,   Hagans   0-4-0   353-357 of 1897.
                          6-8,   Hohenzollern 0-4-0   822-824 of 1895.   "
                          9-16, Hohenzollern 0-4-0   1130-1137 of 1898.   "
                          17-18, Hohenzollern 0-4-0   1301-1302 of 1901.   "
                          19-21, Hohenzollern 0-4-2   1298-1300 of 1900/01.
                          22-25, Henschel   0-6-0   15142-15143, 15147 & 15141 of 1917
                          36-37, Henschel   0-6-0   15148-15149 of 1917.   "

Names. -   A works photo exists of No.19 named "Brühl".

Note. -   The company also owned a large fleet of standard gauge railway locomotives
                   for goods work. Replaced by diesel locos by 1968.

28. CÖLN. (Cöln-Frechen-Benzelrather Eisenbahn A.G.).
Later (Stadtische Vorortbahn Cöln). Now part of Köln municipal tramways.
Some standard gauge goods lines continue to be worked in the name of the old company.
Cöln-Frechen-Benzelrath, 37.9 km. (Connecting with No.7).
S.1893, E.1913. Still Operating. Gauge. 1000 (1435 on electrification).
Locomotives. -   Nos.   1-3,   Hagans   0-4-0 267-269 of 1892.
                   (II)   3-4,   Hohenzollern 0-4-0 845-846 of 1895.   "
                          5,   Hohenzollern 0-4-0   933 of 1896.   "
                          6-7,   Hohenzollern 0-4-0 967 & 992 of 1897.   "
                          8,   Hohenzollern 0-4-0   1187 of 1899.   "

Names. -   Hagans Locos - not known, (II)3-Franz, 4-Benzelrath, 5-Maria, 6-not named.
                   7-Antonie.

Note. -   The Hohenzollern locos were renumbered 51-56. Like No.27, this company
                   owned a large fleet of standard gauge railway locomotives (41 in all).

29. CREFELD. (Crefeld-Uerdingen Lokalbahn A.G.).
Taken over in 1900 by (Crefelder Strassenbahnen) who worked the town system.
Crefeld-Uerdingen, 6.7 km.
Crefeld-Hüls,   6.7 km.
Crefeld-Fischeln,   3.5 km.
S.1883, E.1900, Still Operating. Gauge. 1000.
Locomotives. -   Nos.   1-5,   Hohenzollern 0-4-0 278-282 of 1883.
                          6-9,   Hohenzollern 0-4-0 296-299 of 1883.   "
                          10,   Hohenzollern 0-4-0   301 of 1883.   "
                          11-13, Hohenzollern 2-2-0 639 & 635-636 of 1891/92, ex-No.12. "

30. DARMSTADT. (Firma Bachstein). In 1895 part of S.E.G. Group, See No.99.
From 1912 (Hessische Elektrizitäts A.G.).

Darmstadt-Griesheim,   7.3 km.
Griesheim-Griesheim Lager, 1.0 km ?.
Darmstadt-Arheilgen,   4.2 km.
Darmstadt-Eberstadt,   7.3 km.
S.1886, E.1914/1926, Still Operating. Gauge. 1000.

Locomotives. -   Nos.   1-2,   Krauss   0-4-0   1784-1785 of 1886.(became S.E.G. Nos.51-52).
                         3-4,   Heilbronn   0-4-0   231-232 of 1886.(became S.E.G. Nos.53-54).
                         60,   Karlsruhe   0-4-0   1215 of 1887.
                         61-63, Hohenzollern 0-4-0   464-466 of 1888.   from S.E.G. General Stock.
                         64,   Henschel   0-4-0   2834 of 1889.   "

31. DOBERAN.   (Doberan-Heiligendammer Eisenbahn).
From 1890 (Mecklenburgischen Friedrich-Franz Eisenbahn).
From 1925 (Deutsche Reichsbahn).   Now in East Germany.
Built as a tramway from Doberan to Heiligendam (5.7 km) and later extended
to Ardenseel (now called Kuhlingsborn), as a seaside light railway.
Doberan-Heiligendam-Ardenseel, 15.4 km.
S.1886, R(part) 1900.   Still Operating.   Gauge. 900.

Locomotives. -   Nos.   1,   Hohenzollern   0-4-0   304 of 1886.
                              2,   Hohenzollern   0-4-0   307 of 1887.   "
                              3,   Krauss   0-6-0   2554 of 1891.
                           1004,   Krauss   0-6-0   3788 of 1898.   "
                           1005,   Henschel   0-6-0   9845 of 1910.   "
                           1006,   Henschel   0-6-0   10699 of 1911.   "
                           1007,   Henschel   0-6-0   12884 of 1914.   "
                   99.311-99.312,   Henschel   0-8-0   19747-19748 of 1923.
                        99.313,   Henschel   0-8-0   20223 of 1924.   "
                   99.321-99.323,   Orenstein & Koppel 2-8-2   12400-12402 of 1932.   "
                        99.331,   Karl Marx   0-8-0   30011 of 1951.   "
                        99.332,   Karl Marx   0-8-0   30013 of 1951.   "
                        99.333,   Karl Marx   0-8-0   16501 of 1950.   "

Note. -   Nos.1-3 were later renumbered 1001-1003 and later still 1005-1007
              became 99.301-99.303 in the Deutsche Reichsbahn series.

32. DÖHREN. (Wollwäscherei und Kämerei Döhren). = "Döhren Woollen Mill", Hannover.
A goods only tramway, carrying main line stock on transporters.
Döhren(Bahnhof)-Döhren Wollwäscherei, 2.5 km.
H.1882, S.1882, C.1905.   Gauge. 1000 (Replaced by a standard gauge railway on a
different allignment).

Locomotives. -   Nos.   1,   Winterthur 0-4-0   321 of 1882.
                         2,   Hagans   0-4-0   223 of 1887.   "
                         3,   Hagans   0-4-0   381 of 1899, ex-No.49. "

33. DORTMUND. (Dortmunder Strassenbahn für Pferde und Dampfbetrieb).
Controlled by (Allgemeine Lokalbahn und Strassenbahn A.G.).

Dortmund-Hörde,   8.5 km.
Dortmund-Dorstfeld,   7.9 km.
Dortmund-Fredenbaum, 2.0 km. ?
H.1881, S.1881, E.1897, Still Operating.   Gauge. 1435.

Locomotives. -   Nos.   1-2,   Winterthur 0-4-0   230-231 of 1881.
                         3-4,   Krauss   0-4-0   1024-1025 of 1881.   ∵   "
                         5,   Henschel   0-4-0   1249 of 1881.   "
                         6-7,   Henschel   0-4-0   1386 & 1385 of 1882.   "
                         8,   Henschel   0-4-0   2851 of 1889.   "
                         9,   Henschel   0-4-0   3349 of 1890.   "

91

34. DUISBURG. (Allgemeine Lokalbahn und Strassenbahn A.G.). See No.33.
     Duisburg-Speldorf-Müllheim Broich, 11.1 km.
     S.1882, E.1897, Still Operating. Gauge. 1435.
     Locomotives. - Nos. 1-2, Henschel   0-4-0 1387-1388 of 1882.
                            3-4, Henschel   0-4-0 1390-1391 of 1882.
                     (II)   2 ? Graffenstaden 0-4-0   4592 of 1894 ?
                            6.   Henschel   1386 of 1882, ex-No.33. ⚮

35. DUISBURG. (Strassenbahn Duisburg-Meiderich ?).
     An uncompleted metre gauge steam tramway. The formation was later used
     for a standard gauge electric tramway, belonging to No.34.
     Duisburg-Meiderich, 15.9 km (not completed). Gauge. 1000.
     Locomotives. - Nos. 1-3,? Humboldt 0-4-0, 52-54 of 1900 (See Nos.54, 77A & 79).

36. DÜREN. (Dürener Dampfstrassenbahn A.G.). from 1938 (Dürener Eisenbahn A.G.).
     There was also a "Dürener Kreisbahn" which was a standard gauge railway.
     Düren-Birkesdorf-Merken-Pier, 11.1 km.
     GS.1893, S.1894, E.1913/26, (S again 1945-47), GS to 1952, C.1965. Gauge. 1000
     Locomotives. - Nos.   1,   Henschel 0-4-0   1068 of 1892.*
                            2-3, Henschel 0-4-0 3892-3893 of 1893.
                             4,   Henschel 0-4-0   5276 of 1899. (Preserved).
                            5-6, Henschel 0-4-0 5569-5570 of 1900.
                             7,   Henschel 0-4-0   5847 of 1901.
                             8,   Henschel 0-4-0   7286 of 1905.
                             9,   Henschel 0-4-0   7739 of 1906.
                           10-11, Henschel 0-4-0 8331-8332 of 1907.
                            12,   Hanomag 0-6-0   6453 of 1912.
                           13-14, Henschel 0-6-0 11625-11626 of 1912.

     Names. -   1-Birkesdorf, 2-Industrie, 3-Düren, 4-Rur, 5-Hoven, 6-Merken, 7-Pier.
                    8-Inden, 9-Luchersberg, 10-Schophoven, 11-Lamersdorf, 12-Düren,
                    13-Vilvenich, 14-Pommenich.
                    *Some records show that No.1 was built by Jung, but not confirmed
                    by Works List and too high a number for Jung at that date.

37. EISERN. (Eisern-Siegener Eisenbahn A.G.).
     A steam railway with through running over Siegen tramways (Siegener Kreisbahn), over which
     steam working was retained for goods even after electric operation ceased.
     Kaan Marienborn-Eisern-Siegen, 14.2 km.
     S.1883, Part E.1947, GS only 1957, GD.1961. Still Operating. Gauge. 1435.
     Locomotives. - Nos. 1-3,   Henschel 0-6-0 1608-1610 of 1883.
                             4,   Henschel 0-6-0   2687 of 1888.
                             5,   Henschel 0-6-0   3792 of 1892.
                             6,   Henschel 0-6-0   4576 of 1895.
                            7-8, Henschel 0-6-0 5635-5636 of 1901.
                             9,   Henschel 0-6-0   6706 of 1907.
                           10-11, Henschel 0-6-0   ? - ? of 1913 ?
                     (II) 11-12, Jung   0-8-0 3425-3426 of 1923.
                           13-15, Jung   0-8-0 3709-3711 of 1926/27.
                            16,   Jung   0-8-0   5597 of 1935.

38. EMMERICH. (Stoomtram Maatschappij Zutphen-Emmerik).
     Short section of a Dutch tramway in Germany. See NETHERLANDS No.101.

39. ELTVILLE. (Dampfstrassenbahn Eltville-Schlangenbad A.G.).
     Controlled by (Allgemeine Deutsche Kleinbahnen A.G.)
     Eltville-Schlangenbad, 7.8 km.
     S.1895, C.1933. Gauge. 1000.
     Locomotives. - Nos. 1-3, Henschel 0-4-0 4302-4304 of 1895.
                            4-5, Henschel 0-4-0 5118-5119 of 1899.

     Note. -   Loco No.3 was requisitioned during the 1914 war and subsequently sold
                    to Netherlands No.79.
                                        92

40. EUPEN. (Eupener Kleinbahn Gesellschaft A.G.).
A light railway, partly in Belgium and leased from the outset to the Belgian "Vicinal"
undertaking. They took it over in 1908 and the whole area was ceded to Belgium in
1919, but taken back by Germany in 1940, when the line was worked by the Aachener
Kleinbahn until 1945, when it was returned to Belgium.
Nieder Eupen-Goé-Dolhain, 9.2 km.
S.1891, GS.1945, C.1963. Gauge. 1435.
Locomotives. -   SNCV Nos.803-805, St.Léonard 0-6-0 755-757 of 1887.

41. FILDERBAHN. Stuttgart. (Filderbahn A.G.).
Owned until 1922 by the (Württemburgische Nebenbahn A.G.) then by
(Vereinigte Kleinbahn A.G.).
A light railway with enclosed locomotives, including those which worked on a section
of paved Riggenbach rack track on the streets of Stuttgart. Part was taken over and
electrified by Stuttgart tramways and the rest converted to standard gauge freight railways,
including some mixed gauge.
Stuttgart(Marienplatz)-Bopser-Degerloch, 2.8 km. (Rack, now electric).
Degerloch-Möhringen-Vaihingen,   6.6 km. (now electric, part mixed gauge).
Möhringen-Hohenheim,   5.7 km. (now standard gauge freight line).
Möhringen-Neuhausen,   14.3 km.   "   "
S.1884, Part E.1902/1924, Rest GS.1957 (now GE). Gauge. 1000 (See also above).
Locomotives. -   Nos.   1,   Esslingen   0-4-0z 2000   of 1883. (rack).
                          2,   Esslingen   0-4-0z 2051   of 1884.   "   "
                          3,   Esslingen   0-4-0z 2088   of 1885.   "   "
                        4-5,   Esslingen   0-4-0   2285-2286 of 1888.   "
                          6,   Esslingen   0-4-0   2357 of 1889.   "
                        7-8,   Esslingen   0-6-0   2904-2905 of 1897.   "
                       9-10,   Esslingen   0-6-0   3023-3024 of 1898.   "
                      11-12,   Esslingen   0-4-0z 2544-2545 of 1892. (Intended for Brazil)..
                      13-14,   Esslingen   0-6-0   3147-3148 of 1900.   "
                       1010,   Winterthur 0-4-0z 1192 of 1899 ∵ (ex-Brünig Rly. Switzerland).
                       1012,   Winterthur 0-4-0z 1339 of 1901 ∵ ("   "   ").
                  (II) 10-11,   Esslingen   0-4-0 (VB)2968-2969 of 1899 ∵

Names. -   1-Stuttgart, 2-Degerloch, 3-Filder, 4-Möhringen, 5-Hohenheim, 6-Plieningen,
            7-Echterdingen, 8-Neuhausen, 9-Bernhausen, 10-Aichen, 11-Alb, 12-Aussicht,
            13-Sielmingen, 14-Uhlberg. 1010 & 1012 not named.

42. FLENSBURG. (Dampftram Flensburg ?).
Flensburg(Hauptbahnhof)-Norder Tor ? km.
Steam traction proposed, electrified instead. Locos to Nos.5 & 43.
Locomotives. -   Nos.   1-2,   Orenstein & Koppel 0-4-0 584-585 of 1899.
                          3-6,   Orenstein & Koppel 0-4-0 536-539 of 1899.

43. FLENSBURG. (Kreisbahn Flensburg-Kappeln).
From 1901 (Flensburger Kreisbahn A.G.).
A light railway with enclosed locomotives to the end and street running.
Flensburg-Glücksburg electrified in 1930 by urban tramways.
Flensburg-Glücksburg-Rundhof-Kappeln, 51.5 km.
Flensburg-Satrup-Rundhof,   43.9 km.
S.1885, Part D.1925, Part E.1930, C.1938/1953. Gauge. 1000.
Locomotives. -   Nos.   1-4,   Winterthur   0-6-0 393-396 of 1884.
                          5-6,   Winterthur   0-6-0 427 & 457 of 1886/87. "
                            7,   Winterthur   0-6-0 1106 of 1898.   "
                            8,   Orenstein & Koppel 0-4-0 538 of 1900. ex-No.42. ∵
                         9-12,   Orenstein & Koppel 0-4-0 841-844 of 1901.   "
                        13-14,   Jung   0-6-0 627-628 of 1903.   "
                        15-16,   Jung   0-6-0 1167-1168 of 1907.   "
                        17-20,   Numbers not occupied.
                        21-23,   Orenstein & Koppel 0-4-4-0 838-840 of 1901. (Mallet).
                        24-25,   Jung   0-8-0 1604-1605 of 1910.
                  (II)   1-2,   A.E.G.   0-8-0 3413-3414 of 1926.   "

Names. -   1-Flensburg, 2-Glücksburg, 3-Gelting, 4-Kappeln, 5-Steinberg, 6-Rundhof,
            7-Langballig. Others not named.

93

44. FORST. (Forster Stadteisenbahn). Owned by (Lokalbahn A.G., München).
Later (Dienstleitung des Rates der Stadt Forst).
A freight only steam tramway, serving various textile factories in the town of
Forst. Carried standard gauge wagons on transporters, with own standard gauge
locomotives to shunt them on and off.
Forst(Bahnhof)-Forst(Stadt) & industrial sidings, 24.0 km.
GS.1893, C.1965. Gauge. 1000 with 1435 connections.
Locomotives. -
(Metre Gauge)   Nos. 32-37,   Krauss 0-4-0   2792-2797 of 1893.   ⊏⊐
                        1,   Krauss 0-4-0   7990 of 1922.   "
                      2-3,   Krauss 0-4-0   8328-8329 of 1922.   "

(Standard Gauge)   6,   Krauss 0-6-0   2050 of 1889. ⁖   ⊢⊐
                       50,   Krauss 0-6-0   1690 of 1888. ⁖   "
                       31,   Krauss 0-6-0   939 of 1881. ⁖   "
                       38,   Krauss 0-6-0   2417 of 1891. ⁖   "

Note. -   Locomotives numbered in L.A.G. general series except Nos.1-3, built
                    after the Municipality took over. No.36 is preserved in Dresden Museum.

45. FRANKFURT. (Frankfurter Lokalbahn A.G.).
 •   Frankfurt(Eschenheimer Thurm)-Eschenheim, 5.7 km.
H.1888, S.1888, E.1908. Still Operating. Gauge. 1435.
Locomotives. -   Nos.   1-3,   Henschel 0-4-0   2508-2509 & 2620 of 1888.   ⊏⊐
                          4,   Hagans   0-4-0   413 of 1899.   "
                          5,   Henschel 0-4-0   5571 of 1902 ?

46. FRANKFURT. (Frankfurter Waldbahn A.G.).
Frankfurt-(Untermainbrücke)-Niederrad-Schwannheim,11.5 km.
Short branch at Niederrad,   1.0 km.
Frankfurt(Lokalbahnhof)-Neu Isenburg,   6.0 km.
S.1889, E.1925/29, Still Operating. Gauge. 1435.
Locomotives. -   Nos.   1-2,   Henschel 0-4-0   2510-2511 of 1888.   ⊏⊐
                        3-5,   Henschel 0-4-0   2617-2619 of 1888.   "
                        6-7,   Henschel 0-4-0   2806-2807 of 1888.   "
                        8-9,   Henschel 0-4-0   2840-2841 of 1889.   "
                      10-12,   Henschel 0-4-0   6025-6027 of 1902.   "
                      13-15,   Henschel 0-4-0   2508-2509/2620 of 1888, ex-No.45. ⁖   "
                         16,   Hagans   0-4-0   413 of 1899.   "
                         17,   Henschel 0-4-0   5571 of 1902.   "

Note. -   Nos.1,3,4 & 6 were sold to the Łódź Industrial railway, Poland in 1923.
                    See POLAND No.5.

47. GERA. (Geraer Stassenbahn A.G.).
Owned by (Vering und Waechter Eisenbahnbau und Betriebs A.G.).
An electric tramway using steam for freight in the early days.
Gera Pforten-Gera Stadt, 3.3 km.
H.1886, E & GS.1892, (GE.1903), Still Operating. Gauge. 1000.
Locomotives. -   Nos.   1-2,   Henschel 0-4-0   3483-3484 of 1891.   ⊏⊐
                          3,   Henschel 0-4-0   3655 of 1892.   "
                          4,   Henschel 0-6-0   3973 of 1893.   "

48. GÖRLITZ. Görlitz did not have a steam tramway, but the Berlin-Görlitz railway ran
a line in the suburbs of Berlin with enclosed locomotives. See No.14.

49. HADERSLEBEN. (Kleinbahn des Kreises Hadersleben).
Ceded to Denmark in 1919, then called (Haderslev Amstbaanen).
Hadersleben(Haderslev)-Aarösund(Aarøsund),   km.)
Hadersleben(Haderslev)-Scherrebek(Skaerbaek), km.) 70.5 km.
Hadersleben(Haderslev)-Rödding(Rødding),   km.)

94

S.1899, C.1939. Gauge. 1000.

Locomotives. -	Nos.	1-7,	Hagans	0-4-0	369-375 of 1898.	⌐
		8-9,	Hagans	0-4-0	381-382 of 1899.	"
		10-11,	Not known			
		12-13,	Jung	0-6-0	551-552 of 1902.	╚╝
		14-16,	Jung	0-6-0	614-616 of 1903.	"
		17-24,	Jung	0-6-0	654-660 of 1903.	"
		25-29,	Jung	0-6-0	757-761 of 1904/05.	"
		30,	Jung	0-6-0	790 of 1905.	"
		31-37,	Jung	0-6-0	942-948 of 1906.	"
		38-43,	Jung	0-6-0	1142-1147 of 1909.	"
		44-45.	Jung	0-6-0	2198-2199 of 1914.	"

50. HAMBURG. (Hamburger Pferdeeisenbahn).
From 1881 (Hamburger Strasseneisenbahn A.G.).
Hamburg-Wandsbek, 5.0 km. (approx).
H.1866, S.(Trials only)1875, S.1878, E.1897, C.1978. Gauge. 1435.

Locomotives. -	(Trials) -		Falcon (Hughes)	0-4-0	11 of 1878.	⌐
			Krauss	0-4-0	865 of 1880 (later at Brünn).	"
			Kitson	0-4-0	T2 (2376) of 1878.	"
	Nos.	1-2,	Winterthur	0-4-0	126 of 1878 & 150 of 1879.	"
		3-5,	Winterthur	0-4-0	167-169 of 1879.	"
		6-11,	Winterthur	0-4-0	300-305 of 1882.	"
		12-17,	Winterthur	0-4-0	308-310 & 318-320 of 1882.	"
		18-19,	Winterthur	0-4-0	329 of 1882 & 350 of 1883.	"
		20-21.	Winterthur	0-4-0	765-766 of 1892.	"

51. HEILIGENHAUS. (Bergische Kleinbahn A.G.) worked by (Elberfelder Strassenbahnen).
Owned by (Continentale Gesellschaft für Elektrische Unternehmungen).
Part of the Elberfeld tramway system too remote from a substation,
to justify electrification and worked as a steam light railway
Heiligenhaus-Hösel, 6.8 km.
S.1899, E.1923, C.1952. Gauge. 1000.

Locomotives. -	Nos.	1-3,	Orenstein & Koppel	0-4-0	327-329 of 1898.	╚╝
		4-5,	Orenstein & Koppel	0-4-0	314 & 316 of 1898.	
	(II)	1-2,	Hanomag	0-4-0	6228-6229 of 1911 ex-Mörchingen
					⁖ (Alsace-Lorraine No.5).

52. HASPE. (Kleinbahn Voerde-Haspe GmbH.).
From 1906 (Kleinbahn Haspe-Voerde-Breckerfeld).
Taken over by Hagen Tramways and electrified in 1926.
Haspe-Voerde-Breckerfeld, 18.4 km.
S.1903, E.1926, C.1963. Gauge. 1000. (Closed for reconstruction 1921-1926).

Locomotives. -	Nos.	21-23,	Henschel	0-6-0	5970-5972 of 1902.	╚╝
		24,	Henschel	0-6-0	7751 of 1907.	"
		25,	Henschel	0-6-0	8905 of 1908.	"
	(II)	21.	Karlsruhe	0-4-4-0	2051 of 1918. ⁖	"

53. HERFORD. (Herforder Kleinbahn A.G.).
A steam light railway with street running in Herford, later electrified and
worked by tramcars.
Vlotho-Herford-Wallenbruck, 42.4 km.
S.1900, E(GS).1930, GD.1951, C.1966. Gauge. 1000.

Locomotives. -	Nos.	1-5,	Hagans	0-4-2	422-426 of 1900.	╚╝
		6-7,	Borsig	2-6-0	5179-5180 of 1903.	"
		8-10,	Borsig	0-8-0	10838-10840 of 1920. (9-10 renumbered 5 & 8).
	(II)	6,	Borsig	0-8-0	11836 of 1924. ⁖ ex-Bielefelder Krb.	"
	(II)	1.	Borsig	0-8-0	11396 of 1922.	"

Names. -   1-Herford, 2-Enger, 3-Vlotho, 4-Salzuflen, 5-Spenge, 6-Georg von Borries,
7-Exter, 8-Enger, 9-Spenge, 10-Loose, (II)6-Georg von Borries, (II)1-Herford.

54. HOHENLIMBURG. (Hohenlimburger Kleinbahn A.G.).
A freight only steam tramway using transporter trucks.
Hohenlimburg-Hobrackerweg, 3.1 km. (11.5 including industrial sidings).
GS.1900, GD.1961, Still Operating. Gauge. 1000.

Locomotives. -

	Nos.				
	1-3,	Hohenzollern	0-4-0	1170-1172 of 1899/1900.	🔁
	4,	Hohenzollern	0-4-0	992 of 1897. ⋇	"
	5,	Humboldt	0-4-0	52 of 1900 (intended for No.35).	"
	6,	Henschel	0-4-0	12480 of 1913.	"
	7,	Henschel	0-4-0	? 4302 of 1895 ex-No.39. ⋇	"
	8,	Henschel	0-6-0	? of , ex-No.52. ⋇	🔁
(II)	1,	Jung	0-6-0	4055 of 1927.	🔁
(II)	2,	Henschel	0-4-0	22737 of 1935.	🔁
(II)	3,	Jung	0-4-0	7042 of 1937.	🔁
(II)	4,	Jung	0-6-0	3726 of 1925.	"
(II)	5,	Hohenzollern	0-4-0	1798 of 1894. ? ⋇	"
(III)	5,	Jung	0-4-0	8638 of 1939.	"

Names. - 1-Hohenlimburg, 2-Nahmer, 3-Lenne, (II)5-(Kanal).

55. KARLSRUHE. For Karlsruhe, Kassel, Köln & Krefeld, See CARLSRUHE, CASSEL, CÖLN
and CREFELD, as the "K"s were not adopted until the 1920s.

56. KAYSERSBERG. See COLMAR, Alsace Lorraine, Chapter 4. No.3.

57. KATTOWITZ. (Oberschlesische Dampfstrassenbahn GmbH.).
In area ceded to Poland in 1919. Electrified and converted to standard gauge over an
extended period, by both German and Polish administrations. There were also extensive
narrow gauge railways in the area.
Kattowitz(Katowice)-Königshütte(Chorzow), 9.0 km.
Gleiwitz(Gliwice)-Königshütte-Deutsch Piekar(Piekary), 33.0 km.
Königshütte(Chorzow)-Laurahütte(Siemianowice), 6.0 km.
S.1894, E.1898, Still Operating. Gauge. 785. (to 1435 between 1928 & 1944).

Locomotives. -

	Nos.				
	1-10,	Hohenzollern	0-4-0	738-747 of 1893.	🔁
	11-17,	Hohenzollern	0-4-0	758-764 of 1894.	"
	18-20,	Hohenzollern	0-4-0	815-817 of 1895.	"
	21-30,	Hohenzollern	0-4-0	859-868 of 1895.	"

58. KEHDINGEN. (Kehdinger Kreisbahn) originally owned by (Haverstadt & Contag A.G.).
A light railway with the first batch of locomotives enclosed.
Stade-Brunshausen-Frieburg-Itzworden, 51.8 km.
Brunshausen-Glasfabriek(Glass Works), 2.0 km.
S.1899, Part P.1923, C.1937. Gauge. 1000.

Locomotives. -

	Nos.				
	1-5,	Hohenzollern	0-4-0	1155-1159 of 1899.	🔁
	6,	Hohenzollern	0-4-0	? of 1907.	"
	7, ?	Hohenzollern	0-4-0	? of ?	"
(II)	3,	Hagans	0-4-2	424 of 1900 ex-No.53. ⋇	🔁
(II)	4,	Hagans	0-4-2	425 of 1900 ex-No.53. ⋇	"
(II)	1,	Hagans	0-4-2	422 of 1900 ex-No.53. ⋇	"
(II)	5,	Orenstein & Koppel	0-6-0	10859 of 1925.	"
(II)	7,	Orenstein & Koppel	2-6-0	11700 of 1928.	"
(III)	1,	Orenstein & Koppel	2-6-0	11181 of 1926.	"
(III)	3,	Orenstein & Koppel	2-6-0	11338 of 1927.	"

Names. - 1-Kehdingen, 2-Frieburg, 3-Stade, 4-Elbe, 5-Üste, 6-Drochtersen,
7-Brunshausen ?, (II)3-(Vlotho), (II)4-(Salzuflen), (II)1-(Herford).
Others not named.

59. KREUZNACH. (Kreis Kreuznacher Kleinbahn).
Owned from 1904 by (Westdeutsche Eisenbahn Gesellschaft).
A light railway with 4.9 km street running and locos with enclosed wheels.
Bad Kreusnach(Holzmarkt)-Lohrermühle-Winterburg, 20.5 km.
Lohrermühle-Wallhausen,   6.9 km.
S.1896, C.1936. Gauge. 750.

Locomotives. -	Nos.	1-3,	Jung	0-6-0	243-245 of 1896.	🔁
		4,	?	0-6-2	? of ?	🔁
		5,	Krauss	0-6-2	3530 of 1896. (Numbers as per Krauss list).	"
		6,	Krauss	0-6-2	3685 of 1898. " " " " "	"
		7,	Krauss	0-4-2	3698 of 1898. " " " " "	"
		8,	Krauss	0-6-2	4031 of 1899.	"
	(II)	1.	Krauss	0-6-2	7651 of 1920. (Sold to Austria).	"

Names. -   1-Kremmler, 2-Agricola, 3-Mathee. Others not named.

60. LAHR. (Lahrer Strassenbahn Gesellschaft).   From 1917 (Lahrer Eisenbahn Gesellschaft).
From 1923 (Mittelbadische Eisenbahn A.G.) worked as part of Strassburg system.
See Chapter 4, ALSACE LORRAINE, No.11.
Seelbach-Lahr-Ottenheim, 16.4 km.
S.1894, D.1934, C.1959. Gauge. 1000.

Locomotives. -	Nos.	1-4,	Carlsruhe	0-4-0	? - ? of 1894.	🔁
		5,	Graffenstaden	0-4-0	4900 of 1900.	"
		6.	Graffenstaden	0-4-0	5097 of 1901.	"

61. LEVERKUSEN.   (Farbenfabriken Bayer A.G.) Worked in conjunction with (Kleinbahn
Köln-Mühlheim-Leverkusen) under same ownership.
An industrial railway in a works, with enclosed locomotives.
Industrial sidings only.
S.1898, D.1968, Still operating ?.   Gauge. 1000 (Kleinbahn 1435).

Locomotives. -	Nos.	1-3,	? - ?			
		4-6,	Hohenzollern	0-4-0	1064-1066 of 1898.	🔁
		7-8,	Hohenzollern	0-4-0	1264-1265 of 1899.	"
		9-10.	Hohenzollern	0-4-0	1402-1403 of 1900.	"

62. LUDWIGSHAFEN.   (Königlisch Bayerisch Pfalzische Eisenbahn).
Later (Königlisch Bayerische Staatsbahn).
From 1925, (Deutsche Reichsbahn).
Ludwigshafen-Frankenthal-Grosskarlbach, 25.3 km.
Ludwigshafen-Dannstadt-Meckenheim,   18.8 km. (See No.58).
S.1890, C.1935, Gauge. 1000.

Locomotives. -	Nos. XI-XVII,	Krauss	0-6-0	2082-2088 of 1889.	🔁
	XVIII-XX,	Krauss	0-6-0	2448-2450 of 1891.	"
	XXI-XXII,	Krauss	0-6-0	4213-4214 of 1899.	"
	XXVIII,	Krauss	0-6-0	5758 of 1907 ?	"
	XXIX,	Krauss	0-6-0	6403 of 1910.	"

Names. -   XI-Dannstadt, XII-Maudach, XIII-Mundehheim, XIV-Friesenheim,
XV-Oppau, XVI-Dirmstein, XVII-Grosskarlbach, XVIII-Hessheim,
XIX-Heuchelheim, XX-Laumersheim, XXI-Edigheim, XXII-Schauernheim,
XXVIII- ?, XXIX-Schwegenheim.

Note. -   Locomotives with intervening numbers used on Nos.67 & 92 to which some
of the above were transferred when this line closed.   Under Deutsch
Reichsbahn management, these locomotives were renumbered from 99.081, etc.

63. MAGDEBURG. (Magdeburg Tramway Company Ltd. - British owned).
Heumarkt-Friedrichstadt-Herrenkrug, 4.8 km.
S.1886, E.1900, C.1973 (this line only). Gauge. 1435.

| Locomotives. - | Nos. 2-7, | Schwartzkopff | 0-4-0 | 992-997 of 1878 ex-Berlin No.9. | 🔁 |

64. MAINZ. (Mainzer Vorortbahn). Owned by (Herman Bachstein Group).
From 1895 (Süddeutsche Eisenbahn Gesellschaft A.G.). See No.99.
From 1919. (Strassenbahnen der Stadt Mainz).
Mainz(Fischtor)-Finthen, 9.0 km.
Mainz(Fischtor)-Zalbach-Hechtsheim, 4.2 km.
Zalbach-Bretzenheim, 4.8 km.
S.1891, E.1923, Still Operating. Gauge. 1000.
Locomotives. - Eleven of S.E.G. General stock, including:-
No. 69, Henschel 0-4-0 2839 of 1889.
96-100, Henschel 0-4-0 3473-3477 of 1891.

Note. - The urban electric tramways of Mainz and Wiesbaden, were physically
connected across the Rhine and could be used for the exchange of
steam locomotives between the two S.E.G. steam tramways at these
towns. From 1923 to 1927, the Mainz steam stock was used on a
French Military railway from Finthen to Wackernheim.

65. MANNHEIM. (Martin Lutz & Cie.). Worked by the Municipality from 1898.
From 1904 (Strassenbahnen der Stadt Mannheim).
Mannheim-Feudenheim, 6.5 km.
S.1884, E.1914, Still Operating. Gauge. 1000.
Locomotives. - Nos. 1-3, Carlsruhe 0-4-0 1109-1111 of 1884.
4, Carlsruhe 0-4-0 1146 of 1885. "
5, Carlsruhe 0-4-0 ? of ? "
(II) 2 & 4. ? 0-4-0 ? of ? ex-Strassburg in 1912. "

66. MANNHEIM. (Konsortium für den Bau und Betrieb der Mannheim-Weinheimer Nebenbahn).
Owned by (Eisenbahn Konsortium Herman Bachstein).
From 1895 part of (Süddeutsche Eisenbahn Gesellschaft), organization.
From 1911 (Oberrheinische Eisenbahn Gesellschaft). "O.E.G."
Mannheim-Käfertal-Weinheim 12.7 km.
Weinheim-Schriesheim-Heidelberg, 16.5 km. (Part diesel 1953-1956).
Schriesheim-Heidelberg Bahnhof, 8.4 km. (Mixed gauge freight line).
Heidelberg-Edingen-Seckenheim-Mannheim, 20.0 km.
Edingen-Neckarhausen-Seckenheim, 6.6 km.
Käfertal-Heddesheim, 6.5 km.
S.1887, Part D.1953, E.1915/1956. Still Operating. Gauge. 1000 (with 1435 freight).
Locomotives. - Nos. 55-58, Carlsruhe 0-4-0 1167-1170 of 1886. (56 preserved).
59-60, Carlsruhe 0-4-0 1202 & 1215 of 1887. "
61, Hohenzollern 0-4-0 464 of 1888. (commandeered 1914). "
(II)61, Borsig 0-4-0 4475 of 1895, ex-No.71. "
66, Henschel 0-4-0 2836 of 1889.
75-82, Henschel 0-4-0 3144-3151 of 1890. "
100-102, Henschel 0-4-0 3477 & 3617-3618 of 1891. (102 preserved).
104, Henschel 0-4-0 5252 of 1899. "
(II) 100-101, Krauss-Maffei 0-4-0 17625-17626 of 1947 (for freight).
(101 sold to M.E.G. 1958).
Standard Gauge. -
Locos 341-342, Henschel 0-6-0 6842-6843 of 1905. (for freight). "

Note. - Locomotives numbered in S.E.G. stock from 1895 to 1911. See No.99.

67. MECKENHEIM. (Königlisch Bayerisch Pfalzische Eisenbahn). etc.
A light railway under the same management as No.62, sharing the same locomotives
when steam worked. Most locomotives enclosed or part enclosed.
Meckenheim-Mundesheim, 15.5 km.
S. ?, D.1950, C.1956. Gauge. 1000.
Locomotives. - Pfalzische Eisenbahn general stock, including those of No.62.

68. MINDEN. (Mindener Strassenbahn Gesellschaft).
From 1914, (Strassenbahn Minden GmbH.).
There was also a Mindener Kreisbahn, a standard & metre gauge railway.
Minden-Porta Westfalica, 6.7 km.

S.1893, E.1920, C.1959. Gauge. 1000.
Locomotives. -   Unnumbered   Hagans   0-4-0   276-277 of 1893 (returned to manufacturer). ⊑
                                Hagans   0-4-0   287-288 of 1894.   "
                                Hagans   0-4-0   293 of 1894 & 316 of 1896.   "
                                Hanomag   0-6-0   5324 of 1908.   "

Names. -   276-Minden, 277-Porta, 287-Witkind, 288-Westfalen, 293-Hausberge,
                  316-Minden, 5324-Porta.

69.   MITTELBADISCHE EISENBAHN A.G.
       A company formed in 1923, to take over that part of the Strassburg tramways remaining
       in Germany after 1919, together with some light Railways.   See Chapter 4 ALSACE LORRAINE
       and GERMANY No. 60, LAHR.

70.   MOERS.   (Königlisch Preussische Eisenbahn Verien) "K.P.E.V."
       Later (Strassenbahn Moers-Homberg).
       Roadside light railway, taken over and electrified as a tramway.
       Moers-Homberg, 6.6 km.
       S.1882, E.1908, C.1954.   Gauge. 1435 (1000 on electrification).
       Locomotives. -   From KPEV general stock.   ⊔⊐

71.   MÜLLHEIM, Baden.   (Lokalbahn Müllheim-Badenweiler).
       Worked by (Deutsche Eisenbahn Betriebs Gesellschaft).
       From 1914 (Müllheim-Badenweiler Eisenbahn A.G.).
       Müllheim-Badenweiler, 7.6 km.
       S.1896, E.1914, C.1955.   Gauge. -1000.
       Locomotives. -   Nos.   1-3,   Borsig 0-4-0   4474-4476 of 1895.   ⊔⊐
                         (II)   1.   Borsig 0-4-4-0   4644 of 1898. (Mallet).   "

72.   MÜNCHEN.   (Munich).   (Strassenbahn München-Nymphenburg).
       München(Stiglmaierplatz)-Nymphenburg, 4.0 km. approx.   (rerouted in ?).
       S.1883, E.1900, Still Operating.   Gauge. 1435.
       Locomotives. -   Nos.   1-2,   Krauss 0-4-0   949-950 of 1881.   ⊑
                                 3-4,   Krauss 0-4-0   1028-1029 of 1883.   "
                                 5,   Krauss 0-4-0   1674 of 1888. (ex-various trials). See No. 6 "
                                 6-7,   Krauss 0-4-0   2433-2434 of 1891.   "

73.   MÜNCHEN.   (Munich).   (Lokalbahn A.G., München).   "L.A.G."
       A holding company controlling several light railways and tramways,
       and itself a subsidiary of the Krauss organisation.   See Nos.44, 81 & 83.
       The tram locomotives were numbered in a common list with the railway locos.
       However, they are shown under the individual tramways concerned.

74.   NAUMBURG.   (Naumburger Strassenbahn).
       Naumberger Bahnhof-Wendelstor, 3.1 km.
       S.1892, E.1907, Still Operating.   Gauge. 1000.
       Locomotives. -   Three unnumbered Krauss 0-4-0   2770-2772 of 1892.   ⊑

       Names. -   Naumburg, Saale, Unstrut.

75.   NEUÖTTING.   (Königliche Bayerische Staats Eisenbahn).
       Later (Deutsche Reichsbahn).
       A roadside tramway owned by a main-line railway undertaking.
       Neuötting-Altötting, 4.9 km.
       S.1905, C.1930.   Gauge. -1000.
       Locomotives. -   Nos. 1101-3,   Krauss 2-6-0   5510-5512 of 1906. *   ⊔⊐
                              1104,   Krauss 2-6-0   7986 of 1922.   "

                  *From maker's photograph in "Krauss Lokomotiven" by Bernard Schmeister
                  1977, it looks as if these locos were intended to have enclosed motion.

76. NIEBÜLL. (Kleinbahn Gesellschaft Niebüll-Dagebüll).
From 1910 (Nordfriesische Verkehrsbetriebe A.G.).
Niebüll-Dagebüll(Mole), 13.8 km.
S.1895, R.1925/26, D.1953. Still Operating. Gauge. 1000 (to 1435 in 1926).
Locomotives. -   Nos.   1-2,   Jung   0-4-0   214-215 of 1895.
                            3,   Jung   0-4-0   372 of 1899.
                          4-5,   Jung   0-6-0   1715 & 1962 of 1912/13.
                            -,   A.E.G. 0-6-0   2833 of 1924.

Subsequently worked by six standard gauge railway locomotives.

77. OBERSCHLESIEN. (Oberschlesische Dampfstrassenbahn GmbH). See KATTOWITZ, No.57.

77A. OTTENSEN. (Ottensener Industriebahn).
Large number of dockside and industrial sidings, with steam, electric and
diesel locomotives. Two tram locos.
H.1897/8, Part S.1901, Part P.1903/4, D. ? , Still Operating ?, Gauge. 1000.
Steam Locomotives. -   No,.3,   Borsig   0-4-0   7388 of 1910.
                          4,   ?   0-4-0   ? of   Sold 1914.
                          5,   Humboldt   0-4-0   53 of 1900. (ex.No.35).
                          6,   Orenstein & Koppel 0-4-0   7818 of 1917.
                          7,   ?   0-4-0   ? of
                          8,   Henschel   0-4-0 19764 of 1923.
                          9,   Henschel   0-4-0 20387 of 1924.
                         12,   Henschel   0-4-0 28387 of 1949.

78. PFALZISCHE Eisenbahn. See LUDWIGSHAFEN, No.62, MECKENHEIM, No.67 and
SPEYER, No.92.

79. PLETTENBERG. (Plettenberger Strassenbahn A.G.).
From 1942 (Plettenberger Kleinbahn A.G.).
Plettenberg Bahnhof-Uhlandstrasse,   2.8 km.
Plettenberg(Maiplatz)-Hirschestrasse,   0-6 km.
Hirschestrasse-Holthausen(Elsetal),   2.1 km. (GS in 1912).
Uhlandstrasse-Wiesenthal(Österau),   6.5 km. (GS in 1960).
S.1896, D(WS & GS).1952, C.1962. Gauge. 1000.
Locomotives. -   Nos.   1-2,   Jung   0-4-0   230-231 of 1895.
                          3,   Hohenzollern   0-4-0   925 of 1896.
                          4,   Hohenzollern   0-4-0   1613 of 1902.
                          5,   Hagans   0-6-0   445 of 1901.
                          6,   Humboldt   0-4-0   54 of 1900 (Built for No.35).
                          7,   Borsig   0-6-0   ? of 1915.
                          8,   Henschel   0-4-0   16930 of 1919. (Centre & side buffers).
                          9,   Henschel   0-4-0   20381 of 1924.   "   "   "   "
                         10,   Henschel   0-4-0   20475 of 1925.
                 (II)   3-4,   Henschel   0-4-0   20822-20823 of 1927. (Centre & side buffers).
                 (II)   5,   Henschel   0-4-0   11949 of 1913.

Names. -   Nos.1-2 not named, 3-Else, 4-not named, 5-Österau,6 & 7 not named,
                8-W.Seissenschmidt, 9-Plettenberg. Others not named.

80. PRIEN. (Chiemseebahn Gesellschaft Ludwig Fessler & Cie.).
Prien Bahnhof-Stock, 1.9 km.
S.1887, Still Operating (Summer only). Gauge. 1000.
Locomotive. -   Unnumbered   Krauss 0-4-0 1813 of 1887. (Rebuilt by Jung 1960).

Note. -   The same company once operated a standard gauge light railway as well
                Prien-Aschau, with locomotive Krauss 1812.

81. RAVENSBURG. (Lokalbahn A.G., München). See No.73. Later (Deutsche Reichsbahn).
Ravensburg-Weingarten-Baienfurt, 6.7 km.
S.1888, E.1910, C.1959. Gauge. 1000.
Locomotives. - Nos. 1-2, Krauss 0-4-0 1814 & 1817 of 1888.

Note. - Locomotives numbered in L.A.G. general list. See No.73.
There was a 4.89 km. standard gauge goods connection, BAIENFURT-NIEDERBIEGEN.

82. REES. (Stadt Reeser Anschlussbahn). Worked by (Firma Haverstadt & Contag).
Rees-Empel Bahnhof, 5.8 km.
S.1897, E.1915, GE.1966, C.1967. Gauge. 1000 (1435 on electrification).
Locomotives. - Nos. 1-2, Hagans 0-4-0 338-339 of 1897.
3. ? 0-4-0 ?

83. REGENSBURG. (Ratisbon), "Walhallabahn" (Owned by Lokalbahn A.G., München).
From 1938 (Deutsche Reichsbahn) and from 1947 (Deutsche Bundesbahn).
Regensburg(Stadt am Hof)-Donaustauf("Walhalla"), 8.8 km.
Later extended to Wörth as a light railway, 24.0 km.
S.1889, R.1909, DG.1964, C.1965. Gauge. 1000.

Locomotives. -	Nos. 13-14,	Krauss	0-4-0	2104-2105 of 1889.	
	39,	Krauss	0-4-0	3146 of 1895.	"
	1-2,	Krauss	0-4-0	1814 & 1817 of 1888 ex-No.81.	"
For Railway. -	61,	Krauss	0-6-2	4823 of 1902 (D.R. No.99251).	
	62,	Krauss	0-6-2	5929 of 1908 (" " 99253).	"
	63,	Krauss	0-6-0	2019 of 1889 (not to D.R.)	"
	64,	Maffei	0-8-0	4200 of 1926 (D.R. No.99264).	"
	67,	Krauss	0-6-2	5173 of 1904 (" " 99252).	"
	-,	Weidknecht	0-6-0	?165 of 1910 (" " 99281) ex-104.	
	-,	Orenstein & Koppel	0-6-0	4801 of 1911 (" " 99291) ex-104.	

Note. - Locomotives numbered in L.A.G. general list and in 99 series by D.R.
No.62 preserved in the open.

84. REICHENBACH. (Königlisch Sachsiche Staatseisenbahn).
Later (Deutsche Reichsbahn) now in East Germany.
Reichenbach-Oberheinsdorf, 5.4 km.
S.1902, GS.1961, C.1963. Gauge. 1000.
Locomotives. - Nos.251-253, Chemnitz 0-4-4-0(Fairlie) 2647-2649 of 1902 (D.R.99161-99163).
99.5803, Güstrow 0-4-0 165 of 1896 in 1962.

Note. - All-over roofs later removed. 99162 is now preserved.

85. REMSCHEID. (Wermelskirchen-Burger Eisenbahn).
Taken over by (Westdeutsche Eisenbahn Gesellschaft) in 1897.
Wermelskirchen-Remscheid(Talsperre)-Burg-Krahanhohe, 11.2 km.
S.1890, E.1900, C.1962. Gauge. 1000.

Locomotives. -	Unnumbered	Hohenzollern	0-6-0	497-498 of 1889.	
	No. 11,	Vulcan	0-6-0	1374 of 1894.	"
	Unnumbered	Krauss	0-6-0	2694-2695 of 1892 ex-No.86.	"

Names. - 497-Wermelskirchen, 498-Burg, 1374-not named, 2694-Barmen,
2695-Luttringhausen.

86. RONSDORF. (Ronsdorf-Müngstener Eisenbahn). Later as No.85 above.
On electrification, 84 & 85 were divided up between the municipal tramways of
Barmen, Remscheid and Solingen.
Barmen(Tölleturm)-Ronsdorf Süd-Müngsten, 19.9 km.
Ronsdorf Süd-Ronsdorf Stadt, 1.1 km.
S.1891, E.1897/1903, C.1954/1959. Gauge. 1000.

Locomotives. -	Unnumbered	Krauss	0-6-0	2260-2261 of 1890.	
		Krauss	0-6-0	2555 of 1891.	"
		Krauss	0-6-0	2694-2695 of 1892.	"

```
            Nos.   1-2,    Vulcan  0-4-0    1704-1705 of 1899.          ⌐⌐
                   11,     Vulcan  0-6-0    1374 of 1894. ex-No.85 in 1900.    "
```

Names. -   2260-Ronsdorf, 2261-Remscheid, 2555-Solingen, 2694-Barmen, 2695-Luttringhausen.
            Others not named.

87. RENDSBURG. (Rendsburger Kreisbahn).
     Rendsburg-Hohenweststedt, 30.7 km.
     Hohenweststedt-Schenefeld, 14.2 km.
     S.1901, P.1925, D(GS).1941, C.1957. Gauge. 1000.
     Locomotives. -   Nos. 1-5,   Jung   0-4-0   452-456 of 1900/01. (A.Koppel order).
                            6-7,   Jung   0-6-0   1898-1899 of 1914.   ⌐⌐
                            8,   Linke Hofmann 0-6-0   2858 of 1924.   "
                            9,   Linke Hofmann 0-6-0   2963 of 1925.   "

88. REUTLINGEN. (Lokalbahn Reutlingen-Eningen).
     Later (Württembergische Eisenbahn Gesellschaft).
     A roadside light railway electrified as part of Reutlingen tramways.
     Reutlingen-Eningen, 4.9 km.
     S.1899, E.1912, C.1970. Gauge. 1000.
     Locomotives. -   Nos. 1-3,   Krauss   0-4-0   4149-4151 of 1899.   ⌐⌐
                            4,   Heilbronn 0-4-0   ?   ?   "

89. SAARBRÜCKEN. (Vering & Waechter A.G.). See No.47 for full title.
     From 1893, (Gesellschaft für Strassenbahnen in Saartal A.G.).
     Saarbrücken(St.Johan)-Burbach-Louisenthal, 8.5 km.
     Saarbrücken-Volkingen-Brebach,   1.5 km.
     S.1890, E.1899, C.1965. Gauge. 1000.
     Motive Power. - Nos. 1-5,   Borsig   "Rowan" Cars, 4312-4316 of 1890.   ⌐⌐⌐
                            6-10, Schwartzkopff "Rowan" Cars, 1673-1677 of 1890.   "
                            11,   ?   ?
                            12,   Henschel   0-6-0   3973 of 1893. ex-No.47 ⌐⌐

     Note. -   There was some steam working with borrowed industrial locomotives in 1945.

90. SAARLOUIS. (Kleinbahn Ensdorf-Saarlouis-Wallerfangen-Fraulautern).
     Owned by (Vering & Waechter A.G.). See No.47 & No.89 above.
     Saarlouis-Fraulautern-Ensdorf, 3.5 km.
     Saarlouis-Wallerfangen,   7.0 km.
     S.1898, E.1913, EG.1961, C.1963. Gauge. 1435.
     Locomotives. -   Nos. 1-2,   Hanomag 0-4-0 2839-2840 of 1897.   ⌐⌐
                            3-5,   Henschel 0-4-0 4785-4787 of 1898.   "
                            6?   Henschel 0-4-0   13007 of 1914.   "

91. SIEGEN. See EISERN, No.37.

92. SPEYER. (Königlisch Bayerisch Pfalzische Eisenbahn). See No.62 for later ownership.
     A light railway under the same administration as the Ludwigshafen tramway.
     See Nos.62 & 67. Had some partly enclosed locomotives and took some enclosed
     machines from No.62 when that closed.
     Speyer-Neustadt, 29.1 km.
     S.1905, C.1955. Gauge. 1000.
     Locomotives. -   Nos.
                      XXIII-XXIV,   Krauss 0-4-0   4920-4921 of 1903.   ⌐⌐
                      XXV-XXVII,   Krauss 0-4-0   5198-5200 of 1905.   "
                      XXVIII,   Krauss 0-6-0   5758 of 1907.   ⌐⌐
                      XXX,   Maffei 0-4-0   3637 of 1916.   ⌐⌐
                      XXXI-XXXIII,   Krauss 0-6-0   7987-7989 of 1923/24. (partly enclosed). ⌐⌐

                                        102
```
```

93. SPREMBERG. (Spremberger Stadtbahn). Freight only in steam days.
Owned by (Vering & Waechter A.G.) See No.47 for full title.
Spremberg Bahnhof-Spremberg West, 17.0 km. (including sidings).
GS.1896, P.1924, D. ? C. ? Gauge. 1000 (plus 3.5 km.1435 connections).
Locomotives. - Nos. 1-2, Hanomag   0-4-0   2785-2786 of 1896 (1435 gauge).
                     3, Borsig   0-6-0   5262 of 1903   "   "   "
                   4-5, Borsig   0-4-0   4541-4542 of 1896 (1000 gauge).   "
                     6, Borsig   0-4-0   4474 of 1895 Ex-No.71.
                     7, Borsig   0-4-0   5182 of 1903.   "
                     8, Jung   0-4-4-0(Mallet), 252 of 1896.   "
                     9, Borsig   0-4-0   6651 of 1908.
                    10, Orenstein & Koppel 0-4-0 10321 of 1922.
                    11, Borsig   0-4-0   11870 of 1920.   "
                    12, Orenstein & Koppel 0-4-0 13178 of 1928.   "

94. STADE. See KEHDINGEN, No.58.

95. STRASSBURG. See Chapter 4, ALSACE LORRAINE.

96. STRAUSBERG. (Strausberger Kleinbahn A.G.).
From 1930 (Strausberger Eisenbahn). Now in East Berlin.
Strausberg Bahnhof-Strausberg Stadt, 6.2 km.
S.1893, E.1921, Still Operating. Gauge. 1435.
Locomotives. - Nos. 1-2, Hohenzollern 0-4-0, 720-721 of 1893.
                     3, Hohenzollern 0-4-0,   ? of ?   "

97. STUTTGART. (Stuttgarter Pferde Eisenbahn Gesellschaft).
Trials with a Merryweather locomotive from Cassel, and possibly one from
Strassburg, on the urban horse tramways.
H.-?, S.-only, E. Still Operating. Gauge. 1000.

98. STUTTGART. (Filderbahn A.G.). See No.41.

99. SÜDDEUTSCHE Eisenbahn Gesellschaft.
Formerly (Eisenbahn Konsortium für Handel und Industrie, Herman Bachstein A.G.)
Became "S.E.G." in 1895.
A holding company which controlled a number of light railways and the following
tramways - Carlsruhe (No.23), Darmstadt (No.30), Mainz (No.64) and Wiesbaden (No.105).
Its tram locomotives were numbered between 51 and 104 and appear to have been moved
around between them from time to time. "O.E.G." at Mannheim (No.66) was also in the
group for a time. See individual systems for other details.
Locomotives. - Nos. 51-52, Krauss   0-4-0   1784-1785 of 1886 at Darmstadt.
                    53-54, Heilbronn   0-4-0   231-232 of 1886 "   "   "
                    55-58, Carlsruhe   0-4-0   1167-1170 of 1886 at Mannheim.
                    59-60, Carlsruhe   0-4-0   1202 & 1215 of 1887 at Mannheim. "
                    61-63, Hohenzollern 0-4-0   464-466 of 1888 at Darmstadt
                    64-69, Henschel   0-4-0   2834-2839 of 1889 °
                    70-72, Henschel   0-4-0   2881-2883 of 1889 °
                    73-74, Krauss   0-6-0   2023-2024 of 1889 on light railway
                    75-82, Henschel   0-4-0   3144-3151 of 1890 at Mannheim.
                    83-84, Henschel   0-4-0   3241-3242 of 1889 at Wiesbaden.   "
                    85-88, Henschel   0-4-0   3152-3155 of 1890 Wiesbaden & Mainz.
                    89-95, Carlsruhe   0-4-0   1278-1284 of 1890 at Carlsruhe.   "
                   96-100, Henschel   0-4-0   3473-3477 of 1891 at Mainz.   "
                  101-102, Henschel   0-4-0   3617-3618 of 1891 at Mannheim.   "
                     103, Graffenstaden 0-4-4-0   4738 of 1898 on a light railway.
                     104, Henschel   0-4-0   5252 of 1899 at Mannheim.

Note. -   Other numbers in the series were occupied by metre and standard gauge
                 locomotives for light railways in the group. See No.66.
                 ° 64 at Darmstadt, 65, 68, 72 at Carlsruhe, 66, 67, 70, 71 at Wiesbaden & 69 at Mainz.

100. SYLT. (Dampfspurbahn Westerland-Munkmarsch).
From 1903, (Sylter Dampfspurbahn) & from 1917 (Sylter Betriebsvereinigung).
A light railway on a Friesian island with some enclosed locomotives.
Classified as a tramway for legal reasons in 1952.
Westerland-Munkmarsch, 4.2 km.
Westerland-List, 17.5 km.
Westerland-Keitum, 4.9 km.
S.1888, D.1950, C.1970. Gauge. 1000.

Locomotives. -	Nos.				
	1-2,	Krauss	0-4-0	1975-1976 of 1886.	
	3,	Krauss	0-4-0	4360 of 1900.	
	4,	Krauss	0-6-0	5514 of 1906.	"
	5,	Krauss	0-6-0	6414 of 1911.	"
	6,	Krauss	0-6-0	6714 of 1913.	"
	7,	Jung	0-4-0	454 of 1900 ex-No.87. ❖	
	8,	Krauss	0-6-0	6858 of 1916 (intended for Greece)	
(II)	7-9,	* Freudenstein	0-6-0	67-69 of 1901 ex-No.101.	"
(II)	1,	Krauss/ Maffei	0-8-0	15518 of 1935 (too large ?).	"
(II)	2,	Orenstein & Koppel	0-6-0	10859 of 1925 ex-No.58. ❖	"
	10,	Hagans	0-4-2	379 of 1936 ex-Minden Krb.	"
	11,	Jung	0-8-2	1658 of 1911 " " "	"
	12,	Orenstein & Koppel	0-6-0	4031 of 1910 ❖	"
	13,	Borsig	0-6-0	7166 of 1909 ❖	"
	14,	Hohenzollern	0-4-0	999 of 1897 ❖	"
	15,	Orenstein & Koppel	2-6-0	11338 of 1927 ex-No.58. ❖	"
	16,	Hohenzollern	0-4-0	1011 of 1898 ❖	"
	17,	Krauss	0-6-0	2082 of 1889 ex-No.62. ❖	
	18,	Krauss(Linz)	0-6-2	4364 of 1900 ex-Austria No.2. ❖	

Names. - 1-Präsident von Maybach, 2-Herzog Maximilian von Württemberg, 3-von Koller,
4-Jungnickel, 5-Emil Kurt. Others not named.
*J.Freudenstein was taken over by Orenstein & Koppel in 1905.

101. SYLT. (Sylter Südbahn A.G.). Amalgamated with No.100 in 1917 and tracks connected.
Westerland(Sud)-Hornum, 18.3 km.
S.1901, D.1950, C.1970. Gauge. 1000.

Locomotives. -	Nos.			
	1-3,	Freudenstein 0-6-0	67-69 of 1901.	
	11-15.	of No.100 worked on this line after the amalgamation.		

102. UETERSEN. (Uetersener Eisenbahn A.G.).
A standard gauge light railway with street running and enclosed locomotives.
Through goods working with main line railway at Tornesch.
Uetersen-Tornesch, 4.5 km. (9.3 including sidings).
H.1873, S.1908, D(GS).1924, DG only 1965. Still Operating. Gauge. 1435.

Motive Power. -	No.				
	1,	Borsig	0-4-0	6793 of 1908.	
	2-3,	Borsig "Rowan cars"		6791-6792 of 1908.	
	4-5,	Borsig "Rowan cars"		4235-4236 of 1889 ex-No.13. ❖	"
	(6-7,	Passenger trailers for Rowan cars, also ex-No.13).			
	8-9,	Hanomag	0-4-0	5919 of 1910 & 6738 of 1912.	
(II)	1,	Hagans	0-6-0	665 of 1910. ❖	
(II)	2,	Henschel	0-6-0	3773 of 1893. ❖	"
(II)	3,	Orenstein & Koppel	0-6-0	1101 of 1903. ❖	"
(II)	4,	Henschel	0-6-0	5220 of 1899. ❖	"
(II)	5,	Schwartzkopff	0-6-0	1564 of 1888. ❖	"
	10.	Henschel	0-4-0	2958 of 1889 ex-No.2. ❖	

Note. - Wagons were sometimes carried on the Uetersener line on very short wheel
base standard gauge transporter trucks to get round very sharp curves on
industrial sidings, hence the locomotives had two sets of side buffers, one
above the other.

103. VORGEBIRGSBAHN.   See Cöln No. 27.

104. WANGEROOGE.   (Inselbahn Wangerooge).   Owned by (Grossherzoglich Oldenburgischen Eisenbahn).
An island light railway with one enclosed locomotive.
Later worked by (Deutsche Reichsbahn) now (Deutsche Bundesbahn).
Westturm-Dünen-Ostanleger,   8.9 km.
Westanleger-Dünen,   1.9 km.
S.1897, D.1952, Still Operating.   Gauge. 1000.
Locomotives. -   Nos.   1,   Märkische   0-4-0   148 of 1896.
                          2,   Heilbronn   0-4-0   358 of 1898.   "
                          3,   Freudenstein   0-4-0   194 of 1904 (became 99.021). "
                          4,   Hanomag   0-4-0   5876 of 1910 (became 99.022). "
                          5,   Hanomag   0-4-0   6930 of 1913 (became 99.023). "
                   99.211,   Henschel   0-6-0   21443 of 1929.   "
                   99.081,   Krauss   0-6-0   2082 of 1889
                                                                       ex-No.62 ("Dannstadt").
                   99.271,   Jung   0-4-0   2483 of 1918
                                                                       ex-Netherlands No.84
                   99.291,   Orenstein & Koppel 0-6-0   4801 of 1911 Later to No.83.
                   99.281,   Weidknecht   0-6-0   ?165 of 1910 :·
                                                                       Later to No. 83 "

105. WIESBADEN.   (The Wiesbaden Tramway Co., London).
From 1895, (Süddeutsche Eisenbahn Gesellschaft).   See No. 99.
Biebrich-Wiesbaden-Nerotal Park(Beausite), 10.0 km. ?
H.1875, S.1889, C.1900.   Reopened E.1900, C.1955.   Gauge. 1000.
Locomotives. -   Nos.   1-3,   S.E.G. 0-4-0, 464-466 of 1888. (became S.E.G. 61-63)
                       Later eleven of S. E.G. general stock, (See No.99) 66, 67, 70, 71 & 83-88. "

Note. -   See Note against MAINZ, No. 64.

NOTE. -   Lengths of lines are based on "Reichs Kursbuch" for 1930 and "Deutsche
                    Klein und Privat Bahnen" by Gerd Wolff, 1973.

Heilbronn loco No.4 with enclosed wheels and motion for Reutlingen.
Heilbronn Catalogue.   Courtesy: late F. Kemper.

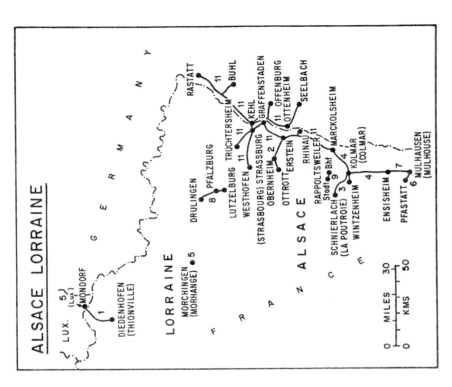

ALSACE LORRAINE

LUX.
MONDORF 5(Lux)
DIEDENHOFEN (THIONVILLE) 1

LORRAINE

MORCHINGEN (MORHANGE) 5
DRULINGEN
PFALZBURG 8
LUTZELBURG TRUCHTERSHEIM 11
WESTHOFEN 11
(STRASBOURG) STRASSBURG 2 11
OBERNHEIM
OTTROTT ERSTEIN
RHINAU
SCHNIERLACH (LA POUTROIE) 3
RAPPOLTSWEILER 11
Bhf 4
Stadt 9
WINTZENHEIM
KOLMAR (COLMAR) 4
ENSISHEIM
PFASTATT 6
MULHAUSEN (MULHOUSE) 7

RASTATT
BUHL 11
KEHL 11
GRAFFENSTADEN 11
OFFENBURG 11
OTTENHEIM
SEELBACH
MARCKOLSHEIM 11

ALSACE

FRANCE

MILES 0 30
KMS 0 50

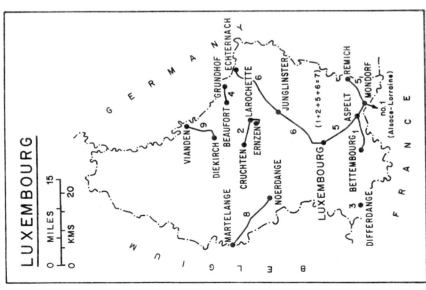

LUXEMBOURG

MILES 0 15
KMS 0 20

GERMANY

VIANDEN 9
DIEKIRCH
BEAUFORT
GRUNDHOF 4
ECHTERNACH
LAROCHETTE 6
ERNZEN 2
CRUCHTEN
JUNGLINSTER
MARTELANGE 8
NOERDANGE
LUXEMBOURG (1+2+5+6=7)
6
ASPELT 5
REMICH 5
MONDORF
no.1 (Alsace-Lorraine)
BETTEMBOURG 1
DIFFERDANGE 3

FRANCE
BELGIUM

4. ALSACE LORRAINE & LUXEMBOURG
1. ALSACE LORRAINE

This largely industrial area on the banks of the River Rhine and known in German as Elsass Lothringen, was in French territory until the early 1870s, when it was annexed by Germany, not long before the introduction of steam tramways. It remained in Germany until it was returned to France by the Treaty of Versailles in 1919. The principal city and owner of the largest tramway system, is Strasbourg. Its steam tramway system probably had the most complicated history of any in Europe. Steam traction was introduced early, when in 1878, suburban extensions were added to the existing horse tramway system, which was laid to standard gauge. Small Winterthur enclosed engines took over from the horses at the city gates and pulled the cars out into the suburbs. The year 1886 saw the beginning of a much larger interurban system of steam tramways based on Strasbourg, but this was of metre gauge, with lines starting at the standard gauge termini. Both networks belonged to the same company, which subsequently absorbed an independant line between Erstein and Ottrott.

Electrification of the urban system was undertaken by the turn of the century and at the same time the lines were converted to metre gauge, so that the interurban trains could run through to the city centre. These latter remained steam operated until after the 1914-1918 war, when the Treaty of Versailles had the most unfortunate effect of cutting the system in two. The city of Strasbourg and its suburbs on the west of the Rhine were handed back to France, but across the Pont de Kehl, the lines on the east of the Rhine remained in Germany. The Ottrott-Erstein line was already abandoned in 1919, but was later replaced by a direct electric line from Strasbourg to Ottrott. This was followed by the electrification of most of the lines on the French side in 1920s. On the other hand, the German lines based on Kehl, at first run by a caretaker administration, were handed over in 1923 to the Mittelbadische Eisenbahn, which took in a physically connected line at Lahr and owned some other lines of purely light railway character. This undertaking did not go in for electrification, but has gradually over the years replaced the steam by small diesel railcars. Although the French system closed down completely after the 1939-45 war, there is still some operation on the Kehl lines, largely because of the existence of some heavy transporter freight traffic.

Of the four metre gauge lines based on Colmar, two were really tramways and the other two light railways. Over much of their life they were controlled by the Alsace Lorraine Railways, who tended to use the enclosed and unenclosed locomotives indescriminately on them. Later, under French administration, one of these lines was handed over to the urban tramway system and electrified.

The tramway system at Mulhouse is notable principally because steam was retained for goods working even on the urban lines long after the electrification of the passenger services. In fact, the steam engines were finally replaced by diesel locomotives in the late 1930s. The two inter-urban lines belonged to a nominally independant company but both were financed by Swiss capital and it is reported that the Winterthur Bank and the Winterthur Locomotive Works were prominent among the shareholders. There was also a steam tramway at Pfalzburg, which just before 1914, was converted to a light railway and extended. It then shared in the common pool of narrow gauge engines owned by the

Alsace Lorraine railway administration, and those used thereafter on this line included some heavy 0-8-0 side tank engines. Morchingen and Rappoltweiler were each served by a single steam tram route, in each case linking the town with the main line railway station. The latter relied mainly on goods traffic and was rebuilt from metre gauge to standard gauge in 1894, so that loaded main line wagons could be run right into factories in the town. There is thought to have been a similar standard gauge steam tramway at Puttelange in 1911, but no details are available.

Locomotives

Most of the locomotives used on the standard gauge lines and the earliest on the metre gauge lines at Strassburg, were small four-coupled Winterthur machines with Brown patent boilers. Not surprisingly, in view of the financial interest, Winterthur machines were used exclusively at Mulhouse; they were also used at Pfalzburg and Rappoltsweiler. Those at Mulhouse were of a peculiar design with a flexible wheelbase; some were 2-2-2s and others 2-4-2s, with the outer wheels on pony trucks in each case. [1] They appear to have been shared by the two undertakings. Colmar went in mainly for Krauss engines, some of their standard enclosed type and others with only the wheels and motion enclosed. There were also a few Krauss engines at Strassburg and the two at Morchingen came from Hanomag; they also had enclosed wheels and motion. They were sold to the Bergische Kleinbahn when Morchingen closed after a short life.

Alsace Lorraine boasted its own locomotive manufacturing works the "Elsassische Maschinenbau Gesellschaft" at Graffenstaden, near Strassburg. This company bought out the other works at Mulhouse and Belfort. Tram engines of quite a distinctive design were turned out from the Graffenstaden and the Mulhouse works. They were 0-4-0s with outside frames and inside cylinders, so that the only moving parts that showed were the coupling rods and they were regarded as locomotives with enclosed motion. They had comodious cabs at the rear and wing tanks alongside the smokebox. In later years some were made to look even more peculiar by the arrangement of a Westighouse brake pump on top of the boiler, behind the chimney, to which it was fixed by brackets. Electric lighting jumper cable attachments were fixed to the front of the chimney. Several were retained to the end of the French system, for goods work, and one took part in the final parade on the closing day. Prior to that they had made a brief re-appearance in passenger traffic in the 1930s on the occasion of a power failure and during the 1939-1945 war. On the German side, two were seen quite recently at the back of a shed, and may be there yet. [2]

When the area passed to France after the war, the German name of the Graffenstaden Works was replaced by a French title "La Societé Alsacienne de Constructions Mécaniques", and new works plates bearing this name, but with the old works numbers and dates, were cast for all locomotives then in French hands.

2. LUXEMBOURG

The Grand Duchy of Luxembourg is a sovereign state lying between France, Belgium and Germany. It had its own main-line railways and tramways, most of which used enclosed locomotives at some stage in their career. These were let out on concessions to several private companies. At first, two lines were leased to the "Winterthur Locomotive Company" and two others to one of the subsidiary companies of the Belgian "Vicinal" organization. "Les Chemin de Fer Cantonaux" worked two other lines, and one other plus a purely industrial line was conceded to the "Prince Henri" main line railway company. Operation never appears to have been profitable and the State had to take over the Cantonaux lines in 1924, and the "Secondaires" lines (those originally leased to Winterthur) in 1934. All were of the metre gauge.

The two most important lines both started in the forecourt of Luxemburg City railway station and ran in opposite directions out of town. Of these, that which ran northwards to Echternach, ran for quite a considerable distance over the city tramway tracks; consequently in 1928, two powerful electric cars were obtained, to pull goods trains and carry passengers between the Station and Dommeldingen on the outskirts of the town, where passengers had to change to steam trains. These two tractor cars, which incidentally ran on eight wheels, not bogies, (another Winterthur invention!),[3] lasted until 1944, when one was destroyed in an air-raid, and the other was too worn out to carry on alone. From then onwards, steam trains were again permitted to run through the town. However, in order to work electrically controlled points at junctions, a small electric passenger car, running empty had to precede every steam train as far as the last junction, to alter the points. This line was always known as "Charly" after the minister, Charles Rischard, responsible for its construction. By contrast, the other line covered very little of the city electric tram tracks and the depot for both was on this one, at Bonnevoie just south of the main-line station. This line met another at Aspelt, and a line from Thionville in Alsace Lorraine at Mondorf. Another line met the Belgian S. N. C. V. at Martelange. (The tracks were close together but not connected).

Petrol railcars were introduced on at least one of the lines as early as 1912 and when several of them were taken over by the state controlled "Réseau des Chemins de Fer à Voie Etroite", in 1934, they were converted to diesel. There were eventually 9 of these cars running on a number of lines. During the 1939-1945 war, Luxemburg was occupied by Germany and all the railways were compulsorily absorbed into the Deutsche Reichsbahn, and after the war they were included in the "Chemins de Fer Luxembourgeois" as a unified undertaking. All the narrow gauge lines survived the war with some damage to bridges and the Bonnevoie depot, but after the war, they were gradually replaced by the ubiquitous motor bus, the last line closing in 1957.

Locomotives

Luxemburg had no locomotive manufacturers of its own, and not unexpectedly in view of the working agreement which they had, the Swiss locomotive Works at Winterthur provided the motive power for the earliest lines. Later there were some Winterthur locomotives of the 0-6-0 arrangement, similar to those used in Geneva and elsewhere, and some unenclosed locomotives second-hand from Swiss light railways being electrified.

In its early days, the Aspelt-Bettemberg line was managed by a Belgian S. N. C. V. subsidiary and their three locomotives were built by Tubize to the standard S. N. C. V. Class 4 design. In the 1930s, they were replaced by railcars and transferred to another line, where they underwent a complete transformation, receiving rear cabs and bunkers, larger side tanks and the removal of the covering over the wheels and motion, rendering them quite unrecognizable as former-enclosed machines.

The longest line of all, the Luxemburg-Echternach, which was the last to open, although managed by the S. N. C. V., was notable for the powerful Mallet articulated locomotives built at Graffenstaden. They were the mainstay of this line and when reboilered in the 1930s, were even more impressive looking as they made their way through the streets of Luxemburg city. When the Winterthur tram-engines began to wear out, several were replaced by other Winterthur locomotives, but these were larger and not enclosed; they came again, second hand from two important narrow gauge railways in Switzerland. The last two engines to be acquired were taken into stock in 1926 and 1930 respectively and were very chunky looking 0-6-0 side tank engines, built new by Haine St. Pierre.

Not unexpectedly, with the various changes in control, which have been mentioned, the locomotives suffered re-numberings, when they came into the hands of the "C. F. Voie Etroite" and its successors. They were numbered in the "99" series by the Deutsche Reichsbahn and in the 300s after the war. "Voie Etroite" locomotives were painted dark green with black wheels and red buffer beams. Latterly they were plain black with yellow numbers.

Carriage Stock etc.

The carriages used on the shorter lines tended to be four-wheeled vehicles of the Belgian style, but the two longer lines starting in Luxemburg City, were worked by some fairly large bogie cars of plain exterior, rather after the Dutch style. At one time dark green, latterly they were painted in a two colour livery, of blue and cream.

Although the Luxemburg City terminus was in the open street, at other places, there were some quite elaborate station buildings.

Notes

1. See "Tramway & Railway World" December 1896, page 325 for drawing.

2. See "Stephenson Locomotive Society Journal" for April 1960, page 21.

3. See "Transport World" November 1933, page 260 for description of electric cars. See also "Chemins de Fer Regionaux et Urbains" Nos. 136 & 137, 1976.

Table 4, ALSACE LORRAINE

Note. - German names of places are given first, as the area was in Germany (1870-1919) when steam tramways were developed. French names are shown in brackets where different.

1. DIEDENHOFEN. (Thionville) (Vering und Waechter Eisenbahnbau und Betriebs Gesellschaft).
    From 1924 (Société Générale des Chemins de Fer Economiques).
    Diedenhofen(Thionville)-Mondorf, 25.6 km.
    (A roadside light railway with street running in towns. The Mondorf terminal was in
    Luxemburg and connected with Luxemburg No. 5.)
    S.1903, C.1934. Gauge. 1000.

Locomotives. -	Nos.	1-3,	Borsig	0-6-0	5103-5105 of 1902.	
		4,	Henschel	0-4-0	3484 of 1891. ex-Gera. ∵	
		5,	Henschel	0-6-0	3973 of 1893. ex-Gera. ∵	"
		51,	Hohenzollern	0-4-0	845 of 1895. ex-Gera ? ∵	"
		3759,	Corpet Louvet	0-6-0	1140 of 1909.	

2. ERSTEIN. (Strassenbahn Obernheim-Erstein-Ottrott).
    Later part of (Strassburger Strassenbahnen). See No. 9.
    Erstein-Obernheim(Obernai)-Ottrott, 19.0 km.
    S.1907, C.1919. Gauge. 1000.
    Locomotives. -   Nos.   1-3,   Borsig 0-4-0   6208-6209 & 6480 of 1907.

3. KOLMAR. (Colmar). (Kaysersbergertalbahn).
    Later (Chemin de Fer de la Vallée de Kaysersberg).
    Finally, part (S.A. des Tramways de Colmar).
    Kolmar-Wintzenheim, 5.4 km.
    Kolmar-Kaisersberg-Schnierlach(La Poutroie), 24.6 km. (to No.4 in 1932).
    S.1885 E.(to Wintzenheim) 1935, C.1960. Gauge. 1000.

Locomotives. -	Nos.	1-3,	Krauss	0-6-0	1552-1554 of 1884/85.	
		4-5,	Krauss	0-4-0	1650-1651 of 1885.	"
		6-7,	Krauss	0-6-0	1686 of 1886 & 4104 of 1899.	"
		8,	Krauss	0-6-0	5759 of 1907.	"
		9,	Krauss	0-8-0	6499 of 1911.	
		?,	Pinguély	0-6-0	355 of 1921.	
		?,	Pinguély	2-6-0	370 of 1923.	

4. KOLMAR. (Colmar). (Reichseisenbahn Elsass Lothringen). (Schmalspurnetz).
    Later (Chemins de Fer d'Alsace Lorraine).
    Finally (Société Nationale des Chemins de Fer).
    Kolmar-Marckolsheim, 22.2 km.
    Kolmar-Ensisheim, 24.0 km. (Converted to standard guage railway).
    S.1890 R. ? C.1947. Gauge. 1000.

Locomotives. -	Nos.					
		541-543,	Krauss	0-6-0	2266-2268 of 1890.	
		550,	Graffenstaden	0-6-0	4199 of 1891.	"
		675-681.	Krauss	0-6-0	3951-3954 of 1899.	"

    (These locomotives were renumbered in the 3000s in 1906 and 1-8
    in a separate series in 1912. Later they were absorbed into the
    Alsace Lorraine Railways general narrow gauge stock, from which
    other locomotives were also used on this line. See No. 10 for
    details).

5. MORCHINGEN. (Morhange). (Morchinger Strassenbahn).
   Morchingen Bahnhof-Morchingen Stadt, 2.0 km ?
   S.1911, C.1920. Gauge. 1000.
   <u>Locomotives.</u> -   Nos. 1-2, Hanomag 0-4-0   6228-6229 of 1911. (Sold to Germany 🔚
                                                         No. 51).

6. MULHAUSEN. (Mulhouse). (Société des Tramways de Ribeauville) See No. 9, Swiss owned.
   From 1884, (Tramways de Mulhouse S.A.). Some lines used for freight only remained steam,
   later diesel, but not electrified.
   Hauptbahnhof(Gare Imperial)-Dornach,   3.6 km. (passenger service).
   Hauptbahnhof(Gare Imperial)-Pfastatt,   4.9 km. (passenger service).
   Hauptbahnhof(Gare Imperial)-Nordfeld,)   5.0 km. (freight only).
   Lavoisierstrasse & other short branches,)
   S.1882, E(GS).1894, GD.1930, C.1956.   Gauge. 1000.
   <u>Locomotives.</u> -   Nos. 1-4, Winterthur 2-4-2 255-258 of 1882. (flexible wheelbase). 🔚
                            5-8, Winterthur 2-4-2 314-317 of 1882. (flexible wheelbase). "
                            9-12, Winterthur 2-2-2 325-328 of 1883. (flexible wheelbase). "
                            13,   Winterthur 0-6-0   336 of 1883.   "
                            16,   Winterthur 0-6-0   457 of 1886. ex-Germany No.43.   "
   Names. -   1-?, 2-Dornach, 3-Lutterbach, 4-Muelhausen, 5-Elsass, 6-Lothringen,
                  7-?, 8-Rhone. Others not named.

7. MULHAUSEN. (Mulhouse). (S.A. des Tramways de Mulhouse-Ensisheim-Wittenheim).
   Always managed with No. 6 and formally amalgamated in 1930.
   Mulhausen-Ensisheim, 16.4 km.
   Mulhausen-Wittenheim, 8.0 km.
   S.1885, E.1931, C.1957. Gauge. 1000.
   <u>Locomotives.</u> -   Nos.14-17, Winterthur 2-4-2 416-419 of 1886. (flexible wheelbase). 🔚
                      (II) 9, Winterthur 0-6-0   864 of 1894. ex-Switzerland Nos. ⋎ ⋎
                                                                                  2 & 3. "
                      (II)10, Winterthur 0-6-0   1144 of 1898. ex-Switzerland No. 3.   "
                      (II)11, Winterthur 0-6-0   1145 of 1898.   "   "   "
                      (II)12, Hanomag   0-6-0   5324 of 1908. ex-Germany No.68.   "

8. PFALZBURG. (Phalsbourg). (Pfalzburger Strassenbahn Gesellschaft).
   Later (Reichseisenbahn Elsass Lothringen) to 1919, See No. 10.
   Finally (Société du Chemin de Fer d'Alsace Lorraine), France.
   Extended to Drulingen in 1914, as a metre gauge railway, then worked by 0-8-0 tank engines
   from the railway's metre gauge stock, See No. 10.
   Lutzelburg-(Bahnhof)-Pfalzburg-Wilsburg, 9.3 km.
   Lutzelburg-(Bahnhof)-Lutzelburg(Kanal),   1.0 km.
   S.1883, R.1914, C.1953. Gauge. 1000.
   <u>Locomotives.</u> -   Nos. 1-3, Winterthur 0-4-0   342-344 of 1883.   🔚
                           For subsequent locomotives, See No. 10.

9. RAPPOLTSWEILER. (Ribeauville). (Société des Tramways de Ribeauville) Swiss owned.
   This company also worked No. 6 at first.
   Rappoltsweiler Bahnhof-Rappoltsweiler Stadt, 3.8 km.
   S.1879, C.1938. Gauge. 1000 until 1895, then 1435.
   <u>Locomotives.</u> -   Nos. 1-2, Winterthur   0-4-0 154-155 of 1879. (Metre gauge). 🔚
                           3, Winterthur   0-4-0   157 of 1880.   "   "   "
                  (II) 1-2, Graffenstaden 0-4-0 4591 & 4590 of 1894. (1435   "
                                                                           gauge).

   Names. -   (II) 1-Taenschel, (II) 2-Rappolstein. (Names and numbers given as
                                                         per Graffenstaden Works List).

10. REICHSEISENBAHN ELSASS LOTHRINGEN.
    Later (Chemins de Fer d'Alsace Lorraine (France)).
    Finally (Société Nationale des Chemins de Fer Français).
    Owned No. 4 and acquired part of No. 3 and No. 8. It had a combined fleet of narrow
    gauge locomotives shared between them.

                                    112

Locomotives. -	Nos. 541-543,	Krauss	0-6-0	2266-2268	of 1890	for No. 4.
	544-545,	Krauss	0-4-0	1650-1651	of 1885	ex-No. 3.
	546,	Krauss	0-4-0	?	of 1890	.'''
	547-549,	Winterthur	0-4-0	342-344	of 1883	ex-No. 8.
	678-681,	Krauss	0-6-0	3951-3954	of 1899	for No. 4. "
	868-869,	Hagans	0-8-0	483-484	of 1903	later - 111-112. "
	870,	Hagans	0-8-0	488	of 1903	" 113. "
	976-978,	Hagans	0-8-0	514-516	of 1904	" 114-116. "
	117-118,	Hagans	0-8-0	580-581	of 1908.	"
	119-120,	Hagans	0-8-0	599-600	of 1908.	"
	121-122,	Hagans	0-8-0	639-640	of 1910.	"
	123,	Hagans	0-8-0	724	of 1913.	"

Note. -   Between 1906 and 1912, these locomotives were renumbered 3001-3042 in order of construction dates. From 1912, Nos. 541-543, 550 and 675-681 were renumbered 1-8 in a separate series and the Hagans locos became 111-123 as shown above. The French SNCF numbered them 040.TB.111-123.

11.   STRASSBURG (Strasbourg).   (Strassburger Pferde-Eisenbahn Gesellschaft).
Later (Strassburger Strassenbahn Gesellschaft).
From 1919 (S.A. des Tramways de Strasbourg).

(a).   Standard Gauge suburban lines.

Strassburg(Metzger Thor)-Kehlerbrucke,   4.0 km.
Strassburg(Stein Thor)-Hoenheim,   ? km.
Strassburg(Metzger Thor)-Neuhof,   4.0 km.
Strassburg(Spital Thor)-Graffenstaden,   7.8 km.
Strassburg(Bahnhof)-Koenigshofen-Wolfisheim,   ? km.
S.1878, E.1898/1904, C.1960. Gauge. 1435 (1000 on electrification).

Locomotives. -	Trials with	Winterthur	0-4-0	124 of 1877.
	Nos. 1-6,	Winterthur	0-4-0	127-132 of 1878.
	7-9,	Winterthur	0-4-0	147-149 of 1878.
	10 & 12,	Winterthur	0-4-0	151-152 of 1879.
	11,	Winterthur	0-4-0	153 of 1879 (not delivered).
(II)	11,	Winterthur	0-4-0	124 of 1877 (ex-Trials).
	13,	Winterthur	0-4-0	158 of 1879.
	14,	Winterthur	0-4-0	190 of 1800.
	15,	Krauss	0-4-0	910 of 1883.
	16,	Carlsruhe	0-4-0	1084 of 1883.
	17-20,	Winterthur	0-4-0	378-381 of 1884.
	25-29,	Winterthur	0-4-0	436-440 of 1886.

(b).   Metre Gauge lines which passed to France in 1919.

Koenigshoffen-Dingsheim-Truchtersheim,   15.0 km.
Dingsheim-Westhoffen,   19.0 km.
Graffenstaden-Erstein-Boofsheim-Marckolsheim,   47.0 km. (See No. 4).
Boofsheim-Rhinau (Ferry),   2.5 km. (Usually horse worked).
Erstein-Obernheim(Obernai)-Ottrott,   19.0 km. (ex-No. 2).
S.1885, E.1925, C.1955. Gauge. 1000.

(c).   Metre Gauge lines which remained in Germany after 1919 and were taken over in 1923 by the (Mittelbadische Eisenbahn A.G.).

Kehl-Schwartzach-Buhl,   39.0 km.
Schwartzach-Rastatt,   19.5 km.
Kehl-Altenheim-Ottenheim,   24.7 km.
Altenheim-Offenburg,   11.5 km.
Ottenheim-Lahr-Seelbach,   16.4 km. (ex-Germany No. 60).
S.1886, D.1934, GD.1970. Gauge. 1000.

Metre Gauge for (b) & (c).

	Nos.						
	21,	Carels ?	0-4-0		?	of 1885 (Brown Patent).	
	22,	Unknown	0-4-0			of 1885 (Industrial type).	
(II)	21-22,	Mulhausen	0-4-0	4724-4725		of 1895/96.	
	23,	Number not occupied.					
	24,	Krauss	0-4-0		1630	of 1885.	
	30,	Krauss	0-4-0		1770	of 1886.	"
	31-34,	Mullhausen	0-4-0	3985-3988		of 1886.	
	35,	Graffenstaden	0-4-0 fireless	3824		of 1886 (System "Uhry")	
	36-37,	Winterthur	0-6-0	468 & 445		of 1886.	"
	38-40,	Graffenstaden	0-4-0	3846-3848		of 1888.	
	41-44,	Graffenstaden	0-4-0	4331-4334		of 1891.	"
	45-48,	Graffenstaden	0-4-0	4804-4807		of 1897/98.	"
	49,	Graffenstaden	0-4-0		4899	of 1899.	"
	50-51,	Graffenstaden	0-4-0	5070-5071		of 1901.	"
	52-53,	Borsig	0-4-0	6688-6689		of 1908.	"
	67,	Borsig	0-6-0		8960	of 1914 (ex-military).	

Nos. 16-20, 25, 26, 28 & 29 are said to have been rebuilt from
standard to metre gauge in 1900 and worked on the above-mentioned
lines.

Note. -   Mullhausen, Belfort and Graffenstaden used a common works list.

Most of the locomotives numbered between 20 and 40 passed to France and No. 32 was used
for the final parade on closing. Those numbered above 40 remained in Germany and the
Mittelbadische Eisenbahn brought in the following from its other lines :-

	Nos.				
	5-6,	Graffenstaden	0-4-0	4900 & 5097 of 1900.	
				(ex-Lahr, Germany No. 60).	
	53-55,	Krauss Maffei	0-4-0	17586-17587 of 1948.	
	101,	Krauss Maffei	0-4-0	17626 of 1947	
				(ex-Germany No. 66).	"
	103,	Graffenstaden	0-4-4-0 (Mallet) 4738 of 1896		
				(ex-Zell-Todtnau Light Rly).	"

12.   THIONVILLE.   See DIEDERHOFEN, No. 1.

Hanomag loco for Morchingen, Alsace-Lorraine.
Hanomag Official Postcard.

LUXEMBOURG

<u>Note</u>.- French names are shown first as French was used for all official titles of tramways and light railways. German names are shown in brackets where also in common usage.

1, ASPELT. (Chemins de Fer Vicinaux de L'Etat de Luxembourg). Worked at first by a subsidiary of the Belgian SNCV (Société Anonyme pour l'Exploitation des Chemins de Fer Regionaux en Belgique).
From 1911 (Société des Chemins de Fer Secondaires Luxembourgeois).
From 1934 controlled by the State (See No. 7 for further details).
Aspelt-Bettemberg, 10.2 km. (Connecting with No. 5).
S.1899, D.1936, GS.1952, C.1957. Gauge. 1000.

<u>Locomotives</u>.-   Nos.A.1-A.2,   Tubize 0-6-0   1176-1177 of 1899 (Like SNCV

                                                                       Class 4).

                            A.3,   Tubize 0-6-0   1262 of 1901   "   "

Note.-   The letter "A" was used to distinguish these locomotives from those of No. 6.

2. CRUCHTEN. (Société des Chemins de Fer Secondaires Luxembourgeois).
Worked by (Schweitzerische Lokomotiv-und Maschinen Fabrik, Winterthur).
From 1934, by State as No. 1 above.
Cruchten-Larochette(Fels)-Ernzen, 16.3 km.
S.1882. C.1948. Gauge. 1000.

<u>Locomotives</u>.-   Nos. 1-2,   Winterthur 0-4-0   227-228 of 1881 (Renumbered 11-12

                                                                        in 1900)

                          3-5,   Winterthur 0-4-0   232-234 of 1881 ex-No.5 in 1910.

Names.-   1-Fels, 2-Cruchten, 3-Luxemburg, 4-Remich, 5-Mondorf.

Note.-   Nos. 8 & 9 (as rebuilt) of No. 9 worked on this line in the final years.

3. DIFFERDANGE (Differdingen) (S.A. Luxembourgeoise des Chemins de Fer et Minières du Prince Henri). An entirely industrial 700 mm gauge line, not open to the public.

4. GRUNDHOF. (S.A. Luxembourgeoise des Chemins de Fer et Minieres du Prince Henri).
Taken over by Germany in 1943. See No. 7.
Grundhof-Beaufort, 6.7 km. (Three reversals en route). Goods carried on transporters.
GS.1904, S.1911, C.1948. Gauge. 1000.
<u>Locomotives</u>.-   Nos.311-312, La Meuse 0-6-0, 1848-1849 of 1904.

Note.-   Locomotives numbered in "Prince Henri" general stock.

5. LUXEMBOURG. (Luxemburg). (Société des Chemins de Fer Secondaires Luxembourgeois).
Ownership and working as No. 2 above.
Luxembourg Gare-Aspelt-Mondorf-Remich, 27.1 km.
(Connecting with No. 1 at Aspelt and with Alsace Lorraine No. 1 at Mondorf).
S.1882, Part P.1912-1913, Part D.1936. GS.1953, C.1955. Gauge. 1000.

<u>Locomotives</u>.-   Nos. 1-3,   Winterthur 0-4-0   232-234 of 1881.

                             4,   Winterthur 0-4-0   322 of 1883.   "

                          5-6,   Winterthur 0-6-0   888-889 of 1893.   "

                          7-8,   Winterthur 0-6-0   1269-1270 of 1900.   "

                       9-10,   Winterthur 0-6-0   862&867 of 1894 ex-Bern, Switzerland " "

                    11-12,   See CRUCHTEN, No. 2 above.

                    13-14,   Winterthur 0-6-0   1512-1513 of 1903 ex-M.O.B. Switzer-

                                                                land 1906.

                   15-16,   Haine St. Pierre 0-6-0 1540 of 1926 & 1671 of 1930.(new)   "

115

Names. -   1-Luxemburg, 2-Remich, 3-Mondorf, 4-Alzette, 5-Altweis,
                 6-Aspelt, 7-Ellingen, 8-Scheuerberg, 9-Hesperingen,
                 10-Weiler la Tour, 11-Fels, 12-Cruchten, 13-Bonnevoie(Montreux),
                 14- (Zweisimmen),   15-16-Not named.

Note. -   Locomotives of Nos. 5 & 6 were worked as a combined fleet in later
                 years.

6.   LUXEMBOURG (Luxemburg).   (Chemins de Fer Vicinaux de l'Etat de Luxembourg).
     Worked by Belgian SNCV Subsidiary as No. 1 and latterly by No. 7.
     Luxembourg Gare-Dommeldange(Dommeldingen)-Junglinster-Echternach. 45.8 km.
     (Proposed connecting line Junglinster-Larochette not built).
     S.1904. Part P.1912. Part E.1928-1944, GS.1954. C.1957.   Gauge.   1000.
     Locomotives. -   Nos. B1-B4,   Graffenstaden 0-4-4-0   5250-5253 of 1902. (Mallet).
                          53-55,   Winterthur   2-6-0   579-581 of 1889.
                                                                   ex-Rhaetischebahn.

     Former names. -   53-(Davos), 54-(Flüela), 55-(Egadin).

7.   LUXEMBURG. (Réseau des Chemins de Fer à Voie Etroite).
     The state owned undertaking which took over Nos. 1, 2, 5 & 6 in 1934. This and the
     other lines were seized by the Deutsche Reichsbahn during the German occupation in 1940
     and became part of the Chemins de Fer Luxembourgeois in 1945.
     Locomotives were numbered thus :-

Original Number	Reichsbahn Number	C.F.L. Number	Class	Description
8-10,	99.233-235.	301-303	C	ex-Vicinaux. Rebuilt from Tubize tram locos.
1-5,	99.236-240.	311-315	G	ex-Cantonaux, St. Léonard 0-6-0.
6-7,	99.241-242.	321-322	H	" " "
11.	99.243.	331	J	" ? La Meuse "
13-14.	99.244-245.	341-342	D	ex-Secondaires Winterthur 0-6-0.
53-55.	99.271.273.	351-353	B	ex-Vicinaux Winterthur 2-6-0.
311-312,	99.291-292.	361-362	F	ex-Prince Henri La Meuse 0-6-0.
15-16,	99.246-247.	371-372	E	ex-Secondaires Haine St. Pierre 0-6-0.
B1-B4,	99.281-284.	401-404	A	ex-Vicinaux Graffenstaden 0-4-4-0.

Note. -   Other locomotives not included in the above renumbering were either
                 already scrapped or war vicitims. (Some may have been in store not
                 in working order).

8.   MARTELANGE. (S.A. des Chemins de Fer Cantonaux Luxembourgeois).
     Worked by State from 1924. See No. 7 above.
     Noerdange-Martelange, 29.5 km. (Near but not connected to Belgian SNCV).
     S.1890, C.1953, Gauge. 1000.
     Locomotives. -   Used Nos. 1, 5, 6 & 11 of No. 9 below.

9.   VIANDEN. (S.A. des Chemins de Fer Cantonaux Luxembourgeois). See Nos. 7 & 8 above.
     Vianden-Diekirch, 14.1 km.
     S.1889, P.1925, D.1936, C.1948. Gauge. 1000.
     Locomotives. -   Nos. 1-5,   St. Léonard 0-6-0   773-775 of 1887.
                          6-7,   St. Léonard 0-6-0   1128 of 1898 & 1167 of 1899.
                          8-9,   Tubize   0-6-0   1176-1177 of 1889 rebuilt ex-No1, 1930
                          10,   Tubize   0-6-0   1262 of 1899 "   "   "
                          11,   La Meuse   0-6-0   2734 of 1919 Possibly ∵.

Note. -   Lengths of lines extracted by R.C. Riley from official booklet "Les
                 Chemins de Fer Luxembourgeois" of 1950.

116

Graffenstaden loco No. 46 for the large Strassburg system, part of which passed to the Mittelbadische Eisenbahn at Kehl.

Photo: H. Urselmann.

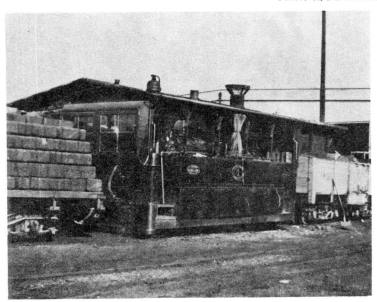

Tubize loco No. 1 of the Aspelt-Bettemburg tramway in Luxemburg.
Photo: Science Museum London - Whitcombe Collection 1208.

International Steam Tram. Belgian SNCV loco No. 7 (Class 3) and train across the Dutch border at Sluis, on 5th September 1930. It is on a through service with the Breskens-Maldegem tramway.

Photo: late F. Merton-Atkins 30068.

One of the post 1914-18 war Class 18 locos, No. 1039 of the SNCV at Antwerpen-Zuremborg Station.

Photo: J. H. Price 645.

One of the standard gauge locos of the SNCV, No. 805 (Class 10), the large square buffers denoting that it was one of those used at Eupen (803-805).

Photo: Lance King.

One of the unenclosed locos of the SNCV No. 443 (Class 14) seen on the scrap dump at Waremme, near Liége, probably in 1950.

Unknown Photographer.

B E L G I U M

S.N.C.V. STEAM TRAMWAY
WITH CAPITAL REFERENCE
NUMBER.

121 ——o (1000mm.)

17 ——o (1435mm.)

```
0    10    20 MILES
0  10  20  30 KMS.
```

ABBREVIATIONS

AD. AARDOOIE	IZ. IZEGHEM	MZ. MOERZEKE	VT. VINALMONT
AN. ANDENNE	JM. JEMEPPE	RS. RUISELEDE	WT. WETTEREN
AR. AARSELE	MB. MOERBEKE	SG. SOTTEGEM	ZH. ZANDHOVEN
AS. AARSCHOT	MG. MANAGE	SI. SICHEM	
BQ. BRACQUEGNIES	MO. MONTIGNY	SO. SOIGNIES	
BR. BRASSCHAAT	MV. MAINVAULT	TN. TIENEN	
BV. BOVESSE	MW. MORLANWELZ	TV. TERVUREN	
BW. BIERWART	OG. OORDEGEM	NV. NIVELLES	
BY. BRAY	OI. OVERIJSSCHE	OM. OVERMERE	
ES. ESTINNES	OU. OUGREE	TA. TAVIERS	
EZ. EGHEZEE	PV. PROFONDEVILLE	WV. WAVRE	
HM. HAMME MILLE	RO. ROESELARE		

FL. FLEURUS
GX. GEMBLOUX
HT. HANNUT
IN. INCOURT
MF. MEEFE

NORTH

N E T H E R L A N D S

G E R M A N Y

F R A N C E

LUX'G

5. BELGIUM

The present writer's first acquaintance with a steam tram was made in Belgium, one misty morning during the war. After passing through an industrial area near Tournai, our convoy came to a halt on the grass verge of a country road for the usual "brew up" and although there were narrow gauge rails among the grass, we assumed that it was only an industrial line that extended further out of town than others. No sooner had we settled down to enjoy our tea, than the whistle of a steam engine was heard faintly in the distance and we could just discern a puff of smoke. We hardly had time to get our vehicles off the track when an enclosed locomotive slid silently past, pulling three small dark green carriages.

The steam tram came late to Belgium, but when it did arrive, development there was on a more intensive scale than in any other European country. Belgium was the only one to have a unified system organized on a national basis. However, even before any steam tramways were constructed in Belgium itself, Belgian financiers were sponsoring the construction of tramways in the Netherlands, Italy, France and Spain, to all of which they exported locomotives and rolling stock. At home, by 1884, one light railway had been opened in the south (Taviers-Ambressin, to the peculiar gauge of 750mm) and suburban steam tramways had just opened in Brussels and Liège - that was all! The government alarmed by the lack of progress at home and the investment of Belgian capital abroad, set up a commission to look into the position. The Bruxelles-Ixelles line and lines at Charleroi, already in hand, they permitted to be completed and worked independently, but pursuant of an Act of Parliament, dated 20th May 1884, it was decreed henceforth, all new interurban tramways and light railways should be owned by a national undertaking, known in French as "La Société Nationale des Chemin de Fer Vicinaux" and in Flemish as "De Nationale Maatschappij van Buurtspoorwegen". This body started operations by constructing a metre gauge line along the coast from Ostend to Nieuwpoort, opened on 15th July 1885 and before many years had passed, they had built up a network covering the whole country. The Flemish speaking north is flat and mainly agricultural; here the network, although not dense was continuous without breaks. In the French (or Wallon) speaking south-west, which is heavily industrialized, and around Brussels, there were very dense networks, particularly between Mons and Charleroi and at Liège. Only in the hilly far south, were there any single disconnected lines and they usually formed feeders to the main-line railways. Although in fact most lines were either street or roadside tramways, worked by enclosed locomotives, all were classed officially as light railways, as signified in the title of the undertaking.

Those who knew it are inclined to think of the "Vicinal" or "S.N.C.V" as a vast unified metre gauge system using standardized designs of enclosed six-coupled engines and small four-wheeled carriages. However, in many ways, this uniformity was only 'skin-deep'. On the one hand, the original powers provided for the S.N.C.V. to act in the capacity of a holding company, in which the capital was provided proportionately by the State, Provincial and Local authorities. The S.N.C.V. itself provided the rolling stock and fixed equipment from a pool, but the day to day running was left to one or other of over fifty subsidiary companies, who leased lines ᴀɴᴅ acted as agents.

The locomotives were certainly of a limited number of standardized designs, most of which looked very much alike, but there were a few interesting exceptions, which will be described in the appropriate section. Likewise, passenger and goods stock was highly standardized.

Nor was the whole network laid uniformly to metre gauge; one of the first subsidiary companies to get going had financial ties with a steam tramway over the border in the Netherlands, who wished to make contact with Antwerp. They took over the standard gauge horse tramway "Les Tramways du Nord d'Anvers" and extended the line northwards as a 3' 6" (1067mm) gauge steam tramway to link up at the frontier with their own line to Bergen op Zoom. A joint through service was worked, some of the rolling stock nominally belonging to the Dutch company and the rest to the Belgian subsidiary. Arising from this, all the Vicinal lines constructed in the Province of Antwerp were laid to the 1067 gauge, with a view to through running with other Dutch tramways. On the other hand, on five widely separated SNCV lines on which the interchange of goods traffic with the main line railways was considered to be of major importance, the standard gauge was adopted. (The Sichem line was in SNCV hands for a short while only). In addition, there were a number of examples of lengthy sections of mixed gauge track, over which Vicinal metre gauge locomotives could pull standard gauge wagons. The earlier examples had four rails and specially adapted locomotives, with side and centre buffers were used; the later ones had three rails and match trucks were interposed between the locomotive and any standard gauge wagons.[1] Transporter trucks are only known to have been used on one line.

Between Malines (Mechelen) and Pasburg, where the 1067 gauge Antwerp lines met and overlapped the metre gauge Brussels area lines, four rail gauntleted track had to be used as the two gauges were too closely similar to permit the more usual arrangement. The six larger towns in Belgium, each had their own urban electric tramway system, Brussels and Liége adopted the standard gauge and there was a good deal of three rail mixed gauge working with the SNCV in their suburbs and to terminals in the city centres. In spite of the SNCV, the Antwerp town system adopted the metre gauge, but in steam days the SNCV lines terminated at two tram stations in the suburbs, without mixed running. However, the standard gauge dock lines at Merxem, in the northern outskirts were worked by the SNCV, who provided a special small fleet of locomotives. Thus tramways of three gauges were to be found in the Merxem area.

Gradually, over the years, the SNCV took over operation of its lines from the various subsidiary companies, a move hastened when many of them got into financial difficulties during the 1914-1918 war, and by the end of the 1939-1945 war only the two subsidiary companies at Ostend and the Grottes de Han were still functioning. One frontier crossing has already been mentioned and the SNCV was probably unique in that it had as many as eighteen physical connections with Dutch steam tramways, over several of which regular through workings were provided, both on the 1000 and 1067 mm gauges.[2] A short line to the west of Mons, for much of its life unconnected with the rest of the SNCV, but connected with the French system at Valenciennes, was worked by the latter and there were connections with other French light railways in the Sedan area, over which through services do not appear to have been provided, as

French and Belgian coupling arrangements and braking were usually incompatible, as the Allies discovered when attempting to work through trains during the 1914-1918 war. There was also a connection at Martelange, between the SNCV and a line in the Principality of Luxembourg. Among the lines ceded from Germany in 1919, in the Eupen area, was one standard gauge steam, part was already in Belgium and the rest seems to have been leased to the SNCV from the outset. (The other lines had already been electrified by the Germans, before being absorbed in Belgium).

Everyone must know of the tremendous destruction wrought in Belgium during the 1914-1918 war and not the least to suffer was the SNCV, who lost, among other equipment, 427 locomotives, almost half of the total fleet. It is greatly to that undertaking's credit, that reconstruction followed swiftly when the war was over. In 1917, even when the war was still in progress, British and American firms built about 70 metre gauge locomotives for use behind the allied lines, and with unusual foresight they had them built similar to the SNCV's then standard design and they were handed over to them at the conclusion of hostilities. At the same time the SNCV had 85 more built by Belgian firms in 1919 & 1920 to take the place of those destroyed. So much of the track in the Antwerp area had been destroyed that it was decided to relay it all to metre gauge, as by that time through working over the rest of the SNCV network and the Antwerp town system, was considered to be more important than the connections with a few minor tramways in the Netherlands. The last 1067 gauge line, from Turnhout to Poppel, was converted in October 1921. Some of the British built locomotives were fitted with air brakes and electric headlights in 1924 to provide an express service from Antwerp to Turnhout and two of the American locos were fitted with side buffers and screw couplings for use on the mixed gauge line from Mol to Donk sand quarries.

Even before the 1914 war, the lines in and around the larger towns had been electrified and other new electric lines opened. The first electrified in 1894, ran from Brussels to Espinette in the woods to the south and other lines in the Brussels, Liége, Mons and Charleroi areas soon followed. Electrification in the Antwerp area was somewhat delayed because of the gauge problem. By 1936, all passenger workings had been replaced by electric cars or by small diesel railcars. Petrol railcars first entered service in 1925, followed by diesel cars in 1934 on the lines with insufficient traffic for electrification. Nevertheless, a large number of steam locomotives was retained for goods work, particularly the heavy autumn sugar-beet traffic. This was indeed fortunate, as when Belgium was occupied by the Germans from 1939 to 1945 and liquid fuel became desperately short, so that the railcars could not be used, the old steam locomotives were put back into passenger service with all the old trailer cars that could be found. This brings us back to the scene depicted at the beginning of this chapter, a scene which soon became quite familiar to the writer and his colleagues in 1944. However with the return of peacetime conditions, the steam passenger trains were soon retired and even a number of the older railcars were equipped with engines recovered from enemy tanks and used as goods locomotives. As the years have progressed the ubiquitous motor-bus has made great inroads into a very large part of the SNCV services, including those electrified. In recent years two steam locomotives were hired to a colliery, but one has now been handed over to a preservation society to run on a museum line in the Ardennes at Dochamps. Several others survived until the early 1970s and ran on a hitherto little known standard gauge line to the south of Liége, between.

Poulseur and Sprimont, when an unexpected revival of stone traffic from a quarry, was brought about by the reconstruction of a mole in the harbour at Ijmuiden over the border in the Netherlands.

One feature of Belgian life, which perplexes strangers, is the dual language problem. The Flemish language, which is closely akin to Dutch is spoken throughout the northern part of the country and the Wallon dialect of French is spoken in the south. Although all large towns except Charleroi have names in both languages, only in Brussels and its suburbs are both languages spoken indescriminately.

Locomotives

Just as Belgian capital was invested in overseas tramways before there were any steam tramways in Belgium itself, Belgian manufacturers were turning out locomotives for tramways in other countries before any were built for orders in the home market. There were a few experiments at home, among which was a geared "Brotherhood" engine tried at Brussels in 1875, but the first batch for which a definite order is recorded, comprised some 0-4-2 tram engines with Vaessen's fan condensers, built by St. Léonard of Liége for Paris in 1877. They were followed by various 0-4-0 enclosed machines built by St. Léonard, Carels of Ghent and other firms for French, Dutch, Italian and Spanish tram-ways. Most of these had inside cylinders, well tanks and the German layout of controls for driving from one side of the boiler, features which were not perpetuated when Belgian manufacturers came to build locomotives for use at home.

In 1880, the Tubize works of the "Ateliers Métallurgiques S. A." organization, produced a batch of heavy 0-6-0 (some reports say 0-4-2) side tank engines with outside cylinders and duplicated controls for the standard gauge Milan-Pavia tramway in Italy. These must have been the largest tramway engines in use at that time and soon afterwards a batch of similar machines, but for metre gauge, were built for the Valenciennes-Anzin tramway just over the border in France. They were 0-6-0s with outside Walschaerts valve gear and square-topped Belpaire fireboxes, both Belgian inventions. Further engines of this type were built for the Ixelles tramway in the suburbs of Brussels and one of these gained a prize at the Antwerp Exhibition of 1884. It accounted so well for itself, that when the SNCV started operation, it was decided that this was the locomotive for them. Although thought in certain other countries, to be too heavy, this design was evidently ideally suited to the rolling country and heavy sugar-beet traffic encountered in Belgium, so that eventually the SNCV acquired over 1000 machines basically of this design. Known by Tubize as their "Model No. 20", they were built not only by them, but by every other Belgian manufacturer and when the needs of the SNCV were satisfied, some were built for export. Thus about 300 were built at Tubize, including some for France, Germany, Italy, the Netherlands, Spain, Luxembourg, Egypt and Algeria. (We have already recounted how about 300 more were built at the subsidiary works at Blanc Misseron in France and a few by other French manufacturers). The second largest exporter was St. Léonard of Liége, who built 174 tram engines, mainly for the SNCV, but also some for France, Italy, Spain, Indo-China and Lebanon. Smaller numbers were built by Couillet (who also continued building machines of an earlier type for Italy), Cockerill, who built some for Russia and a large number of vertical boilered semi-enclosed locomotives intended for industry,[3] but three found their way onto tramways. As its name implies the Franco-Belge organization built locomotives for both France and Belgium. These included "Tubize" type machines, which were also supplied by Halot (22 all for SNCV), Thiriau for SNCV and Dutch tramways, Gilain - 90 mainly for SNCV, Gilly - 24 for SNCV, Boussu - 200 for SNCV & 1 for France. A few "Tubize" type engines were built for Belgian industrial establishments (one is preserved, erroneously under the number SNCV - 1000). Even three German firms turned out a few "Tubize" type machines. Jung and Humbolt each built some for the SNCV and Henschel some for a Dutch tramway. A few more were built by smaller Belgian manufacturers not mentioned above. All were heavy six coupled machines with side tanks and controls at both ends. However the SNCV works at Louvain, as well as turning out 12 standard locomotives for their own use, also built two of a four coupled version for a Dutch tramway.

Thus, all told there were a very large number of "Tubize" type locomotives in use in Western Europe, all closely similar in appearance, but varying in weight and performance. The last of this design to be built appeared in 1928, when La Meuse produced three for a French tramway, as war "reparations". (See French chapter).

Although Tubize produced a standard gauge version of their "Model No. 20", for some French and Italian tramways, the standard gauge locomotives of the SNCV were of rather different appearance, some had the skirting over the wheels swept sharply inwards. Apart from these, engines of the SNCV which were not of the Tubize standard design, were few in number, but nevertheless interesting. There were four, outwardly of the normal design but with the 2-6-0- wheel arrangement; three of these were for the steeply graded Boillon-Paliseul line, and the fourth was built to the order of the then independant Ans-Oreye line. There were two small batches of unenclosed 0-6-0 tank engines, with the cab at the rear and they had both centre and side buffers with dual couplings at both ends, so that they could pull standard gauge stock on four rail mixed gauge track. The second batch was in fact, an export reject built for Spain. A few of the enclosed locomotives were also fitted with side and centre buffers. Mention has already been made of the enclosed 0-4-0 locomotives used on the Antwerp-Merxem tramway and provided by its Dutch counterpart. Nos. 6-11 came in due course to the SNCV and continued to work on that line for some time, but apart from these, the 1067 gauge locomotives were indistinguishable from their metre gauge counterparts; indeed some batches included locomotives built for both gauges. What few of the 1067 gauge machines remained after the war, were quickly converted to metre gauge, as the lines on which they worked were altered.

So that they could work with main-line stock, the standard gauge locomotives of the SNCV were equipped with side buffers, screw couplings and air brakes; the latter a luxury denied to all but a few of the metre gauge machines. The SNCV provided the standard gauge locomotives used at Merxem docks. The original machines were side tank 0-4-0s of varying origins, but they were replaced in the early 1920s, by Tubize standard industrial type 0-6-0 tank engines and in 1924, one similar but larger machine was built by Couillet; this enjoyed a fairly short life at Groenendael and was sold to industry. (The Groenendael-Overijssche line near Espinette to the south of Brussels was connected to the main line railway, but not to other SNCV lines and carried passenger and table grape traffic).

Two experimental locomotives were built in 1909/1910 for an exhibition. One was of standard "Tubize" appearance and the other unenclosed. They passed to the SNCV after the exhibition and were notable in being the only superheated engines the SNCV ever possessed. By far the most unusual locomotives designed and built for the SNCV were two Garratt articulated tram engines, produced by St. Léonard in 1929/30 for the coal traffic on the hilly Bassenge-Glons line. The upper parts and the two motor bogies were enclosed in the usual way and the water tanks over the bogies were sloped to give better visibility.

To the casual observer, the numbering of SNCV locomotives may appear to be rather chaotic. In fact the first 46 machines acquired were numbered strictly in order of acquisition, irrespective of gauge or type. Subsequently engines were numbered according to gauge and the original machines renumbered to fit into that scheme. The numbers 1-699 were allocated to the metre gauge, 700-799 to the 1067 gauge and 800-823 to the standard gauge machines. In later years when the numbers 1-699 were filled up, a few metre gauge machines took numbers in the higher 700s and when the Ans-Oreye line was taken over in 1929, its locomotives took the number 793-799. Two then unidentified locomotives of Tubize design from French tramways, were repatriated to Belgium by mistake after the 1914-1918 war and they became Nos. 658 & 737. One was Blanc Misseron 143 from the Tramways de l'Artois, and the other was Tubize 461, originally belonging to the Bruxelles-Ixelles tramway and sold via a contractor to the Chemins de Fer Economiques du Nord group. The British built wartime locomotives received SNCV numbers in the 900s, the corresponding American locomotives became 1001-1020 and the Belgian built postwar replacements became 1021-1105.

SNCV steam locomotives were always painted dark green, but in the early days were lined out in light green with polished brasswork. They carried large oval brass number plates painted red and inscribed in French or Flemish (sometimes in both), according to the area in which they were intended to work. There was a broad red stripe across the buffer beam.

Passenger and Goods Stock

The Métallurgique Company which owned the Tubize locomotive works, also owned a carriage & wagon works at Nivelles, where the carriages were built that accompanied the original Milan-Pavia locomotives to Italy. They were of rather light construction with peculiar lattice underframes: some had drop side windows and others were open above the waist. Similar vehicles were supplied to other early Italian tramways and to Barcelona in Spain. Subsequently Nivelles supplied a large proportion of the vehicle for the SNCV and for Belgian controlled tramways in other countries, except France, where the Blanc Misseron works undertook the construction of passenger and goods stock as well as locomotives. The group also owned large factories at La Sambre and Bellecourt near Charleroi, from which fixed equipment for railways and tramways was available, so that they could claim in their catalogues that they could completely equip any railway or tramway except for the rails. Among other Belgian manufacturers who supplied large quantities of rolling stock, may be mentioned "La Brugeoise" and "Baume et Marpent".

Passenger carriages on the SNCV steam lines were also of a fairly limited number of standardized designs, usually with about six small drop windows, plain curved roofs and the earlier models had open end platforms with fancy metal gates, the whole mounted on short two axle underframes.[4] Later ones had enclosed end platforms and some looked rather coffin-like. The earlier cars had a coke stove in one corner and a chimney protruding through the roof, but later models had patent underfloor "Charpentier" charcoal burners. Bogie cars were not regarded as generally suitable for SNCV traffic and very few were built in steam days; there were a few centre entrance bogie cars with two second class compartments, one first and a baggage compartment, so designed that each car could be worked as a single unit, replacing a train of several four wheeled cars. The latter, on busier lines were often worked with as many as six and a matching baggage van, forming a train. Carriages and baggage vans on the standard gauge lines, were only enlarged versions of the contemporary open platform narrow gauge stock. The livery for steam stock was normally very dark green, with a transfer of the arms of Belgium on the side. During the 1914 war, a few carriages were turned out in a natural grained teak livery. Continuous braking was not normally provided on narrow gauge stock and trains relied on the locomotive's steam brakes, with rather bumpy stops.

Like the locomotives and passenger coaches, the narrow gauge goods stock, which was quite extensive, was limited to a few standardized types of vehicle. As a large proportion of the traffic carried consisted of sugar-beet and other agricultural products, the commonest vehicle was a high sided open truck, often with a raised brakeman's seat at one end. There were also flat trucks, closed vans and tank cars as well as the open platform baggage vans already mentioned. Special vehicles included transporter bogie trucks for conveying narrow gauge stock over the main line to the central workshops. On the other hand, the standard gauge lines had very little stock of their own, since the whole reason of their being built to that gauge, was to permit the through running of main-line stock, over them.

Station buildings where they existed (mainly at terminals), were usually large plain brick structures, with the exception of some in the Ardennes and around Ostend, which were quite elaborate. Otherwise, wayside halts often comprised no more than a rudimentary platform and a pedestal stop sign. The latter were similar to the famous "clover leaf" signs favoured by the London County Council Tramways. Those in the Brussels area were inscribed "Arrêt du Train" on one face and "Trein Stilstand" on the other. Apart from red discs protecting level crossings with railways, there were no signals on the SNCV steam lines.

Note on Tables

Because Belgium, unlike all the other countries described in this book, was served mainly by one undertaking which operated by far the largest part of the tramways within its boundaries and the other steam tramways which it did not control, were of comparatively minor importance, it has been found necessary to arrange the tables of undertakings in this chapter, somewhat differently to the others. They are divided into two parts; the first part deals with the independently owned tramways and is set out similarly to the other chapters, but the second part, devoted to the SNCV is of necessity set out differently. A sum of money was put up for the construction of each line, its Capital and each line was given a capital number, allocated approximately in order of opening date. After 1919, for management purposes, a number of lines was worked together as a "Groupe" and the sphere of influence of each Groupe roughly corresponded with the confines of a particular administrative Province of the country. Thus the lines are shown in the tables under the headings of the Groupes and each is prefixed by its capital number and followed by a letter indicating the name of the operating subsidiary company. Two of these companies had names which might be confused with tramways in other countries. They were the "Limburgsche Stoomtramweg Maatschappij" and the "Société d'Exploitation de Tramways en Luxembourg Belge". It will be noted that titles could be in either Flemish or French.

Different types of locomotive were originally distinguished by class letters, but after 1918, they were known by class numbers. In the tables locomotives are shown in order of post-1918 class numbers, with the old letters in brackets.

Places in the north of Belgium are shown with the Flemish name first, followed by the French name and in the south, French names are shown first. Places in the Eupen area have German names. Unfortunately the language boundaries do not correspond with any particular groupes and many lines had one terminal in a French speaking town and the other in a Flemish town.

Notes

1. See "The Locomotive Magazine" for February 1941, page 40 for a short article on mixed gauge working on the SNCV. (A match truck is preserved at Schepdaal).

2. See "Op de Rails", Vol. 27, pages 37-48, May 1959, article on through working by M. van Witsen, A. D. de Pater and H. de Herder.

3. See "Industrial Railway Record" for December 1965, article by K. W. Clingan on Cockerill and similar vertical-boilered industrial locomotives.

4. No. A. 1635 of the Ostend Groupe was specially adapted in 1900 as a Royal Saloon and is now preserved in Schepdaal Museum.

Standard gauge coach No.1503 of the SNCV at Groenendael. Built 1894.
Photo: G. Desbarax.

Table 5 BELGIUM

I INDEPENDENT TRAMWAYS
Not forming part of the SNCV Organisation

1. ADINKERKE. (Messieurs Chapel et Pluntz). Taken over by SNCV in 1932.
   Adinkerke-De Panne, 3.7 km.
   H.1901, P.1914, S.1920. E.1932, C.1944. Gauge. 600 (1000 on electrification).
   Locomotives. -   Nos. 1-2, Unknown 0-4-0   ? of ?

   Names. -   1-Adèle, 2-Laura.

2. ANS. (S.A. du Chemin de Fer Vicinal de l'Ans à Oreye et Extensions).
   Taken over by SNCV in 1929 and later electrified.
   Ans-Alleur-Oreye, 17.0 km.
   S.1888, E.1931, C.1959. Gauge. 1000.
   Locomotives. -   SNCV 40, 16 & 29, St. Léonard 0-6-0 748-750 of 1887 on loan
                                                                        from SNCV.
                         Nos. 1-3,   St. Léonard 0-6-0 827-829 of 1890.   "
                              4,   St. Léonard 2-6-0   877 of 1891 (as SNCV   "
                                                                         Class 9)
                              5,   Jung   0-6-0   360 of 1899)Similar to "
                              6-7,   Unknown   0-6-0   ? of   ?)SNCV class 7 "

   Note. -   Ans-Oreye locomotives became SNCV 793-799 in 1929.

3. ANTWERPEN (Anvers). (S.A. des Tramways du Nord d'Anvers).
   From 1887 (S.A. du Tramway d'Anvers à Merxem), worked as part of (Stoomtramweg
   Maatschappij Antwerpen-Bergen op Zoom-Tholen).
   See Netherlands No. 11. Belgian part taken over by SNCV in 1894.
   Antwerpen(Merksem)-Blauhof-Ekeren-Zandvliet, km.) 38.7 km.
   Blauhof-Lillo,   km.)
   H.1878, S.1887, E.1908/1932, C.1966. Gauge. 1067 (to 1000 in 1921).
   Locomotives. -   Nos. 6-10, Cockerill 0-4-0 1497-1501 of 1887/88.
                              11,   Breda   0-4-0   54 of 1889.   "

   Note. -   Locomotives numbered with A.B.T. stock, later became SNCV
                         Nos. 732-737.

4. BRUXELLES (Brussel). (Belgian Street Railway Co.).
   Later (S.A. des Tramways Bruxellois).
   Trials with steam locomotives on urban horse tramway routes.
   Petit Cienture circular route, 4.7 km.
   Place Stephanie-Uccle Globe, 4.0 km. (Approx).
   H.1872, S.1874-1878 intermittently, E.1894, Still Operating. Gauge. 1435.
   Locomotives. -   Yorkshire Engine Co. (Loftus Perkins) 0-4-0   ? of 1874. *
                         Métallurgique (Brotherhood)   0-4-0   ? of 1875.   "
                         St. Léonard   0-4-2   ? 475 of 1877 for Paris. "
                         Winterthur   0-4-0   ? 111 of 1877 for Geneva. "
                         Nos. 1-3, St. Léonard   0-6-0 483-485 of 1878.   "
                              4-7, St. Léonard   0-6-0 497-500 of 1880.   "

   Note. -   * Manufacturer "Yorkshire" confirmed from photo. No works number.

5. BRUXELLES (Brussel). (Compagnie du Chemin de Fer à Voie Etroite de Bruxelles,
   à Ixelles et Boendael). See also SNCV No. 32.
   Taken over by (Tramways Bruxellois) and electrified in 1897.
   Porte de Namur-Chaussée d'Ixelles-Place Saint Croix,   2.0 km.
   Porte de Namur-Chaussée de Wavre-Place Saint Croix,   3.0 km.
   Place Saint Croix-Boendael-Hippodrome,   2.0 km.
   H.1884, S.1885, E.1897, Still operating. Gauge. 1000 (1435 on electrification).

Locomotives. -   Nos. 1-8,   Tubize 0-6-0 459-466 of 1884.   ⊟
                          9-10, Tubize 0-6-0 538-539 of 1884.   "
                          11,   Tubize 0-6-0   601 of 1885.   "
                          12-14, Tubize 0-6-0 742-744 of 1889.   "
                          25-27, Tubize 0-6-0 853-855 of 1892. (Nos. 26-27 became "
                                                    SNCV 422 & 424).

6.   BRUXELLES (Brussel). (Compagnie des Tramways de l'Est de Bruxelles).
     From 1887, (Compagnie du Tramway de Bruxelles-Evère et Extensions).
     From 1891, worked by No. 5 for SNCV and converted to metre gauge.
     Later handed over to Tramways Bruxellois and electrified to 1435 gauge.
     Bruxelles(Place Madou)-Schaerbeek-Evère Cimitière, 4.1 km.
     S.1883, C.1889(temporarily), E.1906, Still operating. Gauge. 1435 (see above).
     Locomotives. -   Nos. 1-6, Krauss   0-4-0   1275, 1280, 1365 & 1390-1392 of 1883 ⊟
                              7-8 ? Cockerill 0-4-0   1582 & 1625 of 1889/1890.   ⊡

7.   CHARLEROI. (Société Anonyme des Chemins de Fer Vicinaux Belges "Tramway de Charleroi
     -Gilly-Montigny"). Later taken over by SNCV and electrified.
     Charleroi-Gilly,   ? km.
     Charleroi-Montigny sur Sambre, 15.7 km.
     S.1885, E.1905, Still operating ? Gauge. 1435 (to 1000 on electrification).
     Locomotives. -   Nos. 1-9,   Unknown   0-4-0   ? - ? of 1885 (Carels ?).   ⊟
                              10-12, St. Léonard 0-4-0 884-886 of 1891.   "

8.   EKEREN. Title ? (Property company developing area).
     Ekeren-Sainte Mariaburg, 4.0 km. (Crossed No. 3 at right angles).
     S. ?, C.1914, Gauge. 750.
     Locomotives. -   Nos. 1-3,   Unknown 0-4-0   ? of ?   ⊔⊐

9.   LIEGE (Luik). (S.A. des Tramways à Vapeur de Liége-Seraing et Extensions).
     Later (S.A. des Railways Economiques de Liége-Seraing et Extensions).
     Liége-Seraing, 8.8 km.
     S.1882, E.1905, C.1968. Gauge. 1435.
     Locomotives. -   Nos. 1-12, Tubize 0-6-0 483-494 of 1881/82.   ⊟
                              14-15, Tubize 0-6-0 535-536 of 1883.   "

10. MALDEGEM. (Stoomtram Maatschappij Breskens-Maldegem).
     Small part of Dutch tramway in Belgium. See Netherlands No. 16.
     Ede-Maldegem, 4.3 km.
     S.1887, Part E.1929, C.1951. Gauge. 1000.
     Locomotives. -   See Netherlands No. 16.

11. QUIEVRAIN. (Compagnie des Chemins de Fer Economiques du Nord, - France).
     Section of SNCV track on frontier worked by France No. 159.
     Quievrain-Roisin,   10.9 km.
     Quievrain-Blanc Misseron,   1.0 km. (Connecting with FRANCE No. 159).
     S.1890, E.1918, C.1939. Gauge. 1000.
     Locomotives. -   Supplied by France No. 159.   ⊟

12. TAVIERS. (Chemin de Fer d'Interêt Local Taviers- Ambresin).
     Taviers-Ambresin, 9.5 km.
     A light railway replaced by a SNCV metre gauge line in 1926.
     S.1879, C.1918. (see above). Gauge. 720. (also 1435 gauge freight connection).
     Locomotives. -   Nos. 1-2, Tubeffe   0-4-0   -   - of 1879.   ⊔⊐
                              3.   Cockerill 0-4-0   ? of 1880.   "
                              4.   Cockerill 0-4-0   1914 of 1895.   "

13. ZEEUWSCH VLAANDEREN. (Zeeuwsch Vlaamsche Tramweg Maatschappij).
Through goods only services on two short sections of a Dutch tramway in Belgium.
See NETHERLANDS No. 84.
Grens(Frontier)-Selzaete,   1.0 km.   (Owned by ZVTM).
Roode Sluis-Moerbeke,   2.0 km.   (Owned by SNCV).

S.N.C.V. SECTIONS OF MIXED GAUGE TRACK.

(a) Worked by metre gauge engines fitted additionally with side buffers and screw
couplings.   FOUR RAIL track.

Mol-Donk (for sand quarries),	Antwerpen Groupe.
Chimay-Forges,	Hainaut Est Groupe.
Baudour-Hercies,	Hainaut Ouest Groupe.
Neufville-Neuf Carrières,	Hainaut Ouest Groupe.
Espièrre- ?	Courtrai-Tournai Groupe

(b) Through working of passenger trains on 1000 and 1067 gauges. FOUR RAIL gauntleted
track.

Mechelen(Malines)-Pasburg,   Antwerpen Groupe.

(c) Worked by metre gauge locomotives and match trucks, with offset side buffers &
screw couplings above metre gauge buffer-couplings (centred).
THREE RAIL track.

Rixensart-Maransart,	Bruxelles Groupe.
Gramont-Goeferdingen,	Hainaut Ouest Groupe.
Taviers- ?	Liége-Limbourg Groupe.

(d) After electrification, for bringing railway exhibits to Brussels exhibition.
THREE RAIL track.

Grimbergen-Londerzeel(Main-Line Station),   Bruxelles Groupe.

(e) Metre gauge through passenger service
(Standard gauge locos from Poulseur worked
freight traffic).
Ouffet-Comblain au Pont.   Liége-Limbourg Group.

(f) Standard gauge coal wagons carried on metre gauge transporters for Trembleur Colliery.

Dalhem-Warsage.   Liége-Limbourg Group.

Bruxelles-Boendael-Ixelles tramway.   Loco from the batch Nos.12-14.   These
were the forerunners of the standard "Vicinal" design.
Tubize Catalogue.   Courtesy: Prof. A.D. De Pater.

II Steam Tramways & Light Railways controlled by the:-
SOCIETE NATIONALE DES CHEMINS DE FER VICINAUX- SNCV
NATIONALE MAATSCHAPPIJ VAN BUURTSPOORWEGEN-NMVB

List of Subsidiary Companies.

(a) Antwerpsche Maatschappij voor den Dienst van Buurtspoorwegen.
(b) S.A. pour l'Exploitation des Chemins de Fer Vicinaux.
(c) Kempische Stoomtram Maatschappij.
(d) S.A. du Tramway d'Anvers à Merxem. - See No. 3 & Netherlands 11.
(e) S.A. pour l'Exploitation des Voies Ferrées en Belgique.
(f) S.A. des Transports Urbains et Vicinaux.
(g) S.A. des Vicinaux en Flandres.
(h) S.A. pour l'Exploitation des Chemins de Fer Régionaux.
(k) S.A. Naamloze Maatschappij voor de Uitbating der Buurtspoorwegen van den Omtrek
     Dixmuide-Yper. (even longer name at first).
(l) S.A. de Chemins de Fer Provinciaux.
(m) S.A. Intercommunale Courtrai.
(n) Maatschappij tot Uitbating der Buurtspoorwegen van het Noorden van West Vlaanderen.
(p) S.A. des Chemins de Fer Vicinaux Montois.
(r) S.A. Pour l'Exploitation du Chemin de Fer Vicinal d'Ans-Oreye et Extensions.
(s) S.A. pour l'Exploitation des Chemins de Fer Vicinaux du Centre.
(t) Compagnie des Chemins de Fer du Nord.
(u) Société pour l'Exploitation des Tramways dans Luxembourg Belge.
(v) S.A. pour l'Exploitation des Chemins de Fer Vicinaux Rochefort-Grotte de Han-Wellin
     et Extensions.
(w) S.A. pour l'Exploitation des Chemins de Fer Vicinaux de Namur et Extensions.
(y) S.A. Limburgsche Stoom Tramweg Maatschappij.
(z) S.A. pour l'Exploitation du Chemin de Fer Vicinaux de Liége-Barchon et Extensions.
(bb) Société du Chemin de Fer à Voie Etroite de Bruxelles-Ixelles-Boendael et Extensions.
(tb) S.A. des Tramways Bruxellois.
(ls) S.A. des Railways Economiques de Liége-Seraing et Extensions.
(bn) S.A. Belge-Neerlandais de Transports et Travaux.
(tg) Electrische Tram van Gent. (Tramways Electriques de Gand).
(ob) Maatschappij tot Exploitatie der Buurtlijnen van Oostende en de Belgische Badplaatsen.
     (formerly longer name).
(cc) S.A. Liégeoise des Chemins de Fer Vicinaux Chimay-Couvin et Extensions.
(rr) S.A. Ruche pour l'Exploitation des Chemins de Fer Vicinaux en Belgique.
(pp) S.A. pour l'Exploitation du Chemin de Fer Vicinal de Bruxelles à la Petite Espinette et
     ses Extensions.
(kk) S.A. pour l'Exploitation du Chemin de Fer Vicinal de Saint Nicolas, Kieldrecht et
     Extensions.
(hh) S.A. pour l'Exploitation du Chemin de Fer Vicinal de Hooglede-Tielt.
(zz) S.A. Naamloze Maatschappij tot Uitbating van de Buurtspoorweg Brugge-Zwevzele.
(ii) S.A. des Chemins de Fer Vicinaux de Binche-Bracquegnies et Extensions.
(jj) S.A. Messieurs Janssens et Surny.
(dd) S.A. du Condroz pour l'Exploitation des Chemins de Fer Vicinaux.
(ww) S.A. de l'Exploitation du Chemin de Fer de Huy-Waremme et Extensions.
(uu) Naamloze Maatschappij tot Uitbating van de Buurtspoorweg Maaseick-Weert en Uitbreiding.
     (see NETHERLANDS No. 95).

Capital Numbers were allocated as near as possible in order of opening dates and are shown
in the left hand column below, while the letters in brackets on the right, indicate the
operating companies as listed above. Lines without letters were worked by the SNCV itself
from the outset.

(A) STANDARD GAUGE LINES (1435 mm).

17	Poulseur-Sprimont-Trooz,	22.2 km.	(b)	Liége Group.
36	Dolhain-Goé-Eupen,	9.2 km.	(cc)	(Formerly Eupener Kleinbahn).
55	Groenendael-Overijssche,	6.7 km.	(rr)	Bruxelles-Brabant Group.
-	Merksem Docks-Ijskelder,	2.4 km.	-	Antwerpen Group (on behalf of S.A. des Etablissements Industriels et Commerciaux de Merksem).
-	Sichem-Scherpenheuvel (Montaigu) 3.8 km.			for C.F. Grand Central Belge. (Transferred to State Railways in 1898),

(B) 3ft. 6 in. GAUGE LINES (1067 mm).

Antwerpen Group

1	Antwerpen (Anvers)-Oostmalle-Turnhout, 40.8 km. (a)	
	Oostmalle-Hoogstraeten, 12.0 km. (a).	
12	Mechelen(Malines)-Heyst op den Berg-Itegem)	73.2 km. (b) later (c).
	Westerloo-Geel-Turnhout,)	
21)	Antwerpen(Anvers)-Brasschaat-Wernhout(frontier) 40.0 km. (d) later (a).	
22)	(Through working with Netherlands No. 14)	
23	Antwerpen(Anvers)-Ekeren-Sandvliet(frontier))	56.2 km. (d) See Netherlands 11.
	Ekeren-Lillo,)	
31	Antwerpen(Anvers)-Broechem-Lier(Lièrre))	41.2 km. (a).
	Broechem-Zandhoven-Oostmalle,)	
57	Turnhout-Arendonck(Dutch frontier), 16.7 km. (a) No through running.	
64	Turnhout-Oostmalle-Sichem)	58.9 km. (a).
	Oostmalle-Westerloo,)	
70	Brasschaat-Oostmalle-Herenthals-Westerloo, 58.9 km. (a).	
77	Antwerpen(Anvers)-Boom-Rumst-Mechelen(Malines))	48.4 km. (a).
	Rumst-Lier(Lièrre),)	
84	Turnhout-Merxplas-Rijkevorsel-St. Leenaarts(St. Léonard))	57.2 km. (a).
	Merxplas-Brecht,)	
	Hoogstraeten-Meersel(Dutch frontier) (See Netherlands 78A)	
105	Itegem-Zandhoven, 19.0 km. (c).	
133	Turnhout-Poppel(Dutch frontier), 22.9 km. (a) No through running.	
147	Lier(Lièrre)-Putte-Werchter, 25.3 km. (c).	
154	Aarschot(Aerschot)-Westerloo, 15.0 km. (c).	

Note. -   All the above 3ft 6in gauge lines were converted to metre gauge 1919-1921.

(C) METRE GAUGE LINES (1000 mm).

Antwerpen(Anvers) Group.

148   Mechelen(Malines)-Pasbrug-Keerbergen-Aarschot(Aerschot), 29.5 (c).
(Mechelen-Pasbrug was mixed gauge 1067/1000 until 1919).

Bruxelles(Brussel) Group.

13	Bruxelles(Brussel)-Dilbeek-Schepdael-Ninove, 38.4 km. (e).
14	Wavre(Wavre)-Incourt-Jodoigne(Geldenaken), 29.3 km. (b).
16	Bruxelles(Brussel)-Leerbeek-Enghein(Edingen), 33.0 km. (e).
18	Bruxelles(Brussel)-Grimbergen-Humbeek, 17.2 km. (e).
47	Bruxelles(Brussel)-Espinette(Hut)-Waterloo-Mont St. Jean, 31.2 km. (pp).
61	Grimbergen-Londerzeel, 15.2 km. (e). (Mixed gauge after electrification).
74	Braine l'Alleud(Eignebrackel)-Mont St.Jean-Wavre(Waver), 21.5 km. (b).
	(Rixensart-Maransart section mixed gauge).
78	Courcelles-Incourt-Gembloux(Gembloers), 67.7 km. (b).
106	Braine l'Alleud(Eignebrackel)-Bois Seigneur-Nivelles).)
	Bois Seigneur-Virginal-Braine le Comte's Gravenbrackel) 40.1 km. (b).
	Virginal-Rebecq Rognon (for Tubize),)
111	Hal(Halle)-Leerbeek-Ninove, 27.3 km. (e).
191	Bruxelles(Brussel)-La Roue(Het Rad)-Hal(Halle), 18.4 km.

Brabant-Leuven(Louvain) Group.

32	Brussel(Bruxelles)-Haacht(Haecht), 30.6 km. (bb). later (tb) then (b).
-	Ixelles(Elsene)-Pl.St.Croix-Schaerbeek-Eglise Ste. Marie, 6.0 km. as above.
	(See No. 5 page Some time mixed gauge).
44	Leuven(Louvain)-Hamme Mille-Jodoigne(Geldenaken), 30.8 km. (b).
46	Bruxelles(Brussel)-Sterrebeek-Vossem/Cimetière, 16.7 km. (as No. 32).
58	Leuven(Louvain)-Tielt-Diest, 29.9 km. (b).
72	Haacht(Haecht)-Werchter-Aarschot(Aerschot)-Tielt-Tienen(Tirlemont), 46.4 km. (b).
76	Leuven(Louvain)-Vossem-Tervueren, 18.4 km. (b).

80	Vossem-Hamme Mille-Tienen(Tirlemont), 42.8 km.
129	Jodoigne(Geldenaken)-Tienen(Tirlemont)-Sint Truiden(St. Trond), 37.7 km. (f).
138	Diest-Beringen-Koersel, 19.4 km. (f).

Oost Vlaanderen(Flandre Est) Group.

8	Gent(Gand)-Somergem-Ursel, 21.1 km. (1s) Later (tg).
19	Gent(Gand)-Oostakker-Saffelaare, 18.0 km. (g).
28	Deinze-Oudenaarde(Audenarde), 19.9 km. (h) Later (f).
38	Gent(Gand)-Wetteren-Hamme, 39.1 km. (g).
39	Eekloo-Watervliet(frontier.) 19.0 km. (worked by Netherlands No. 56).
59	Sint Niklaas(St. Nicolas)-Kieldrecht-Doel, 24.2 km. (kk) (Isolated line).
-	Waterland-Oudeman, ? km. (branch of No. 39).
98	Aalter-Ursel-Erkloo, 12.7 km. (1) (Through running with Netherlands No. 56).
100	Overmere-Saffelaare, 19.5 km. (g).
102	Wetteren-Oordegem-St.Lievenshouten-Sottegem, 21.1 km. (1).
103	Geeraardsbergen(Gramont)-Oudenaarde(Audenarde), 26.3 km. (f).
110	Antwerpen Linker Oever(Anvers Rive Gauche)-Hamme-Moerzeke, 37.8 km. (g).
120	Aasche-Aalst(Alost)-Oordegem, 26.0 km. (1).
126	Gent(Gand)-Loochristi, 10.0 km.
128	Gent(Gand)-Merelbeke-Geeraardsbergen(Gramont), 40.7 km.
136	Gent(Gand)-Evergem-Bassevelde, 27.0 km.
158	Gent(Gand)-Nevele-Ruiselede, 27.0 km.
185	Moerbeke-Dreischouwen(frontier), 5.7 km. (worked by Netherlands No. 84 for goods).

West Vlaanderen (Flandre Ouest) Group.

2	Oostende (Ostend)-Nieuwpoort-Veurne(Furnes), 30.0 km.) Nieuwpoort-Nieuwpoort Bad-Groendijk, ?) 83.5 km. (1s) later (ob).
7	Oostende(Ostend)-Blankenberghe-Knokke-Westkapelle-Brugge(Bruges)) 87.1 km. as above. Westkapelle-Sluis (frontier), (through working with Netherlands No. 16))
6	Tielt-Ruiselede-Aalter, 19.0 km. (1s) later (1).
29	Veurne(Furnes)-Oostvleteren-Ieper(Ypres), 36.5 km. (1s) later (k).
33	Hooglede-Roeselare(Roulers)-Aardooie(Ardoye)-Tielt, 32.8 km. (hh).
41	Kortrijk(Courtrai)-Moorsele-Geluwe-Meenen(Menin)-Wervik, 38.3 km. (m).
65	Brugge(Bruges)-Zwevzele, 20.0 km. (zz).
75	Ieper(Ypres)-Waasten(Warneton)-Le Seau-Steenwerck(France), 30.6 km. (1s).
85	Aarsele-Kortrijk(Courtrai)-Moeskroen(Mouscron)-Mont à Leux-Meenen(Menin), 54.8 km. (m).
107	Diksmuide-Wommen-Merkem-Ieper(Ypres),) Merkem-Oostvleteren-Poperinge,) 40.4 km. (k).
113	Brugge(Bruges)-Ursel, 21.5 km. (n).
115	De Panne-Veurne(Furnes)-Poperinge, 47.4 km. (1s) later (ob).
119	Brugge(Bruges)-Middelburg-Dutch frontier-Aardenburg, 23.3 km. (n)
121	Ieper(Ypres)-Geluwe, 18.2 km. (m).
132	Oostende(Ostend)-Leke-Diksmuide, 25.2 km. (k).
137	Brugge(Bruges)-Leke, 32.0 km. (m).
150	Wommen-Roeselare(Roulers)-Langemark, 43.0 km. (not completed to Bikschoote).
151	Kortrijk(Courtrai)-Bellegem-Pecq, 19.1 km. (m).
152	Aardooie(Ardoye)-Izegham, 6.7 km. (11).
153	Izeghem-Wevelghem, 14.0 km. (m).
166	Kortrijk(Courtrai)-Deerlijk-Berchem, 24.2 km. (m).

Hainaut Ouest (West Henegouwen) Group.

25	Saint Ghislain-Tertre-Hautrage-Stambruges.) Tertre-Baudour,) 32.2 km. (p). Hautrage-Boussu, (Goods only)) (Baudour-Hercies mixed gauge).
27	Banlieue de Mons:- Mons(Bergen)-Saint Symphorien-Bray,) Mons(Bergen)-Ghlin- Baudour,) 51.2 km. (p). Mons(Bergen)-Gasteau-Neufvilles,)
35	French frontier-Quievrain-Roisin, 10.9 km. (worked by France No.159).
66	Lens-Thoricourt-Edingen(Enghein),) 32.2 km. Lens-Soignies,)
67	Boussu-Dour-Fayt le Franc(French frontier), 14.7 km. (p).

95	Banlieue de Tournai:-
	Tournai(Doornijk)-Templeuve-Toufflers,) (Connecting with Lille Electric Tramways, France)
	Tournai(Doornijk)-Mainvault-Ath,)
	Tournai(Doornijk)-Rumillies,)
	Tournai(Doornijk)-Hertain(Frontier),) 135.8 km. (f).
	Tournai(Doornijk)-Peruwelz,)
	Tournai(Doornijk)-Wez Welvain,)
	Tournai(Doornijk)-Pecq,)
	Ath-Flobrecq(Floesberg), 18.6 km. -
104	Casteau-Neufville-Louvignies Bifurcation)
	Neufville-Carrières, (Mixed gauge 4 rail)) 16.7 km. (p).
125	Casteau-Bracquegnies, 12.1 km. (p).
127	Lignes du Borinage:-
	Mons(Bergen)-Harveng-Quevy-Eugies,)
	Givry-Harveng-Frameries,) 76.1 km.
	Quevy-Givry-Estinnes au Mont,)
162	Mainvault-Quevaucamps-Stambruges,)
	Quievrain-Montroeill sur Haine-Canal,) 29.5 km.
183	Flobrecq(Floesberg)-Gramont(Geerardsbergen), 14.0 km. (Gramont-Goefferdingen mixed gauge
	3 rail).

Hainaut Est (Oost Henegouwen) Group.

9	Charleroi-Mont sur Marchienne, 4.3. km (1s).
10/40	Charleroi-Lodelinsart-Châtelet, 8.5 km. (s).
11	Charleroi-Marchienne au Pont-Montigny le Tilleul, 15.7 km. (1s).
43	Morlanwelz-Mariemont-La Louvière-Bracquegnies,) km. (1s).
	Manage-Jolimont-Haine St. Pierre-La Louvière-Famillereux,)
62	Montigny le Tilleul-Thuillies, 11.4 km. (1s).
89	Bracquegnies-La Louvière-Peronnes-Binche,) ? km. (ii).
	Bray-Estinnes au Mont,)
92	Marcinelle Haies-Nalinnes-Bultia, ? km. (1s).
97	Chimay-Forges-Cul des Sarts,) 43.2 km. (cc) (Isolated lines).
109	Couvin-Petite Chapelle-Cul des Sarts,) (Chimay-Forges mixed gauge).
159	Binche-Solre sur Sambre-Bersillies l'Abbaye,) 24.2 km.
	Montignies-Saint Christophe,)
160	Olloy-Oignies, 10.0 km. (Isolated line).
170	Châtelet-Fosses, 15.2 km.

Namur (Namen) - Luxembourg Group.

3	Andenne-Bierwart-Forville-Egherzée, 19.9 km. (t).
63	Egherzée-Saint Denis Bovesse, 16.6 km. (t).
4	Melreux-La Roche, 19.0 km. (u).
5	Poix-St. Hubert-Freux, 19.8 km. (u).
143	Libramont-Freux-Amberloup, 20.5 km. (u).
15	Jambes-Andenne-Huy(Hoei), 32.5 km. (t).
26	Bourcy-Houffalize, 11.6 km. (h). (Isolated line).
34	Paliseul-Bouillon, 15.2 km. (h).
93	Poix-Paliseul, 28.2 km. -.
45	Arlon-Ethe-Virton, 22.1 km. (h).
149	Arlon-Martelange, 30.5 km. (Connecting with Luxembourg No. 8).
49	Grupont-Wellin, 13.5 km. (h). Later (v).
50	Namur lines:-
	Profondeville-Namur(Namen)-Lesves-Saint Gerard,)
	Namur(Namen)-Forville-Meefe,) 92.7 km. (w).
	Namur(Namen)-Onoz,)
123	Lesves-Bioul-Warnant, 15.3 km. (w).
71	Onoz-Fleurus, 12.0 km.
82	Andenne-Ohey-Ciney, 31.3 km. (t).
94	Marche-Amberloup-Bastogne-Martelange, 81.3 km. (l). (Connecting with Luxembourg 8).
112	Rochefort-Han sur Lesse-Wellin-Graide, 37.7 km. (v).

144	Han sur Lesse-Grotte de Han,	3.7 km.	(v). (Summer service only).

144 Han sur Lesse-Grotte de Han,   3.7 km. (v). (Summer service only).
114 Vielsalm-Lierneux,   15.6 km. (h). (Isolated line).
116 Dinant-Florennes,   25.0 km. (jj). (Isolated line).
134 Comblain la Tour-Manhay-Melreux,   64.0 km.
131 Ben Ahin-Ohey-Courrière,   24.5 km. (t).
135 Bouillon-Corbion-Pussemange(France), 21.2 km. (h). (Connecting with French light railways
                                                           at both ends).
141 Etalle-Villiers devant Orval.   30.9 km. (Isolated line).
161 Gedinne-Vresse-Bohan(French frontier),)
    Vresse-Alle sur Semois,   ) 32.5 km. (Connecting with French light rly.).
163 Marbehan-Florenville-Sainte Cecile,   31.0 km. (Isolated line).

Liége-Limburg Group.

20 Huy(Hoei)-Vinalmont-Omal-Waremme,   26.0 km. (ww).
48 Waremme-Oreye(Borgsworm-Oerle),   10.3 km. (ww).
24 Leopoldsburg(Bourg Leopold)-Bree-Maaseik, 44.2 km. (y).
30 Clavier-Val Saint Lambert,   25.3 km. (dd).
60 Clavier-Warzée-Ouffet-Comblain au Pont, 27.0 km. (dd). (Ouffet-Comblain mixed gauge).
51 Glons-Bassenge-Canne(Dutch frontier),   16.0 km. (1s).
53 Sint Truiden(Saint Trond)-Oreye-Ans,   33.4 km. (r). (See part (a) No. 2).
68 Tongeren(Tongres)-Riemst-Vroenhoven(Dutch frontier), 34.0 km. (1s).
"   Riemst-Lanaeken-Maastricht(Netherlands)   ?   (See NETHERLANDS no. 64).
69 Fexhe le Haut Clocher-Villers l'Evêque-Tongeren, 18.8 km.
73 Liége(Luik)-Barchon-Fouron le Comte('s Gravenvoeren), 31.1 km. (y).
81 Hasselt-Kortessem-Oreye(Oerle),   30.5 km. (y).
108 Tongeren(Tongres)-Kortessem,   14.0 km. (y).
82 Maaseick-Lanaeken(Dutch frontier),   26.5 km. (1s). (See NETHERLANDS No. 64).
86 Hasselt-Herk de Stad(Herk la Ville)-Haelen, 18.1 km. (y).
87 Liége(Luik)-Saint Walburge-Vottem,   60.0 km. (z).
"   Saint Walburge-Rocourt-Tongeren(Tongres) 21.0 km. (z).
96 Maaseick-Kessenich(Dutch frontier),   26.5 km. (1s). (See NETHERLANDS No. 79).
117 Hannut-Ambresin-Meefe-Burdinne-Vinalmont,)
"   Burdinne-Bierwart-Seilles-Andenne,   )
"   Bierwart-Couthuin-Statte (for Huy),   ) 59.9 km.
"   Couthuin-Seilles,   )
122 Hannut-Omal-Verlaine-Ampsin,)
"   Verlaine-Saint Georges-Engis,) 72.7 km.
"   Saint Georges-Horion-Jemeppe,)
"   Horion-Fexhe le Haut Clocher,)
130 Maaseik-Molenbeersel(Dutch frontier)-Stramproy-Weert, 11.1 km. (uu). (Connecting with
                                                                    NETHERLANDS No.95)
146 Sint Truiden(Saint Trond)-Brustem-Hannut, 26.2 km. (r).
156 Genck-Zutendaal-Riemst-Bassenge(Bitsingen)-Liége(Luik), 62.0 km.
164 Ougrée-Warzée,   28.0 km.
165 Spa-Tiège ? km. (1s). (Steam only 1909-1910 then electric to Verviers).
168 Sint Truiden(Saint Trond)-Herk de Stad(Herk la Ville), 16.9 km. (y).
194 Taviers-Ambresin, 9.4 km. (See part (a), No. 12).
-   Waterschei-Zutendael-Lanaeken, ? km. (Opened 1933-1941).
-   Koersel-Zolder-Houthalen, ? km. (Opened 1947-1948 & part soon electrified).

S.1885, E.1894/1948, P.1925, D.1934. Some E. Still operating. Gauges. 1435. 1067 and 1000.

LOCOMOTIVE STOCK

The different classes of locomotive were distinguished by letters until 1918, then by numbers. The first 46 machines were renumbered according to gauge in 1887, and the numbers quoted below, are those subsequently in use.

Class 1. (Formerly A).   15 Tonnes.   Metre Gauge.

Enclosed 0-6-0 tram-engines, with short frames, for use on lightly laid track around the Dutch Frontier. Centre buffers and couplings.

Nos.	
30-35,	Tubize 647-652 of 1886.
36-39,	Haine St.Pierre 259-262 of 1887.
171-173,	Haine St.Pierre 438-440 of 1893.
248,	Haine St.Pierre 492 of 1895. (Ex-Netherlands No. 44).

Class 2. (Formerly B).   17 Tonnes.   Metre Gauge.

Enclosed 0-6-0 tram-engines, as class 1 but slightly heavier.

Nos. 167-170, Tubize 900-903 of 1893. (Used at Maastricht, See NETHERLANDS No. 64).

1067 Gauge.

No.   727, Tubize 909 of 1893.

Class 3. (Formerly C).   18 Tonnes.   Metre Gauge.

Earlier standard type of 0-6-0 tram-engine, Centre buffer & coupling.

Nos.	
1-4,	Tubize 613-614, 616-617 of 1885.
5,7,12,	Franco Belge 558, 562, 559 of 1886.
13,19,	Franco Belge 561, 560 of 1886.
6,8,11,	Couillet 832, 835, 831 of 1886.
14,15,	Couillet 833-834 of 1886.
16,29,40,	St.Léonard 748-750 of 1887.
9-10,	Lambert (unknown works numbers) 1886.
25-28,41-46,	Lambert (unknown works numbers) 1886.
17-18,	Haine St.Pierre 241 ? 243 of 1886.
20,	Zimmermann 8 of 1886.
21-24,	Carels 247-250 of 1886.
47-50,	Lambert (unknown works numbers) of 1887.
63-65,	Franco Belge 590-592 of 1887.
59-62,	Franco Belge 608-611 of 1887.
66-69,	Franco Belge 612-615 of 1887.
51-58,	Cockerill 1505-1512 of 1887.
70-77,	Couillet 873-880 of 1887.
78-83,	Carels 262-267 of 1887.
84-89,	Haine St.Pierre 266-271 of 1887.
90-92,	St.Léonard 752-754 of 1887.
93-95,	Zimmermann 17-19 of 1887.
96-97,111-112,	
113-120,	Halot 1-2, 3-4, 7-14 of 1888 & 1890.
109-110,121,	Halot 16-17 & 15 of 1890.
98-99,	La Meuse 501-502 of 1887.
100,102-106,)	
107-108,122-125,)	
131-136,)	Boussu 13, 14-18, 19-20,
126-129,130,)	27-32, 5-8 & 10. of 1890.
141-142,143-146,	
& 158-166 & 174,	Boussu 25-26, of 1891, 33-36 of 1892, 37-45 of 1893 & 46 1893.

Nos.137-140,	Couillet 1019-1022 of 1891.
177-179,	
175-176,	Halot 18-20,21-22 of 1894.
180-181,	
182-183,184-185,	Boussu 50-51, 53-54, 56-57 of 1894.
186-189,	Haine St.Pierre 495-498 of 1895.
190-194,	Cockerill 1916-1920 of 1895.
195-198, 199,	Tubize 990-993, 995 of 1896.
200,	Cockerill 1938 of 1895.
201-210,211-212,	Boussu 58-67, 68-69 of 1896 & 1897.

(1067 Gauge).   <u>1067 Gauge.</u>

700,701,	
702,703-708,	Tubize 609,612,615618-623 of 1885.
709,	Zimmermann 12 of 1886.
710-711,	Haine St.Pierre 242 ?, 244 of 1886.
712-719,	Tubize 667-674 of 1887.
720-721,	Flenu (unknown works numbers) of 1889 ?.
722-725,	
726,728-729,	Boussu 1-4, 9,11-12 of 1889 & 1890.
730-731,	Halot 5-6 of 1890.
738-740,	Boussu 47-49 of 1894.
741,742,	Boussu 52,55 of 1894.
743.	Tubize 994 of 1896.

<u>Class 4. (Formerly C).</u>   <u>18 Tonnes.</u>   Metre Gauge .

As type 3, but higher boiler pressure.

Nos.

213-221,222-223,	Jung 285-293, 283-284, 294, 295 of 1897
224-225,	
226-227,	318-319 of 1898.
228-230&247,	Cockerill 2061-2063, 2064 of 1898.
231-237,	Boussu 79-85 of 1897.
238-242,249-251,	St.Léonard 1106-1110, 1111-1113 of 1898.
243-246,	La Meuse 1413-1416 of 1898.
252-254,	Franco-Belge 1213-1215 of 1899.
255-258,	La Meuse 1487-1490 of 1898.
259-261,	St.Léonard 1149-1151 of 1899.
262-264,	Tubize 1164-1166 of 1899.
268-270,	Cockerill 2140-2142 of 1899.
271-275,	Boussu 91-95 of 1898.
276-279,	Couillet 1249-1252 of 1898.
265-267,	Haine St.Pierre 652-654 of 1900.
280-285,	St.Léonard 1219-1224 of 1900.
286-288,	Franco Belge 1309-1311 of 1900.
289-291,	Couillet 1276-1278 of 1900.
295-299,310,	Cockerill 2255-2259, 2260 of 1901.
312-316,	Humboldt 85-89 of 1901.
276-279,	Couillet 1249-1252 of 1898.
280-285,	St.Léonard 1219-1224 of 1900.
286-288,	Franco Belge 1309-1311 of 1900.
289-291,	Couillet 1276-1278 of 1900.
295-299&310,	Cockerill 2255-2259 & 2260 of 1901.
312-316,	Humboldt 85-89 of 1901.
311,320,339-341,	Boussu 131, 132 & 145-147 of 1902.
321,	Thiriau 30 of 1902.
327-330,	Cockerill 2381-2384 of 1902.
331-332,	
368 & 379,	St.Léonard 1352-1353 of 1902, 1427, 1426/1905.
334-338,	La Meuse 1801-1805 of 1903/04.
342-346.	Couillet 1373-1377 of 1903.

(II) 208, 333 & 347,	Zimmermann 607-609 of 1903.
349-351,	La Biésme 13-15 of 1904.
352-355,	Gilain 1-4 of 1905.
356-359,	Haine St.Pierre 799-802 of 1904.
360-363,	Tubize 1403-1406 of 1904.
366-367,	Detombay 158-159 of 1905.
371-376,	Haine St.Pierre 831-836 of 1905.
377-378,380-382,	Thiriau 61-62, 64-66 of 1905.
379-380,	St.Léonard 1426-1427 of 1900.
383-387,	Tubize 1438-1442 of 1905.
388-390,	Boussu 168-170 of 1905.
391-392,394,	La Meuse 1947, 1948, 1950 of 1906.
444-447,	Gilain 13-16 of 1907.
448,449,	Thiriau 88,86 of 1907.
450-453,	Energie 147-150 ? of 1907.
454-455, & 504-507,	Tubize 1501-1502 of 1907, 1568-1571 of 1909.
456,458-459,	La Biésme 32, 34-35 of 1907.
393,460-462, 463-469,	Gilly 309, 310-312, 314-320 of 1907.
473-474,457, 470-472,	Boussu 191, 200 of 1907, 203-206 of 1908.
475-478,502-503,	Haine St.Pierre 947-950 of 1908, 982-983/1909.
486-487,488-493,	Grand Hornu 12-13 of 1907, 14-19 of 1908.
494-497,	Gilly 337-340 of 1908.
498-501,516-517,	Zimmermann 670-673 of 1908, 675-676 of 1909 ?
457,470-472,	Boussu 203, 204-206 of 1908.
504-507,547-550, 508-511,607, 608-611,	Tubize 1568-1571 & 1585-1588 of 1909. Boussu 207-210 of 1908, 211,226-228/1911.
512-515,	Franco Belge 1752-1755 of 1908.
519-530,	Grand Hornu 20-31 of 1909.
531-534,	Gilain 32-35 of 1909.
535-538,	Detombay 180-181, 183-184 of 1909.
539-542,581-584,	Franco Belge 1815-1818 of 1909, 1886-1889/10.
543-546,577-580,	Haine St.Pierre 1007-1010, 1078-1081 of 1909/10.
551-554,	St.Léonard 1582-1585 of 1909.
555-558,	La Biésme 49-52 of 1909.
559-560,562,	Thiriau 125-126, 128 of 1910.
23(II),574-576,	Tubize 1672-1675 of 1910.
561,589-591,	Thiriau, 176-179 of 1911.
585-588,	Gilly 370-373 of 1908.
592-599,	Tubize 1696-1699 of 1911 & 1701-1704 of 1911.
603-605,	Thiriau 180-182 of 1911.
607-610,	Boussu 211, 226-228 of 1911.
611-614,	Louvain (SNCV Works) 61,60,62-63 of 1913.
615-618,	Grand Hornu, 52-55 ? of 1912.
619-620,	Haine St.Pierre 1090-1091 of 1911.
637-641,	Boussu 236-240 of 1912.
642-646,	Grand Hornu 64-68 of 1913.
647-649, 650 & 651,	La Hestra 13-15,16 ? & 17 ? of 1912.

1067 Gauge.

744-746,747,	Jung 296-298 & 301 of 1898.
750-752,	Haine St.Pierre 612-614 of 1899.
756-760,	Boussu 102,101,100, 103-104 of 1900.
761-764,	Thiriau 6-9 of 1901.
765,	Cockerill 2261 of 1901.
766-768,	Boussu 128-130 of 1902.
769-770,	St.Léonard 1354-1355 of 1902.
771,	Thiriau 63 of 1905.
772,	Detombay 160 of 1905.
773,	St.Léonard 1428 of 1905.
774-775,	Thiriau 87,85 of 1907.
776-777,	Tubize 1499-1450 of 1907.
778,	La Meuse 1949 of 1906.

```
        779,    Gilly 313 of 1907.
        780,    La Biesme 33 of 1907.
    781-782,    Boussu 192-193 of 1907.
    783-786,    Couillet 1504-1507 of 1908.
    787-788,    Haine St.Pierre 984-985 of 1909.
(II)732 & (II)735,  Thiriau 127 of 1910 and 183 of 1911.
  (II)733-734,  Haine St.Pierre 1092-1093 of 1911.
```

Note. -
    (II)732-735, Replaced Cockerill 0-4-0s ex-Nord Anvers line. See part (a) No.3.

Class 5. (No old classification).   **20 Tonnes.**   **1000 Gauge.**

Unenclosed 0-6-0 side tank engines with rear cabs. Both side buffers and centre buffer couplings at both ends for working stock on four rail mixed gauge lines.

```
Nos.419-420,   St.Léonard 1440-1441 of 1906.
       483,    St.Léonard    1481 of 1907. (for Chimay-Couvin line).
       518,    St.Léonard    1479 of 1908.   "      "       "      "
```

Class 6. (Formerly D).   **22 Tonnes.**   **1000 Gauge.**

Enclosed 0-6-0 tram-engines with centre buffers and couplings.

```
Nos.400-404.   Tubize    745-749 of 1889.
    405-408,   Tubize 1135-1138 of 1897.
    409-413,   Thiriau       1-5 of 1901.
    414-417.   Tubize 1345-1348 of 1902.
       418.    Zimmermann 635 of 1906.
       421.    Tubize      750 of 1889.
```

(II)423 425-426, (II)433 (II)436, Zimmermann 629-631, 636-637 of 1905/06.
(II)429, 431, 432 & 434, Thiriau 26-29 of 1902.
(II)435 & (II)437-438. Tubize 1349-1351 of 1903.

Note. -
    (II)432-438. Replaced Class 13 locomotives found unsuitable and sold.

Class 7. (Formerly H).   **27 Tonnes.**   **1000 Gauge.**

Enclosed 0-6-0 tram-engines of a heavier type. Centre buffer and coupling.

```
Nos.
300-303 & 304,  Tubize 701-704 & 707 of 1888. (303 is now preserved at Schepdael).
       305,     Tubize 1020 of 1900.
    306-309,
     & 322-326, Tubize 1213-1216 of 1900 & 1311-1315 of 1902.
348 & 369-370,  Louvain (SNCV Works) 52 of 1904 & 53-54 of 1905.
    364-365,    Tubize 1407-1408 of 1904.
    395-399,    Energie 120-124 of 1905.
    479-482,    Energie 164-167 of 1907.
    484-485,
     & 563-565, Louvain 57-58 of 1909 & 60, 62, 61 of 1910.
    566-568,    La Meuse 2181-2183 of 1909.
    569-571,    Energie 208-210 of 1909.
    621-622,
     & 627-628, Haine St.Pierre 1113-1114 of 1911 & 1115-1116 of 1912.
    631-633,    Tubize 1734-1736 of 1911.
    629-630,
     & 634-636, Franco Belge 1969-1973 of 1912.
    659-662,    Franco Belge 2208-2211 of 1915.
    663-665,
     & 687-689, Haine St.Pierre 1266-1268 of 1915 & 1277-1279 of 1915.
```

666-668, Boussu 254-256 of 1915.
690-692, Franco Belge 2214-2216 of 1915.
797, Jung 360 of 1899. (Formerly No. 5 of Ans-Oreye Tramway). ⁖

Class 8. (Formerly B).   17 Tonnes.   1067 Gauge.

Enclosed 0-6-0 tram-engines with centre buffers & couplings and bell on roof. Larger boiler
than Class 2, but narrow tanks for through working into the Netherlands.

Nos.
  748-749,
  & 753-755, Haine St.Pierre 561-565 of 1898. (Turnhout-Hoogstraten-Rijsbergen).

Class 9. (Formerly I).   30 Tonnes.   1000 Gauge.

Enclosed 2-6-0 tram-engines for use on heavily graded lines. Centre buffer & coupling.

Nos.600-602, St.Léonard 808-810 of 1890 (for Bouillon-Paliseul line).
     796,   St.Léonard   877 of 1891 (formerly No.4 of Ans-Oreye Tramway).

Class 10 (Formerly F).   28 Tonnes.   1435 Gauge.

Enclosed 0-6-0 tram-engines with skirting over wheels inclined inwards. Low overall height
(except No.813). Side buffers, screw couplings and air brakes.

Nos.803-805, St.Léonard 755-757 of 1887 (for Eupen line).
    806-808, St.Léonard 939-941 of 1894 (for Groenendael-Overijssche line).
    813,   St.Léonard   1468 of 1906 ("   "   "   "). (Preserved).

Class 11. (Formerly not classified).   28 Tonnes.   1435 Gauge.

Enclosed 0-6-0 tram-engines as class 10 but with straight skirting over wheels. Side buffers,
screw couplings and air brakes.

Nos.800-802, St.Léonard 730-732 of 1886. (for Poulseur-Sprimont-Trooz line).

Class 12. (Formerly G).   28 Tonnes.   1435 Gauge.

Enclosed 0-6-0 tram-engines as Class 11, but with higher roof like No.813.

No.   810,   St.Léonard 1125 of 1898 (for Poulseur-Sprimont-Trooz line).
        812,   St.Léonard 1392 of 1905.
    816-817,   Franco Belge 2084 of 1913 & 2143 of 1914. (816 at Poulseur, 817 at
                Groenendael).

Class 13. (Formerly E).   24 Tonnes.   Metre Gauge.

Enclosed 0-6-0 tram engines, with high pitched boilers. Centre buffers and couplings.
These locomotives were withdrawn at an early date and sold.

Nos.422-427, Tubize 830-835 of 1891.   (422 sold to Spain & 427 to Germany No.7).
    428-433, Couillet 1023-1028 of 1891.   (429 sold to Germany No.7).
    434-439, La Meuse 1204 - 1209 of 1891. (437 sold to Spain & 438 to Germany No.7).

Class 14.   30 Tonnes.   Metre Gauge.

Side tank 0-6-0 engines with rear cab. Built for an undertaking in Spain but not delivered.
Fitted by the SNCV with side & centre buffers for use on mixed gauge lines.

Nos.440-443, Haine St.Pierre 890-893 of 1906.

Class 15.   21 Tonnes.   1435 Gauge.

Industrial type 0-4-0 side tank engines with rear cabs, screw couplings and side buffers for use
on Antwerp Docks at Merxem.

Nos.   809.   St.Léonard 1000 of 1895.
        811.   Corpet Bourdon (unknown works No.) Named "La Force".
               (acquired second hand in 1897).
    814-815,   St.Léonard 1526-1527 of 1908.
        818.   St.Léonard 1758 of 1915. (Sold to industry, possibly preserved).

Class 16.   19 Tonnes.   Metre Gauge.

Enclosed 0-6-0 tram engine of conventional appearance with centre buffer and coupling,
superheater and air brakes.   Prototype locomotive built for an exhibition and sold to the
SNCV afterwards.

No.   572,   Tubize 1650 of 1909.

Class 17.   22 Tonnes.   Metre Gauge.

Unenclosed 0-6-0 tank engine with rear cab. Centre buffer & coupling, superheated. Prototype
locomotive built for an exhibition and sold to the SNCV.

No.   573,   St.Léonard 1643 of 1910. (destroyed in 1914-1918 war).

Class 18.   22 Tonnes.   Metre Gauge.

Enclosed 0-6-0 tram engines of larger type. Centre buffer & coupling.

Nos. 623-624,   Haine St.Pierre 1106-1107 of 1911.
     625-626,   Tubize 1717-1718 of 1911.
606,652,655,   Tubize 1785, 1786-1789 of 1914.
     656-658,   Louvain (not completed), because of 1914-1918 war).
     669-672,   La Meuse 2798-2801 of 1915.
     736 (2nd), Tubize 1790 of 1914 (1067 gauge).
     673-675,   Thiriau 247-249 of 1915.
     677-680,
     696-698,   St.Léonard 1870-1873, 1875-1877 of 1915.
     789-791,   Tubize 1858-1860 of 1915.
676,681-682,
     792,699,   Cockerill 2908-2912 of 1915.
     683-685,   Gilain 72-74 of 1915.
     690-692,   Franco Belge 2214-2216 of 1915.
         686,   Haine St.Pierre 1276 of 1915.
     693-695,   Detombay 206-208 of 1919.
   1001-1002,   Cockerill 2913-2914 of 1915.
   1021-1026,
   1045-1056,   Tubize 1899-1904, 1864-1876 of 1919/1920.
   1027-1033,   St.Léonard 1891-1897 of 1920.
   1034-1038,   Haine St.Pierre 1291-1295.
   1039-1044,   Gilain 76-81 of 1920. (1039 preserved at Schepdaal).
   1057-1062,   Thiriau 258-263 of 1920.
   1063-1064,   Franco Belge 2219-2220 of 1920.
   1065-1067,   Haine St.Pierre 1296-1298 of 1920.
   1068-1071,   Tubize 1887-1890 of 1921.
   1072-1076,   Grand Hornu 91-95 of 1920.
   1077-1087,   Boussu 257-267 of 1919/1920.
   1088-1093,   Franco Belge 2221-2226 of 1920.
   1094-1105,   Cockerill 2921-2932 of 1920.

Class 19.   21 Tonnes.   Metre Gauge.

Locomotives supplied by the British War Department for use behind the allied lines and handed
over to the SNCV at the end of hostilities.   0-6-0 tram engines with centre buffer & coupling.
Similar to Class 18.   (W.D. Numbers 201-230 & 231-250 in Works number order; two locos
did not survive to come into SNCV hands).

Nos. 968, 997, 992, 971, 969, 950,   Stephenson (3663, 3666, 3667, 3669, 3670,
                                                        (3671 of 1916.
    956, 980, 972, 962, 974, 981, 975,   Stephenson (3675-3678, 3680, 3681, 3683,
    987, 955, 993, 970, 963, 995, 966,   (3685-3694 of 1917.
    990, 965, 957.
    961, 982, 986, 989, 994.   Stephenson (3664, 3665, 3668, 3672, 3679, 3682,
                                                        (3684 of 1917 (two missing).
    964, 988, 954, 983, 984, 978, 977,   Hawthorn Leslie 3215-3225 of 1917.
    952, 991, 976, 958.
    985, 979, 953, 973, 996, 967, 951,   Hawthorn Leslie 3227-3232, 3234, 3226, 3233
    959, 960.   of 1917.
                                           (Last two numbers may have been reversed).

Note. - Stephenson 3673 & 3674 did not pass to SNCV, therefore Nos. 998 & 999 remained blank.

Class 20.   38 Tonnes.   Standard Gauge.

Industrial type 0-6-0 tank engines with side buffers, and screw couplings, for use on Antwerp
Docks at Merxem, replacing Class 15.

Nos. 819-820,   Tubize 1828-1829 of 1922.
     821, 822.   Tubize 1970, 1993 of 1924.   (822 at first at Groenendaal).

Class 21.   27 Tonnes.   1000 Gauge.

Enclosed 0-6-0 tram-engines, similar to Class 19 but heavier. Supplied by the American army
for use behind the allied lines and handed over to the SNCV at the conclusion of hostilities.
Fitted with centre buffers and couplings, but Nos. 1009 & 1010 had side buffers and screw
couplings as well, for use on the mixed gauge track between Mol and Donk sand quarry.

Nos.
    1001-1020,   American Locomotive Co. 55227-55246 of 1915.
                 (Nos. 1013, 1015 and 1020 were resold in 1920 to ZVTM, See Netherlands 84).

Class 22.   43 Tonnes.   1435 Gauge.

Industrial type 0-6-0 tank engine, larger and of more modern appearance than Class 20.
Fitted with side buffers, screw couplings and air brakes. Used at Groenendael. Sold to
industry in 1953.

No.   823,   Couillet 1791 of 1926.

Class 23.   60 Tonnes.   1000 Gauge.

Garratt Articulated 0-6-0+0-6-0 enclosed tram-engines, with sloping tanks front and rear. Built
for the heavy coal traffic on the Bassenge-Glons line.

No.   850,   St.Léonard 2121 of 1929.
         851,   St.Léonard 2140 of 1930.

Unclassified locomotives.

This group comprises locomotives acquired from other undertakings in Belgium, which did not fit into SNCV standard classes and two repatriated by mistake from France in 1919, as they resembled SNCV machines.

1000 Gauge.

Nos.
422 & 424,	Tubize 854-855 of 1892, ex-Ixelles Co. (See Part (a), No.5.	
658,	Tubize 461 of 1884? originally Ixelles Co. then contractor in France.	
(II) 737,	Tubize/BM 1001(143) of 1896. Ex-France No.11. (Tramways del'Artois).	
793-795,	St.Léonard 827-829 of 1889. ex-Part (a) No.2 (Ans-Oreye Nos.1-3).	
796-797,	See classes 7 & 9. " " " " (" " Nos.4-5).	
798-799,	Unknown (like Class 7). " " " " (" " Nos.6-7).	

1067 Gauge.

Nos.
732-735,	Cockerill 0-4-0, 1497-1500 of 1887. (ex-Part (a) No.3 Antwerpen 6-9).	
736,	Cockerill 0-4-0, 1501 of 1888. (" " " " " 10).	
737,	Dutch Breda 0-4-0, 54 of 1889. (" " " " " 11).	

Steam "Rowan" Cars.   1000 Gauge.

Steam passenger cars with a driven bogie at the front and a single axle at the rear. Tried on the Bruxelles-Ninove line and at Antwerp.

Nos.
900-901, Franco Belge 666-667 of 1886/88.

SNCV loco No.797, formerly No.5 of the Ans-Oreye tramway, built by Jung.
Photo: "AMURTA".

(Upper). Small Breda loco No.9 "Groede" of the Breskens-Maldegem tramway
at Sluis, photographed at the same time as SNCV No.7 at the same place.
(Lower). Again photographed on the same day, Breskens-Maldegem No.21 at
Breskens. This is identical to the SNCV Class 18.

Photos: late F. Merton Atkins 30073 & 30074.

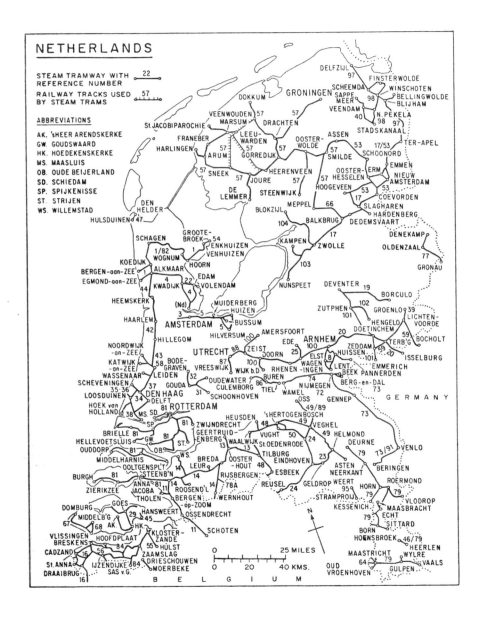

NETHERLANDS

STEAM TRAMWAY WITH REFERENCE NUMBER

RAILWAY TRACKS USED BY STEAM TRAMS

ABBREVIATIONS

AK. 'SHEER ARENDSKERKE
GW. GOUDSWAARD
HK. HOEDEKENSKERKE
MS. MAASLUIS
OB. OUDE BEIJERLAND
SD. SCHIEDAM
SP. SPIJKENISSE
ST. STRIJEN
WS. WILLEMSTAD

25 MILES

20   40 KMS.

B E L G I U M

146

6. THE NETHERLANDS

Mention of steam tramways in the Netherlands[1] conjures up in the writer's mind, a country scene with a dead straight brick road, lined with tall trees and a few tidy gabled houses, in front of which there would be a small group of young ladies in winged caps, flowing skirts and clogs. The picture would almost certainly be completed by a single tram track running along one side of the road, with on it a small "Breda" locomotive pulling a large bogie carriage. In fact, apart from the early urban lines at the Hague, Rotterdam and Nijmegen, most Dutch steam tramways were interurban and kept to the grass verge of country roads, except where they took to the towpath of a canal. Lifting bridges with tram-tracks were quite commonplace and sometimes tram-engines like drunkards, had to be hauled ignominiously out of canals into which they had fallen when derailed. Although there exists a word "Buurtspoorweg" meaning local railway, it was but little used and all secondary lines were known as "Stoom Tramwegen". In point of fact, only those railway branch lines which had been down-graded to the status of tramway, had much track on private right of way.

The first tram-engine arrived in the Hague in 1878 and hereafter development was rapid, so that by the turn of the century, the country was covered by a network as dense as that in Belgium, but with the important difference that, while Belgium had a unified undertaking, laid mainly to the metre gauge, the Netherlands were served by a large number of companies, whose ownership and gauges were as varied as the patches on the proverbial Dutchman's trousers. The 3' 6" gauge, 1067 mm, which was quite popular was known as "kaapspoor" as it was thought to have originated in South Africa. - Kaap = Cape of Good Hope.[2]

City tramways were electrified early and by the 1920s some lengthy inter-urban lines had also been electrified, particularly the Noord-Zuid Holland, which contrived to retain two gauges even after electrification. There was also the Nederlandsche Buurtspoorweg at Zeist and the Limburgsche Tramwegen which served the Coal Mining area in the deep south, most of whose electric line was additional to its existing steam lines. In the same period, many of the other tramways were experimenting with a varied assortment of petrol and diesel rail-cars and locomotives. By 1939, the steam tram in passenger service had all but disappeared, in favour of the ubiquitous motor-bus, but a few lines retained steam for goods trains. The outstanding exception was the Rotterdamsche Tramweg Maatschappij, (Maatschappij = Company) which having been ousted from the city, when the concession to electrify was given to another company, set about constructing a large network of 1067 gauge lines serving the South Bank of the Maas and the islands to the south. These lines flourished until a few years ago, when those on the islands were destroyed in post-war flooding, and the others hung on with a peculiar assortment of diesel tractors and rail-cars, but a few steam locomotives until 1966. Strangely the RTM named its diesel units but not its steam locomotives.

On the other hand, the 1939-1945 war brought back a meagre service on some other companies' lines, where locomotives were still available and many had to pull "dead" diesel cars, for which fuel was unobtainable. Several of these lines, such as the Maasbuurtspoorweg, were destroyed in the fighting, while after the war, with the return of normal conditions, the rest soon closed down again. Until recently, all that was left, was the occasional goods train, hauled by a main-line diesel loco, on some of the Westland and the Netherlands Tramway lines. (Both standard gauge, with main-line connections). One still sees motor buses bearing the titles of former steam tramways; and what strange names some of them had: "De Meijerij" (The Small Holding) "De Graafschap' (The Dukedom), "Eerste Drentsche Stoomtramweg" (First Drente Steam Tramway) or "Tweede Noord Holland Stoomtramweg" (Second North Holland Steam Tramway), the latter so named because the original owning company made no provision in its Articles of Association for any branches or extensions and a second company had to be formed to own the Purmurend branch. Hence the "Tweede" in its title.

One peculiar feature of the steam tramways in the Netherlands, was that several of them were owned or worked by the main-line railways. The Hollandsche Ijzeren Spoorweg Maatschappij, (known as the HYSM), owned or controlled 14 steam tramways, mainly in the North West,[3] but in addition, they down graded a number of their branch lines with light traffic and worked them in effect as tramways. The Nederlandsche Centraal Spoorweg Maatschappij, (NCS) operated three steam tramways, one of which, the Zwolle-Blokzijl, owned jointly with a local company was of narrow gauge. The Nederlandsche Rhijn Spoorweg Maatschappij[4] also constructed two tramways, one of which, the Hague-Scheveningen, was the first steam tramway in Holland. The NRS, became part of the State owned, company worked system in 1890 (Maatschappij tot Exploitatie van Staatsspoorwegen, known as S.S.), which acquired one other steam tramway. The various railways and their dependant tramways came under unified management in 1921 and in due course obtained financial control over even more tramways. Unfortunately this new management showed a strong bias towards motor buses, which spelt the doom of most Dutch steam tramways, nevertheless, one of the former HYSM lines, that between Bergen aan Zee and Alkmaar, survived until 1956, using tramway type carriages hauled by small railways engines, during the holiday season.

Although steam tramways came quite early to the Netherlands, several systems started surprisingly late; the "Oostelijk Groningen" began in 1915, but took over an existing horse tramway, which it worked as a branch. The large Limburg system, in the far South, was formed as such only in 1921, but incorporated three narrow gauge lines, themselves opened in 1915 and an extensive standard gauge system, partly steam and partly electric, constructed between 1922 and 1925 to serve a mining area. One of these lines, between Maastricht and Vaals, was one of the few true light railways, boasting some considerable earthworks and a lengthy steel viaduct at Gulpen. On it ran The Netherlands only Garratt articulated locomotive. These lines disappeared by 1937, after an equally short life.

Two of the lesser steam tramways were owned by ferry-boat companies, to which they acted as feeders. The various cross-frontier connections with Belgium have already been mentioned, but it should also be noted that in the Gelderland area, there were also some lines penetrating into Germany, but not connecting with any German systems. (See chapter 5).

Locomotives

The earliest locomotives to run on Dutch tramways were constructed in London by Merryweather & Co. in 1878. There were 19 of these for the Hague-Scheveningen tramway, followed by 5 more for the Leiden-Katwijk line in 1881/82. As mentioned in the previous chapter, Carels of Ghent, built some larger machines for the first-named line in 1882, before there were any steam tramways in Belgium itself. Soon afterwards, some Hohenzollern engines appeared on other tramways; those for the narrow gauge Geldersche tramway were very small indeed. Also from Germany, the ubiquitous "Square 'Henschel' was not long in making its presence felt in the Netherlands, but strangely enough the Krauss machine, so popular elsewhere was only represented by three examples, in spite of its success at the "Wedstrijd te Arnhem". (See below).

In the early days, the Netherlands seem to have had rather more than their fair share of peculiar tram engines. Some of the Hohenzollerns were single-drivers (see German chapter). Most of the experimental designs tried by Winterthur were to be found, a good many having Brown's patent boilers (see chapter 8), while the oddest were fireless engines built by van Duyl of Delfshaven for the short-lived West Friesian tramway; they had rocking-shaft drive like the Winterthur engines, and when the line closed, they were returned to the makers for rebuilding as conventional steam engines and sale elsewhere. At this time they were fitted with "Brown" boilers, completing the likeness to the Winterthur machines. Two of the Krauss engines were imported as reserve power for this illfated tramway. Although the narrow gauge Hohenzollern locomotives were very small, two Breda engines for the Bathing-beach tramway at Den Helder were quite tiny almost like toys. For those who can read Dutch, these and many other interesting locomotives are described in a book by Ir. Overbosch[5] even those with no knowledge of the language would find much of interest in the many illustrations, drawings and tables.

Two important events affected the history of Dutch steam tramways: the first was the "Wedstrijd te Arnhem", a sort of miniature "Rainhill Trials" held on the Arnhem horse tramway tracks in April and May 1881. Winterthur, Krauss, Merryweather and Hohenzollern locomotives were matched against each other, while Hagans & Henschel, although invited to compete, were unable to spare the necessary machines. The gold medal was awarded to the Krauss engine. The other event occurred in 1910, when Dr. Verhoop, "Ingenieur van de Raad van Toezicht op de Spoorwegdiensten" (Chief Inspecting Officer of Railways) issued a report, setting down a number of improvements in the design of tram-engines which he recommended.

The principal ones were :-

1. Normal speed 35 Kph. but capable of doing 50 Kph. with comfort.
2. Simple construction.
3. Easy to maintain.
4. Economical on fuel.
5. Easy for one man to control.
6. Capable of pulling a train of 160 tons on the flat.
7. Adequate water capacity with a low centre of gravity.
8. Fitted with a superheater and a feed water heating system.

Five standard gauge machines incorporating these features, were built by Hohenzollern in 1911 for the Westlandsche tramway. They were four coupled with inside cylinders and the water tanks forming a vallance under the footplate. They were designed for one-man drive and had the smokebox door visible in the front-sheet. Later, Verhoop narrow gauge engines were built for the Zutphen-Emmerik tramway and the Maasbuurtspoorweg. These had Verhoop patent feedwater heating apparatus.

Although some of the more prosperous of the tramways ran "Boat Trains" of 12 or 14 cars, connecting with important ferries, most Dutch tramways preferred to run light trains, often of only one large bogie coach. Hence the general demand was for a light locomotive, which could be driven and fired by one man; it is pleasing to note how adequately this demand was met by the Dutch firm "Backer en Rueb" of Breda, which after 1884, traded under the name N. V. Machinefabriek "Breda", who between 1883 and 1910 built 216 engines for Dutch tramways 34 for the Dutch Indies, 8 for Spain and one for South Africa. The standard Breda locomotives were pretty little things, with large oval end windows and the operators title and number on an oval plate, under which the works plate appeared in the form of a scroll. Most of them carried names and small brushes on the buffer-beam for sweeping away stones and other obstructions from the track. Another Dutch locomotive builder, who who made tram engines was the Nederlandsche Fabriek van Werktuigen en Spoorwegmaterieel, trading under the name "Werkspoor" and who built between 1901 and 1908, 22 locomotives for Dutch tramways, and 35 for tramways in the Dutch Indies. Of the former, six were of the Breda design, two of the Henschel design and the rest 0-6-0s with enclosed motion for the Rotterdam Tramways (RTM). By 1912 German manufacturers had undercut Breda's prices and they had gone out of the locomotive business.

Their weight and the necessity to carry two men did not endear the Belgian type six-coupled engines to the Dutch and their use was confined to the Belgian owned tramways in the South-West, where there was heavy sugar-beet traffic. The only four-coupled versions of the Belgian "Tubize" design, known to have been built, were to the order of two Dutch tramways. Of these the Haarlem-Alkmaar tramway had a ferry at Velsen across which they had to be carried. A turntable was at one end of its line and a triangle at the other, so that it could always run its engines fire-box leading and thus be worked by one man. In due course the cabs at the smoke-box end were closed up and the controls removed, but a regulator handle was fixed on the outside of the windscreen, so that the guard, riding on the platform of the front coach could cut off steam in an emergency.[6] From 1905 onward, the Rotterdam tramway adopted 0-6-0 well tank locomotives, with only the wheels and motion enclosed; their example was later followed by a number of tramways in the east, who bought similar but four coupled engines. Some built after the war, had no more than iron bars over the wheels. These included the 0-8-0s for the heavy goods traffic on the Geldersche tramways at Doetinchem.

Unfortunately, the history of the locomotives in use on the tramways controlled by the main-line railways, is far from clearcut. The HYSM, although it acquired a number of enclosed engines, also used its own 0-4-0 and 0-6-0 shunters on its tram lines and down graded lines, moving them around from time to time, changing the brake and coupling gear to suit. Two types of locomotive used on down-graded lines do call for special mention; there was a batch of 42 Borsig 0-4-0s with inside cylinders and disc wheels, which had the cabs closed in at the back and open at the front; the side tanks extended beyond the front of the smokebox and stood out from the boiler just sufficiently for a man to walk round inside them. These engines were named after small animals and insects, but were always known as "Ezeltjes" (little asses)[7]. The other type, built by Breda, also had inside cylinders and disc wheels, but were enclosed above the footplate in an all-over cab, with a single large window opening either side, through which the crew had to climb, as there were no doorways. They were not named but the staff knew them by the grim title "Doodkisten" (Coffins).

Passenger Stock and Miscellaneous Items

The earlier Dutch steam tramways had very lightly built coaches with turtle-back roofs, obviously based on horse tramway practice if not actually converted from horse cars. Some of the earlier bogie cars had centre entrances. R. Stockvis en Zonen, Falcon's agent in Rotterdam was very active in importing Falcon and Brush cars, including some open platform bogie cars for Nijmegen, which were elaborately lined out and had the title on the rocker panel. Naturally, the Belgian controlled companies tended to use standard Nivelles cars, but the Zuider Stoomtramweg was equipped by Winterthur; its stock included two-wheeled luggage trailers and transporters (in 1880!) The use of the latter was the reason for the choice of the 3' 6" (1067mm) gauge, as it was then thought that a transporter with a standard gauge wagon would be unsteady on any lesser gauge. In later years, Dutch tramways showed a preference for solidly built grained teak bogie vehicles, many of which came from Allan of Rotterdam. The Breskens-Maldegem tramway had an elaborately decorated Royal Saloon on bogies. On the subject of liveries, it believed that the Dutch Central Railway had some financial connection with the London, Brighton & South Coast Railway, at all events, its locomotives were painted in the same yellow-ochre colour, even with green and red lining; its tram-engines were included in this livery! The Geldersche tramways painted their engines a very pleasant shade of apple green, but many others adopted a dark bluish shade. Maasbuurtspoorweg locomotives were black lined out in red, when seen by the writer in 1945.

Terminal stations were sometimes quite elaborate and that at Rosestraat, Rotterdam, with two tracks in a proper station and two more out in the street, where they were mixed up with some standard gauge industrial lines, was rather peculiar. The North Amsterdam terminus of the Noord Holland tramway was on the end of a jetty, so that passengers arriving by ferry from the city could step straight out of the boat on to a tram. Tickets issued varied considerably in size and the quantity of information they contained,[8] while fares were often shown in "Stuivers" (slang for 5 cents) and were still shown thus in the RTM timetable for 1952. It was not unusual to give the conductor a small tip.

Notes

1. The title "The Netherlands" was used at the request of the writer's Dutch advisers, since to them, Holland is but one Province of the whole country.

2. In Dutch and Flemish the letter "Y" is usually replaced by "IJ" and placed near the end of the alphabet, but is shown under "I" in the tables overleaf. The prefixes De, Den, 's and 't meaning "the", "of the" and "to the" do not affect the alphabetical order.

3. See "Locomotive Magazine" 15th August 1936, page 260, "The Holland Railway Company and its Locomotives" by L. Derens.

4. See "Locomotive Magazine" 15th June 1920, page 136, "The Dutch Rhenish Railway and its Locomotives" by L. Derens.

5. See "De Stoomlocomotiven der Nederlandsche Tramwegen", Ir.S. Overbosch, 1957, 2nd edition 1967.

6. See "Op de Rails", August 1967, Article on the Haarlem-Alkmaar Tramway.

7. See "The Holland Railway Company and its Locomotives" by L. Derens, in "Locomotive Magazine", 15th February 1935, page 51.

8. See "Dutch Stoomtramwegen" in "Locomotive Magazine" of 10th October 1903, page 216.

The last tram-loco built at Breda, was "Para" for the Paramaribo Tramway in Surinam, Central America. Shown here with two of their Borsig locos.

Photo: J. G. Todd.

152

Table 6 NETHERLANDS

1. ALKMAAR. (Hollandsche Ijzeren Spoorweg Maatschappij). "H.Y.S.M"
   This group was worked through the following subsidiaries:-
   (a). (Stoomtramweg Maatschappij Egmond-Alkmaar-Bergen).
   (b). (Noorderstoomtramweg Maatschappij).
   (c). (Stoomtramweg Maatschappij "West Friesland").
   (d). (Spoorweg Wieringen-Schagen).
   (e). (Spoorweg Maatschappij "de Zuider Kogge").

   (a). Egmond-Alkmaar-Koedijk-Bergen aan Zee, 19.6 km.
   (b). Koedijk-Warmenhuisen-Schagen, 27.9 km.
   (c). Schagen-Nibixwoud-Wognum-Hoorn, 25.3 km. (See No.82, to HYSM in 1909).
   (d). Nibixwoud-Van Ewijksluis, 15.2 km.
   (e). Hoorn-Veenhuizen-Grootebroek,18.9 km. (Partly replacing No.54).
   S.1898, C.1930/1955. (Bergen-Alkmaar last). Gauge. 1435.
   Locomotives. -   Part of HYSM's general stock. See No.52.
                     (Mainly railway locomotives used on these lines).

2. ALKMAAR. See Haarlem, No.44.

3. AMSTERDAM. (Stoomtram Maatschappij Amsterdam-Sloterdijk C.V.).
   Amsterdam(Willems Poort)-Sloterdijk, 2.5 km.
   S.1882, H.1889, E.1916, C.1951. Gauge. 1435.
   Locomotives.-   Nos.   1-2,   Winterthur 0-4-0, 307 & 306 of 1882.

   Names. -   1-Amsterdam, 2-Sloterdijk.

4. AMSTERDAM. (Noord Hollandsche Tramweg Maatschappij).
   From 1893 (Tweede Noord Hollandsche Tramweg Maatschappij).
   From 1932, part of N.Z.H., No.75.
   Amsterdam Noord-Zunderdorp-Edam,   21.5 km.
   Zunderdorp-Schouw-Purmerend-Alkmaar, 35.2 km. (Purmerend-Alkmaar C.1932).
   S.1888, E.1932, C.1956. Gauge. 1000.
   Locomotives.-   Nos.   1-2,   Breda 0-4-0 38-39 of 1887.
                           3-5,   Breda 0-4-0 51-53 of 1888.   "
                           6-7,   Breda 0-4-0 96-97 of 1893/94.   "
                           8-11,   Breda 0-4-0 108-111 of 1895.   "
                           12-13, Breda 0-4-0 114-115 of 1895.   "
                           14-16, Breda 0-4-0 214-216 of 1903.   "

   Names. -   1-Amsterdam, 2-Edam, 3-Monikkendam, 4-Buiksloot, 5-Broek in Waterland,
                   6-Purmerend, 7-De Rijp, 8-Beemster, 9-Schermerhorn, 10-Schermer,
                   11-Alkmaar, 12-Ilpendam, 13-Zunderdorp, 14-President Krüger,
                   15-President Steijn, 16-Generaal de Wet.

5. AMSTERDAM. (Gooische Stoomtram). Later (N.V. Gooische Tramweg Mij).
   Amsterdam(Weesperpoort)-Naarden-Laren, 27.5 km.
   Hakkelaarsbrug-Muiderberg,   1.0 km.
   Hilversum-Laren-Huizen,   10.7 km.
   Bussum-Naarden-Huizen,   6.3 km. (Owned by HYSM, No.52).
   S.1881, D.1925, C.1947. Gauge. 1435.
   Locomotives. - Nos.   1-8,   Henschel 0-4-0 1205-1208 & 1230-1233 of 1881.
                           9-16,   Henschel 0-4-0 1234 & 1250-1256 of 1881.   "
                   (II)   5,9,   Henschel 0-4-0 6213-6214 of 1902.   "
                   (II)   10,   Henschel 0-4-0 6479 of 1903.   "
                   (II)   7-8,   Henschel 0-4-0 6897-6898 of 1904.   "
                   (II)   1-2,   Werkspoor 0-4-0 192-193 of 1907 (Henschel type). "
                   (II)   13-14, Henschel 0-4-0 12189-12190 of 1913.   "
                   (II)   15,   Henschel 0-4-0 17737 of 1920.   "
                   (II)   16-18, Henschel 0-4-0 18774-18776 of 1921. (No.18 preserved). "

HYSM 229-230 acquired and 179 & 231 hired 1917.   See No.52.
NTM. 45,47 & 50 hired 1940-1949.   See No.57.

Steam Railcar. -   No.   1,   Henschel bogie car 8624 of 1908.

Note. -   This undertaking was on the point of closing in 1940, but steam working
          was kept on during the war, on a route Laren-Huizen-Naarden, with
          hired locomotives.   Taken over by No.71 in 1944.

6.   ANTWERP.   (Belgium). - See Bergen op Zoom, No.11.

7.   ARNHEM.   (Arnhemsche Tramweg Maatschappij).   See page 14 9 for details.
     Tests carried out with steam locomotives on an existing horse tramway.
     Buitensocietiet-Station-Velperplein, 2. 0 km.
     H.1880, S.1881 only, E.1911, C.1944 (war destruction).   Gauge. 1435.
     Locomotives. -   Merryweather 0-4-0 109 of 1881 from No.58.
                         Krauss 0-4-0 909 of 1881, later to No.81.
                         Hohenzollern 0-4-0 153 of 1880, from No.43.
                         Winterthur 0-4-0 203 or 204 of 1881 for No.81.

8.   ARNHEM.   (Betuwsche Stoomtramweg Maatschappij).   To No.20 in 1933.
     Arnhem-Elden-Elst-Lent (for Nijmegen), 16.1 km.
     Elden-Huissen-Bemmel-Lent,   17.7 km.
     Huissen-Doornenbrug,   7.2 km.
     Elst-Bemmel,   5.6 km.
     Bemmel-Pannerden,   10.2 km.
     S.1908, Part P.1924, GS.1933, C.1935.   Gauge. 1067.
     Locomotives. -   Nos.   1-6,   Breda 0-4-0 267-272 of 1908.
                              7-9,   Breda 0-4-0 273-275 of 1909.
                             10-11, Breda 0-4-0 276-277 of 1910.

     Name. -   1-Baron van der Feltz. (others not named).

9.   ARNHEM.   See Doetinchem, No.20 and Zeist, No.100.

10. ASSEN.   See Hoogeveen, No.53 and Leeuwaarden, No.57.

11. BERGEN OP ZOOM.   (Stoomtramweg Bergen op Zoom-Tholen).   See Belgium No. 3.
     Extended into Belgium in 1886, with new title:-
     (Stoomtramweg Maatschappij Antwerpen-Bergen op Zoom-Tholen).
     Worked by No.12, from 1934.
     Antwerpen(Merksem)-Ossendrecht-Bergen op Zoom-Tholen, 23.5 km.
     S.1882, C.(Dutch Section)1934.   Gauge. 1067.
     Locomotives. -   Nos.   1-2,   Winterthur 0-4-0 296-297 of 1882.
                              3-5,   Van Duyl 0-4-0 - of 1882, ex No.54 in 1887.
                             6-10,   Cockerill 0-4-0 1497-1501 of 1887/88(Belgium).
                               11,   Breda   0-4-0 54 of 1889. (Belgium).
                            12-15,   Breda   0-4-0 70 of 1889 & 80 of 1891.
                            14-15,   Thiriau   0-6-0 12 of 1901 & 91 of 1906. (SNCV type).
                            16-18,   Breda   0-4-0 212-213, 210 of 1903. (Intended for No.31)

     Note. -   The fleet was owned jointly with Belgium No.3, until 1894, when the
                      section in Belgium was taken over by the SNCV, with Locos Nos.6-11.

12. BRABANT.   (N.V. Brabantsche Buurtspoorwegen en Autobusdiensten). "B. B. A. "
     An amalgamation of Nos.11, 13, 14, 23, 24 & 49. 397 km in all.
     Acquired 78 locomotives from constituents, but added no new ones. Last
     tram line, Veghel-Oss, then goods only, closed in 1939.

154

13. BREDA. (Zuider Stoomtramweg Maatschappij). See No.12 above.
    Breda-Oosterhout-Geertruidenberg, 18.0 km.
    Oosterhout-Tilburg,   20.1 km.
    S.1880, D.1923, C.1934, Gauge. 1067
    Locomotives. - Nos. 1-3,   Winterthur 0-4-0 192-194 of 1880.   ⊔
                          4-6,   Winterthur 0-4-0 215, 222-223 of 1881.   "
                            7,   Breda 0-4-0 67 of 1889.   "
                            8,   Hanomag 0-4-0 3652 of 1901. (Henschel type).   "
                         9-10,   Hanomag 0-4-0 3991-3992 of 1902. ("   ").   "
                           11,   Hanomag 0-4-0 4241 of 1904. ("   ").   "
                        12-13,   Hanomag 0-4-0 5010-5011 of 1907. ("   ").   "
                        14-15,   Hanomag 0-4-0 5449-5450 of 1909. ("   ").   "

14. BREDA. (Zuid Nederlandsche Stoomtramweg Maatschappij). - See No.12.
    Breda-Rijsbergen-Wernhout(Belgian Frontier), 24.8 km. (Through running with SNCV).
    Breda-Steenbergen-Halsteren, ? km. (Connecting with No.11 & 81).
    Vaarkant-Leur,   1.0 km.⎫
    Gastelveer-Roosendaal,   6.4 km.⎬ Total - 96.4 km.
    Gastel-Willemstad,   ? km.⎭
    S.1890, C.1935. Gauge. 1067.
    Locomotives. - Nos. 1-5,   Tubize 0-6-0 787-791 of 1890 (like SNCV Class 2)   ⊔
                          6-8,   Tubize 0-6-0 885-557 of 1893 ("   "   )   "
                         9-10,   Tubize 0-6-0 1174-1175 of 1899("   4)   "
                           11,   Thiriau 0-6-0 18 of 1901.   ("   "   )   "
                        12-14,   Tubize 0-6-0 1464-1466 of 1906("   "   )   "
                           15,   Tubize 0-6-0 1562 of 1908.   ("   "   )   "
                           16,   Breda 0-4-0 211 of 1903, ex-No.31 in 1928.   "
                   "Moselle",   Hagans 0-4-0 ? of 1876 in 1890 ex-Contractor. ⌵   ⊔⌷

15. 's BOSCH. (Short name for 's Hertogenbosch. - See Nos.48, 49 & 50).

16. BRESKENS. (Stoomtram Maatschappij Breskens-Maldegem).
    The Maldegem-Ede section was in Belgium and another section although in the Netherlands
    was worked as an extension of a SNCV electric line.
    Breskens-Oostburg-Draaibrug-Ede-Maldegem, 28.5 km. (Part in Belgium).
    Draaibrug-Sluis-St. Anna ter Muiden(Frontier), 5.8 km. (Part E.1934).
    Oostburg-Cadzand, 3.0 km. ?
    Breskens-Cadzand-Retranchment-Sluis, 20.0 km.
    Retranchment-Belgian Frontier, 1.0 km. SNCV through running (steam).
    S.1887. Small Part E.1929/34, GS.1949, C.1951. Gauge. 1000.
    Locomotives. - Nos. 1-5,   Breda   0-4-0 29-33 of 1886/87.   ⊔
                          6-7,   Krauss   0-4-0 1300-1301 of 1883, ex-No.54. "
                            8,   Boussu   0-6-0 65 of 1896, ex SNCV (No.208). "
                         9-11,   Breda   0-4-0 265-266 of 1908 & 287 of 1911. "
                        12-13,   Hanomag   0-6-0 6741-6742 of 1912.   "
                           14,   Carels   0-6-0 248 of 1886, Ex-SNCV (No.22). "
                        15-16,   Breda   0-4-0 190-191 of 1901, Ex-No.44.   "
                        17-21,   Tubize   0-6-0 1988-1992 of 1924. (as SNCV C1.18). "
                    (II) 1 & 5, Haine St.Pierre 0-6-0 490-491 of 1895, ex-44. ⌵   "

    Note. -   SNCV No.207, Boussu 0-6-0 64 of 1896, hired 1897-1901.   ⊔
                 No.39, Tubize 0-6-0 1897 of 1919 hired from Contractor in 1945.   ⊔⌷

    Names. -   1-Breskens, 2-Schoondijke, 3-Oostburg, 4-Aardenburg, 5-Sluis, 6-Draaibrug,
                 7-Maldegem, 8-not named, 9-Groede, 10-Eede, 11-Cadsandria,
                 12-Zuidzande, 13-Cadzand, 14-21-not named.

17. DEDEMSVAART. (Dedemsvaartsche Stoomtramweg Maatschappij).
    Worked No.66. Amalgamated with No.53 in 1936.
    Zwolle-Balkbrug-Dedemsvaart, 29.8 km.
    Dedemsvaart-Lutten-Slagharen-Nieuw Amsterdam-Ter Apel, 66.7 km.
    Lutten-Harderberg, 6.0 km.

Slagharen-Hoogeveen, 16.2 km.
Amsterdamsch Veld-Griendsveen, 7.3 km. (Goods only).
S.1886, Gs.1947, C.1948. Gauge. 1067.

Locomotives. - Nos.   1-4,   Breda 0-4-0   25-28 of 1886.
                         5-7,   Breda 0-4-0   101, 100, 99 of 1894.
                         8-10, Breda 0-4-0   134-136 of 1896/97.
                         11,   Breda 0-4-0   161 of 1899.
                         12,   Breda 0-4-0   181 of 1900
                         13-14, Breda 0-4-0   112-113 of 1895/99. (Exhibition).
                         15-16, Breda 0-4-0   192-193 of 1902.
                         17-18, Breda 0-4-0   217-218 of 1903.
                         19-20, Breda 0-4-0   224-225 of 1904.
                         21-22, Breda 0-4-0   230-231 of 1905.
                         23-25, Breda 0-4-0   234-236 of 1905.
                         26-27, Breda 0-4-0   237 of 1905 & 242 of 1906.
                         28,   Breda 0-4-0   247 of 1907.
                         29-30, Breda 0-4-0   288-289 of 1911.
                         31,   Breda 0-4-0   294 of 1912.
                         101-105, Henschel 0-4-0   12887-12891 of 1914.

Names. -   1-Jhr.Junius van Hemert, 2-Baron van Dedem, 3-Overijssel,
                4-Dedemsvaart, 5-Zwolle, 6-Coevorden, 7-Heemse Hardenberg,
                8-Avereest, 9-de Krim, 10-Drenthe, 11-Nieuw Amsterdam,
                12-Amsterdamsche Veld, 13-Erica, 14-Emmen, 15-Balkbrug,
                16-Lutten, 17-Slagharen, 18-Klazienaveen, 19-Hoogeveen,
                20-Hollandsche Veld, 21-Jhr.Junius van Hemert (II),
                22-Baron van Dedem (II), 23-Overijssel, 24-Ter Apel,
                25-Groningen (or De Schere ?), 26-Emmer Compascuum,
                27-Dedemsvaart (II), 28-Vlagtwedde, 29-Landbouw, 30-Nyverheid,
                31-Handel, 101-105 not named.

18.   DELFT. See 's Gravenhage, No.34.

19.   DEVENTER. (Geldersch Overijsselsche Stoomtram Maatschappij).
      Amalgamated with No.20 in 1934.
      Deventer-Epse-Borculo, 32.8 km.
      (Deventer-Epse mixed gauge with No.101 until 1934).
      S.1885, GS.1931, C.1945. Gauge. 1067 (Reduced to 750 in 1934).

Locomotives. - Nos.   1-5,   Breda   0-4-0   16-20 of 1885.
                        6,   Breda   0-4-0   35 of 1887. (Sold 1894 to No.86).
                (II)   6,   Henschel 0-4-0   6207 of 1902.
                        7,   Henschel 0-4-0   6298 of 1903.
                        8,   Henschel 0-4-0   6962 of 1905.
                        9-11, Henschel 0-4-0   18771-18773 of 1921.
                        12,   Henschel 0-4-0   20655 of 1926.

Names. -   1-Deventer, 2-Laren, 3-Lochem, 4-Barchem, 5-Borculo,
                6-(Both)Gorssel, 7-Gelderland, 8-Overijssel, 9-Deventer,
                10-Lochem, 11-Borculo, 12-Laren.

20.   DOETINCHEM. (Geldersche Stoomtramweg Maatschappij).
      From 1929 (Geldersche Tramweg Maatschappij).
      which acquired Nos. 8, 19, 59, 101 & 102 in 1934, with their locomotives.
      One further locomotive was acquired.
      Arnhem-Doetinchem-Genderingen-Isselburg, 56.0 km. (last section in Germany).
      S.1881, P.1926, GS.1949, C.1957. Gauge. 750.
      (Jubilee Passenger service Doesburg-Doetinchem, worked 1956-1957).

Locomotives. - Un-numbered   Hohenzollern 0-4-0   163-166 of 1881.
                Un-numbered   Hohenzollern 0-4-0   194-195 of 1882.
                No.   7,   Hohenzollern 0-4-0   273 of 1883.
                       8-9,   Breda   0-4-0   36-37 of 1887.
                       10-11, Breda   0-4-0   71 of 1890 & 79 of 1891.
                       12-13, Breda   0-4-0   116 of 1895 and 182 of 1900.

	6,	Hohenzollern	0-4-0	1499 of 1901. (Breda type).	
5 & 14,		Hohenzollern	0-4-0	1616-1617 of 1902 "	"
	15,	Hohenzollern	0-4-0	2242 of 1907.	"	"
	3-4,	Hohenzollern	0-4-0	2601-2602 of 1909 "	"
	2,	Hohenzollern	0-4-0	2989 of 1912. "	"
	1,	Orenstein & Koppel	0-4-0	6044 of 1913.	
	18,	Vulcan 0-4-0 1484 of 1895 ∵ in 1916.			
(II)	18-20,	Orenstein & Koppel	0-4-0	9251, 7915, 9254 of 1919.	"
	16-17,	Orenstein & Koppel	0-8-0	6381-6382 of 1913.	"
	23,	Orenstein & Koppel	0-8-0	10556 of 1923.	"
	26,	Orenstein & Koppel	0-8-0	12000 of 1930.	"
	21-22,	Breda 0-4-0, 255 & 257 of 1907/08. ex-No.59. ∵			
	(24-25	were diesel locos).			
	-	Jung 0-4-0 5503 of 1933 in 1941 ∵			

Names. -
-Doetinchem, -Keppel, -Doesburgh, -Dieren, -Drempt, -Terborgh.
1-Tekkel, 2-Doetinchem, 3-Terborgh, 4-Drempt, 5-Keppel,
6-Dieren, 7-Wisch, 8-de Steeg, 9-Ellecom, 10-Gendringen,
11-Velp, 12-Ulft, 13-Silvolde, 14-Anholt, 15-Rheden, 16-Isselburg,
17-Doesburgh, 18(both)Roskam, 19-Gaanderen, 20-De Pol,
21-Middachten, 22-Groot Zande, 23-G. H. van Hengel,
24-H. M. Erdbrink, 25-G. A. van Everindingen, 26-Mr. J. Coops.

Note. -
Locomotives from No.59 took Numbers 401-409 when acquired.
"   "   No.101   "   "   601-616   "   "
in the same order as their old numbers. Those from Nos. 8, 9 and
102 were not retained long enough to have new numbers.

21. DRENTHE. See Hoogeveen, No.53.

22. EDAM. (Hollandsche Ijzeren Spoorweg Maatschappij).
From 1921 (N.V. Nederlandsche Spoorwegen).
Kwadijk-Edam-Volendam, 7.4 km.
S.1906, C.1933. Gauge. 1435 (see Note below).
(Edam-Volendam mixed gauge 1932-33, then electrified as an extension of No.4).
Locomotives. -   Part of HYSM general stock, See No.52. (Three of 1-5 of 103 ran in 1931).

23. EINDHOVEN. (Tramweg Maatschappij Eindhoven-Geldrop).
Eindhoven-Geldrop-Helmond-Asten, 35.3 km.
(Worked by No.24 from 1908 and taken over in 1922. There was a branch line
Geldrop-Heeze which was mainly horse worked).
H.1888, S.1904, C.1935. Gauge. 1067.
Locomotives. -   Nos. 13-16,   Breda 0-4-0   220-223 of 1904.
                      17-18,   Breda 0-4-0   245-246 of 1906.

Names. -
13-Geldrop, 14-Mierlo, 15-Asten, 16-Helmond, 17-18 not named.
Locomotives numbered in series with No.24.

24. EINDHOVEN. (Tramweg Maatschappij "De Meyerij").
Worked No.50 from the outset and took it over in 1906.
Worked No.23 from 1908 and took it over in 1922.
All the above taken over by No.12 in 1934.
Eindhoven-Reusel(Belgian Frontier), 29.5 km. (no through running with SNCV).
Eindhoven-Sint Oedenrode-Veghel, 24.7 km. (connecting with No.50).
S.1897, D.1923, C.1935. Gauge. 1067.
Locomotives. -   Nos.   1-6,   Breda   0-4-0   126-131 of 1896.
                       7-12,   Breda   0-4-0   155-160 of 1898.
                      13-18,   - See No.23 above.
                         19,   Maffei   0-4-0   4131 of 1920.
                      20-23,   Henschel 0-4-0   6300-6303 of 1903.
                               (Acquired two each from Nos. 53 & 97. Intended
                               for contractor who was to have built No.31).

Names. -   1-Eindhoven, 2-St.Oedenrode, 3-Veghel, 4-Noord Brabant, 5-Veldhoven,
6-Bladel, 7-Schijndel, 8-St.Michielsgestel, 9-Vught, 10-J.F.Pompen van
Sterksel 11-'s Hertogenbosch, 12-J.T.Smits van Oijen, 19-23 not named.

25.   EDE. (Nederlandsche Rijnspoorweg Maatschappij).
From 1890 (Maatschappij tot Exploitatie van Staatspoorwegen). "SS"
From 1921 (N.V. Nederlandsche Spoorwegen). "NS"
Ede-Wageningen, 7.2 km.
S.1882, GS.1937, GD.1956 ?,   Still operating.   Gauge. 1435.
Locomotives. -   At first various Merryweathers from No.35.
Later part of SS general tramway stock. See No.35.

26.   ENKHUIZEN. See Hoorn, No.54 (See also No.1).

27.   FLUSHING. English name for Vlissingen.   See No.68 also No.67.

28.   GELDERLAND. See Doetinchem, No.20.

29.   GOES. (Spoorweg Maatschappij Zuid Beveland).
Taken over in 1951 by (Nederlandsche Spoorwegen).
Goes-Hoedekenskerke-'s Heer Ardenkerke, 37.8 km.
Goes-Wemeldinge,   8.2 km.
Goes-Wolphaartsdijkse veer,   10.2 km.
P.1927, S.1927, GS.1949, GD. ? Still operating.   Gauge. 1435.
Locomotives. -   Hired from Nederlandsche Spoorwegen.
(after brief trials with petrol cars).

30.   't GOOI. (Gooische Stoomtram). - See Amsterdam, No.5.

31.   GOUDA. (Ijsel Stoomtramweg Maatschappij).   See also Nos.37, 80 & 87.
Bankrupt 1891, then (Maatschappij tot Exploitatie van Tramwegen). "M.E.T."
Gouda-Oudwater, 13.6 km.
Gouda-Schoonhoven, (Not completed as tramway - later railway).
(The Schoonhoven line was built as a standard gauge railway with S.S. Merryweather
tram-engines, working on it). (See No.35).
S.1883, C.1907. Gauge. 1067.
Locomotives. -   Nos.   8-11,   Ij.S.M. General stock, See No.37.
21-24,   Breda 0-4-0 210-213 of 1903 (Not delivered
See Nos. 11 & 14. For locomotives intended for
the contractors who were to build the Schoonhoven
line, see No.24).

32.   GOUDA. (Tramweg Onderneming Gouda-Bodegraven).
Later (Stoomtramweg Maatschappij "Gouda"). (Later "ALGEMEENE Tramweg
Maatschappij). Finally "M.E.T." See No.31.
Gouda-Bodegraven, 8.8 km.
S.1882, H.1892, C.1917. Gauge. 750.
Locomotives. -   Nos.   1-2,   Winterthur 2-2-0   253-254 of 1881.
3.   Hagans 0-4-0, 146 of 1883. "Gouda".

33.   De "GRAAFSCHAP". - See Zutphen, No.102.

34.   's GRAVENHAGE. (The Hague). Société Anonyme des Tramways de la Haye).
Later (Haagsche Tramweg Maatechappij).
's Gravenhage-Delft, 8.5 km.
H.1866, S.1887, E.1924, Still operating. Gauge. 1435.

Locomotives. -	Trials		Carels 0-4-0	87 of 1878 (Winterthur type).	⏚
	Nos.	1-5,	Henschel 0-4-0	1864-1866,2419,2521 of 1887.	"
		6,	Henschel 0-4-0	3347 of 1890.	"
		7-8,	Breda 0-4-0	226-227 of 1904. No.8 preserved at Breda	"
		9-10,	Breda 0-4-0	243-244 of 1906.	"
		11-12.	Breda 0-4-0	278-279 of 1909.	"

| Names. - | 1-'s Gravenhage, 2-Rijswijk, 3-Reineveld, 4-Delft, 5-Vrijbaan, 6-Zuid Holland, 7-Eend, 8-Ooievaar, 9-Gans, 10-Snip, 11-R.v.Hasselt, 12-Kieviet. |

35. 's GRAVENHAGE.   (The Hague) (Nederlandsche Rhijnspoorweg Maatschappij).
From 1890 (Maatschappij tot Expolitatie van Staatspoorwegen). From 1921
(N.V. Nederlandsche Spoorwegen).
S.1879, E.1924 (by No.75), C.1957. Gauge. 1435.
's Gravenhage (SS.Stn)-Scheveningen (Bad Paleis) ? km.

Locomotives. -	No.	1,	Merryweather 0-4-0	82 of 1878.	⏚
		2-7,	Merryweather 0-4-0	88-90,91,93,92 of 1899.	"
		8-12,	Merryweather 0-4-0	96-100 of 1880.	"
		13-17,	Merryweather 0-4-0	115-119 of 1881.	"
		18-19,	Merryweather 0-4-0	173-174 of 1892.	"

36. 's GRAVENHAGE.   (The Hague) (Hollandsche Ijzeren Spoorweg Maatschappij). See No.52.
's Gravenhage(Station HYSM)-Scheveningen(Strand), 7.8 km.
Laan van Meerdervoort-Anna Paulonastreet (branch), 1.7 km.
S.1886, C.1926, reopened E.1927, Still operating. Gauge. 1435.
Locomotives. -   Part of HYSM general stock, See No.52.   Particularly Nos.201-214 & 231 ⏚

37. 's GRAVENHAGE.   (The Hague) (IJsel Stoomtramweg Maatschappij). Bankrupt 1891.
Taken over by (Maatschappij tot Exploitatie van Tramwegen). "M.E.T."
See also Nos.31,80 & 87.   Taken over by No.75 in 1924.
's Gravenhage- Voorburg- Voorschoten- Leiden, 18.0 km.
Voorschoten-Wassenaar,   3.8 km.
S.1882, E.1924, C.1962. Gauge. 1067. (to 1435 on electrification).

Locomotives. -	Nos.	1-7,	Hohenzollern 2-2-0	216-222 of 1882/83.	⏚
		8-10,	Hohenzollern 2-2-0	225-227 of 1883.	"
		11-12,	Hohenzollern 2-2-0	229-230 of 1884.	"
		13-17,	Hohenzollern 2-2-0	231 & 235-238 of 1884.	"
		18,	Hohenzollern 2-2-0	232 of 1885.	"
	(II)	5 & 15,	Hohenzollern 0-4-0	635-636 of 1892 ex-Germany No.12. ⁚ "
	(II)	12.	Hohenzollern 2-2-0	639 of 1891.	"

Note. -   Locos Nos.1-4, 13, 14 & 18 used on this line, rest on Nos.31, 80 & 87.

38. 's GRAVENHAGE.   (The Hague), (Westlandsche Stoomtramweg Maatschappij).
Worked by No.52 until 1885, then with own stock.
's Gravenhage-Loosduinen-Poeldijk-Maaslandsche Dam.-Maasluis. 24.0 km.
Poeldijk-Monster-'s Gravenzande-Hoek van Holland.   11.0 km.
Maaslandsche Dam-Delft (connecting with railway).   9.9 km.
Loosduinen-Kijkduin, (summer service only).   2.0 km.
S.1882, D.(GS).1923, GD.1956, C.1967. Gauge. 1435. (Steam passenger
service reinstated 1942-1943).

Locomotives. -   Until 1885, part of HYSM general stock, See No.52.

Then. -	Nos.	1-5,	Winterthur	0-4-0	410-414 of 1885.	⏚
		6-7,	Winterthur	0-4-0	307,306 of 1882, ex-No.3.	"
	(II)	6-7,	Breda	0-4-0	95 of 1893 & 180 of 1900.	"
		8-9,	Hohenzollern	0-4-0	537-538 of 1890.	"
		10-14,	Breda	0-4-0	200-204 of 1903.	"
		15-20,	Hohenzollern	0-4-0	2808-2813 of 1911 (Verhoop design).
		21-22,	Hohenzollern	0-4-0	4084-4085 of 1921.	彐
		23,	Orenstein & Koppel	0-4-0	8319 of 1918 ⁚ ex-industry.	彐
		24-25.	Orenstein & Koppel	0-4-0	12282-12283 of 1931.	"

31,	Hanomag	0-4-0	10209 of 1925, ex-No.79. ∵ 🝧
168.	Borsig	0-4-0	4107 of 1885, hired from No.52.🝧

Names. -   Nos.1-5 all named Westland, 6-(Amsterdam), 7-(Sloterdijk),
(II)6-'s Gravenhage, (II)7-Loosduinen, 8-Naaldwijk, 9-'s Gravenzande,
10-Phoenix, 11-Appolo, 12-Odin, 13-Laga, 14-Minerva, 15-Dr.G.van Diesen,
16-F.W.Conrad, 17-N.Th.Michaelis, 18-J.L.Cluysenaer, 19-A.K.P.F.R.
van Hasselt, 20-Dr.C.Lely, 21-Jhr.Verspijck, 22-P.R.van de Kasteele,
23-H.J.H.Modderman, 24-25 & 31 not named. 168-Tor.

Note. -   A works photograph exists of one of the Nos.15-20 class with the name plate
"Westland". No.23 is now preserved in working order at Hoorn.

39.   GROENLO. (Stoomtramweg Maatschappij Lichtenvoorde-Groenlo).
Worked by (Hollandsche Ijzeren Spoorweg Maatschappij).
From 1915 ("Groenlosche Tram")
Groenlo-Lichtenvoorde Station, 4.0 km. (Connecting with No.59).
(Originally worked as a tramway branch line of the HYSM, but closed in 1911.
It was reopened by local interests in 1915 and worked for a short time with an
articulated petrol railcar).
S.1883, C.1911, P.1915, H.1917, C.1922. Gauge. 1435.
Locomotives. -   Part of HYSM general stock - See No.52.

40.   GRONINGEN. (Eerste Groninger Tramweg Maatschappij).
(Experiments with a light steam locomotive on a very long horse tramway).
Zuidbroek-Veendam-Stadskanaal-Ter Apel, ? km.) 49.9 km.
Veendam-Pekela,   ? km.)
H.1880, S.1884 only, C.1923. Gauge. 1435.
Locomotive. -   Krauss 0-4-0. 864 of 1881. (Hired from manufacturer).   🝧

41.   GRONINGEN. (Stoomtramweg Maatschappij "Oostelijk Groningen").
See Winschoten - No.97.

42.   HAARLEM. (Haarlemsche Tramweg Maatschappij).
(Experiments with a light steam locomotive on the urban horse tramway).
Haarlem Station-Dreef, 2.3 km.
H.1878, S.1878 only, C.1913, Gauge. 1435.
Locomotives. -   Merryweather 0-4-0   ? of 1878 (Hired from manufacturer).   🝧

43.   HAARLEM. (Noord-Zuid Hollandsche Stoomtramweg Maatschappij).   "NzH".
Various minor changes in title, see No.75 for details.
Controlled by HYSM from 1909.
Haarlem-Hillegom-Leiden, 28.0 km.
S.1881, E.1932, C.1949. Gauge. 1435.
Locomotives. -   Nos.   1-6,   Hohenzollern 0-4-0   153-158 of 1880.   🝧
                          7,   Hohenzollern 0-4-0   105 of 1878 (Stock).   "
                        8-9,   Winterthur   0-4-0   346-347 of 1883.   "
                         10,   Hohenzollern 0-4-0   1603 of 1902.   "

Names. -   1-Haarlem, 2-Leiden, 3-Hillegom, 4-Heemstede, 5-Lisse
6-Sassenheim, 7-Bennebroek, 8-Zuid Holland, 9-Noord Holland,
10-Oestgeest.

44.   HAARLEM. (Société Anonyme Belge de Tramways Néerlandais, Haarlem et Extensions).
Controlled by HYSM from 1902.
Worked by (Maatschappij tot Exploitatie van Tramwegen), and by NzH, No.43 from 1909.
Haarlem-Beverwijk-Alkmaar, 30.0 km.
S.1895, C.1924. Gauge. 1000.
Locomotives. -   Nos.   I-II,   Haine St.Pierre 0-6-0   490-491 of 1895.   🝧
                        III-IV,   Haine St.Pierre 0-4-0   517-518 of 1895.   "
                            V.   Haine St.Pierre 0-6-0   492 of 1895 (Sold).   "

```
                VI-VII,   Haine St.Pierre 0-4-0  526-527 of 1886.
                7-8,      Breda 0-4-0, 190-191 of 1901
                9.        Hohenzollern 0-4-0  639 of 1891 ex-No.37.
```

Note. -   Nos. I, II & V were of the SNCV Class 1 type. No.V was found to be
                surplus to requirements and sold to the SNCV, becoming their No.248.
                Nos.VI & VII were then renumbered V & VI. They and Nos.III-IV were
                four-coupled versions of the SNCV type, and had to be light enough to
                cross over on the North Sea Canal Ferry at VELSEN.

45. HANSWEERT. (Stoomtramweg Hansweert-Vlake). Owned by the (Provinciale
     Stoombootdienst op de Westerschelde).
     Vlake Station-Hansweert, 3.3 km.
     (Ferry Connection Hansweert-Walsoorden with No.55).
     S.1913, C.1933. Gauge. 750.
     Locomotives. -   Nos.   1-2,   Decauville 0-4-0   842-843 of 1912.

46. HEERLEN. (Limburgsche Electrische Spoorweg Maatschappij).
     Worked a line belonging to the Staatsmijmem(State Mines)
     with steam locomotives. Handed over to No.79 in 1922.
     Heerlen-Hoensbroek(Mijn Emma), 5.5 km.
     S.1918, E.1923, C.1954. Gauge. 1435.
     (Electrified as part of a through route Sittard-Kerkrade/de Locht).
     Locomotives. -   No.   1,   Orenstein & Koppel 0-4-0   2706 of 1907.
                            10-12, Winterthur 0-4-0 412-413 of 1885 ex-No.38.
                            13-15, Breda 0-4-0, 22-24 of 1886 ex-No.52. ("Doodkisten").
                            18,   Karlsruhe 0-4-0   942 of 1877.

47. Den HELDER. ("Tram Helder-Huisduinen" owned by Mijnheer J.Pot).
     Den Helder-Huisduinen, 4.2 km. (Summer operation only).
     S.1896, C.1907. Reopened S.1911, C.1917. Gauge. 700.
     Locomotives. -   Nos.   1-2,   Breda 0-4-0   121-122 of 1896.
                                    (Very small type, later rebuilt with normal boilers).
                            3,   Maffei, 0-4-0   3837 of 1913.

48. 's HERTOGENBOSCH. (S.A. "Vicinaux Hollandais") Known in the Netherlands as
     (Hollandsche Buurtspoorwegen).
     Taken over by No.12 in 1935.
     's Hertogenbosch-Drunen-Waalwijk, 18.0 km.
     Tilburg-Waalwijk, 22.0 km. (No.86 re-opened in 1898).
     Tilburg-Esbeek(Belgian Frontier), 19.8 km. (Connecting with SNCV).
     Drunen-Heusden, ? km.
     S.1896, C.1938. Gauge. 1067.
     Locomotives. -   Nos.   1-5,   Winterthur 0-4-0 212-214 of 1881)
                                                        226,292 of 1882) ex-No.86.
                              6,   Breda 0-4-0 35 of 1887, ex-No.19 in 1894.
                      (II) 3,6,12 & 5, Cockerill 0-6-0 1960-1963 of 1896.
                              7-8,   Hanomag 0-4-0 2630 & 2748 of 1895.
                              9-11,   Tubize 0-6-0 1167-1169 of 1899.
                      (II)   4 & 13. Haine St.Pierre 0-6-0 1376-1377 of 1922.

Note. -   Nos.(II) 3,6,12 & 5 were as the SNCV Class 2. They were originally
                un-numbered. Nos.9-11 and 4 & 13 were more enclosed than SNCV
                locomotives with cab doors etc., See Note on "Mobile Chests of Drawers"
                in Chapter I.

49. 's HERTOGENBOSCH. (Stoomtramweg Maatschappij 's Bosch-Helmond).
     Took over No.89 in 1899 but went bankrupt in 1918 and a new company was formed:-
     ("Stoomtram 's Hertogenbosch-Helmond-Veghel-Oss).
     This was taken over by No.12 in 1934.
     's Hertogenbosch-Veghel-Helmond, 52.0 km.
```
```

's Hertogenbosch-Vught, 6.5 km. (Later sold and horse operated).
Veghel-Oss, 15.1 km. (ex-No.89).
S.1881, C & reopened 1918, C.1939. Gauge. 1067.

Locomotives. -   Nos.   1-2,   Henschel 0-4-0 1287-1288 of 1881.　　　　　　🔔
               3,   Henschel 0-4-0 1485 of 1882.　　　　　　　　　"
          4-10,   Henschel 0-4-0 1501-1507 of 1883.　　　　　"
       (II)   8,   Breda 0-4-0 135 of 1896, ex-No.17 in 1928. ❖ "
         11-12,   Hohenzollern 2-2-0 234, 233 of 1885. ex-No.89. ❖ "
         13-14,   Hohenzollern 2-2-0 239-240 of 1884. ex-No.89. ❖ "
      (II)   12-13,   Linke Hofmann 0-4-0 2715 & 2467 of 1922.　　　"
   (II)11,14,15,   Breda 0-4-0 270, 272. 274 of 1908/09. ex-No.8 ❖ "

Names. -   1-'s Bosch, 2-Vught, 3-Helmond, 4-Berlicum, 5-Heeswijk,
           6-Dinther, 7-Veghel, 8-Erp, 9-Gemert, 10-Beek, (II)8-Erp,
           11-Uden, 12-Veghel, 13-Oss, 14-Nistelrode, (II)12-Heesch,
           (II)13-Oss, (II)11-Uden, (II)14-Nistelrode, 15-Rosmalen.

50.   's HERTOGENBOSCH.   (Tramweg Maatschappij Sint Oedenrode-'s Hertogenbosch).
Worked by No.24 from outset.
St.Oedenrode-St.Michielsgestel-'s Hertogenbosch, 26.1 km. (Connecting with No.24).
St.Michielsgestel-Vught, 4.0 km. (Connecting with No.49).
6.1898, Taken over by No.24 in 1906. Gauge. 1067.
Locomotives. -   Supplied by No.24. (Nos. 7-10 owned by No.50).

51.   HILVERSUM.   See Gooische Stoomtram, No.5.

52.   HOLLANDSCHE IJZEREN SPOORWEG MAATSCHAPPIJ.   Known as "HYSM".
A main line railway company, which controlled and operated the following
steam tramways:- Nos. 1,5,22,36,39,43,58,77 and 82. It owned a combined
fleet of tram-engines which were moved from one line to another and small railway
locomotives were also used. Gauge. 1435.

Tramway Locomotives.
          Nos.201-206,   Carels 0-4-0 181-186 of 1882.　　　　　　🔔
             207-208,   Carels 0-4-0 209-210 of 1883.　　　　　　　"
             209-210,   HYSM Works 0-4-0 1-2 of 1883. (Carels design). "
             211-214,   Breda 0-4-0 1-4 of 1883   (Carels design). "
             215-218,   Merryweather 0-4-0 109-112 of 1881, ex-No.58. ❖ "
               219,   Merryweather 0-4-0 131 of 1882, ex-No.58. ❖ "
               220,   Carels 0-4-0 211 of 1883.　　　　　　　　　　"
             221-224,   Breda 0-4-0 8,9,11,12 of 1884. (Carels type). "
             225-228,   Breda 0-4-0 21-24 of 1885. "Doodkisten".　"
             229-231,   Breda 0-4-0 41-43 of 1888. "Doodkisten".　"
             136-143,   Borsig 0-4-0 3929-3936 of 1883. "Ezeltjes". 🔔
             160-171,   Borsig 0-4-0 4101-4112 of 1885.　　　"　　"
             172-176,   Borsig 0-4-0 4214-4218 of 1886/87. "　　"
             177-183,   Borsig 0-4-0 4227-4233 of 1887.　　　"　　"
             194-198,   Borsig 0-4-0 4248-4252 of 1888.　　　"　　"
             199-203,   Borsig 0-4-0 4264-4268 of 1889.　　　"　　"
           1061-1063,   Breda 0-4-0 152-154 of 1898, ex-No.82. ❖　🔔

Names of "Ezeltjes":-
          136-Casuaris, 137-Duif, 138-Eend, 139-Faisant, 140-Gier, 141-Hond,
          142-Ibis, 143-Jakhals, 160-Kapel, 161-Leeuwerik, 162-Muis,
          163-Nachtegaal, 164-Otter, 165-Papegaai, 166-Raaf, 167-Snip,
          168-Tor, 169-Uil, 170-Valk, 171-Wachtel, 172-IJsbeer, 173-Zwaluw,
          174-Aap, 175-Baviaan, 176-Colibri, 177-Doffer, 178-Ezel, 179-Frel,
          180-Gans, 181-Haas, 182-Isegrim, 183-Kraai, 194-Lepelaar,195-Musch,
          196-Neuschoor, 197-Os, 198-Patrijs, 199-Reiger, 200-Sijsje, 201-Tortel,
          202-Vink, 203-Wesp.

          Nos.136-171 were slightly smaller than the others and had Grondana
          couplings as well as side buffers and screw couplings.

In addition to the above, the HYSM used ordinary 0-4-0 and 0-6-0 tank engines from its railways, on the tramways. After it was absorbed in Nederlandsche Spoorwegen in 1921, small locomotives from other railways were used as well.

53. HOOGEVEEN. (Eerste Drentsche Stoomtramweg Maatschappij).
Amalgamated with No.17 in 1936.

Hoogeveen-Oosterhesselen-Erm-Emmen-Ter Apel,	km.)	
Erm-Nieuw Amsterdam,	km.)	110.0 km.
Assen-Schoonoord-Oosterhesselen-Coevorden,	km.)	

S.1903, GS.1938, C.1947. Gauge. 1067.
Note. -   Passenger service reinstated in 1940 for duration of war.

Locomotives. -

Nos.	1-5,	Breda	0-4-0	205-209 of 1903.
	6-8,	Breda	0-4-0	282-284 of 1909.
	9-10,	Breda	0-4-0	285-286 of 1910.
	11-12,	Henschel	0-4-0	6300-6301 of 1903. ex-No.31.
	13-17,	Hohenzollern	0-4-0	4352-4356 of 1923.

Names. -   1-Hoogeveen, 2-Sleen, 3-Oosterhesselen, 4-Nieuw Amsterdam, 5-Drenthe, 6-J.E.Scholten, 7-J.Blom, 8-Emmen, 9-Ter Apel, 10-Groningen, Nos.11-17 not named.

54. HOORN. (West Friesche Tramweg Maatschappij). (See also No.1(e)).

Hoorn-Nadorst,	km.)	6.0 km.
Grootebroek-Enkhuizen,	km.)	

(Steam working only on end sections of what was in effect a long through route Hoorn-Nadorst-Grootebroek-Enkhuizen, 18.9 km.)
S.1883, C.1884, H.1887, C.1918. Gauge. 1000.
Locomotives. -

Nos.	1-5,	van Duyl	0-4-0	(fireless) ? - ? of 1882.
	6-7,	Krauss	0-4-0	1300-1301 of 1883.

55. HULST. (Stoomtram-Hulst-Walsoorden).
Worked by No.84 from 1918 and taken over in 1944.
Hulst-Walsoorden, 13.6 km.
Kloosterzande-Perkpolderhaven, 1.9 km. (Built by State in 1940).
S.1902, C.1949. Gauge. 1000.
Locomotives. -   Nos. 1-3,   Henschel 0-6-0 6324-6326 of 1902. (Tubize type).

56. IJZENDIJKE. (IJzendijksche Stoomtramweg Maatschappij).
Taken over by No.84 in 1912.
Schoondijke-IJzendijke-Veldzicht(Belgian Frontier), 11.0 km.
(Through running over Belgian SNCV to Eekloo 19.0 km).
S.1891, C.1949. Gauge. 1000.
Locomotives. -

Nos.	1-2,	Breda	0-4-0	73-74 of 1890.
	3,	Jung	0-4-0	322 of 1897.

Names. -   1-Luctor et Emergo, 2-IJzendijke, 3-Burgemeester de Vos.

57. LEEUWARDEN. (Nederlandsche Tramweg Maatschappij).

Leeuwarden-St.Jacobaparochie,	16.9 km.	
Heerenveen-Joure-Arum-Harlingen,	51.5 km.	
Joure-Lemmer,	15.7 km.	
Arum-Franeker-Marssum,	20.8 km.	
Heerenveen-Gorredijk-Drachten-Groningen,	67.5 km.	
Gorredijk-Oosterwolde-Assen,	? km.	(See No.53).
Oosterwolde-Steenwijk,	? km.	
Meppel-Smilde,	32.8 km.	(See No.66).
Drachten-Dokkum-Veenwouden,	10.2 km.	(Horse worked).

(Between 1913 & 1947, NTM Trams worked over the railway lines from Leeuwarden to Heerenveen, Leeuwarden-Sneek and between Leeuwarden-Veenwouden on the Leeuwarden-Drachten line. Also the trams terminated on railway track in Groningen Station).

H.1880, S.1882, GS.1949, GD.1951. Still occasional use. Gauge. 1435.
(Some goods traffic still worked with main-line Diesel locos).
Locomotives. -   Nos.   1-10,   Henschel 0-4-0 1289-1298 of 1881.
                          11-14,   Henschel 0-4-0 1508-1511 of 1883.
                             15,   Henschel 0-4-0 1512 of 1884.
                          16-18,   Henschel 0-4-0 4995-4997 of 1898.
                          19-21,   Henschel 0-4-0 5391-5393 of 1900.
                          22-23,   Henschel 0-4-0 1230-1234 of 1881) ex-No.5. ⁘
                          24-25,   Henschel 0-4-0 1250,1256 of 1881)
                          26-28,   Henschel 0-4-0 6370-6372 of 1903.
                          29-31,   Henschel 0-4-0 10086-10088 of 1911.
                          32-45,   Henschel 0-4-0 11921-11934 of 1913.
                          46-50,   Henschel 0-4-0 11935-11939 of 1914.
                          51-58,   Maffei   0-4-0   3892-3899 of 1915.
                          59-63,   Maffei   0-4-0   4354-4358 of 1930.
                          64-65,   Maffei   0-4-0   3890-3891 of 1914 ex-No.103. ⁘
              (II)   1,   Hohenzollern 0-6-0 1439 of 1901 Hired.
              (II)   2,   Orenstein & Koppel 0-6-0   1214 of 1903 ⁘

Also hired various locos from HYSM & NS.

58.   LEIDEN. (Rijnlandsche Stoomtramweg Maatschappij).
      Worked by HYSM, No.52 from 1883 - they owned the branch.
      Taken over by NzH, No.75 in 1909.
      Leiden-Rijnsburg-Katwijk, 8.5 km.
      Rijnsburg-Noordwijk,   8.2 km. (Built by HYSM after take-over)
      S.1881, E.1912, C.1960. Gauge. 1435.
      Locomotives. -   Nos.   1-4,   Merryweather 0-4-0 109-112 of 1881.
                                    5,   Merryweather 0-4-0 131 of 1882.
                  "Doodkisten" 225, 232 & 233 also worked on this line (See No.52 for details).

59.   LICHTENVOORDE. (Geldersch Westfaalisch Tramweg Maatschappij).
      Amalgamated with No.20 in 1934. See also No.39.
      Lichtenvoorde-Aalten-Heurne-Bocholt, 21.0 km.
      Lichtenvoorde Station-Terborg-Zeddam, 28.0 km.
      (The Heurne-Bocholt section was in Germany).
      S.1908, P.1921, GS.1946, C.1953. Gauge. 750.
      Locomotives. -   Nos.   1-2,   Breda 0-4-0 254-255 of 1907.
                                  3-5,   Breda 0-4-0 256-258 of 1908.
                                  6-9,   Hanomag 0-6-0   5768-5771 of 1910.

      Names. -   1-Lichtenvoorde, 2-Varsseveld, 3-Terborg, 4-Etten, 5-Zeddam,
                         6-Gelderland, 7-Aalten, 8-Westfalen, 9-Bocholt.

60.   LIMBURG. See Roermond (Limburgsche Tramweg Maatschappij). No.79.

61.   LIMBURG. (Limburgsche Stoomtramweg Maatschappij). Not in the Netherlands, but a
      subsidiary company of the Belgian SNCV.

62.   LOOSDUINEN. (Westlandsche Stoomtramweg Maatschappij). See No.38.

63.   MAAS. (Maasbuurtspoorweg Maatschappij).   - See Nijmegen, No.73.
             (Stoomtram Maas en Waal).   - See Nijmegen, No.74.

64.   MAASTRICHT. (Gemeente Maastricht).
      Lines belonging to the municipality, but worked by subsidiaries of the Belgian SNCV as
      part of through routes.

(Société Anonyme des Railways Economiques de Liége Seraing et Extensions).
Until 1911, then by :-
(Société Anonyme Belge-Néerlandais de Transports et Travaux). and from 1922, by
the SNCV itself.
Maastricht-Smeermaas, 6.0 km. (for Maaseik).
Maastricht-Montenaken, 1.4 km. (for Tongeren).
Maastricht-Oud Vroenhoven, 1.0 km. (for Glons).
S.1894, D.1936, C.1943. Gauge. 1000.
Locomotives. - SNCV
                        Nos.167-170, Tubize 0-6-0 900-903 of 1893. (Class 2).

65.   MALDEGEM (Belgium). (Stoomtramweg Maatschappij Breskens-Maldegem).
      See Breskens, No.16.

66.   MEPPEL. (Spoorweg Maatschappij Meppel-Balkbrug). (Worked by No.17).
      Meppel-Balkbrug, 21.5 km.
      S.1908, GS.1934, C.1939. Gauge. 1067.
      Locomotives. -   Nos.   1-4,   Breda 0-4-0 248-251 of 1907.

      Names. -   1-Minister Kraus, 2-Meppel, 3-deWyk,4-Bloemberg.
                         (These locomotives were identical to Nos. 23-28 of No.17).

67.   MIDDELBURG*. (Stoomtram Walcheren N.V.)
      Middelburg-Koudekerke-Domburg, 21.0 km.
      Koudekerke-Vlissingen(Flushing),   6.3 km.
      S.1906, C.1937. Gauge. 1067.
      Locomotives. -   Nos.   1-5,   Hohenzollern, 0-4-0 1885-1889 of 1905.

      Note. -   No.3 was named "Vlissingen" for a works photograph, but these
                         engines did not carry names in service.

      * There is also a Middleburg (West Vlaanderen) on the Belgian/Dutch frontier near Brugge.

68.   MIDDELBURG. (Chemins de Fer Economiques Néerlandais).
      From 1885 (S.A. des Tramways à Vapeur de Flessingue,
      Middelbourg et Extensions). Belgian owned.
      Middelburg-Vlissingen(Flushing), 7.7 km.
      S.1881, E.1910, C.1944 (War destruction). Gauge. 1435.
      Locomotives. -   Nos.   1-2,   Carels 0-4-0   ? - ? of 1881.
                               3,   Carels 0-4-0 178 of 1882.   "
                               4,   Black Hawthorn 0-4-0 842 of 1885 ? "
                       (II)   4,   Carels 0-4-0 268 of 1887.   "
                               5,   Tubize 0-4-0   1401 of 1904.   "
                               6-7, SNCV Works, Louvain, 0-4-0 55-56 of 1908. "

      Note. -   Nos. 5-7 were shortened versions of the standard SNCV type.

69.   "De MEIJERIJ" See Eindhoven, No.24.

70.   NEDERLANDSCHE Tramweg Maatschappij. See Leeuwaarden, No.57.

71.   NEDERLANDSCHE Buurtspoorweg Maatschappij. See Zeist, No.100.

72.   NIJMEGEN. (Nijmeegsche Tramweg Maatschappij).
      Nijmegen-Berg en Dal,   5.0 km. (Electrified by different route).
      Nijmegen-Beek,   7.3 km.
      Nijmegen-Neerbosch,   3.3 km. (Handed to No.74 in 1913).
      S.1889, E.1912, C.1956. Gauge. 1067.

Locomotives. -   Nos.   1-3,   Hanomag 0-4-0   2115-2117 of 1899.   🖸
                   4,   Van Duyl 0-4-0   - of 1882. ex-No.54 in 1889. ⋮   "
          (II)   4,   Hanomag 0-4-0   2334 of 1891.   "
                   5,   Hanomag 0-4-0   2915 of 1897.   "
                   6.   Hanomag 0-4-0   4011 of 1903.   "
         (No.4 rebuilt from a Fireless loco).

73.   NIJMEGEN. (Maasbuurtspoorweg Maatschappij).
       Nijmegen-Gennep-Venlo, 63.6 km.
       Venlo-Beringen, 20.2 km. (Taken over from No.79 in 1929).
       S.1913, D.1934, C.1944 (War destruction). Gauge. 1000.
       Locomotives. -   Nos.   13-16,   Hohenzollern 0-4-0   2835-2838 of 1911. ex-No.91. ⋮   🖸
                           17,   Hohenzollern 0-4-0   1122 of 1898. ex-No.84. ⋮   "
                       40-45,   Hohenzollern 0-4-0   3041-3046 of 1913.   "
                       46-47,   Hohenzollern 0-4-0   4079-4080 of 1920.   "

       Names. -   13-Venlo, 14-Panningen, 15-Helden, 16-Maasbree, 17-de Hengst,
                           40-Nijmegen, 41-Plasmolen, 42-Gennep, 43-Bergen, 44-Arcen,
                           45-Venlo*, 46-Mook, 47-Velden.

       *Note. -   For the purposes of a Works Photo, No.45 carried the name "Gennep"
                           but ran as "Venlo" in service. 40-47 were "Verhoop" type locos and
                           were numbered in the same series as the Noord Brabantsch Duitsche
                           railway company's locomotives.

74.   NIJMEGEN. (Stoomtram Maas en Waal).
       Nijmegen-Neerbosch-Wamel, 30.3 km.
       (Working of Nijmegen-Neerbosch taken over from No.72 in 1913).
       S.1902, C.1934. Gauge. 1067.
       Locomotives. -   Nos.   1-5,   Breda 0-4-0   183-187 of 1901.   🖸
                     (II)   5-6,   Hanomag 0-4-0   2915 of 1897 & 4011 of 1903.   "
                           (Hired from No.72, 1913-1922 then purchased). ⋮

75.   Noord-Zuid Hollandsche Stoomtramweg Maatschappij. "NzH".
       Later (Noord-Zuid Hollandsche Stoomtramweg Maatschappij "Haarlem-Leiden).
       From 1932 (Noord-Zuid Hollandsche Tramweg Maatschappij N.V.).
       From 1909, this company was controlled by the H.Y.S.M. and its successors. It in turn
       controlled and operated at various periods, Nos.4, 35, 37, 43, 58 and part of No.22.
       Renumbering of locomotives. -
                           Haarlem-Leiden Nos.1-10 became   A. 1 - A.10. (See No.43).   🖸
                           Leiden-Katwijk No.225 (ex-HYSM)   A.11. (See No.58).   "
                           Rijnsburg-Noordwijk Nos.232-233   A.12 - A.13. (See No.58).   "
                           Leiden-Heemstede   (II)   A.11 - A.14. (ex-No.34). ⋮   "
                           Leiden-Katwijk Nos.1-5 became   A.14 - A.18. (See No.58).   "
                           Haarlem-Alkmaar Nos.1-9   A.51 - A.59. (See No.44).   "

76.   OLDAMBT. See Winschoten, No.98.

77.   OLDENZAAL. (Nederlandsche-Westfaalsche Stoomtram Maatschappij).
       Worked by HYSM until 1921 then by Nederlandsche Spoorwegen. Taken over
       by the State in 1936.
       Oldenzaal-Gronau (Germany), 14.4 km.
       Oldenzaal-Denekamp,   10.4 km.
       S.1896, C.1938. Gauge. 1435.
       Locomotives. -   Part of HYSM and NS general stock.   🖽

78.   OOSTELIJK GRONINGEN. See Winschoten, No.97.

78A. RIJSBERGEN. (Exploitatie van Buurtspoorwegen in Nederland).
Worked by a Belgian SNCV subsidiary:-
(Antwerpsche Maatschappij voor den dienst van Buurtspoorwegen). From 1901 until
1920, then by the SNCV itself as part of a through route from Hoogstraten.
The gauge was changed with other SNCV lines after war destruction, in 1920.
Rijsbergen-Meersel(Frontier), 4.0 km.
S.1901, C.1934. Gauge. 1067 until 1920, then 1000.
Locomotives.-   SNCV
　　　　　　　　Nos.748-749.   Haine St.Pierre 0-6-0   561-562 of 1898 (Class 8).
　　　　　　　　　753-755.   Haine St.Pierre 0-6-0   563-565 of 1898 ("   ).

79. ROERMOND. (Centrale Limburgsche Spoorweg (Stoomtramweg) Maatschappij.
From 1921. (Limburgsche Tramweg Maatschappij). which took over the above, also
Nos.46 & 91 and built some new standard gauge lines.

(a). Narrow Gauge Lines of C.L.S.
Roermond-Vlodrop,   13.1 km.
Roermond-Horn-Kessenich(Belgian Frontier), 17.5 km. (no through running).
Horn-Meijel-Deurne,   30.5 km.
Venlo-Beringen,   20.2 km. (ex-No.91, handed to No.73 in 1929).
                                              (intended Meijel-Beringen connection
                                              not built).
S.1915, C.1935. Gauge. 1000.
Locomotives.-   Nos.   1-4,   Orenstein & Koppel 0-4-0   7723-7726 of 1915.
                         5,   Hohenzollern 0-4-0   846 of 1895. ex-Germany No.28. ❖
                         6,   Hohenzollern 0-4-0   933 of 1896. ex-Germany No.28. ❖
                         7,   Henschel 0-4-0   4304 of 1895. ex Germany No.39. ❖
                         8,   Henschel 0-4-0   13793 of 1915 ❖ in 1919.
                      9-12,   Hanomag 0-4-0   9446-9449 of 1920.
                     13-16,   Hohenzollern 0-4-0   2835-2838 of 1911. ex-No.91. ❖
                        17,   Hohenzollern 0-4-0   1122 of 1898. ex-No.91. ❖
                    "Karl",   Krauss 0-4-0   2062 of 1888, ex-Contractor. ❖
                  (II)   1,   Orenstein & Koppel 0-4-0   6398 of 1914.

(b). Standard Gauge lines, ex-No.46 and built new from 1921.
Heerlen-Hoensbroek,   5.5 km. (ex-No.46 (E.1923, see No.46).
Roermond-Echt-Born-Sittard,   29.5 km.
Echt-Echt Station,   0.7 km.
Echt-Maasbracht Haven,   6.0 km. ?
Echt-Roosteren (for Maaseick),   1.0 km. ? (Not connected with Belgian SNCV).
Roosteren Dorp-Roosteren Maas,   1.0 km.
Born-Grevenbicht,   2.5 km.
Maastricht-Gulpen-Vaals,   25.0 km.) Separate lines.
Gulpen-Wylre,   2.5 km.)
S.1921, Part E.1923, C.1938/1950. Gauge. -1435.
Locomotives.-   Nos. 21-30,° Hanomag 0-4-0   9857-9866 of 1922.
                      31-35,   Hanomag 0-4-0   10209-10213 of 1925.
                      51-52,   Linke Hofmann 0-6-0   2542 & 2547 of 1922.
                         53,   Krupp 0-6-0   737 of 1924 ❖ in 1932.
                   (II) 51,   Hanomag 0-6-6-0   Garratt 10758 of 1931.
                              (Completed as Henschel 22063).
                         64,   Henschel 0-4-0   17698 of 1920, ❖ in 1923.

          ° No.21 is now preserved at Hoorn.

80. ROTTERDAM. (IJsel Stoomtramweg Maatschappij). Closed in 1886 after accident.
Reopened by No.81, but not steam worked by them.
Two locomotives were taken over but used elsewhere.
Rotterdam(Slagveld)-Overschie, 4.9 km.
S.1884, C.1886, H.1890, P.1925, C again 1928. Gauge. 1067.
Locomotives.-   Nos. 15-17,   of IJ.S.M. general stock, see No.37.

81.   ROTTERDAM.   (Rotterdamsche Tramweg Maatschappij).
Originally operated urban and suburban standard gauge lines by horse and steam in
Rotterdam, but the concession was handed to another company for electrification, whereupon
the RTM turned its attention to the construction of a large rural narrow-gauge network on
the marshes and islands to the south of Rotterdam. The island lines were linked by
miniature train ferries.

The RTM also took over No.80, but did not continue to work it by steam.

(a).   Standard Gauge Steam Line.
Rotterdam-Schiedam, 6.5 km.
S.1881, Part H.1903, E.1906, Still operating. Gauge. 1435.
Locomotives. -   Nos.   1-3,   Winterthur 0-4-0 203-205 of 1881.
                          4-7,   Winterthur 0-4-0 249-252 of 1882.
                          8,   Krauss 0-4-0 909 of 1881. ex-trials on No.7. ⁖
                          9.   Winterthur 0-4-0 337 of 1883.

(b).   Narrow Gauge Steam Lines.
Rotterdam-Blaakschedijk-Krooswijk-Numansdorp Haven,   30.8 km.
Blankschedijk-Strijen,   11.5 km.
Middeldijk-Zwijndrecht (for Dordrecht),   11.9 km.
Krooswijk-Goudswaard (Ferry to Middelharnis),   14.8 km.
Numansdorp-Zuid Beijerland,   4.1 km.
Rotterdam-Spijkenisse-Brielle-Oostvoorne(Strand),   35.9 km.
Spijkenisse-Hellevoetsluis (Ferry to Middelharnis),   15.4 km.
Middelharnis Haven-Middelharnis Dorp-Ouddorp,   22.4 km.
Middelharnis Dorp-Ooltgensplaat, (Ferry to Numansdorp), 19.6 km.
Burgh-Zierikzee-Zijpe (Ferry to Anna Jacopa),   42.3 km.
Anna Jacopa-Steenbergen. (Connecting with No.14).   21.0 km.
S.1898, D.1925 (Some S. to 1961) C.1966. Gauge. 1067.
Locomotives. -   Nos.   10-11,   Hohenzollern 2-2-0 237-238 of 1884. ex-No.80. ⁖
                         12-15,   Breda 0-4-0 138-141 of 1897. (See 41-44).
                         16-22,   Breda 0-4-0 162-163 & 174-178 of 1899.
                         23-24,   Hagans 0-4-0¹ 269 & 267 of 1893. ex-Germany No.28. ⁖
                         25-26,   Breda 0-4-0 188-189 of 1901.
                         27-32,   Breda 0-4-0 194-199 of 1902.
                         33-34,   Breda 0-4-0 228-229 of 1904.
                         35-40,   Werkspoor 0-4-0 166-171 of 1906. (Breda type).
                         41-44,   - 12-15 renumbered in 1908.
                         45-46,   - 10-11 renumbered in 1908.
                         47-50,   Henschel 0-6-0   11719-11722 of 1913.
                         51-55,   Orenstein & Koppel 0-6-0   8062-8066/1915.
                         56-58,   Orenstein & Koppel 0-6-0   9193-9195/1920.
                 (II)   1-6,   Werkspoor 0-6-0 137-142 of 1905.
                 (II)   7-14,   Werkspoor 0-6-0 201-208 of 1908.
                 (II)   15,   Hohenzollern 0-4-0   4354 of 1923. ex-No.53. ⁖
                 (II)   44-45. Henschel   0-4-0 12887 & 12889 of 1916. ex-No.17 ⁖
                                                                             in 1947 "

82.   SCHAGEN.   (Stoomtramweg Maatschappij "West Friesland").
Worked by (Maatschappij tot Exploitatie van Tramwegen),
to 1909, then by HYSM. See Nos. 1 and 52.
No connection with "West Friésche Tramweg Maatschappij", for which see No.54.
Schagen-Wognum, 23.3 km.
S.1898, C.1930. Gauge. 1435.
Locomotives. -   Nos.   1-3,   Breda 0-4-0 152-154 of 1898.
                          (Given HYSM numbers 1061-1063 in 1909 and given NS
                          numbers 6601-6603 in 1921).

83.   STAAISMIJNEN.   (State Mines Department). See Heerlen, Nos.46 & 79.

84.   TERNEUZEN.   (Zeeuwach Vlaamsche Tramweg Maatschappij N.V.)
Worked No.55 from 1918 and took it over in 1944.
Took over No.56 in 1912. (Before its own lines were open).

Schoondijke-IJzendijke-Veldzicht(frontier), 11.0 km. (Ex-No.56).
IJzendijke-Stroopuit, 3.0 km. (Goods only).
Hulst-Kloosterzande-Walsoorden, 13.6 km. (Ex-No.55).
Kloosterzande-Perkpolderhaven, 1.9 km. (Built by State in 1940).
IJzendijke-pyramide-Philippine-Sas van Gent, 21.2 km.
Pyramide-Tol-Breskens, 16.2 km. (Goods connection with No.16).
Tol-Hoofdplat, 1.2 km.
Philippine-Terneuzen-Zaamslag, 16.6 km.
Sas van Gent-Zaamslag-Kloosterzande, 29.7 km.
Drieschouwen-Roode Sluis-Moerbeke(Belgium), 10.3 km. (Goods only).
Zaamslag-KamperscheHoek, 3.9 km. (Goods only).
Sas van Gent-Selzaerte(Belgium), 4.3 km. (Goods only).
S.1915 (new lines), D.1935, C.1950. Gauge. 1000.

Locomotives. -	Nos.	1-2,	Breda 0-4-0 73-74 of 1890. ex-No.56.	🚂
		3,	Jung 0-4-0 322 of 1897. ex-No.56.	"
	(II)	3,	Hohenzollern 0-4-0 1122 of 1898. ex-Germany No. 17 ·:	
		4,	Orenstein & Koppel 0-4-0 359 of 1899. ·:	🚃
		5,	Orenstein & Koppel 0-4-0 7625 of 1914. ·:	"
		6,	Hohenzollern 0-4-0 757 of 1893, ex-Germany No.17.·:	🚂
		7-9,	ALCo. 0-6-0 55239-55241 & 55246 of 1915.	
			(ex-Belgian SNCV Class 21).	
		10-13,,	Jung 0-4-0 2271-2274 of 1916.	🚃
		14-16,	Jung 0-4-0 2476-2478 of 1917.	"
		17,	Jung 0-4-0 2479 of 1918.	"
		18-21,	Jung 0-4-0 2480-2483 of 1917. (Light type).	"
		22-26,	Jung 0-4-0 3147-3151 of 1920.	"
		27-29,	Henschel 0-4-0 21371-21373 of 1929. (Light type).	"
	(II)	5-6,	Hohenzollern 0-4-0 846 of 1895 & 933 of 1896.	🚂
			(Hired from No.79)	
	SNCV	360,	Tubize 0-6-0 1403 of 1904 borrowed 1916-1918.	"
		-	Vulkan 0-4-0 1704 of 1898. Hired from a contractor.	🚃

85. TIEL. (Stoomtram Tiel-Buren-Culemborg).
Tiel-Buren-Culemborg, 25.5 km. (Ferry connection with No.74).
S.1906, C.1915. Gauge. 1067.

| Locomotives. - | Nos. | 1-4, | Breda 0-4-0 238-241 of 1906. | 🚂 |
| | | | (Sold to No.97 on closure). | |

86. TILBURG. (Noord-Brabantsche Stoomtramweg Maatschappij). Bankrupt 1893.
Bought out by No.72, and operated as (Stoomtramweg Tilburg-Waalwijk").
Taken over by No.48 in 1898.
Tilburg-Waalwijk, 22.0 km.
S.1881, C.1938. Gauge. 1067.

Locomotives. -	Nos.	1-4,	Winterthur 0-4-0 212-214 & 226 of 1881.	🚂
		5,	Winterthur 0-4-0 292 of 1882.	"
		6.	Breda 0-4-0 35 of 1887, ex-No.19 in 1894. ·:	"

Names. - 1-Tilburg, 2-Waalwyk, 3-Loon op Zand, 4-Amsterdam, 5-Capelle
6-Gorssel.

87. UTRECHT. (IJsel Stoomtramweg Maatschappij).
Taken over in 1888 by (Reederij "Vereeniging"), and then known as (Stoomtram en
Bargedienst Vereeniging).
Utrecht-Vreeswijk, 12.0 km.
S.1883, H.1893, C.1929. Gauge. 1067.

| Locomotives. - | Nos. | 5, | | 🚂 |
| | | 7 & 12, | of IJ.S.M. general stock - See No.37. | |

88. UTRECHT. (Nederlandsche Centraal Spoorweg Maatschappij).
(Experiments with a steam car on an existing horse tramway).
Utrecht-Zeist, 11.6 km.
H.1879, S.1903, E.1909, C.1949. Gauge. 1435.

| Motive Power :- | No. | 1. | Hohenzollern steam car, 1625 of 1903. | 🚎 |
| | | | (Later rebuilt as an 0-4-0 locomotive for No.103). | |

89. VEGHEL. (Compagnie des Chemins de Fer Provinciaux Néerlandais).
Taken over by No.49 in 1899 and by No.12 in 1934.
Veghel-Oss, 21.0 km.
S.1885, C.1939. Gauge. 1067.
<u>Locomotives.</u> -   Un-numbered   Hohenzollern 2-2-0   233-234 of 1884.
                                    Hohenzollern 2-2-0   239-240 of 1884.

Names. -   Veghel, Uden, Oss, Nistelrode. ("Veghel" changed to "Heesch").
              by No.49 as they already had a loco named "Veghel").

90. VENLO. (Maasbuurtspoorweg).   - See No.73.

91. VENLO. (Stoomtramweg Maatschappij Venlo-Maasbree-Helden).
Taken over by No.79 in 1923 and handed over to No.73 in 1929.
Venlo-Maasbree-Helden-Panningen-Beringen, 20.2 km.
S.1912, C.1935. Gauge. 1000.
<u>Locomotives.</u> -   Nos.   1-4,   Hohenzollern 0-4-0   2835-2838 of 1911.
                              5.   Hohenzollern 0-4-0   1122 of 1898 ∵   (Ex-Germany No.15)."

Names. -   1-Venlo, 2-Panningen, 3-Helden, 4-Maasbree, 5-(II) Venlo.

92. VLISSINGEN. (Flushing). - See Nos. 67 & 68.

93. WAALWIJK. See Nos. 48 & 86.

94. WALCHEREN. See Nos. 67 & 68.

95. WEERT. (Naamlooze Maatschappij tot Uitbating van den Buurtspoorweg Maaseyck-Weert
en Uitbreiding). A Belgian SNCV subsidiary, worked as an extension of their Maaseick-
Molenbeersel line, except during the 1914-1918 war, when it was worked by the two
municipalities (Gemeenten Weert en Stramproy). Using three Belgian locomotives left
behind when war broke out.
Weert-Stramproy(Frontier), 8.7 km. (Connecting with Belgian SNCV).
S.1910, C.1934. Gauge. 1000.
<u>Locomotives.</u> -   SNCV general stock.

96. WESTLAND. See No.38.

97. WINSCHOTEN. (Stoomtramweg Maatschappij "Oostelijk Groningen").
Delfzijl-Winschoten-Ter Apel, 70.0 km. (Connecting with Nos.17 & 53).
Blijham-Bellingwolde, 9.6 km. (Formerly horse worked).
H.1900, S.1915, GS.1934, C.1949. Gauge. 1067.
(A passenger service was reinstated during the 1939-1945 war).
<u>Locomotives.</u> -   Nos.   1-3,   Hanomag 0-4-0   2115-2117 of 1889. Ex-No.72. ∵
                              4,   Hanomag 0-4-0   2334 of 1891.
                            5-8,   Breda 0-4-0   138-141 of 1897. Ex-No.81. ∵
                           9-10,   Henschel 0-4-0   6303, 6302 of 1903 ∵
                                   (Ex-Contractor building No.31).
                          11-14,   Breda 0-4-0, 238-241 of 1906. Ex-No.85.
                          15-20,   Linke Hofmann 0-4-0   2568-2573 of 1922.
                          21-24,   Linke Hofmann 0-4-0   2831-2834 of 1924.

98. WINSCHOTEN. (Stoomtramweg Maatschappij "Oldambt").
From 1895 (Stoomtramweg Maatschappij Oldambt-Pekela).
Winschoten-Finsterwolde-Scheemda, 24.0 km.
(Finsterwolde-Scheemda section closed in 1884).

Winschoten-Oude Pekela-Nieuwe Pekela-Stadskanaal, 17.6 km. (S.1885).
S.1882, D.1932, GS.1934, C.1939. Gauge. 1067.
Locomotives. -   Nos.   1-6,   Henschel 0-4-0 1462-1467 of 1882.
                          7,   Breda 0-4-0 82 of 1891.
                          8,   Orenstein & Koppel 0-4-0 6828 of 1913.

99.   ZEEUWSCH VLAANDEREN.   See Terneuzen, No.84.

100.   ZEIST. (Ooster Stoomtram Maatschappij).
       From 1927 (Nederlandsche Buurtspoorweg Maatschappij). "NBM".
       Zeist-Driebergen-Doorn-Rhenen-Wageningen-Arnhem, 74-8 km.
       Doorn-Wijk bij Duurstede, 8.8 km.
       Zeist-Amersfoort, 13.8 km.
       H.1882, S.1882, P.1910, Part E.1911/1924, C.1949. Gauge. 1067.
       (Took over No.88 for electrification in 1909 and No.5 in 1944).
       Locomotives. -   Nos.   1-2,   Hohenzollern 2-2-0 223-224 of 1882.
                                    3,   Hohenzollern 2-2-0 228 of 1883.
                                  4-6,   Breda 0-4-0 5-7 of 1883.
                                    7,   Breda 0-4-0 10 of 1884.
                                 8-10,   Breda 0-4-0 13-15 of 1885.
                                11-12,   Breda 0-4-0 34 & 40 of 1887.
                                13-14,   Breda 0-4-0 102-103 of 1894.
                                   15,   Breda 0-4-0 179 of 1899.
                                16-17,   Breda 0-4-0 232-233 of 1905.
                         (II)   12,   Breda 0-4-0 ? hired from No.17 in 1918/19
                                   27,   Hanomag 0-4-0 7345 of 1914 hired from No.104.
                                   29.   Breda 0-4-0 288 of 1911 hired from No.17.

       Names. -   Nos.1-3 not named, 4-Arnhem, 5-Renkum, 6-Amerongen, 7-Doorn,
                          8-Wijk bij Duurstede, 9-Wageningen, 10-Oranje Nassau, 11-Rhenen,
                          12-Grebbe, 13-Zeist, 14-Oosterbeek, 15-Driebergen, 16-Leersum,
                          17-Heelsum, (II) 12-not named, 27-not named, 29-Landbouw.

       Note. -   Loco No.5 was rebuilt as an electric locomotive in 1928. Later it was
                          sold to Germany No.66 and again rebuilt.

101.   ZUTPHEN. (Tramweg Maatschappij Zutphen-Emmerik).
       Taken over by No.20 in 1934.
       Deventer-Zutphen-Doetinchem-Emmerich(Germany), 57.0 km.
       (Deventer-Epse, mixed gauge with No.19).
       S.1902, GS.1949, C.1954. Gauge. 750.
       Locomotives. -   Nos.   1-6,   Henschel 0-4-0 6012-6017 of 1902.
                                    7,   Henschel 0-4-0 6848 of 1904.
                                  8-9,   Breda 0-4-0 280-281 of 1909.
                                   10,   Hohenzollern 0-4-0 3291 of 1914.
                                11-15,   Hohenzollern 0-4-0 4166-4120 of 1921.
                                   16.   Hohenzollern 0-4-0 4549 of 1925.

       Names. -   1-Zutphen, 2-Steenderen, 3-Hummelo, 4-Doetinchem, 5-'s Heerenberg,
                          6-Emmerik, 7-Vrijland, 8-Zeddam, 9-Baak, 10-Gelderland, 11-Deventer,
                          12-Gorssel, 13-Overijssel, 14-Nederland, 15-Duitschland, 16-Montferland.

       Note. -   When taken over by No.20, the locomotives were numbered 601-616.
                          Nos.10-16 were of the Verhoop type.

102.   ZUTPHEN. (Tramweg Maatschappij "De Graafschap").
       Taken over by No.20 in 1939.
       Zutphen-Warnsveld-Hengelo, 18.9 km.
       H.1889, S.1903, P.1926, GS.1933, C.1938, Gauge. 750.
       (A short section in Zutphen remained used by No.101 until 1942.

Locomotives. -	Nos.	1-4,	Henschel 0-4-0 6367-6369 & 6316 of 1903.
		5,	Hohenzollern 0-4-0. 2801 of 1911.
		8-9,	Breda 0-4-0 280-281 of 1909 hired from 101.
		11,	Breda 0-4-0. 79 of 1891, hired from No.20.
	(II)	1,	Orenstein & Koppel 0-4-0 6044 of 1913)
			Hired from No.20.

Names. -   1-Zutphen, 2-Warnsveld, 3-Vorden, 4-Hengelo G.
5-B.Cuperus. (Hired locos - see owners for names).

Note. -   Nos.1-4 had the external appearance of Breda locos.

103.   ZWOLLE. (Nederlandsche Centraal Spoorweg Maatschappij). "NCS".
Later (Nederlandsche Spoorwegen).
These lines known as "Zuiderzee Stoomtram".
Zwolle-Hattembroek-Nunspeet, 29.0 km.
Wezep-De Zande-Kampen Zuid, 2.2 km.
(Worked over the railway lines, Zwolle-Hattembroek & De Zande-Kampen).
S.1908, C.1931. Gauge. 1435.

Locomotives. -	Nos.	1-5,	Breda 0-4-0 260-264 of 1908. (Centre & side buffers).
		6,	Hohenzollern 0-4-0, 1625 of 1903.
			(Rebuilt from steam railcar. See No.88).
		7-8,	Maffei 0-4-0 3890-3891 of 1914.
		- -	Maffei 0-4-0 3892-3899 of 1915.
			(Built for N.C.S. but hired to No.57 on delivery and later sold to them).

104.   ZWOLLE. (Spoorweg Maatschappij Zwolle-Blokzijl).
Worked by N.C.S. and its successors. See No.103.
Zwolle-Blokzijl, 33.2 km.
S.1914, C.1934. Gauge. 1067.

Locomotives. -	Nos.	20-24,	Hanomag 0-4-0 6540-6544 of 1913.
		26-27,	Hanomag 0-4-0 7344-7345 of 1914.

Note. -   Nos.20-24 belonged to No.104, the number 25 was left blank and 26-27 belonged
to the N.C.S. All were numbered in the N.C.S. series later becoming 41-47
and under the N.S. they were Nos.51-57.

105.   ZWOLLE. See Dedemsvaart No.17.

NOTE :- Lengths of lines are in most cases derived from "Beknopt Overzicht van de Nederlandse
Spoor - en Tramwegsbedrijven", by Ir.J.W.Sluiter, Leiden 1961. The remainder were
supplied by Ir.S.Overbosch.

Standard gauge Breda loco No.11 "Apollo" of the Westland Tramway.
Unknown Photographer.

Zeeuwsch Vlaamsche Tramweg No.19 on the other side of the fence at Breskens
Ferry; taken at the same time as the previous two photos. There was a physical
connection between the tracks of the ZVTM and the Breskens-Maldegem, by
which a special train chartered by the Light Railway Transport League made a
through journey from Terneuzen to Ostend in 1947.

Photo: late F.Merton-Atkins 30072.

Maasbuurtspoorweg No.47, "Velden" amid the ruins of the loco shed at Venlo
in August 1944. The writer saw this scene, but was in a convoy and unable
to stop. Fortunately Dick Riley was there with his camera.

Photo: R.C.Riley.

173

Rotterdam Tramweg No. 8 about to depart from Rosestraat terminus in Rotterdam South, pushing its way between ice-cream vendors and a standard gauge diesel loco making for the dockside lines. There was a small tram station behind the building on the left and a large depot just down the road. July 1956.

Photo: G. E. Baddeley 10021.

Probably the smallest of tram engines, the two little Breda locos for the Den Helder bathing beach tramway originally had vertical boilers, but had been rebuilt with horizontal boilers by the time this photo was taken.
Courtesy: Ir. S. Overbosch.   Unknown Photographer.

The first tram loco built in Italy, "L'Italiana" by "BAMAT".
Courtesy: Sartori Brothers.   Official Photo.

No. 102.
Locomotivfabrik Hagans in Erfurt (Deutschland).

One of the rather primitive looking Hagans locos built for Brescia in 1879.
Hagans Catalogue.   Courtesy: Helmuth Hinze.

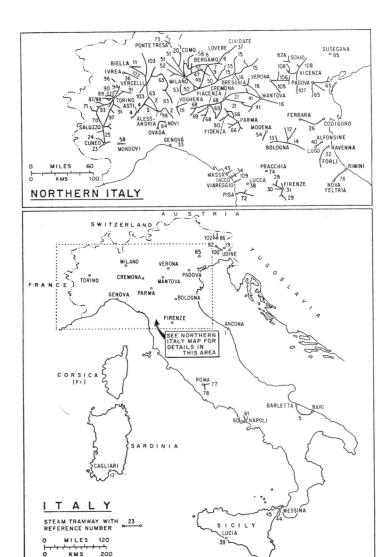

NORTHERN ITALY

ITALY

STEAM TRAMWAY WITH ‒‒‒‒ 23
REFERENCE NUMBER

176

7. ITALY

Although most readers will be aware of the extensive development of steam tramways in Belgium and the Netherlands, the rapid spread of steam tramways in Italy, before the turn of the century may come as a surprise to many.

The first steam tramway in Italy opened in 1878 and ran east from Milan to Vaprio, with a depot at Gorgonzola; no doubt it went a long way towards introducing the well known product of this small town to the households of Europe. By 1885 official statistics show that there were 384 tramway locomotives at work in Italy - in fact the steam tram spread like wildfire. However, this expansion was not evenly spread throughout the country and there developed a large concentration of lines in the North, stretching in an almost continuous network, with but few breaks, across the Lombardy Plain and the Po Valley. This is the flat part of Italy between the Alps and the Appenines, where agriculture and industry flourish. To the south where the country is more mountainous, there were a number of separate systems, some quite large and other isolated routes, but no connected networks. There were even steam tramways at Messina in Sicily and at Cagliari in Sardinia. In fact the only important town never to be served by them was Palermo, Sicily. One interesting fact about Italian steam tramways, was that apart from some early experiments at Ancona, Bergamo and Genoa, all were inter-urban and like Italian light railways, a marked preference was shown for the standard gauge, but some in the more mountainous parts chose the gauges of 1100, 950 and 750 mm. By comparison the metre gauge was quite rare. Some of the 750 gauge lines were inherited from Austrian military railways of the 1914-1918 war and were to be found in the Dolomites.

In Italy as in Great Britain, there does exist a legal distinction between a tramway laid on or beside the street and a railway laid on its own right of way. Railways are regulated by the State and if considered sufficiently deserving, receive a subsidy there-from. On the other hand, a tramway receives its concession and subsidy if any, from the Provincial Council. The financial history of most Italian transport undertakings is extremely complicated, and this complication is in no way lessened by the facility with which an impecunious operator could go bankrupt and arrange for the tramway to be reopened under a new title and collect a fresh subsidy ! Italy did not become an united kingdom until 1861 and the hang-over from the previous unsettled conditions no doubt affected the availability of local capital. Hence we find that several of the early enterprises were financed from Great Britain or Belgium. This accounts for such titles as "The Lombardy Road Railway Company" with offices at Copthall Buildings, London and Via Farini, Milan, or the "Société des Chemins de Fer Tessins (Bruxelles)", a holding company, known in Italy as the "Società Ferrovie del Ticino". It will be noted that right down to the 1920s, the Italians seemed to be undecided whether to use the word "Tramway" "Tranvia" or "Tramvia" to describe a tramway. The word tranvia is now standard. A number of tramways were financed locally and in several cases, by an individual rather than a company. Thus, the "Tramvie Ferdinand Pistorius" was not named after a Roman Emperor, but after a wealthy landowner, Cav. (Sir) Ferdinand Pistorius, who put up the capital. Pistorius died in 1885 and his tramway undertaking, serving the south-east of Milan, amalgamated with the Milan-Vaprio, forming the second largest steam tramway undertaking in Europe, with eventually about 80 locomotives and exceeded only by the Belgian "Vicinal" with over 1000 engines.

Italy would appear to be a transport operator's paradise. It is a densely populated country, where restless people seem to have to make frequent calls on friends and business connections in neighbouring towns, so that no matter what transport services are provided, they are never quite adequate. However, conditions for operators are not quite as rosy as they seem, since because the dense population was accompanied by low standards of living, fares had to be kept to a very low level, and by our standards, transport undertakings were very much over-staffed; there was no question of "one-man" locomotives here.[1]

No doubt the early development of steam tramways, particularly in the Milan and Turin areas considerably helped the industrialization of these cities by bringing the rural population to work daily in factories located in their suburbs. Workmen always comprised the heaviest traffic on Italian tramways and the services provided were suitably bunched at peak hours accordingly. Nevertheless, the attractively named "Tranvie del Chianti" at Florence and others opened up the picturesque country-side to the tourist. There was also a not inconsiderable goods traffic on many lines, composed largely of industrial and market produce. Interchange was greatly facilitated by the widespread adoption of the standard gauge on the interconnected systems in the north. Italian steam tramways formed an association in the early 1880s, which acted as a clearing-house for goods and was said to be responsible for the construction of the "Circumvallazione" line round the walls of Milan, linking the various tramways starting from that city.[2]

Rome as the cultural rather than the business capital of Italy, was served only by one proper steam tramway, that to Tivoli,[3] but far to the South there were two steam tramway systems serving Naples, one of which started out of the City on a gradient which was steep enough to require a section of rack rail, one of the five in Europe with this feature. Many of the tramways around Milan, Turin, Florence and Naples, where traffic was always dense, were electrified at an early date, while others were replaced by diesel railcars (often second-hand from the State Railways), in the early 1930s when motor bus competition became acute; the substitution of battery-electric railcars was perhaps more extensive in Italy than elsewhere, and at least two lines kept going with this form of traction until the late 1950s, with steam for extra workmen's journeys.

Most other steam tramways succumbed to motor-bus competition by the 1930s, but the Milan-Magenta, Monza-Trezzo-Bergamo, Bologna-Malalbergo, Novi-Ovada, Pisa-Pontedera and Udine-San Daniele survived the 1939-1945 war with some steam workings. The first two mentioned lasted until 1957/58, but the very last to close was the narrow-gauge Bari-Barletta tramway, which was replaced by a standard gauge railway on a slightly different course in 1959; and even then, an enclosed locomotive (from Padua) was used by the contractors who built the line. Other tram-engines were seen in industrial use or shunting in tramway company's goods yards until the late 1960s. Those brought to the writer's attention included the Bologna Sugar factory, Falk Steel works at Monza, the Piacenza-Bettola Railway and Vicenza Tramways. An ex-tramway locomotive converted to a battery locomotive was seen shunting in a goods yard at Lonigo on the Verona interurban tramway, even after the steam tramways had been replaced by electric and the electric trams by trolleybuses. There were two un-enclosed locomotives in a factory yard at Asti, which are said once to have worked on the local tramway.

Locomotives

The first tramway to be worked by steam in Italy, the Milan-Vaprio, experimented with a number of different locomotives of various origins. Their initial fleet comprised a Fox Walker 0-4-2 from Bristol, a Henschel, two Krauss from Germany and a peculiar 0-4-0 produced in Italy under the name "Bamat" also a Baldwin steam railcar from America. These were followed by six Winterthur 0-4-0s. Likewise, a number of other Italian tramways opened in the early days started with Winterthur machines. Subsequently, Italian tramways showed a marked preference for German built locomotives, among which Henschel and Krauss predominated but most of the other German builders of tram engines were represented; even the British owned tramways used Henschel engines, but not unnaturally, the Belgian owned systems preferred the products of their own country, using Tubize, St. Léonard, Couillet and La Meuse locomotives as far as possible.

During the early period, when the tramways were expanding most rapidly, Italian locomotive manufacturers were not sufficiently developed to compete on equal terms with their German and Belgian rivals and we find Italian built engines in a very small minority. It might be mentioned that the firm which produced the "Bamat" machine, normally made agricultural machinery and only turned out the one locomotive under that name, after which the title was changed to "Cerimedo all' Elvetica" who were credited with 50 tram engines, but it would appear that some were in fact German machines assembled under license in Italy, 15 of these being Henschels and 5 from Hohenzollern. The remainder although probably built in their own works, followed very closely to the basic Henschel design. By 1888, Cerimedo had become "S. A. Ernesto Breda" of Milan, who although going in for locomotive building in a big way, is only known to have turned out a further 25 enclosed locos, all for Italian tramways and still keeping broadly to the Henschel or Krauss designs. Although there are other well known locomotive builders in Italy, there is no evidence that they turned their hands to building enclosed locomotives, but in later years when enclosure regulations were less strictly observed, a few of their industrial machines did find their way onto tramways, particularly if intended nominally for goods traffic. Thus, Ansaldo of Sampierdarena near Genoa, supplied two of their standard 0-6-0 well tank engines to the Bologna-Malalbergo tramway. (When overhauled in the 1930s in a State Railway workshop, they reappeared numbered 813.10 & 813.11, as they resembled the State Railways' 813 class). Likewise, the works at Saronno, formerly a subsidiary of the German works at Esslingen, supplied two unenclosed locomotives to a tramway at Asti (the two that were seen recently at work in industry there). Around 1910 several tramways with heavy workmens traffic acquired large Henschel, Borsig or Breda 0-6-0 enclosed engines (Vicenza had closely similar machines from all three manufacturers).

In later years, Italian tramways tended to remove the covering from the wheels and motion of enclosed locomotives, as it was thought to cause overheating and as already mentioned industrial locomotives were accepted on tramways. In this connection, we should not pass without mention of Glauco Greco of Reggio Emilia, who bought up engines and rebuilt them, using parts canibalized from other machines, changing the appearance considerably and even changing the gauge on occasion; in so doing, unfortunately for the historian, attempting to trace previous ownership, they were invariably turned out bearing Greco works plates, without number or date: two such examples were to be seen on the Monza-Trezzo-Bergamo tramway as late as the 1950s. The dislike of enclosed locomotives goes back to quite early days, as the Pisa-Pontedera tramway opened in 1884, very soon stripped the covering off their Henschel locomotives and the long lived Bari-Barletta line used St.Léonard 0-6-2s with side tanks and enclosed motion, although the latter was soon removed.[4]

A high proportion of the locomotives bore names, particularly if of German manufacture. They were usually named after places served, but the Pisa-Pontedera line was an exception and named theirs after famous people. Sometimes when early locomotives were withdrawn, their name plates were transferred to replacement machines.

Passenger Stock, Stations, etc.

Much of the earliest passenger stock in Italian tramways was supplied by Felice Grondana of Milan. His steam stock was similar to that already in use on horse tramways with the underframes suitably strengthened. In general, they were small four wheelers with clerestorey roofs, six small side windows and end platforms closed by fancy metal gates. In deference to Italy's sunny climate, some were open from waist to roof level and equipped with side curtains; there were also metal bodied postal vans and various freight trucks. As well, Grondana invented a practical heavy-duty centre buffer coupling, which was used on many Italian tramways and on some Dutch and German systems.[5]

The carriages used on the Milan-Pavia tramway were among the first exported by the Nivelles works in Belgium and most Belgian owned tramways were equipped with their stock. Subsequently Breda, Reggiane, Casaralta and other Italian builders produced rather solid looking four wheeled cars, either with open or enclosed end platforms; some had a luggage compartment at one end, as separate luggage vans were rare in Italy. The Pisa-Pontedera tramway had some Orenstein & Koppel centre-entrance cars. Passenger carriages mounted on bogies were also rare on Italian steam tramways, but did include three enormous bogie cars for the Monza-Trezzo-Bergamo tramway, evidently built in the 1930s as trailers for the accumulator cars, but rather heavy for them and used in steam workmen's trains as well. Like France, the most common livery was dark green, but some Italian tramways adopted a medium brown and the M.T.B. was perhaps the most daring, painting its passenger stock white with brown edging. Some others, like the Milan-Magenta, distinguished first class cars with white upper panels. This latter finished in 1957 with over 60 solid looking four wheeled cars, many second-hand, including some wartime "utility" bodies on older chassis. When taken over by the municipality the livery became two shades of green, separated by red and white lining. There was a transfer of the coat of arms and under-frames were light grey.

Plans in old Italian technical books [6]   show that many of the steam tramways had most elaborate and improbable terminal layouts, cramped into confined spaces, with traversers and turntables all over the place, where shunting of stock must have been a nightmare.   Urban terminals in yards enclosed by high walls were quite common but the Milan terminus of the Magenta line was in a court between high buildings, only accessible through a narrow doorway, while the tracks at Magenta ended in a fan of sidings in a field, just short of the town.   Many of the old walled towns of the Lombardy Plain had a tram-station alongside the main line station and the tram lines ran round outside the walls to reach the points where they branched off.   Some tramways had quite substantial station buildings at intermediate points, others used small buildings like ornate cabmen's shelters, but many "station houses" were just conveniently sited shops or cafés with telephone communication and entitled to sell tickets. Outside towns the track was laid at the side of the road and rough ballasted to discourage other traffic from using it except in an emergency.   Several Italian tramways developed an early form of container system for the carriage of bricks and others used tank containers for the disposal of sewage (Concimi) [7]

Notes

1.   A Milan-Magenta train would have a driver, fireman, guard and about three conductors. There were crossing-keepers with red flags at several points.

2.   See "The Engineer" for 22nd March 1895 page 253.

3.   There were complaints that British steam tramways were dirty, but weekly season tickets on the Rome-Tivoli tramways included the price of a bath each day at Acque Albule. The Baths were owned by the tram company.   (See "Orario Generale" for 1921).

4.   See article in "La Vie du Rail" for May 1966. (No.1044).

5.   See "Locomotive, Railway Carriage & Wagon Review" 15th March 1935 (Drawing)

6.   See "La Costruzione ed Esercizio delle Tramvie", A. Viapiani, Turin, 1893, and "L'Impianto e l'Esercizio dei Tramways nella Provincia di Milano",G. Bianchi, Milan, 1885.

7.   See "The Engineer", "Steam Tramways in Italy", P. Amoretti, March 1895, p253

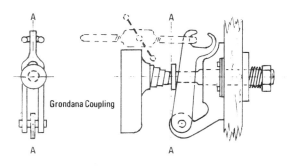

Grondana Coupling

Table 7 ITALY

1. ANCONA. (Signor Marotti).
    Possibly only experiments on urban horse tramway.
    Stazione-Piazza Teatro-Piazza Cavour, 1.0 km. (approx.).
    H.1881, S.1881 only, E.1908, C.1949/51, Gauge. 1435.
    Locomotives. -   Nos.   1-2,   Winterthur 0-4 0, 224 225 of 1881.

2. ALESSANDRIA. (Signori Belloli e Bellisomi).
    Later (Società Belga dei Tramways Alessandrini).
    In 1920s (S.A. Tramways a Vapore della Provincia d'Alessandria).
    Alessandria-San Salvatore-Casale, 31.7 km.
    Allessandria-Marengo-Sale,   24.7 km.
    Marengo-Spinetta-Mandrogne,   8.4 km. (Closed in 1883 and reopened later).
    Sale-Tortona,   12.4 km. (Taken over from No.98).
    Tortona-Monleale,   10.3 km. ("   "   "   ").
    Camagna-Casale,   10.4 km. (Sold to No.3 in 1886).
    Alessandria-Altavilla,   19.2 km. ("   "   "   "   ").
    S.1880, C.1933. Gauge. 1435.
    Locomotives. -   Nos.   1-2,   Winterthur 0-6-0 170-171 of 1880.
                            3-8,   Winterthur 0-4-0 172-177 of 1880.
                            9,   Winterthur 0-4-0 195 of 1880.
                            10,   Hagans   0-4-0 118 of 1881.
                            11-12, Winterthur 0-4-0 206 207 of 1880.
                            13,   Winterthur 0-6-0   235 of 1881 ? (ex-No.98). ∴
                            14-15, Winterthur 0-4-0 208-209 of 1881.
                            16-18, Cerimedo   0-4-0 (Henschel 1619-1621 of 1883).
                    (II)   18-19, Krauss   0-4-0 1032-1033 of 1882, (ex-No.98). ∴
                            20-22, Krauss   0-4-0 1155 1157 of 1882, (ex-No.98). ∴
                    (II)   14-15, Krauss   0-4-0 5332 of 1905 & 6105 of 1908.
                    (II)   16-17, Krauss   0-4-0 6523 of 1911 & 6899 of 1914.

3. ALTAVILLA. Originally part of No.2.
    Sold to Vincenzo Remolti in 1886 and to No.4 in 1900.
    Altavilla-Alessandria, 19.2 km.
    Altavilla-Camagna,   15.4 km.
    S.1883, C.1933. Gauge. 1435.
    Locomotives. -   Nos. 16-18, Cerimedo 0-4-0 (Henschel 1619-1621 of 1883). Ex-No.2 ∴
                           ?   Henschel 0-4-0 2485 of 1887.

4. ASTI. (Signor Berrier de la Leu, Belgium). (Bankrupt in 1885).
    Later (Società Astese Monferrina di Tramvie e Ferrovie).
    (a). Narrow Gauge Lines.
          Asti Cortanze, 18.7 km.
          Asti Canale,   24.0 km.

    (b). Standard Gauge Lines.
          Asti-Montmagno-Altavilla-Casale, 45.3 km. (Part ex-No.3).
          Altavilla-Alessandria,   19.2 km. (Ex-Nos. 2 & 3).

    S.1883, C.1936. Gauges. 1435 & 1100.
    Locomotives. -   Nos.   1-4,   Winterthur 0-4-0 288-291 of 1882. (for 1100 mm gauge).
                            5-7,   Krauss   0-4-0 Not confirmed in Krauss works list. ? .
                            8-9,   Krauss   0-4-0 1312-1313 of 1884. ("   "   "   ").
                            10-12, Krauss   0-4-0 1717-1718 & 1722 of 1886.("   ").
                            13-14, Saronno   0-4-0 133-134 of 1897 (for 1435 mm gauge).
                            15-18, Henschel   0-4-0 2485, 1619-1621 of 1883/87 (for 1435 mm gauge
                                                                              ex-No.3). ∴

                            19,   Henschel   0-4-0   7503 of 1908. (Standard Gauge).
                            20,   Henschel   0-4-0 10085 of 1910. ("   ").
                            21,   Hanomag   0-4-0   6300 of 1911. (Narrow Gauge).

22, ?	Henschel 0-4-0	9485 of 1909. (Standard Gauge).
23,	Henschel 0-4-0	20453 of 1929. (" ").
24.	Henschel 0-4-0	20454 of 1929. (" ").

<u>Names.</u> -   1-Canale, 2-S. Damiano, 3-Asti, 4-Montechiero*, 5- ?, 6- ?, 7- ?,
8-Alfieri, 9-Malabaila, 10- ?, 11- ?, 12-Tanaro, 13- ?, 14-Castagnole Monf.
15- ?, 16- ?, 17- ?, 18- ?, 19-Vignole Monf., 20-Italia, 21-S. Damiano.

<u>Note.</u> -   * Works photo exists showing No.4 as "S. Damiano".

5.   BARI. (Società Generale dei Tramways di Bruxelles).
Later (Società Anonima Ferrotranviaria).
Bari-Barletta, 65.0 km.
S.1881, C.1959. Gauge. 750.
Replaced by a standard gauge railway on a different course.

<u>Locomotives.</u> -	Nos.	1-7,	St. Léonard 0-6-2	537-543 of 1881.
		8-9,	St. Léonard 0-6-2	564-565 of 1881.
		10-11,	St. Léonard 0-6-2	535-536 of 1881. (loaned first to No.11)"
		12,	Hunslet 4-6-0	1308 of 1918, ex-British Army.
		13,	Wiener Neustadt 0-8-0	4800 of 1908, ex-Austrian Army.

<u>Names.</u> -   1-Bari, 2-Bitonto, 3-Andria, 4-Barletta, 5-Gravina, 6-Terlizzi, 7-Corato,
8-Ruvo, 9-Altamura, 10-Trani, 11-Canosa.

<u>Note.</u> -   Wheel covers removed and some name plates changed round in later years.
S. V.No. 149 ex-No. 65 used for construction of replacing railway.

6.   BERGAMO. (Impresa A. Ferretti). Later (S. A. Tranvie e Funicolare di Bergamo).
Bergamo (Stazione Ferrovia)-Stazione Funicolare, 1.4 km.
H.1875, S.1887, E.1898, C.1950. Gauge. 1435. (1000 on electrification).

<u>Motive Power.</u> -	Borsig "Rowan" car, 4204 of 1886, ex-Naples, No. 60.
	Borsig "Rowan" car, 4311 of 1892, ex-?

<u>Names.</u> -   Serio, Brembo.

7.   BERGAMO. (Società Tranvia Bergamo-Sarnico). Later (Tranvie Provinciale di Bergamo).
Bergamo-Trescore-Sarnico, 32.0 km.
S.1901, C.1931. Gauge. 1435.

<u>Locomotives.</u> -	Nos.	1-2,	Krauss 0-4-0	4573-4574 of 1901.
		3-4,	Krauss 0-6-0	5519-5520 of 1906.
	Possibly	51,	Orenstein & Koppel 0-4-0	3069 of 1908 ? (7 locos by 1907
	(II)	1,	Breda 0-6-0	2136 of 1924, "Brianza". See No.57).

8.   BERGAMO. (Società Tranvia Valle Cavallina). Later as No.7.
Trescore-Lovere, 29.0 km. (Access to Bergamo over No.7 from Trescore).
(Extended Lovere-Bersaglio, 2.0 km, parallel to No.37 after 1917).
S.1904, C.1931. Gauge. 1435.

<u>Locomotives.</u> -	Nos.	1-3,	Borsig 0-6-0	5374-5376 of 1904.
		4.	Borsig 0-6-0	5561 of 1905.

<u>Names.</u> -   1- ?, 2- ?, 3-Borgo di Terzo, 4-Sovere.

9.   BERGAMO. (Società Belga di Ferrovie Economiche).
Worked by Ferrovia Valle Seriana, under same ownership.
Bergamo-Ghisalba-Soncino, 42.0 km. (Connecting with Nos.15 & 50 at Soncino).
S.1884, C.1931. Gauge. 1435.

<u>Locomotives.</u> -	Nos.	1-3,	Esslingen 0-4-0	2062-2064 of 1884.
		4,	Esslingen 0-4-0	2116 of 1884.
		5.	Breda 0-4-0	1526 of 1915.

<u>Names.</u> -   1-Italia, 2-Seriate, 3-Romano, 4-Soncino, 5-Ghisalba.

10. BERGAMO. (Tranvia Monza-Trezzo-Bergamo). See MONZA, No. 57.

11. BIELLA. (Società Generale dei Tramways di Bruxelles).
Biella-Cossato, 9.3 km.
S.1880, R.1891, C.1961. Gauge. 750 (1000 as railway).
Locomotives. - Nos. 1-2, St.Léonard 0-6-2 535-536 of 1881.
(Intended for No.5 but delivered first to this line).

12. BOLOGNA. (S. A. Tranvie Bologna-Pieve di Cento-Malalbergo) until 1946, then
(Cooperativa fra il Personale della Tranvia Bologna-Pieve di Cento-Malalbergo).
Bologna(Porta Galliera)-Dozza-Pieve di Cento, 29.7 km.
Dozza-Malalbergo,   34.3 km.
S.1889, A. ?, D.(GS).1936, C.1958. Gauge. 1435.
Locomotives. - Nos. 1-5, St.Léonard 0-4-0 822-826 of 1889.
                 6-7, Henschel 0-4-0 1862-1863 of 1884 ∵ ex-S.V.Rly.
                 8, Orenstein & Koppel 0-4-0 942 of 1902.
                 9, Henschel 0-6-0 8125 of 1907.
                 10-11, Ansaldo 0-6-0 1173 & 1169 of 1923.
                 C.31, Henschel 0-4-0 1118 of 1880 ex-No.78 ∵
                 C.32, Henschel 0-4-0 1937 of 1884 ∵ ex No.77.
                 C.34, Henschel 0-4-0 11686 of 1912 ∵   "

Names. - 1-Argile, 2-Pieve, 3-Minerbio, 4-Baricella, 5-Malalbergo, 6-Galvani,
7-L.Maglietti, 8-Cento, 9-Bologna, 10- ?, 11-Polesine, Others not named.
(Nos. 9 & 11 said to be preserved).

13. BOLOGNA. (Ditta Rotondi e Almagia) (Later as Nos.51 & 77).
In 1911 (Société des Tramways de Bologne).
Later (S.A.Ferrovie e Tranvie dell'Emilia).
Finally (Tranvie Provinciale di Bologna, Casalecchio e Vignola). "T.B.V."
Bologna-Casalecchio, 5.0 km. (Through running over urban tramways, E.1907 own cars).
Casalecchio-Bazzano-Vignola, 22.5 km.
Bazzano-Castelfranco,   12.5 km. (Formerly part of No.54).
S.1883, ER.1938, destroyed 1944, DR.1951, ER again 1955. Gauge. 1435.
Locomotives. - Nos. 1-2,? Henschel 0-4-0 1559 & 1617 of 1883.
                 3-?, Cerimedo 0-4-0 ? - ?
                 8-10, Breda   0-4-0 267-269 of 1893.   "
                 11-12, Henschel 0-6-0 9520-9521 of 1909.   "
                 13-14, Krauss 0-6-0 5871-5872 of 1908.   "
                 15-16, Henschel 0-6-0 10176 & 10457 of 1910/11. "
                 17, Henschel 0-6-0 11361 of 1912.   "
                 18-19, Breda   0-6-0 1452-1453 of 1913.   "

Names. - 1-14 Not Known, 15-Pragatto, 19-Giacomo.

Note. - No.19 had screw couplings and side buffers, 18 did not.
Ing.Ferretti experimented with small steam cars at Bologna
                                 Exhibition in 1888.

14. BOLOGNA. (Società Veneta per la Costruzione ed Esercizio delle Ferrovie
Secondarie Italiane). Known as "S.V."
Bologna(San Vitale)-Imola, 31.7 km.
S.1886, C.1935. Gauge. 1435.
Locomotives. - Nos.185-187, Esslingen 0-4-0 2182-2184 of 1886. (Henschel type).
                 188-189, Breda 0-4-0 103-104 of 1889.   "   "   "

Names. - 185-Quaderna, 186-Sellustra, 187-Gaiana, 188-Mezzolara, 189-Roveri.

Note. - Works photo of 186 as "Gajana" and reports that 187 was "Albano".
All numbered in S.V.General series, later numbered 160,152,148,153 & 154.

15.　BRESCIA.　(Compagnie Génerale des Chemins de Fer Secondaires. (Belgium ?).
　　From 1907, (Tramways Elettrici e a Vapore della Provincia di Brescia).
　　Brescia(Stazione)-Gardone Val Trompa-Tavernole,　29.2 km.
　　Brescia(Stazione)-Tormini-Salo-Gargnano,　　53.4 km.
　　Tormini-Vestone-Idro,　　27.6 km.
　　Brescia(Stazione)-Orzinuovi-Soncino,　　35.6 km. (Still Steam in 1922).
　　S.1880, E.1909/1922, C.1955.　Gauge. 1435.　　　　　(See No.9).
　　Locomotives. -　　Nos.　1-3,　Hagans　　0-4-0　102-104 of 1879.
　　　　　　　　　　　11-16,　Hagans　　0-4-0　112-117 of 1881.　　　　　　"
　　　　　　　　　　　41-42,　Cerimedo (Henschel) 0-4-0　1135-1136 of 1881.　　"
　　　　　　　　　　　51-52,　Henschel　0-4-0　1733-1734 of 1883.　　　　　　"
　　　　　　　　　　　53-55,　Henschel　0-4-0　2490-2492 of 1887.　　　　　　"
　　　　　　　　　　　61-65.　Krauss　　0-4-0　5950-5954 of 1908.　　　　　　"

16.　BRESCIA.　(Signor Prunieaux).　Later (Societá delle Ferrovie Ticino). See No.63.
　　Under unified management with No.15 in 1884/85.
　　Then (Societá dei Tramways a Vapore Brescia-Mantova-Ostiglia).
　　Owned in 1906 by (S.A. d'Entreprise Génerale de Travaux, Liége).
　　Finally (Societá delle Tranvie de Lombardia e Romagna) from 1922.
　　Brescia(Porta Veneta)-Carpenedolo-Castiglione-Mantova(Mantua), 74.1 km.
　　Castiglione delle Stiviere-Desenzano, 15.1 km. (Opened in 1911).
　　Mantova(Mantua)-Ostiglia, 36.9 km.
　　S.1882, (E to Carpenedolo 1932, C.1952) Rest GS.1932, C.1936.　Gauge. 1435.
　　Locomotives. -　　Nos.　1-3,　Tubize 0-6-0　496-498 of 1882.
　　　　　　　　　　　4-7,　Tubize 0-6-0　505-508 of 1882.　　　　　"
　　　　　　　　　　　8,　Tubize 0-6-0　　534 of 1883.　　　　　　　"
　　　　　　　　　　　9-10,　?　　?　　?　　　　　　　　　　　　　"
　　　　　　　　　　　11-12,　Krauss　0-4-0　1278-1279 of 1883.　　　　"
　　　　　　　　　　　13-16,　Krauss　0-4-0　1329, 1395 & 1435-1436 of 1885.　"
　　　　　　　　　　　17-18,　Krauss　0-4-0　1815-1816 of 1889.　　　　"
　　　　　　　　　(II)　9-10,　Tubize 0-6-0　1493-1494 of 1906. (Belgian SNCV type).　"
　　　　　　　　　(II)　11-12,　Tubize 0-6-0　1577-1578 of 1908.　"　　"　　"　　"
　　　　　　　　　(II)　13-16.　Tubize 0-6-0　1632-1635 of 1909.　"　　"　　"　　"

17.　CAGLIARI.　(Sardinia).　(Societá Tranvie della Sardegna).
　　In 1922 (S.A.Tranvie del Campidano e Poetto).
　　Cagliari-Quartu Sant'Elena, 10.5 km.
　　Cagliari-Campidano-Poetto, 6.5 km.
　　S.1893/1913, E.1925/1930, Still Operating.　Gauge. 950.
　　Locomotives. -　　Nos.　1-2,　Krauss 0-6-0　2806-2807 of 1893.
　　　　　　　　　　　3-4,　Krauss 0-6-0　3040-3041 of 1894.　　　　　"
　　　　　　　　　　　5,　Krauss 0-6-0　5377 of 1905, "Giovanni Merello".　"
　　　　　　　　　　　6.　Krauss 0-6-0　6955 of 1914. "Roma".

18.　CHIANTI.　(Tranvie del Chianti).　See FIRENZE, No.29.

19.　CIVIDALE.　(Societá Veneta) Formerly run by Austrian army.
　　Cividale-Caporetto,　　km.
　　S.1917, to Jugo Slavia 1919, R. ?.　Gauge. 750.
　　Locomotives. -　　Nos.90 & 97,　Breda 0-4-0　1690 & 1697 of 1916.

20.　COMO.　(S.A.Tramways a Vapore Como-Fino-Saronno e Fino-S.Pietro Martire).
　　Later owned by (Ferrovia Nord Milano), from 1888.
　　Como Fino-Saronno, 18.6 km.
　　Fino-S.Pietro Martire, (not completed).　(S.Pietro Martire now called Seveso).
　　S.1880, R.1896, Still operating as railway.　Gauge. 1435.
　　Locomotives. -　　Nos.　1-5,　Esslingen 0 6-0　1784-1787 of 1880 & 1810 of 1880.
　　　　　　　　　　　11-12,　Esslingen 0-6-0　1836-1837 of 1881.　　　　　"

　　Names. -　　　1-Como, 2-Saronno, 3-Camerlata, 4-Lomazzo, 5-Rovellasca,
　　　　　　　　11-Lario, 12-Ceresio.

21. CREMONA. (Cav. E.Belloli), by 1920 (Società Nazionale di Ferrovie e Tranvie).
Finally (Administrazione Tranvie Provinicale Cremonese).
Cremona-Montanara-Ostiano,   20.8 km.
Montanara-Asola,   22.9 km.   (Connecting with No.41).
Cremona-Ca'de'Soresini-Ponte della Maiocche,   47.9 km.   "
Ca'de'Soresini-San Giovanni in Croce,   5.1 km.
S.1888, D.1932, C.1955.   Gauge. 1435.
Locomotives. -   Nos.   1-4,   Henschel 0 4-0   1515-1517 & 1392 of 1887.
                          5,?   Henschel 0-4-0   4308 of 1895.   "
                          6-10,   ?   ?   ?   (Before 1901).
                          11,   Borsig   0-4-0 7737 of 1911.   "
                          12-13, Borsig   0-4-0 8997-8988 of 1914.   "
                          05-07, Krauss   0-4-0 6076-6078 of 1908, ex-No.51. ∵   "

22. CREMONA. (Tranvie Inter-Provinciale di Milano, Bergamo e Cremona).   In spite of its title,
this tramway did not serve the city of Cremona.   See No.49.

23. CUNEO. (Signor Carlo Ciappello).   Later (S.A.Tranvie Cuneo-Borgo San Dalmazzo).
Finally (Dittà Fratelli Vigna-Taglianti), in 1939.
(a).   Cuneo-Borgo San Dalmazzo, 8.0 km.
S.1878, Regauged 1914, C.1948.   Gauge. 1435 (later 1100).
Locomotives. -   No.   1,   Krauss 0-4-0   573 of 1877.
                         2,   Krauss 0-4-0   712 of 1878.   "
                         3,   Krauss 0-4-0   912 of 1880.   "

Names. -   1-Citta di Cuneo, 2-Alto Piemonte, 3-Carlo Ciappello.

(b).   As regauged and extended in 1914.
Cuneo-Borgo San Dalmazzo-Delmonte, 26.2 km.
Locomotives. -   Nos.   1-5,   Breda 0-4-0   1528-1532 of 1914.

Names. -   5-Delmonte.

Note. -   Borsig 0-4-0, 7225-7229 ordered for the regauging in 1909, but delivered to
                  Nos. 71 & 97 instead.

24. CUNEO. (Signori Berrier de la Leu e Bonardi).
Later (Compagnia Generale di Tramways a Vapore Piemontesi) Finally to 97.
Cuneo-Dronero, 18.4 km.
S.1897, C.1948, Gauge. 1100.
Locomotives. -   Nos.   1-3,   Winterthur 0-4-0   164,163 & 178 of 1879.
                         4-5,   Winterthur 0-4-0   201-202 of 1880.   "

Names. -   1-S.Giuseppe.

25. CUNEO. (Signori Berrier de la Leu e Bonardi).   Later as No.24 above, then as No.97.
Cuneo-Saluzzo, 30.2 km.
S.1880, A.1927, C.1948.   Gauge. 1100.
Locomotives. - Unnumbered Winterthur 0-4-0 187-189 of 1880.

26. FERRARA. (Società di Tranvie Ferraresi) ?   Later (S.A.Ferrovie e Tranvie Padane).
Ferrara-Ostellato-Codigoro, 52.3 km.
S.1901, R.1932. Still operating as railway.   Gauge. 1000 (to 1435 as railway).
Locomotives. -   Nos.   1-4,   Krauss 0-4-0   4275-4278 of 1900.
                         11-12, Henschel 0-4-0 5852-5853 of 1901.   "

Note. -   Loco No.4 was transferred to a light railway under the same management
                  at Rimini, was later derelict there for many years and is now preserved for
                  the Blonay-Chamby line in Switzerland.   See No.76

27. FIDENZA. Modern name for Borgo San Donino.   See No.80.

28. FIRENZE (Florence). (Signor Otlet).
Later (Société des Tramways Florentins - Bruxelles).
Firenze(Piazza Stazione)-Sesto Fiorentino, 9.7 km.
Firenze(S.M. Novella)-Le Cascine (Park), 0.8 km. (Public holiday service only).
Firenze(S.M. Novella)-Peretola-Campi-Prato, 21.0 km.
Peretola-Poggio a Caiano, 11.5 km.
H.1874 ?, S.1879, E.1898/1913, C.1956. Gauge. 1435.

Locomotives. -	Nos.	1-2,	Winterthur	0-4-0	159 & 161 of 1879.	(Sesto line).	
		3,	Winterthur	0-4-0	165 of 1879.	(" ").	
		4,	Krauss	0-4-0	617 of 1879.	(" ").	
		1-2,	Krauss	0-4-0	861-862 of 1880.	(Prato line).	"
		3-7,	Krauss	0-4-0	913-917 of 1880.	(" ").	"
		8-10,	Krauss	0-4-0	931-933 of 1881.		"
		11-12,	Krauss	0-4-0	1276-1277 of 1883.		"
		13.	Krauss	0-4-0	1393 of 1883.		"

Names. -   1- ?,
             10-Camro, 11-Firenze, 12- ?, 13-Prato.

29. FIRENZE (Florence). (S.A. Tramvie del Chianti). Taken over by No.28 by 1922.
Firenze(Duomo)-Viale dei Colli-Gelsomino, 9.6 km.
Firenze(Porta Romana)-Gelsomino-Falciani-Poggio Imperiale-Greve, 31.0 km.
Falciani-San Casciano, 4.3 km.
Poggio Imperiale-Campo di Marte, 7.2 km.
S.1889, Part C.1934, Rest E.1907/27. C.1956. Gauge. 1435.

Locomotives. -	Nos.	1-3,	Krauss 0-4-0	2208,2207 & 2206 of 1889.	
		4-8,	Krauss 0-4-0	2205,2204,2203,2202 & 2201 of 1889.	"
		9,	Krauss 0-6-0	? of ?	"
		10.	Krauss 0-6-0	2893 of 1893.	"

Names. -   1-9 not known   10-Greve.

30. FIRENZE(Florence). (S.A. dei Tramways Fiorentine).
Firenze(San Frediano)-La Lastra-Ponte a Signa-Porto di Mezzo, 13.0 km.
S.1881, E.1907/13, C.1956. Gauge. 1435.

Locomotives. -	Nos.	1-2,	Henschel 0-4-0	998-999 of 1879.	
		3-5,	Henschel 0-4-0	1143-1145 of 1880/81.	"
		6,	Henschel 0-4-0	1185 of 1881.	"
		7.	Henschel 0-4-0	2651 of 1888.	"

31. FIRENZE(Florence). (S.A. Tranvia Firenze-San Domenico).
Firenze(Le Cure)-San Domenico (for Fiesole), 7.3 km.
S.1886, E.1891, Trolleybus 1937. Gauge. 1435.
Locomotive.-   Krauss 0-4-0   1652 of 1888.

32. FORLÌ. (Signor Brusaporci). Later (Tacchis, Levie e Brusaporci).
Finally (S.A. dei Tranvie di Romagna).
Officina di Forlì-Forlì-Medola, 13.0 km.
Forlì-Ravenna, 27.0 km.
Ravenna-Classe, 4.3 km.
Forlì-Fondiera, 0.5 km.
S.1881, C.1930. Gauge. 1000.

Locomotives. -	Nos.	1-8,	Cerimedo 0-4-0	(Including Henschel 1302 of 1881).	
		9-10,	Krauss 0-4-0	1431 & 1434 of 1883.	"
		21-23,	La Meuse 0-4-0	2157-2159 of 1907.	
		31-32.	La Meuse 0-6-0	2717-2718 of 1913.	

33. GENOVA (Genoa). (Società dei Tramways Orientali di Genova).
Genova-Cimitero Staglieno, 4.1 km. (Approx.)
(Possibly only experiments on urban horse tramways).
H. ?, S.1883, E.1895, C.1966. Gauge. 1067 (1000 on electrification).

Locomotives. -	Nos.	1-3,	Winterthur 0-4-0	311-313 of 1883.	
		-,	Borsig "Rowan" car, 4263 of 1888.		

34. IACCO. (S.A. dei Tranvie Alta Versillia).
By 1922 (The Carrara'Versilia Electric Railway & Power Co. Ltd.).
In 1939 (S.A. Elettrica Tranviaria Litorena).
Iacco-Arni,   15.9 km. (Opened 1927).
Forte di Marmi-Seravezza-Trambissera,   9.7 km.
Pietrasanta-Seravezza-Pontestazzemese,   11.4 km.
S.1916/1927, C.1939. Gauge. 1000.
Locomotives. -   Nos.   1-3. ?   ?) Possibly Decauville 0-6-0   ex-Vendée   ⊢⊐
                         4-6. ?   ?) Tramways France. No.160.   "

35. ISEO. (Società per la Guidovia a Vapore Iseo-Rovato-Chiari).
Later (Società Nazionale delle Ferrovie e Tranvie, Brescia).
Iseo-Rovato-Chiari, 20.2 km. (Later extended to Soncino, 26.0 km ? See Nos. 9 & 15).
S.1897, R.1932, C.1954. Gauge. 950 (until 1911 ?, then 1435).
Locomotives. -   Nos.   1-2,   ?   ?   of 1897. (950 gauge).
                         3-4, ? Orenstein & Koppel 0-4-0   974-975 of 1902. (1435 gauge). ⊢⊐
                        11-12. Borsig 0-4-0   7087-7088 of 1909. (1435 gauge).   ⊟

36. IVREA. (Società Generale delle Strade Ferrate Economiche - Bruxelles). (Took over No.11).
Ivrea-Santhia, 29.3 km.
S.1882, C.1933. Gauge. 750.
Locomotives. -   Nos.   1-4,   Esslingen 0-4-0 1884-1887 of 1881.   ⊟
                         5,   Esslingen 0-4-0 1895 of 1882.   "
                         6.   Esslingen 0-4-0 1955 of 1883.   "

Names. -   1-Adige, 2-Ticino, 3-Tanaro, 4-Stura, 5-Sesia, 6- ?.

37. LOVERE. (Società della Guidovia della Valle Camuna).
Later owned by the (Provincia di Bergamo e Brescia).
Lovere-Darfo-Cividate, 22.4 km. (No.8 overlapped on a higher level).
S.1901, C.1917. Gauge. 950.
Locomotives. -   Nos.   1-2,   ?
                         3-5,   Orenstein & Koppel 0-4-0   797-799 of 1900.   ⊟
                         6.   Orenstein & Koppel 0-4-0   944 of 1902.   "

Names. -   1- ?, 2- ?, 3-Darfo, 4-Lovere ?, 5-Edolo, 6-Oglio.

Note. -   "Darfo" & "Edolo" were requisitioned in 1917 and operation ceased, but
                  "Orario Generale" for 1921 gives a list of times, with the remark (in Italian)
                  "No service until further notice", therefore, it must then have been
                  hoped to reopen the line.

38. LUCCA. (Signor Balestrieri, operating as "Tranvie Lucchesi").
by 1901, (S.A.Manifattura Italiana di Juta).
Finally (Consorzio Trasporti Secondari, Roma).
Lucca(Stazione)-Ponte a Moriano, 10.6 km.   ⊟
S.1883, C.1932. Gauge. 1435.
Locomotives. -   Nos.   1-4,   Cerimedo 0-4-0 (Hohenzollern 272, 277 & 309-310 of 1883/84) ?

39. LUCIA, Sicily. (S.A.Unio e Italiana fra Consumatori e Fabbricanti di Concimi e
Prodotti Chimici). An industrial line registered as a tramway.
1901 official returns show one passenger carriage. Replaced by narrow gauge railway in 1914.
Lucia-Porto Empedocle, 15.6 km.
S.1897, R.1914, Still Operating. Gauge. 600 (950 as railway).
Locomotives. -   Seven ?   ? (5 locos in 1901, 7 in 1907, possibly Cerimedo). ⊢⊐

40. LUGO. (Signor Filippo Baviani), later (Signori Pasini e Dragoni).
Lugo-Alfonsine, 18.0 km.
S.1885, C.1895. Gauge. 1435.

<u>Locomotives.</u> -   Unnumbered   Krauss 0-4-0   1261-1262 of 1884.
                 "   Krauss 0-4-0   1302-1303 of 1885.

<u>Names.</u> -   Lugo, Fusignano, Alfonsine & Senio (in works number order).

41.   MANTOVA. (Mantua). (S.A.Tramvie Provinciale di Mantova).
      Mantova-Gazzoldo-Asola,   36.3 km. (Connecting with No.21).
      Mantova-Ponte a Maiocche-Viadana, 41.3 km. (Connecting with No.21).
      Gazzoldo-Medole,   10.1 km.
      S.1886, A.1927, C.1933. Gauge. 1435.
      <u>Locomotives.</u> -   Nos.   1-7,   Maffei 0-4-0   1391-1397 of 1885.
                           8,   Maffei 0 4 0   1502 of 1889.
                        9-10,   Maffei 0-4 0   2852-2853 of 1908.

      <u>Names.</u> -   1-Mantova, 2-Virgilio, 3-Belfiore, 4-Montanara, 5-Curtatone, 6-Viadana,
                       7-Asola, 8-Pomponazzo, 9-Sordello, 10-Mincio.

42.   MANTOVA. (Mantua). See BRESCIA-Mantova-Ostiglia, No.16.

43.   MASSA. (S.A.Tramvie di Massa).
      Massa Stazione-Massa-Poggio Piastrone-Forno, 8.6 km.
      Massa-Marina di Massa,   4.4 km.
      S.1890, C.1932. Gauge. 1000.
      <u>Locomotives.</u> -   Nos.   1-3,   Breda   0-4-0   198-200 of 1890.
                         4-5,   Breda   0-4-0   204-205 of 1890 ?
                           6,   Henschel   0-4-0   6220 of 1902.
                           7,   Henschel   0-4-0   8590 of 1907.
                         8-9,   Henschel   0-4-0   12505-12506 of 1914.
                       12-13,   Winterthur 0-6-0   621-622 of 1890, ex-Geneva.᛬ Swiss No.7 "
                       16-19,   Winterthur 0-6-0   625-628 of 1890, "   "   "   " "
                          20,   Winterthur 0-6-0   641 of 1890, "   "   "   " "

      <u>Names.</u> -   1-Chirullo, 2-Frigido.
                       8-Citta di Massa, 9-Poggio Piastrone.

44.   MESSINA. Sicily. (S.A.Tramvie di Messina ?).
      Possibly only experiments on existing horse tramway.
      Route ? ?
      H. ?, S.1884, C. before 1890. Later E. Gauge. 750.
      <u>Locomotives.</u> -   Nos.   1-2,   Winterthur 0-4-0   352-353 of 1884.
                           3,   Krauss   0-4-0   1027 of 1884.

45.   MESSINA. Sicily. (S.A.Tramvie di Napoli). Later (S.A.Tranvie Siciliane).
      Messina-Granatari-Barcellona,   62.4 km.
      Giampilieri-Messina-Faro Superiore, 44.5 km.
      S.1890, E.1917, C.1931/43. Gauge. 950.
      <u>Locomotives.</u> -   Nos.   1-4,   St.Léonard 0-4-0   818-821 of 1889.
                        5-10,   St.Léonard 0-6-0   852-857 of 1890.
                       11-12,   St.Léonard 0-6-0   924-925 of 1892.
                       13-15,   St.Léonard 0-6-0   963-965 of 1894.

      <u>Names.</u> -   1-Nettuno, 2-Pace, 3-Gargieri, 4-Faro, 5-Messina, 6-Corsari, 7-Divieto,
                       8-Spadofora, 9-Meri, 10-Barcellona, 11-Paola, 12-Gazzi, 13-Zacra,
                       14-San Stefano, 15-Giampilieri.

      <u>Note.</u> -   A·works photo exists showing No.9 as "Barcellona".

46.   MESTRE. See PADOVA, No.65.

47. MILANO. (S.A. del Tramway Milano-Gorgonzola-Vaprio).
Amalgamated with No.48 in 1882 to become No.49.
Milano(Porta Venezia)-Cascina Gobba-Gorgonzola-Vaprio, 20.2 km.
Cascina Gobba-Brugherio-Vimercate,   15.5 km. (Connecting with No.57).
Brugherio-Monza Sobborghi,   3.7 km. (Opposite side of railway
                                               from Nos. 56 & 57).
S.1878, E.1922/29, R.1970.   Still operating.   Gauge. 1435.

Locomotives. -	Unnumbered	Bamat	0-4-0	1 of 1878.	
		Fox Walker	0-4-2	411 ? of 1878.	"
		Krauss	0-4-0	713-714 of 1878.	"
		Henschel	0-4-0	975 of 1879.	"
		Henschel	0-4-0	1228 of 1882. (via Cerimedo).	"
	Nos. 1-3,	Winterthur	0-4-0	141-143 of 1878.	"
	4-7,	Winterthur	0-4-0	183-184 of 1880.	"
		Baldwin Steam car 4314 of 1878.			

Names. -   Bamat-"L'ITALIANA", Krauss-Crescenzago, Adda, Baldwin-Cossenzago.

48. MILANO. (Cav. Ferdinando Pistorius). Amalgamated with No.47 in 1882 to form No.49.
Milano-(Porto Romana)-Rogoredo-Melegnano-Lodi, 30.8 km.
Melegnano-Sant'Angelo,   15.2 km. (Connecting with No.53).
Lodi-Treviglio-Bergamo,   25.5 km.
Villa Fornaci-Treviglio-Caravaggio,   16.5 km. (Connecting with No.47).
S.1879, Part E.1918, Part P.1927, C.1937. Gauge. 1435.

Locomotives. -	Nos. 1-2,	Henschel	0-4-0	1005-1006 of 1879.	
	3-4,	Henschel	0-4-0	1048-1049 of 1879.	"
	5-7,	Henschel	0-4-0	1034, 1033, 1035 of 1879.	"
	8-9,	Henschel	0-4-0	1050, 1059 of 1879.	"
	10-16,	Henschel	0-4-0	1016-1022 of 1880.	"
	17-18,	Henschel	0-4-0	1071-1072 of 1879.	"
	19-20,	Henschel	0-4-0	1104-1105 of 1880.	"
	21-24,	Henschel	0-4-0	1127-1128 of 1880 & 1139-1140 of 1880.	"
	25-28,	Henschel	0-4-0	1156-1159 of 1880/81.	"
	29-31,	Henschel	0-4-0	1175-1177 of 1881.	"
	32,	Henschel	0-4-0	1227 of 1881.	"

Names. -   1-Bergamo, 2-Treviglio, 3-Lodi, 4- ?, 5-Stazzano, 6- ?, 7- ?,
8-Arcene, 9- ?, 10- ?, 11-Roma, 12-Milano, 13-Creina, 14-Cassano d'Adda,
15-Melegnano, 16-Sant'Angelo, 17-Arzago, 18-Tuzago, 19-Cernusco,
20-Villa Fornaci, 21-Napoli, 22-Ferdinanda, 23-Adda, 24-Lambro, 25-Serio,
26-Po, 27-Gamboloita, 28-Rogoredo, 29-San Donato, 30-San Giuliano,
31-San Grato, 32-Tavazzano.

Note. -   Milan Municipal tramways electrified the short section Milano-Rogoredo
in 1918 and the company built four electric cars to pull trains over it.

49. MILANO. (S.A. Tramvie Interprovinciale di Milano, Bergamo e Cremona).
Later (S.A. Tranvie Inter-Provinciale Padane, "T.I.P").
An amalgamation of Nos. 47 & 48, plus a short connecting line in Milan.
Milano(Porta Venezia)-Milano(Porta Romana), 3.0 km. (approx.).

Locomotives. -	Nos 1-32,	Those of No.48, which see.			
	33-35,	Winterthur	0-4-0	141-143 of 1878. ex-No.47.	
	36-38,	Winterthur	0-4-0	184-186 of 1880. ex-No.47.	"
	39-40,	Henschel	0-4-0	975 of 1878 & 1228 of 1882. ex-No.47.	"
	41-42,	Krauss	0-4-0	713-714 of 1878. ex-No.47.	"
	43,	Fox Walker	0-4-2	411 of 1878. ex-No.47.	"
	44,	Bamat	0-4-0	1 of 1878. ex-No.47. ?	"
	45-46,	Esslingen	0-4-0	2060-2061 of 1885. Acquired new.	"
	47-49,	Henschel	0-4-0	2557-2559 of 1888. " "	"
	50-51,	Henschel	0-4-0	2879-2880 of 1889. " "	"
	52,	Henschel	0-4-0	3660 of 1892. " "	"
	53-56,	Henschel	0-4-0	5577-5580 of 1900. " "	"
	57-58,	Henschel	0-4-0	2378-2379 of 1887. ex-Naples, No.60.	"
	59,	Henschel	0-4-0	2707 of 1888. " " "	"

60-61,	St.Léonard	0-6-0	678-679 of 1883. ex-Naples, No.60.	⊏╜
62-64,	Tubize	0-6-0	1573-1575 of 1908. Acquired new.	"
65-70,	Borsig	0-6-0	7370-7375 of 1909. " "	"
71-72,	Borsig	0-6-0	7382-7385 of 1909. " "	"
73-80,	-	-	Numbers probably not occupied.	
81-85.	Tubize	0-6-0	1705-1709 of 1911.	⌐╜

Note. -   Nos.67 & 70 exchanged numbers and names after an accident, but not works
             numbers.

Names. -   Nos.1-32 as with No.48.   33-Vimodrone, 34-Trezzo, 35-Concorezzo,
             36-Romanenzo, 37-Ottanengo, 38-Soncino, 39-Ticengo, 40-Crema,
             41-Crescenzago, 42-Adda, 43-Vimercate, 44-Pozzuoli, 45-Monza,
             46-Caravaggio, 47-Salerano, 48-Loreto, 49-Mairano, 50-Colognola, 51-Riolo,
             52-S.Albino, 53-Verdello, 54-Bernareggia, 55-Oglio, 56-Muzza, 57-Saati,
             58-Tusaro, 59-Dogali, 60-Margharita, 61-Toretta, 62-64-not named,
             65-Dovera, 66-Cazzera, 67-Gorgonzola, 68-Martesana, 69-Mulino Nuovo,
             70-San Donato, 71-Vaprio, 72-Ombriano. Nos.81-85 not named.

50.   MILANO.   (Lombardy Road Railway Co. Ltd.), in association with the (Tramways & General
      Works Co. Ltd., of London and Milan).
      Later (Società Trazione Elettrica Lombarda).
      From 1939, (Azienda Tranviaria Municipale Interurbane, Milano).
      (a).   Northern Section :-
      Milano(Porta Volta)-Seregno-Giussano, 24.5 km.
      Seregno-Carate Brianza,   3.5 km.
      Monza(Largo Manzini)-Carate Brianza, 11.3 km. (Not connecting with Nos.56 or 57).
      S.1881, E.1926/1939, Part still operating. Gauge. 1435.
      (b).   Southern Section :-
      Lodi-Sant'Angelo,   10.2 km. (Connecting with Nos. 49 & 53).
      Lodi-Crema-Soncino, 35.2 km. (Worked by No.49 from 1921. Connecting with Nos. 9 & 15).
      S.1881, C.1931. Gauge. 1435.

Locomotives. -	Unnumbered	Henschel 0-4-0	1060, 1062-1063 of 1879/80.	⊏╜
		Henschel 0-4-0	1173-1174, 1180-1184 & 1229 of 1881.	"
		Henschel 0-4-0	1283, 1299-1301 of 1881.	"
		Henschel 0-4-0	1488-1489 & 1560 of 1883.	"
		Henschel 0-4-0	3265-3266 of 1890.	"
		Henschel 0-4-0	9316 of 1909 & 9861 of 1910.	"
		Henschel 0-4-0	10443-10444 of 1911.	"

Names. -   1283-Desio, 1489-Ticengo, 3265-Cinisello, 3266-Monza, 9861-Macherio.

51.   MILANO. (Milan Tramways Co. Ltd., London). Saronno line taken over by (Ferrovia
      Nord Milano) in 1889 and extended to Tradate.
      Rest became (S.A. Tramvie e Ferrovie Economiche di Milano, Roma e Bologna).
      Milano(Parco Sempione)-Saronno-Tradate,   36.0 km.
      Milano(Parco Sempione)-Legnano-Gallarate, 39.9 km.
      H.1877, S.1878, (Tradate line R.1921), Rest E.1914/1922, C.1967. Gauge. 1435.

Locomotives. -	Nos.	1,	Winterthur 0-4-0	119 of 1877. (Saronno line).	⊏╜
		2-4,	Winterthur 0-4-0	140 & 144-145 of 1878.	"
		5, ?	Hagans 0-4-0	85 of 1879.	"
	101-105,		Couillet 0-4-0	415-419 of 1879.	⌐╜
	01-03,		Henschel 0-4-0	1027 of 1879 & 1073-1074 of 1880. (Saronno line)
	04,		Krauss 0-4-0	571 of 1877.	" ⊏╜ "
	05-07,		Krauss 0-4-0	6076-6078 of 1908.	"
	10-11,		Henschel 0-4-0	1223-1224 of 1881. (Gallarate line).	"
	BC 33-34.		Henschel 0-4-0	9716-9717 of 1910. " "	"

Name.-   04-Vittorio Emanuele. (Krauss's first tram engine).

Note. -   Possibly common numbering with Nos. 13 & 77, under same ownership.

191

52. MILANO. (S.A. del Tramway a Vapore Milano-Sedriano-Magenta-Cuggiono-Càstano Primo).
From 1922 (Società del Tranvay Milano-Càstano). "M.M.C.".
From 1939 (Azienda Tranviaria Municipale Inter-urbane, Milano).
Milano(Corso Vercelli)-Sedriano-Magenta, 23.0 km. (including 1.5 km over urban track).
Sedriano-Cuggiono-Càstano Primo, 20.8 km.
S.1879, WS.1954, C.1957. Gauge. 1435.

Locomotives. -	Nos.	1-6,	Krauss	0-4-0	715-716, 823 & 799-781 of 1879.	🔔
		7,	Krauss	0-4-0	860 of 1880.	"
		8,	Krauss	0-4-0	1631 of 1885.	"
		9-10,	?	?	(not known but before 1901).	"
	(II)	2,	Krauss	0-4-0	5195 of 1904.	"
		11,	Krauss	0-4-0	5410 of 1906.	"
		12,14,	Krauss	0-4-0	5839-5840 of 1907.	"
		15-17,	Krauss	0-4-0	6344-6346 of 1910.	"
	Possibly	18,	Esslingen	0-4-0	3610 of 1911. (built at Saronno).	"
		64,	Tubize	0-6-0	1575 of 1908. (SNCV type) ex-No.49. ∵	"
	65,68,70-71,		Borsig	0-6-0	7370,7373,7372 & 7382 of 1909 ex-No.49.	
(Later numbered 80).82,			Tubize	0-6-0	1706 of 1911. ex-No.49. ∵	
	(II)	82,	St.Léonard	0-4-0	1577 of 1909, ex-No.53. ∵	🔔
		108,110,	St.Léonard	0-4-0	1546, 1548 of 1908, ex-No.53.∵	"
		111.	Tubize	0-4-0	1683 of 1912, ex-No.53. ∵	"

Names. - Nos.1-10, not known (Probably plates transferred to later machines as below).
(II)2-Sedriano, 11-Cuggiono, 12- ?, 14- ?, 15-Milano, 16-Inveruno,
17-Vittuone, 18- ?, 64-not named, 65-S.Pietro all'Olmo, 68-Càstano,
70-Magenta, 71-Sedriano, Others not named. (64-111 retained former numbers).

53. MILANO. (Signori Righetti e Lue).
Later (Société des Tramways et Chemins de Fer de la Haute Italie). Belgian.
Finally (Società delle Ferrovie del Ticino). Leased to No.52, 1933/36.
Milano(Porta Lodovica)-Binasco-Pavia, 33.9 km.
Pavia-Sant'Angelo, 23.0 km. (Connecting with Nos. 48 & 50).
S.1880, C.1936. Gauge. 1435.

Locomotives. -	Nos.	1-10,	Tubize	0-4-2	372-381 of 1880.	🔔
		30 & 50-56,	Henschel	0-4-0	1284, 1550-1556 of 1883. (Possibly used	"
		100-107,	Couillet	0-4-0	677-684 of 1882. for a time).	"
		108-110,	St.Léonard	0-4-0	1546-1548 of 1908. (Couillet type).	"
		111,	Tubize	0-4-0	1683 of 1912. " " "	"
		82,	St.Léonard	0-4-0	1577 of 1909 (Transferred from No.63).	"

Note. - Locomotives numbered in S.F.T. general tram and railway series. See No.111.

54. MODENA. (S.A. per la Ferrovia Modena, Mirandola e Finale).
Later (Società Emiliana di Ferrovie, Tranvie ed Automobili).
Worked by Modena-Mirandola Railway then of same gauge.
Modena-Maranello, 16.3 km.
S.1893, C.1938. Gauge. 950.

| Locomotives. - | Nos. | 1, | Krauss 0-4-0 | 1098 of 1883. (Formerly No.9 of railway). | ⌐┘ |
| | | 2-3, | Krauss 0-4-0 | 1066, 1065 of 1882. (Formerly 7 & 6 of railway). | |

Name. - 1-Pico, 2-Finale, 3-Mirandola.

55. MONZA. (Lombardy Road Railway Co. Ltd.). See No.50.

56. MONZA. (Società Anonima della Tramvia Monza-Barzanò).
Replaced in 1915 by a railway on a slightly different course).
Monza(Sobborghi)-Barzanò-Molteno-Oggiono, 31.0 km.
S.1879, Ceased operation 1915, C.1921. Gauge. 1435.

Locomotives. -	Nos.	1,	Cerimedo	0-4-0	(Henschel 1061 of 1880).	🔔
		2-4,	Hagans	0-4-0	86-88 of 1879.	"
		5-6,	Hagans	0-4-0	105-106 of 1880.	"
		7.	Winterthur	0-6-0	1525 of 1903.	"

57. MONZA. (Società Anonima della Tramvia Monza-Trezzo-Bergamo). "M.T.B.".
From 1939 (Azienda Tranviaria Municipale Interurbane, Milano). See also 52.
Monza(Stazione)-Trezzo-Dalmine(Bivio)-Bergamo, 38.9 km. (Connecting with Nos.7 & 47).
Dalmine Bivio-Dalmine Centro, 1.0 km. (Opened in 1930s to serve industrial estate).
S.1890, A(WS).1932, C.1958. Gauge. 1435.

Locomotives. -	Nos.				
	1-4,	Krauss	0-4-0	2186-2189 of 1889? (for agent - Belloli).	🛏
	5,	Henschel	0-4-0	3496 of 1891.	"
	6,	Krauss	0-4-0	2848 of 1893.	"
	7-8,	Breda	0-4-0	316-317 of 1895. (Krauss design).	"
	9-10,	Krauss	0-6-0	6108 of 1909 & 6259 of 1910.	"
	11-12,	Krauss	0-6-0	6152-6153 of 1909. (Intended for No.7 ?).	"
	14,	Krauss	0-6-0	5872 of 1907, ex-No.13. ∵	"
(II)	2,	Breda	0-6-0	2136 of 1924, ex-No.7. ∵	"
(III)	2,	Greco	0-6-0	(No works number or date).	🛏
(II)	4,	Esslingen	0-6-0	1785 of 1880 ex-No.20∵then No.108.∵	"
(II)	6,	Henschel	0-4-0	3660 of 1892, ex-No.49.∵	🛏
	21,	Henschel	0-4-0	6366 of 1903, ex-No.107 ∵then 108.∵	🛏
	22,	Krauss	0-6-0	4901 of 1902, ex-Industry,∵(rebuilt by Greco).	
	23,	Henschel	0-6-0	9720 of 1909, ex-Nos.107/108. ∵	🛏
	24-25,	Henschel	0-6-0	10104-10105 of 1910, ex-No.108. ∵	"
	32,	Henschel	0-4-0	1227 of 1881, ex-No.49. ∵	"
	34,	Henschel	0-4-0	9716 of 1909, ex-No.51. (Preserved).∵	"
	-.	Henschel	0-6-0	20977 of 1927. On loan from Industry in 1945.	
					🛏

Names. -   Nos.1-4, (Possibly - Monza, Trezzo, Bergamo & Vimercate), 5-8 not named.
9- ?, 10-Trezzo, 11- ?, 12- ?, 14-not named, 22-Vimercate, 23-not named,
24-Bergamo, 25-(possibly "Monza"), 34-(later)-Trezzo. (II)2-Brianza,
Unnumbered-Valtellina.

Notes. -   Name plates were transferred as locomotives were withdrawn.
Locomotives 64, 65, 68, 70, 71 & 80 of No.52 worked on this line 1951-58.
No.21 was rebuilt from an enclosed engine and 22 from narrow gauge, both
before acquisition. (II) 4, was rebuilt with a Krauss boiler in 1954,
and No.(III)2 appears to have acquired the boiler of (II)2.
The Alta-Valtellina Railway also had a loco named "Valtellina".

58. MONDOVI. (Felice del Vecchio). From 1885 (Angelo del Vecchio).
Later owned by (S.A. della Ferrovia Fossano-Mondovi-Villanova).
From 1933 (S.A. Tranvie di Mondovi).
Mondovi-San Michele, 10.6 km.
S.1881, E.1923, C.1953. Gauge. 950.

Locomotives. -	Nos.				
	1,	Hagans	0-4-0	148 of 1883.	🛏
	2,	Henschel	0-4-0	1638 of 1883.	"
	3,	Henschel	0-4-0	2043 of 1885.	"
	4,	Henschel	0-4-0	2427 of 1887.	"
	5.	Henschel	0-4-0	9719 of 1907.	"

59. MORTARA. (Società Ferrovie del Ticino). See NOVARA, No.63.

60. NAPOLI. (Naples). (S.A. delle Tranvie di Napoli).
Napoli(Museo)-Via Salvador Rosa-La Torretta, 5.7 km. (Museo-Via S.Rocca - rack).
La Torretta-Pozzueli, 9.7 km.
S.1883, E.1902, C.1948 ?. Gauge. 1435.

Locomotives. -	Nos.				
	1-2,	Henschel	0-4-0	1557-1558 of 1883.	🛏
	3-4,	St.Léonard	0-6-0	678-679 of 1883. (Later sold to No.49).	"
	5-6,	Esslingen	0-4-0z	2119-2120 of 1885.(Rack).	"
	7-8,	Henschel	0-4-0	2378-2379 of 1887.(Later sold to No.49).	"
	9-10,	Henschel	0-4-0	2706-2707 of 1888.	"
	11,	Esslingen	0-4-0z	2310 of 1888.(Rack).	"
	12-13,	Henschel	0-4-0	3970,3969 of 1893.(Later sold to No.93).	"
	14,	Henschel	0-4-0	5880 of 1901. " " " " "	"
	-.	Borsig "Rowan" car,		4204 of 1896.(Later sold to No.6).	🚃

Names. -   1- ?, 2- ?, 3-Margharita, 4-Torretta, 5- ?, 6-Leopoldina, 7-Saati,
8-Tusaro, 9- ?, 10-Dogali, 11-San Severino.

193

61. NAPOLI. (Naples). S.A. dei Tramways a Vapore di Napoli).
Later (S.A. Tranvie Provinicale di Napoli) (Belgian owned).
Napoli(Reclusorio)-Capodicino-Colonne di Giugliano-Aversa, 20.2 km.
Capodicino-Afragola-Caivano,   14.3 km.
Colonne di Giugliano-Giugliano,   1.5 km.
Colonne di Giugliano-Cappelluccia,   3.7 km.
S.1881, E.1899/1901, C.1962.   Gauge. 1435.

Locomotives. -	Nos.	1-5,	Krauss	0-4-0	944-948 & 951 of 1881.
		6-7,	Krauss	0-4-0	986-987 of 1881.
		8-11,	Krauss	0-4-0	1129-1132 of 1882.
		12-13,	Krauss	0-6-0	1133-1134 of 1882.
		14-15.	Krauss	0-4-0	1257-1258 of 1883.

Names. -   1- ?, 2- ?, 3- ?, 4- ?, 5-Caivano.

62. NOVARA. (S.A.Tramvia Novara-Galliate).   Became part of No.63 in 1886.
Novara-Galliate, 8.0 km.
S.1880, Taken over by No.63 in 1886, C.1934.   Gauge. 1435.

| Locomotives. - | Nos. | 1-2, | Winterthur 0-4-0 | 199-200 of 1880. |
| | | 3. | Winterthur 0-4-0 | 248 of 1881. |

63. NOVARA. (Signor Charpillon & Ing.G.Provasi).
Later (Société des Chemins de Fer Lombards) (Belgian owned).
Finally (Società Ferrovie del Ticino).
Novara-Galliate-Vigevano,   31.7 km. (Including No.62).
Vigevano-Ottobiano,   19.3 km.
Mortara-Ottobiano-Pieve del Cairo,   27.2 km.
Novara-Biandriate,   11.8 km.
Vercelli-Biandriate-Fara,   32.1 km.
Vercelli-Casale Monferrato,   28.1 km. (Connecting with No.2).
S.1883, C.1934. Gauge. 1435.

| Locomotives. - | Nos. | 61-79, | Couillet | 0-4-0 | 658-676 of 1882. |
| | | 81-82. | St.Léonard 0-4-0 | 1576-1577 of 1909. (Couillet design). |

Note. -   Probably combined numbering with Nos.53 & 111 and some railways.
               Some of the Henschel locomotives from No.111 may have worked on this system.

64. NOVI LIGURE. (Signor Luigi della Betta).
Later (S.A. per la Tranvia Novi Ligure-Ovada).
Finally (S.A. Ferroviaria Val d'Orba) which also worked the Basaluzzo-Frugarlo Railway
as a branch of the tramway with same stock.
Novi Ligure-Basaluzzo-Ovada, 23.2 km.
S.1881, D(GS).1940, C.1952. Gauge. 1435.

Locomotives. -	Nos.	1,	Merryweather 0-4-0	74 ?	of 1878 ?
		2-3,	Henschel	0-4-0	1379-1380 of 1882.
		4-7,	Henschel	0-4-0	1245-1248 of 1881.
		8.	Henschel	0-4-0	2080 of 1885.

Replacements. -		10-11,	Tubize	0-6-0	1574 & 1573 of 1909. ex-No.49. (SNCV type).
		12-15,	Tubize	0-6-0	1705,1708,1707,1709 of 1911, ex-No.49?.
	(II)	15.	Esslingen	0-6-0	1837 of 1881, ex-No.20.

Note. -   Nos. 10-15 were later renumbered 31-36.

65. PADOVA. (Padua). (Società Veneta - See No.14 for full title).
Padova-Malcontenta-Fusina, 40.4 km. (for ferry to Venice).
Malcontenta-Mestre,   7.1 km.
Padova-Piove di Sacco,   18.9 km.
Padova-Bagnoli di Sopra,   27.5 km.
S.1885, E.1909/1913, C.1954. Gauge. 1435.

Locomotives. -	Nos.171-178,	Henschel 0-4-0	1977-1984 of 1885.	⊟
	179-184,	Henschel 0-4-0	2134-2139 of 1886.	"
	(II) 170-172,	Henschel 0-4-0	2480,2482 & 2484 of 1887 (see below).	"
			(Rebuilt from 211, 213 & 215 of No.107).	

Names. -   171-Dola, 172-Stra, 173-Bagnoli, 174-Conselve, 175-Mira, 176- ?,
                   177-Sillaro, 178-Savena, 179-Ponte di Brenta, 180-Noventa, 181-Oriago,
                   182-Sellustra, 183-Mestre, 184-Cartura.

Note. -   These locos later renumbered 140-143, 150, 144, 151, 145-147, 161-162,
                   149, 160, 152, 148, 163 and 154. (Very wide bodies and side buffers
                   for running over S.V. Railway lines).

66.   PARMA. (Compagna Nazionale di Trasporti e Communicazione).
        Later (Società Riuniti di Trasporti).

Parma(Stazione)-Pilastrello-Montecchio,	17.6 km.	
Pilastrello-Travesetolo,	7.0 km.	(later A).
Parma(Stazione)-Crocetta-Soragna-Busseto,	36.8 km.	
Parma(Stazione)-San Secondo-Busseto,	41.5 km.	(later A).
Parma(Stazione)-Stradella-Fornovo,	22.6 km.	(later E).
Stradella-Marzolara,	17.4 km.	(later E).
Fornace Bizzi-Medesano,	11.6 km.	
Soragna-Borgo San Donino(Fidenza),	9.1 km.	(Connecting with No.80).

S.1893, Part A.1925, Part E.1922/1935, C. ?, Gauge. 1435.

Locomotives. -	Nos.	1-6,	Breda	0-4-0	259-264 of 1892.	⊟
		7-15,	Breda	0-4-0	? ? of ?	"
		16-19,	Henschel 0-4-0	8592-8585 of 1907.	"
		20-22,	Henschel 0-4-0	10101-10103 of 1910.	"
		23-24,	Henschel 0-4-0	11401-11402 of 1912.	"

Names. -   1- ?, 2- ?, 3- ?, 4-Busseto, (preserved privately),
                   16-Noceto, 17- ?, 18-Fornovo.

67.   PAVIA. (Società Ferrovie del Ticino), See No.53.

68.   PIACENZA. (Signor Mackenzie), (Piacenza, Bettola & Cremona Tramways Co. Ltd.).
        Amalgamated with No.69 in 1905 and became :- (Società Italiana di Ferrovie e Tranvie).

Piacenza-Grazzano-Bettola,	35.6 km.	(R. in 1933).
Grazzano-Riverago,	7.9 km.	
Piacenza-Cremona,	33.5 km.	
Piacenza-Borgonovo-Nibbiano,	36.0 km.	(built after amalgamation with No.69).
Borgonovo-Agazzano,	7.3 km.	(" " " " ").

S.1881, (Bettola line ER.1933, C.1967), Rest C.1938. Gauge. 1435.

Locomotives. -	Nos.	1-3,	Winterthur 0-4-0	196-198 of 1880.	⊟
		4-11,	Cerimedo 0-4-0	? ? of 1891/1900.	"
		1-3,	Breda	0-6-0	753-755 of 1905 (for S.I.A.F.T.).	"
		12-24,	?	?	(Locomotives taken over from No.69) ?	"
		25-30,	Jung	0-4-0	1262-1267 of 1908.	"

	Nos.	31-33;	Henschel 0-4-0	10875-10877 of 1911.	⊟
		34-36,	Breda	0-6-0	1643-1645 of 1914.	"
		(II) 33.	Greco	0-4-0	(No date or works number).	⊟

Names. -   1- ?, etc. not known.
                   25-Samarto, 26-Rottofermo, 27-Grazzano, 28-Giovei, 29-Ronecaglio,
                   30-San Nazzaro, 31- ?, 32- ?, 33-Gragnano. (II)33-Not named.

69.   PIACENZA. (S.A. per la Tramvia della Provincia di Piacenza).
        Amalgamated with No.68 in 1905.

Piacenza-Pianello,	37.2 km.
Piacenza-Lugagnano,	37.0 km.
Cremona-Lugagnano,	30.5 km.

S.1893, P.1930, C.1938. Gauge. 1435.

Locomotives. -   Nos.   1-2,   Breda 0-4-0 265-266 of 1892.
                         3-10,   Breda 0-4-0 259-264? of 1893.

Names. -   1-Castel San Giovanni, etc.

70. PINEROLO. (Compagnia Generale dei Tramways a Vapore Piemontesi). Later worked by 97.
     Pinerolo-Cavour-Saluzzo, 30.8 km. (Connecting with Nos. 71 & 93 & 97).
     S.1882, C.1939 ?, Gauge. 1100.
     Locomotives. -   Nos.   4,   Hagans 0-4-0 111 of 1881.
                               5-7, Krauss 0-4-0 1154, 1184-1185 of 1881.

     Names. -   4- ?, 5-Alfieri, 6-Gordini, 7-Malabaila. (Common numbering with No.24).

71. PINEROLO. Owned by (Signor Giuliano).
     Later (S.A. Tranvia Pinerolo-Perosa Argentina).
     Pinerolo-Villar Perosa-Perosa Argentina, 17.9 km.
     S.1886, ER.1921, C.1968. Gauge. 1100.
     Locomotives. -   Nos.   1-3,   Winterthur 0-4-0 285-287 of 1882.
                               4,   Winterthur 0-4-0   345 of 1883.
                               5-6,   Winterthur?0-4-0 ?   ? of ?
                               7,   ?   ?   ? by 1901.
                     (II)   2.   Borsig   0-4-0 (one of 7225-7229 of 1909 intended for No.22).

     Names. -   1- ?, 2- ?, 3- ?, 4-Assietta, 5-Pragelato, 6-Val Chisone,
                     7- ?, (II)2-Perosa.

     Note. -   Photographs of Nos.5-6 show typical Winterthur machines like 1-4, of No.4.
                     works numbers not legible. Possibly ex-No.4.

72. PISA. (Società Italiana delle Ferrovie Economiche e Tranvie a Vapore per la Provincia
     di Pisa). Later (S.A. Imprese e Trasporti di Pisa).
     Pisa-Navacchio-Pontedera, 20.4 km.
     Navacchio-Calci,   5.5 km.
     Pisa-Marina di Pisa,   12.8 km. (Later ER).
     S.1884, (Part ER.1932, C.1960), Rest D.1935, C.1953. Gauge. 1435.
     Locomotives. -   Nos.   1-6,   Henschel 0-4-0 1684-1689 of 1883. (Covering later removed).
                               7,   Henschel 0-4-0   1937 of 1884. Ex-contractors for No.78.
                               8-9,   Henschel 0-4-0 7219-7220 of 1905.
                     (II)   4.   Henschel 0-6-0   2248 of 1887. ᛫

     Names. -   1- ?, 2- ?, 3-Dante Aligheri, 4-Leonardo Fibonacci, 5- ?, 6-Camilla del Lante,
                     7-Andrea di Pontedera, 8-Marina, 9-Nicola Pisano.

73. PONTE TRESA. (Società di Navigazione e Ferrovie del Lago di Lugano).
     A steam light railway later electrified as part of the Varese Tramways.
     Ponte Tresa-Luino, 12.0 km.
     S.1884, E.1910, C.1954. Gauge. 1000.
     Locomotives. -   Nos. 1 & 3,   Esslingen 0-6-0 2026-2027 of 1884.
                       2, 4, 5, 6,   Esslingen 0-6-4 2034-2037 of 1884.

     Note. -   Locomotives shared with Menaggio-Porlezza railway under same management.

74. PRACCHIA. Title ?. Later (S.A. Ferrovia Alto Pistoiese).
     Pracchia-Campo Tizzoro, 5.0 km.
     S. ?, ER.1926, C.1966. Gauge. 1000.
     Locomotives. -   Nos.   1-2,   Henschel 0-4-0 12505-12506 of 1914, ex-No.43.
                               3.   ?   0-4-0   ? of ?

75. RAVENNA. See FORLÌ, No.32.

76. **RIMINI.** (S.A.Ferrovie e Tranvie Padane).
A light railway which used one enclosed locomotive, from No.26 under same management.
Rimini-Mercantino Marecchio (renamed Nova Feltria), 35.5 km.
S.1915, D.1948, C.1962. Gauge. 950.

Locomotives. -   Nos.   4,   Krauss 0-4-0   4278 of 1900.   Now preserved in Switzerland ⊟
                   21   Orenstein & Koppel   0-6-0   3593 of 1910.   ⊞
             61-62.   Breda   0-8-0   1548-1549 of 1915.   "

77. **ROMA** (Rome). (Società Anonima dei Tramways e Ferrovie Economiche di Roma,
Milano, Bologna, ecc.)
From 1928 (Società delle Tramvie e Ferrovie Elettriche di Roma) "S.T.E.F.E.R."
(1932-1934 served only one factory at Ponte Mammalo).
Roma (Pz.Tibertina).Bivio di Roma-Tivoli, 28.4 km.
S.1879, GS.1931, C.1934. Gauge. 1405.

Locomotives. -   Nos.   1-6,   Hohenzollern 0-6-0   178-183 of 1881.   ⊟
           (II)   1,   Krauss   0-6-0   410 of 1876.   ✌ in 1883.   ⊞
           (II)   2,   Winterthur   0-4-0   139 of 1879.   ⊞
          C.31-32,   Henschel   0-4-0   1118-1119 of 1880 ex No.78.
          C.33,   Henschel   0-4-0   10421 of 1911.   "
          C.34,   Henschel   0-4-0   11686 of 1912.

Note. -   No.1 (II) was formerly "Uto" of the Uetlibergbahn of Zurich, Switzerland.

78. **ROMA** (Rome). (Signori Villa e Taddei). From 1883 as No.77.
Bivio di Roma-Ciampino-Marino, 22.0 km. (Connecting with No.77).
S.1882, R.1889. Still operating as railway. Gauge. 1435.
(Ciampino-Marino became part of a through railway to Albano).

Locomotives. -   C.31-C.32,   Henschel 0-4-0   1118-1119 of 1880.   ⊞
          102-105,?   Krauss   0-6-0   1532-1535 of 1884.   "

79. **SALE.** See Alessandria No.2 and Tortona No.98.

80. **SALSOMAGGIORE.** (Tranvia Borgo San Donino-Salsomaggiore).
Owned at first by Signor A.Corradi and Later by Signor Luigi Corazza from 1907 to 1922.
Finally (S.A.Autoguidovie Italiane).
Salsomaggiore-Borgo San Donino(now called Fidenza), 9.3 km. (Connecting with No.66).
S.1890, P.1926, D.1933, R.1938, Still operating as railway. Gauge. 1435.

Locomotives. -   Nos.   1-3,   Dick Kerr   0-6-0   ? - ? of 1890.   ⊞
                 4,   Unknown   0-6-0   ?   of 1902 ?   "
                 5.   Henschel   0-6-0   13003 of 1914.   ⊟

Names. -   1-Salsomaggiore, 2-Mersina, 3-Vittoria, 4-Phoenix, 5- ?.

81. **SANTHIA.** See Ivrea, No.36.

82. **SAN DANIELE.** (S.A. Tranvia San Daniele a Pinzano ?). See No.100.
San Daniele-Pinzano, 13.0 km. (Not completed). Gauge. 1000 proposed.

Locomotive. -   Henschel 0-6-0   10692 of 1911. (Delivered to No.100).   ⊞

82A. **SCHIO** (Tramvie e Ferrovie Economiche di Schio). A "S.V." Subsidiary.
Torrebelvicino-Schio-Arsiero, 15.0 km. (Approx.).
S.1885, Part C.1926, rest R.1933, C.1949. Gauge. 950.

Locomotives. -   60-61,   Henschel 0-4-0   1772-1773 of 1884.   ⊟
          73-74.   Breda   0-4-0   698 & 710 of 1883 ? (also used later).   ⊞

83. **STRADELLA.** See Voghera, No.111.

84. **SALUZZO.** See Cuneo No.25 and Torino No.97.

85. SUSEGANA. (Società Veneta). See No. 14 for full title.
Susegana-Pieve di Soligo, 13.0 km.
S.1913, C.1931. Gauge. 1000.
Locomotives. -   Nos. 71-73,   Unknown 0-6-0.   ⌐┐

86. TOLMEZZO. (Società Veneta). See No. 14 for full title.   (ex-Austrian military line).
From 1919 (Consorzio fra i Comuni della Valle del But).
Tolmezzo(S. V. Station)-Paluzza-Moscardo, 19.7 km.
S.1915, C.1931. Gauge. 750.
Locomotives. -   Nos.101-103,   Krauss   0-6-0 ? - ?. ⁘   └┘
                   2119.   Winterthur 0-4-0   446 of 1886 ⁘   ?
                   -.   Orenstein & Koppel 0-4-0 3798 of 1910.   └┘

87. TORINO. (Turin). (Cav. Giovanni Colli). Colli died in 1877.
Then (S. A. Ferrovie e Tranvie di Torino-Rivoli).
(A roadside light railway electrified as a standard gauge electric tramway).
Torino(Piazza Statuto)-Barriera di Francia-Rivoli, 11.6 km.
SR.1871, E.1914, Trolleybus 1955, Gauge. 1000 (1435 on electrification).
Locomotives. -   Nos.   1-3,   St. Léonard 0-4-0   364-366 of 1871.   └┘
                          4.   St. Léonard 0-4-0   403 of 1873.   "

     Names. -   1-J. Colli, 2- ?, 3-Teresa, 4- ?,

88. TORINO. (Turin). (Dittà Eredi Colli). i.e. "Heirs of Colli".
Later (Società Finanziaria Industriale Torinese).
Closed when No. 87 was electrified.   The exact relationship between Nos. 87 & 88
is not certain, they appear to have shared at least some track.
Torino(Pz. Statuto)-Tesoreria-Rivoli, 12.8 km. (through running over No. 87).
S.1879, C.1914. Gauge. 900 or 1000.
Locomotives. -   Nos.   1,   St. Léonard 0-4-0   496 of 1879. "Giovanni".   ⌐┐
                          2,   Hagans   0-4-0   99 of 1879.   "
                          3,   Krauss   0-4-0 1030 of 1881.   "
                          4,   Henschel   0-4-0 6692 of 1904.   "
                          5,   Henschel   0-4-0 9016 of 1908.   "

89. TORINO. (Turin). (Signor Chiambretta).
Later (S. A. Tranvie Occidentali della Città di Torino e delle Province Torinese).
Finally (Fratelli Chigo fu Pietro).
Torino(Pz. E. Filiberto)-Lucento-Cravetta-Pianezza, 11.6 km.
Cravetta-Druent,   5.3 km.
Lucento-Venaria Reale,   5.2 km. (formerly independent, See No. 90).
S.1884, E.1930, C.1952. Gauge. 1435.
Locomotives. -   Nos.   1,   Henschel 0-4-0 1618 of 1884.   ⌐┐
                          2-3, Henschel 0-4-0 1762-1763 of 1884.   "
                          4,   Henschel 0-4-0 2520 of 1888.   "
                          5,   Henschel 0-4-0 2688 of 1888.   "
                          6,   Henschel 0-4-0 6896 of 1904.   "
                          ? 7. Breda   0-4-0   174 of 1890. (possibly replacing No. 4). "

     Names. -   1-Torino, 2- ?, 3- ?, 4-Venaria, 5-Druent, 6- ?, 7-Venaria.

90. TORINO. (Turin). Owned by (Ferrovia Torino-Cirie-Lanzo).
Later part of 89 above. (Reopened as part of Urban Tramways in 1969).
Torino(Lucento)-Venaria Reale, 5.2 km.
S.1888, E.1930, C.1952. Gauge. 1435.
Locomotives. -   Nos.   1-2, Henschel 0-4-0 2440-2441 of 1887.   ⌐┐

     Names. -   1-Casale, 2-San Maurizio.

91. TORINO. (Turin). (Signor Beckers). Later (Société Anonyme des Tramways de Turin).
Torino(Castello)-Moncalieri-Poirino, 25.5 km. (Still part steam in 1922).
Moncalieri-Real Castello, 0.9 km. (usually worked by horses).
Torino(Castello)-Castagneto-Brusasco, 36.9 km.
Castagneto-Chivasso, 1.4 km.
H.1877, S.1881, E.1904/1922, C.1950. Gauge. 1435.

Locomotives. -	Nos.	1,	Winterthur	0-4-0	146 of 1878.	🚂
		2,	Henschel	0-4-0	1004 of 1878.	,,
		3-5,	Henschel	0-4-0	1037-1038 & 1047 of 1879.	,,
		6-9,	Henschel	0-4-0	1123-1126 of 1879.	,,
		10-12,	Henschel	0-4-0	1186 & 1257-1258 of 1881.	,,
		13-14,	Henschel	0-4-0	1281-1282 of 1881.	,,
		15-18,	Henschel	0-4-0	1678-1681 of 1883/84.	,,
		19.	Henschel	0-4-0	1203 of 1885.	,,

Names. -   10-Torino, 11-Poirino, 18-S.Mauro.

92. TORINO. (Turin). (Signor Berrier de la Leu). Went bankrupt in 1885.
Later (S.A. di Tramways e Ferrovie Economiche di Torino).
Subsequently divided between the Municipal tramways and No.93.
Torino-(Via Sacchi)-Stupinigi-Vinovo-Piobesi, 11.9 km. (own track).
(plus 5.2 km through running over No.93).
S.1882, Part E.1904 & C.1961, rest C.1936. Gauge. 1435.

| Locomotives. - | Nos. | 1-4, | Winterthur | 0-4-0 | 269-272 of 1882. | 🚂 |
| | | ? 5. | Krauss | 0-4-0 | 989 of 1881. | ,, |

Names. -   1- ?, 2- ?, 3- ?, 4-Torino, 5- Teresa.

93. TORINO. (Turin). (Signor Corti). Later (Tranvie a Vapore Provinciali di Torino).
in 1922 (Società Torinese di Tramways e Ferrovie Economiche).
in 1936 (S.A. Tranvie Ovest di Torino).
and finally (S.A. Tranvie Torinese Intercomunali). (S.A.T.T.1).
Torino(Via Sacchi)-Orbassano-Bivio di Cumania-Pinerolo, 36.6 km.
Orbassano-Giaveno, 16.3 km.
Bivio di Cumania-Cumania, 3.6 km.
S.1882, E.1928 (Torino-Orbassano-Giaveno only), C.1939/1956. Gauge. 1435.

Locomotives. -	Nos.	1-4,	Krauss	0-4-0	934, 942-943 & 988 of 1881/82.	🚂
		5-7,	Krauss	0-4-0	1031, 1034-1035 of 1882.	"
		8,	Krauss	0-6-0	1263 of 1883.	"
		9,	Krauss	0-4-0	1790 of 1887.	"
		10,	Krauss	0-4-0	989 of 1881 ex-No.92.	"
		11-12,	Henschel	0-4-0	3970 & 3969 of 1893 ex-No.60. ∵	"
		13,	Henschel	0-4-0	2706 of 1888. ex-No.60. ∵	"
		14,	Henschel	0-4-0	5880 of 1901. ex-No.60. ∵	"
		15-16,	Krauss	0-6-0	5518 of 1906 & 5920 of 1908.	"
		17-18,	Krauss	0-4-0	5921 of 1908 & 6135 of 1909.	"
		19-25.	Krauss	0-4-0	6742-6748 of 1913.	"

Names. -   1-Rita, 2- ?, 3- ?, 4-Pioseasco, 5-Giaveno, 6-Belnasco, 7- ?, 8-Italia,
9-Bruino, 10-Teresa, 11-Pinerolo, 12- ?, 13-Torino, 14- ?, 15-Sangano,
16-Piedmonte, 17-Chisola, 18-Stupinigi, 19-25-not named.

94. TORINO. (Turin). (Fratelli Ghigo fu Pietro) in 1920s under same ownership as No.89.
Worked by No.89 from 1895 and finally by S.A.T.T.I. (See No.93).
Torino (Corso Regina)-Barca-Settimo, 10.7 km.
S.1884, E.1925, C.1952. Gauge. 1435.

Locomotives. -	Nos.	1-2,	St.Léonard	0-4-0	626-627 of 1883.	🚂
		3-4,	?			
		5-6,	Esslingen	0-4-0	2065-2066 of 1884.	"

Names. -   1-Torino, 2-Stura.

Railcars. -   Nos.   1-2, Franco-Belge "Rowan" cars 666-667 of 1887.
("Engineer" for March 1886 says double deck).

199

95. TORINO. (Turin). (Ing. Perincioli).
    Taken over in 1891 by (S.A. Strade Ferrate Centrale del Canavese) and
    run as a feeder to their railway.
    Torino (Corso Regina)-Leyni-Volpiano, 18.1 km.
    S.1884, GS.1929, C.1931, Gauge. 1435.

Locomotives. -	Nos.	1-2,	Krauss 0-4-0	1182-1183 of 1883.	卢
		3-4,	Krauss 0-4-0	1394 of 1884 & 1721*of 1886.	"
		5-6,	Krauss 0-4-0	4534 of 1901 & 5027 of 1903.	"
		7.	Krauss 0-4-0	6082 of 1909.	"

Names. -   1-Botta, 2-Provana, 3-Terrero.
                  *Requisitioned by Army in 1939/45 War and used as yard shunter
                  at Udine in 1946. Seen by P.M. Kalla-Bishop.

96. TORINO. (Turin). (Fratelli Ceriani e Banco). Later as No.95.
    From 1921 (Ferrovie Generale e Tramvie del Canavese).
    Now worked as a branch of the "Nord Torino"railway, owned by 93.
    Rivarolo-Cuorgne, 9.3 km.
    S.1882, R. ?, Still operating. Gauge. 1435.

| Locomotives. - | Nos. | 1-3, | Henschel 0-4-0 | 1430-1432 of 1882. | 卢 |
| | | 4. | Henschel 0-4-0 | 1399 of 1885. (from stock ?). | " |

97. TORINO. (Turin). (S.A.Tranvia Torino-Saluzzo). Took over Nos.24,25 & 70 to form:-
    (La Compagnie Generale des Tramways Piedmontais).
    Finally (S.A.Tranvie Interprovinciale Piemontesi, "S.A.T.I.P. ").
    Torino(Via Nizza)-Pilone Virle-Costigliole-Saluzzo, 53.9 km. (Connecting with No.24).
    Pilone Virle-Carmagnola,   7.6 km.
    Costigliole-Venasca,   7.5 km.
    Saluzzo-Revello-Paesana   12.8 km. (Built 1900).
    Revello-Barge,   11.6 km.
    Cuneo-Boves,   8.2 km. (Built after amalgamation).
    Cuneo-Dronero,   18.4 km. (Ex-No.24).
    Cuneo-Saluzzo,   30.2 km. (Ex-No.25).
    Pinerolo-Cavour-Saluzzo,   30.8 km. (Ex-No.70).
    S.1881, A.1925, C.1950. Gauge. 1100.

Locomotives. -	Nos.	1-3,	Winterthur 0-4-0	164,163 & 178 of 1879, ex-No.24.	卢
		4-5,	Winterthur 0-4-0	201-202 of 1880. ex-No.24.	"
		6-8, ?	Winterthur 0-4-0	187-189 of 1880. ex-No.25.	"
		- -	Krauss 0-4-0	1154, 1184-1185 of 1881 ex-No.70.	"
		10-11,	Henschel 0-4-0	1225-1226 ? of 1881 (Cerimedo ?).	"
		12-17,	Henschel 0-4-0	1189-1194 of 1881.	"
		18,	Hagans 0-4-0	111 of 1881. ex-No.70.	"
		19-22,	Henschel 0-4-0	1341-1344 of 1882.	"
		23,	Henschel 0-4-0	1429 of 1882.	"
		24-27,	Henschel 0-4-0	1546-1549 of 1882.	"
		28-31,	Henschel 0-4-0	2708-2711 of 1888.	"
		32-35,	Henschel 0-4-0	5078-5082 of 1899.	"
		36-37,	Henschel 0-4-0	8140-8141 of 1907.	"
Replacements. -		(II)18,38,	Henschel 0-4-0	9220-9221 of 1909.	"
		(II) 1-2,	Breda 0-4-0	- ? - of ?	"
		(III) 1-2,	Borsig 0-4-0	(two of 7225-7229 of 1909 ex-No.71). ∵	"

Names. -   1-S.Giuseppe, 2-8-Not known, (Krauss)-Alfieri, Goldini, Malabaila,
                  10-Pinerolo, 11-Cavour, 12-Torino, 13-Carignano, 14-Moretta, 15-Monterosa,
                  16-Casalis, 17-Cesare di Saluzzo, 18-Not known, 19-Camillo Cavour,
                  20-Silvio Pellico, 21-Piemonte, 22-Italia, 23-Barbaroux, 24-Garibaldi,
                  25-Ponta di San Martino, 26-Siccardi, 27-Santore di Santarosa, 28-Bruxelles,
                  29-Moncalieri, 30-Venasca, 31-Dronero, 32-Cuneo, 33-Saluzzo, 34-Verzuolo,
                  35-Costigliole, 36-Busca, 37-Boves, (II)18-Belgio, 38-Monviso, (II)-Marco di Saluz
                  (II)2-Camillo Peano, (III)1-Fontestrelle, (III)2-Perosa.

98.   TORTONA. (Signor Bellisomi). Not operating in 1885. In 1907 (Ing. Grattoni
Francesco). In 1911 (S.A.Tranvie a Vapore Sale-Tortona-Monleale).
Finally part of No.2.
Tortona-Sale,   12.4 km. (Connecting with No.2).
Tortona-Monleale, 10.3 km. (Possibly extended to Volpedo).
S.1882, C.1933, Gauge. 1435.

Locomotives. -   Nos.   1,   Winterthur 0-6-0   235 of 1881.
                      2-5,   Krauss   0-4-0   1032-1033 ? & 1156-1157 of 1882.
                                            1033 not confirmed by Krauss works list.
Names. -   1- ?, 2-Ferdinanda, 3-Roma, 4- ?, 5- ?.

99.   TURIN. English and French name for TORINO. See Nos.87-97.

100.   UDINE. (Signor Carlo Neufeld, Vienna).
Later (Società della Tranvia Udine-San Daniele).
1902-1924, worked by (Società Veneta).
In 1939, owned by Signor G.Cantoni.
Finally (S.A.Trasporti Interurbani, Udine).
Udine (Porta Gemona)-San Daniele del Friuli, 29.0 km.
Udine (Porta Gemona)-Udine Stazione,   5.0 km.(approx). (Freight connection).
San Daniele-Pinzano, (Not completed) See No.82.
S.1889, A.1924 WS.1924-1948. C.1955. Gauge. 1000.

Locomotives. -   Nos. 20-22.   Wiener Neustadt 0-6-0 3313-3315 of 1889.
                      23,   Wiener Neustadt 0-6-0 3484 of 1891.   "
                      50,   Winterthur   0-6-0 1018 of 1897 ex-Cherbourg(France No.35).
                      60,   Henschel   0-6-0 10692 of 1911 intended for No.82.

Names. -   20-Udine, 21-Fagagna, 22-San Daniele, 23-Martignacco, 50-Torreano,
               60-Pinzano.

Note. -   Numbers shown above are those allocated by S.V. in 1902, formerly Nos.1-5.

101.   VARESE. See No.73 (All other lines electrified from outset).

102.   VALLE DEGANO. (Consorzio fra i Comuni della Valle Degano). (ex-Austrian Military Line).
(Temporarily in hands of "S.V." 1915-1918 and worked as a Tramway).
Villasantina-Comeglians (Conegliano), 13.8 km.
S.1915, C.1935. Gauge. 750.
Locomotives. -   As supplied by Austrian army.

103.   VERCELLI. (Tay & Co.). Later (S.A. dei Tramways Vercellesi).
Vercelli-Quinto-Aranco, 47.9 km.
Quinto Vercellese-Biella, 35.2 km.
Vercelli-Trino,   17.9 km. (Later electric).
S.1878, (Part E.1927. C.1948) Rest C.1933. Gauge. -1435.

Locomotives. -   Nos.   ?   Baldwin ? 0-4-0? of 1878.
                          Henschel 0-4-0 1160-1161 of 1881.   "
                          Henschel 0-4-0 1843 of 1884.   "
                          Henschel 0-4-0 3327 of 1890.   "
                          Henschel 0-4-0 3482 of 1891. (13 locos in 1901).   "

104.   VERCELLI. See No.63 Novara-Vercelli.

105.   VERONA. (S.A. delle Tranvie Provinciale di Verona).
Verona(Porta Nuova)-Tombetta-Albaredo-Coriano, 35.1 km.
Tombetta-San Giacomo di Tomba,   3.0 km. (Closed before 1922).
S.1898, C.1927. Gauge. 750.

Locomotives. -   Nos.   1-3,   Breda   0-4-0 331-333 of 1896.
                      4-9,   Breda   0-4-0 569-574 of 1901.   "
                      10.   Maffei 0-6-0 3580 of 1909.   "
                    11-12.   Maffei 0-4-0 3682 of 1911 & 3716 of 1913.   "

Names. -   1- ?, 2- ?, 3-Albaredo.

106. VERONA. (Dittà Grondana Alessi).
Later (S.A. delle Tramvie nelle Provincie di Verona e Vicenza). "vTv".
Finally (Amministrazione Provinciale di Verona). Did not serve Vicenza.
Verona(Porta Vescovo)-Caldiero-Sambonifacio, 22.1 km. (E.1912).
Verona(Porta Vescovo)-San Martino,   3.0 km.   "   "
Caldiero-Tregnano,   11.0 km.   "   "
Sambonifacio-Lonigo,   8.9 km. (A.1923).
Lonigo Stazione-Lonigo-Cologna Veneta,   14.0 km.   "   "   (Accumulator Goods).
S.1880. (Part A.1923, AG.1935, C.1968). Rest E.1912, Trolleybus 1961). Gauge. 1435.

Locomotives. -	Nos.	1-8,	Carels	0-4-0	146, etc. of 1880/81 ?
		9,	Henschel	0-4-0	6366 of 1903. (Covering later removed).
		10,	Henschel	0-4-0	9720 of 1908
	(II)	4,	Esslingen	0-6-0	1785 of 1880, ex-No.20 ∵

107. VICENZA. (S.A. della Tranvia Vicenza-Montagnana). Later worked by Società Veneta.
Sold to No.108 in 1911 and converted to standard gauge, leaving Vicenza
by a more direct route.
Vicenza(Campo Marzio)-Borgo Padova-Noventa-Montagnana, 47.0 km.
S.1887, C.1911 (See No.108 below). Gauge. 950. (Later 1435).
Locomotives. -   Nos.211-215,   Henschel 0-4-0 2480-2484 of 1887. (S.V. numbers).

Names. -   211-Montagnana, 212- ?, 213-Noventa Vicentine, 214- ?, 215-Orgiano.

Note. -   Nos.211, 213 & 215 were retained by the S.V. and converted to standard
                   gauge for use at Padova, where renumbered 170-172.

108. VICENZA. (Province of Vicenza Steam Tramways Co. Ltd.).
Later (S.A. Ferrovie e Tranvie Vicentine).
Vicenza(Campo Marzio)-Montecchio-Valdagno-Recoaro, 41.7 km. (E.1928).
Montecchio(San Vitale)-Arzignano-Chiampo,   10.9 km. " " C.1968.
Vicena(Campo Marzio)-Marostica-Bassano del Grappa, 34.2 km. (D.1934, C.1965).
Marostica-Thiene,   ? km. (Closed at an early date).
Vicenza(Campo Marzio)-Vicenza Stazione-Noventa-Montagnana, 45.5 km. ex-No.107.D.1934
Arzignano-Miniere di Pulli, ? km. (Closed at an early date).
S.1880, (Part E.1928), rest D.1934, Still operating. Gauge. 1435.

Locomotives. -	Nos.	1-8,	Cerimedo	0-4-0	- ? - of 1880.
		9,	Breda	0-4-0	- ? - of 1908.
		10-13,	Borsig,	0-6-0	6887-6890 of 1908.
		14-19,	Borsig,	0-4-0	6891-6896 of 1910.
		20 and others,	Breda	0-6-0	1249-1254 of 1910. (20 = 1253).
		24-26,	Henschel	0-6-0	10104-10106 of 1910.
		27.	Borsig	0-6-0	7968 of 1911.

Replacements. -	(II)	1,	Borsig	0-6-0	7375 of 1909. ex-No.49. ∵
	(II)	2,	Henschel	0-4-0	6366 of 1903. ex-No.106 (Rebuilt). ∵
	(II)	3,	Henschel	0-4-0	9720 of 1909. ex-No.106. ∵
	(II)	4.	Esslingen	0-6-0	1785 of 1880. ex-No.106 & 20.∵ (Rebuilt).

Names. -   1-12 not known, 13-Agno, 14- ?, 15- ?, 16-Astico, 17- ?, 18-Montecchio,
                   19-Arzignano, 20-Marostica, 21-25 not known, 26-Montagnana.

Note. -   Steam locos Nos.(II) 1 and 17 used for shunting in Vicenza yard until 1966.
                   (both then without names).

109. VIAREGGIO. (Impresa Tramvia Camaiore-Viareggio, Massagli, Malfatti e Berrettino).
From 1922 (Comune di Camaiore).
Viareggio-Camaiore, 10.1 km.
S.1900, C.1937 ?. Gauge. 1435.

Locomotives. -	Nos.	1,	Breda	0-4-0	366 of 1899.
		2,	Breda	0-4-0	559 of 1900.
		3.	Henschel	0-4-0	9214 of 1909.

110. VIGEVANO. (Società Ferrovie del Ticino). See No.63.

111. VOGHERA. (Société des Tramways et Chemins de Fer, Bruxelles).
Later (Società Ferrovie del Ticino).
Voghera-Stradella,   25.0 km.
Voghera-Rivanezzano-Salice, 9.5 km.
S.1883/1909, C.1931.° Gauge. 1435.

Note. -   ° An electric railway, Voghera-Salice-Varzi on a slightly different course,
                 opened later in 1931.

Locomotives. -   Nos. 30-35,   Henschel 0-4-0   1284 of 1881 (& possibly 1223-1224).
                 50-56,   Henschel 0-4-0   1550-1556 of 1883.   "
                 Various -,   Couillet 0-4-0   transferred from No.63, from time to time. "

Names. -   30-Voghera, 31- ? -Stradella, 32- ? -Broni, etc.

Notes. -   Locomotives numbered in S.F T. General series.

                 An electric railway, Voghera-Salice-Varzi
                 on a slightly different course, opened later in 1931.

                 _____

NOTE. -   Lengths of lines are extracted from "Ministero dei Trasporti"
                 Official Statistics, by Dr.G.Masino of Turin and author.

Esslingen loco No.5 "Soncino" for the Bergamo-Soncino tramway.
Kessler Catalogue.   Courtesy: Deutsches Museum, Munich.

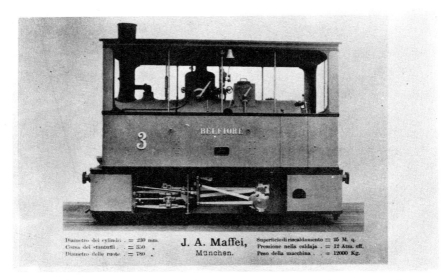

Diametro dei cilindri . = 230 mm.
Corsa dei stantuffi . . = 350 .
Diametro delle ruote . = 780 .

J. A. Maffei,
München.

Superficie di riscaldamento = 25 M. q.
Pressione nella caldaja . = 12 Atm. eff.
Peso della macchina . . = 12000 Kg.

Maffei loco No. 3 "Belfiore" built for the Tranvie Provinciale di Mantova, whose fleet consisted of ten of these.
Maffei Catalogue.   Courtesy: late Friederich Kemper 1264.

Breda loco No. 19 "Giacomo" of 1912 for the Bologna-Castelfranco tramway. Vicenza had batches of closely similar locos built by Henschel, Borsig and Breda respectively.
Breda Catalogue.   Courtesy: Walter Hefti.

19140 · Bagni Albule (Tivoli) Arrivo del Tram

(Upper). Take a tram for a bath! The Rome-Tivoli tram arrives at Bagni Albule, with one of the original Hohenzollern locos, No.4. The tramway and the baths were in the same ownership.
(Lower). Loco No.C.32 of the Rome-Tivoli tramway at Piazzale del Verano, Rome.

Photos: Courtesy G.de Grisantis.

(Upper). Long wheelbase Henschel enclosed loco for the Tranvie Provinciale di Verona e Vicenza "vTv", as new in 1909.
Henschel Catalogue. Photo: Science Museum London - Whitcombe Collection 3612.
(Lower). The same loco forty years later when it had become No. 23 of the Monza-Trezzo-Bergamo tramway. Last seen by the writer in 1957.
Photo: "Farabola", Milan 24758.

(Upper). Krauss loco No.4 of the metre gauge tramway line of the Ferrovie e
Tranvie Padane at Ferrara, as new in 1900.
Krauss Catalogue.   Courtesy: late Friederich Kemper 1972.
(Lower). This same loco was latterly transferred to Rimini, where it lay derelict
for many years, but has recently been retrieved and sent to Blonay, Switzerland
for restoration.

Photo: M.Grillo.

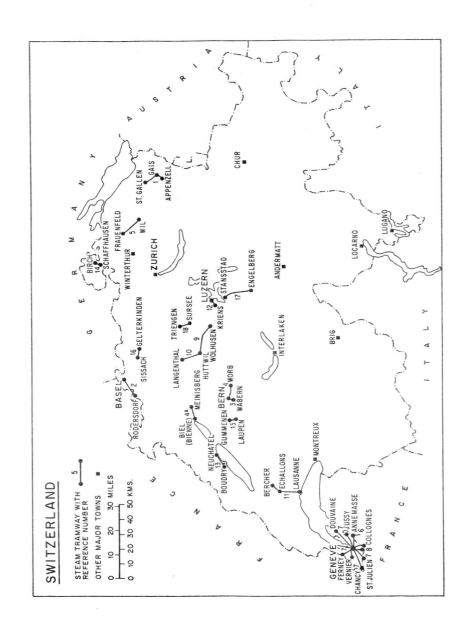

8. SWITZERLAND

To those who regard Switzerland as a country composed entirely of lakes and lofty snow capped peaks, the fact that it once boasted several steam tramways may come as a surprise.

In fact, a glance at a relief map will show that the larger cities are located on the comparatively flat floors of wide valleys, where there is room for development. Even so the two larger were regarded as too hilly for urban tramways. Hence Zurich had no steam tramways at all and Basel had only one inter-urban line. The only city which could claim a network of steam tramways was Geneva, which lies in a Swiss enclave, almost surrounded by French Territory. There, a standard gauge urban horse tramway system was developed by "La Compagnie Générale des Tramways Suisses", who had aspirations of development in other towns as well. However, in 1877, the first steam tramway locomotive in Switzerland was constructed at Winterthur, and was put into service on the "Tramways Suisse" route from the centre of Geneva to Carouge, to the south. Having proved successful, other similar locomotives were acquired and the route extended eastwards from the city to Chêne, and further extended to Moillesulaz in 1881. An extension still further in 1883 took the line across the French Frontier to Annemasse, thus changing it in effect to an inter-urban with international status. It was electrified in 1902 and subsequently converted to metre gauge.

Four other companies operated steam tramways in the Geneva area on Swiss and French territory. All were of metre gauge. The most important of these was "La Compagnie Genèvoise des Chemins de Fer de Voie Etroite", which ran several interurban lines based on Geneva, and modelled itself on the Belgian "Vicinal" system. The line from Geneva to Veyrier, with a short branch belonged to another company and both had sections penetrating into France. Both of these used Winterthur six coupled engines of a much more advanced design than those on the "Tramways Suisses". Entirely on French territory, and really outside the scope of this chapter, were the Ferney-Gex and the Annemasse-Samoëns: the former was at first worked by stock loaned by the "Voie Etroite", one of whose lines it met end-on.

The interurban line at Basel, the Birsigtalbahn also entered France, but re-entered Switzerland before its terminus. At Bern, one urban line was worked by Mekarski compressed air cars and another by conventional Winterthur 0-6-0 steam locomotives, but here electrification came so early that all eight locomotives were sold to other undertakings, still being comparatively new. The interurban Bern-Worb line was also steam worked at first. There was a lengthy lakeside steam tramway at Neuchâtel, with a short branch to Cortaillod, near the Boudry terminus. The line was later extended at the Neuchâtel end to the station, but this section was so steep that a rack was required. The passenger service on a steam tramway from Luzern to Kriens was replaced by a parallel electric tramway at an early date, but although this has now closed, the former steam tramway, now electrified is still open as a goods branch line.

The Stansstad-Engelbergbahn although always an electric railway, recently extended, for many years had two ex-Bern steam tramway locos in reserve for emergency use and fortunately one of them was put aside and not scrapped, so is now an exhibit in the Museum of Swiss Transport at Lucerne. Another is on the Blonay-Chamby Museum line. Two others from the Birsigtalbahn, were used for some time to provide a steam goods service running over an existing electric tram route, between Schaffhausen station and a large iron works, to which they belonged. They have since been replaced by electric locomotives.

Locomotives

It was as a builder and exporter of tram-engines that Switzerland was best known; the single firm of "Schweitzerische Locomotiv und Maschinenfabrik", at Winterthur, near Zurich, during the first years of its existence, specialized in the construction of engines for rack railways and tramways. The former were most successful and world famous and they were one of the earliest continental builders in the tram-engine field, building about 300 between 1877 and 1903. They constructed about 50 locomotives for German tramways, 50 for Dutch, 50 for Italian and 50 for Swiss tramways and smaller numbers for Greece, France, Luxemburg, Spain, Portugal, Russia and Brazil. There was even one for Great Britain (Sunderland). The earlier machines usually had four coupled wheels and many had Brown's Patent boilers, with a vertical dome cum-firebox, behind a short horizontal part, said to be derived from the early British "Haystack" design: Charles Brown was a director of the Company.[1] Various parts of the locomotive were so designed that they could not make unnecessary noise by working loose and rattling. The first was supplied to the Geneva standard gauge tramway in 1877; it was a success, but the reputation of many of the other early tram-engines was marred by their being used for some not entirely successful experimental features, for which they were used as "Guinea-Pigs". Some of the earlier machines, including those for Brazil, had the wheels uncoupled, while two for Holland also had vertical boilers. Those for Mulhouse had a flexible wheelbase, while those for Barcelona were six-wheeled with chain drive. A feature common to all Winterthur tram engines, except the above for Barcelona, and derived from the rack engines, was the drive through a rocking shaft, from cylinders placed above the footplate, usually midway along the boiler-side. This did have the advantage of keeping the motion clean, when working on wet or muddy roads, but the rocking shafts caused many to shake themselves to pieces after a comparatively short life. The earlier machines usually had brass capped chimneys and roof condensers, while the later ones often had a chimney cap incorporating a small spark arrestor. Controls were duplicated on platforms at both ends of the locomotive. (See page 19 of Introduction).

Locomotives for tramways in later years were of a standard six-coupled design, which was much more reliable than the earlier machines. These were supplied to all Swiss systems except the Geneva standard gauge line and Neuchâtel but also to Cherbourg, Flensburg, Luxemburg, Marseille, Lyon and Athens. They gave long service on the systems which had them and their characteristic appearance was given by very low side sheets extending without a break into waist-high end sheets. The cylinders and motion were "amid-ships" and drove through a rocking-shaft at the front.[2] The underframes were by now suitably strengthened.

Not unnaturally, the majority of Swiss tramways employed Winterthur locomotives, but there were a few Krauss and one Jung, to be found on the Luzern-Kriens and the Neuchâtel tramways.[3]   When Swiss tramways were electrified, some of the engines were sold abroad.   Some went only just over the border to the Ferney-Gex line, which although in France, was connected with the Geneva system; others went to Luxembourg, Paris and Mulhouse.   It is believed that many of the Geneva metre gauge engines were sold to industry in Austria, and others went to Massa, the marble quarrying town in Italy.[4]

We should not pass without mention of some other enclosed locomotives used in Switzerland.   Although intended for standard gauge light railways and not for tramways, they had the upper parts enclosed in a casing resembling a metal bodied brake-van, but the wheels and motion were not enclosed.   One was in use until fairly recently on the Sursee-Triengen light railway which also had an extraordinary four wheeled steam railcar, with a corridor along one side, enclosed only by iron railings.

Passenger Stock & Stations

The original carriages on the standard gauge line at Geneva, appear to have been just horse tramway cars adapted for steam haulage.   On the other hand, the "Voie Etroite" undertaking is said to have modelled itself on the Belgian "Vicinal" system and their carriages certainly resembled the small open platform four-wheelers once so common in Belgium; like the Vicinal, they even had some matching baggage vans.   Bern and Neuchâtel both used bogie cars with open platforms which were rather long in relation to the saloon, while the Birsigtalbahn had bogie cars of rather Dutch aspect and Appenzall had some peculiar six wheelers.

As a matter of policy, it was decided that the stations in Geneva should be as simple as possible.   City centre terminals comprised no more than a run-round loop and a water column, while country halts were furnished with only a name board.   Most of the "Voie Etroite" locomotives were housed in one large depot at Acacias, in a southern suburb of Geneva and were parked by means of a traverser.

After the "Tramways Suisses" line had been electrified and converted to metre gauge, a goods transfer service which it had formerly provided between the French and Swiss main line stations, was maintained with the aid of "Voie Etroite" locomotives pulling standard gauge trucks mounted on transporter bogies. This continued until some powerful electric tractor cars were acquired.[5]   As a matter of fact, only the "Tramways Suisses" and Luzern-Kriens lines were constructed to the Standard gauge, as soon after their opening, a law was passed which decreed that all tramways must be laid to metre gauge.

Three languages, German, French and Italian are spoken in different parts of Switzerland, but the majority of the steam tramways were in the German part; two, Geneva and Neuchâtel were in the French speaking part and none in the Italian part.

Notes

1. Charles Brown (1827-1905) an Englishman was the Company's Chief Engineer. He returned to England in 1880 and joined R. W. Hawthorn & Co. His son (1863-1924) remained in Switzerland and was one of the founders of the Brown-Boveri electrical organisation.

2. See "Tramway & Railway World" 1895, page 74. Article on Geneva, with map and illustration of locomotive No. 22 "Crepy".

3. See "Chemins de Fer Secondaires" No. IV, 1966, for an article on early steam rack locomotives in Switzerland and photo of Neuchatel Jung locomotive by J. Chapuis.

4. See "Der Dampfbetrieb der Schweitzerischen Eisenbahnen" by A. Moser (second edition 1967).

5. See "Les Transports en Commun a Genève" by Pierre Bertrand, 1963.

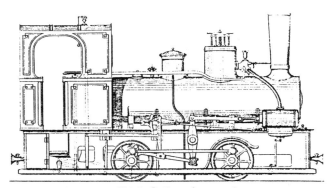

Types of Light Railway Locomotives

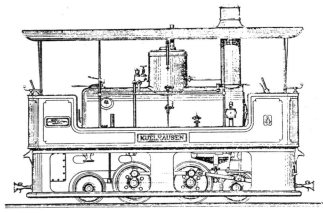

Table 8 - SWITZERLAND

1. APPENZELL. (Appenzeller Strassenbahn) No connection with "Appenzellerbahn" which is
   a railway.
   St. Gallen-Gais-Appenzell. 19.4 km
   S.1888, E.1931. Still operating. Gauge 1000.
   Locomotives. - Nos. 1-3. Winterthur 0-4-2 z   523-525 of 1888 (rack)
                          4. Winterthur 0-4-2 z   636 of 1890   "
                        5-6. Winterthur 2-4-2 z   1561-1562 of 1904   "
                        7-8. Winterthur 2-4-2 z   2006-2007 of 1909   "

   Names. -   1-Gais, 2-Teufen, 3-Bühler, 4-St. Gallen, 5-Appenzell, 6-Saentis, 7-Gaebris,
                8-Fröhlichsegg.

2. BASEL. (Birsigtalbahn).
   Basel (Heuwage) - Leymen-Rodersdorf. 16.1 km. (Leymen is in France),
   S.1887, ER1905/10, Still Operating. Gauge. 1000.
   Locomotives. - Nos. 1-2. Winterthur 0-6-0   473-474 of 1887.
                          3. Winterthur 0-6-0   548 of 1888.   "
                          4. Winterthur 0-6-0   635 of 1890.   "
                          5. Winterthur 0-6-0   976 of 1896.   "

   Names. -   1-Basel, 2-Blauen, 3-Birsig, 4-Landskron, 5-Blochmont.

3. BERN. (Berner Tramway Gesellschaft).
   Turbinestrasse-Hollingen, 2.9 km. (Compressed air cars).
   Längasse-Wabern,   4.9 km (Steam locomotives).
   H.1865, Compressed air 1890, S.1894, E.1902, Part Still Operating. Gauge. 1000.
   Air Cars. Nos. 1-10. Mekarski 1890.
   Locomotives. - Nos. 11-17. Winterthur 0-6-0   862-868 of 1894.
                          18. Winterthur 0-6-0   890 of 1894.   "

4. BERN. (Bern-Muri-Gümlingen-Worbbahn).
        Later (Vereinigte Bern-Worbbahn).
   Bern (Helvetia Platz)-Muri-Gümlingen-Worb, 9.7 km.
   S.1897, ER.1910, Still Operating. Gauge. 1000.
   Locomotives. - Nos. 1-2. Winterthur 0-6-0   1144-1145 of 1898.
                          3. Winterthur 0-6-0   864 of 1894 ex-No.3.   " "

4A. BIEL. (Biel-Meinisbergbahn). In French (Chemin de Fer Bienne Meinisberg).
    Through running over town tramways, whose cars replaced steam cars in 1926.
    Biel-Meinisberg, 6.9 km + through running.
    S.1913, C.1923, E.1926, C.1940. Gauge. 1000.
    Motive Power. - CFm/2/4/1-2 Winterthur steam cars 2319-2320 of 1913.

5. FRAUENFELD. (Frauenfeld-Wilbahn).
        A roadside light railway with some street running and two secondhand
        enclosed locomotives.
   Frauenfeld-Wil. 18.0 km.
   S.1887, E.1921, Still Operating. Gauge. 1000.
   Locomotives. - Nos. 1-3. Winterthur 0-6-0   461-463 of 1887
              (II)   3. Winterthur 0-6-0   864 of 1894 ex-Nos. 3 & 4.   "
                          4. Winterthur 0-6-0   617 of 1890
                          5. Winterthur 0-6-0   635 of 1890 ex-No.2.   "

   Names. -   1-Frauenfeld, 2-Wyl, 3-Murg, 4-Hornli, 5-not named.
                No.2 later carried the name plates "Hornli".

6. GENÈVE. (Geneva). (Compagnie Générale des Tramways Suisses.)
   Carouge-Marché-Moillesulaz-Annemasse, 10.0 km. (4.6 km in France.)
   Annemasse-Entrembières, 1.7 km. (Entirely in France.)
   H.1862, S.1877, E.1901, Still Operating.Gauge. 1435.(1000 after E.)

Locomotives. - No. 1, Winterthur 0-4-0   111 of 1877.
          2, Winterthur 0-4-0   338 of 1883. (Renumbered 5.)
          3, Winterthur 0-4-0   425 of 1885.   "
          4, Winterthur 0-4-0   467 of 1887.   "
          5, Winterthur 0-4-0   477 of 1887. (Renumbered 2.) "
          6, Winterthur 0-4-0   588 of 1889.   "
        7-8, Winterthur 0-4-0   717-718 of 1892.   "

7.   GENÈVE. (Geneva). (Compagnie Genevoise des Chemins de Fer à Voie Etroite.)
     Genève (Quai des Postes)-Lancy, 3.2 km.
     Genève (Quai des Postes)-St. Julien, 10.4 km. (1.5 km in France.)
     Genève (Quai des Postes)-Chancy, 17.1 km.
     Genève (Quai des Postes)-St. Georges, 18.8 km.
     Genève (Place des VII Cantons)-Vernier, 4.9 km.
     Genève (Place des VII Cantons)-Ferney, 6.0 km. (Connecting with France N.54.)
     Genève (Rond Point du Rive)-Corsier-Douvaine, 18.1 km. (7.5 km in France.)
     Genève (Rond Point du Rive)-Jussy, 11.5 km. (Not completed.)
     S.1889, E.1900/15, C.1929/39. Gauge. 1000.
     Locomotives. - Nos. 1-7, Winterthur 0-6-0   564-570 of 1889.
               8-10, Winterthur 0-6-0   590-592 of 1889.   "
              11-19, Winterthur 0-6-0   620-628 of 1890.   "
              20-22, Winterthur 0-6-0   641-643 of 1890.   "
     Serpollet Cars. -   1-5, Werkst. Genf Maschinenbau Ges., Basel 1897.

     Names. -   1-St. Georges, 2-Bernex, 3-Laconnex, 4-Carouge, 5-St. Julien, 6-Mont Sion,
              7-Rhône, 8-Beauregard, 9-Ferney, 10-Vernier, 11-Voirons, 12-Chablais,
              13-Léman, 14-Savoie, 15-Faucille, 16-Allinges, 17-Dole, 18-Jura, 19-Gex,
              20-Douraine, 21-Môle, 22-Crépy* (* - Confirmed by photo in "Tramway &
              Railway World" 1895. Moser's Book says "Crepi".)

8.   GENÈVE. (Compagnie du Chemin de Fer à Voie Etroite Genève-Veyrier.)
     Genève (Rond Point du Rive)-Carouge-Veyrier, 5.5 km.
     Carouge-Croix de Rozon, 4.8 km.
     Veyrier-Collognes, 4.8 km. (4.0 km in France.)
     S.1887, E.1899/1911, C1957. Gauge. 1000.
     Locomotives. - Nos. 1-3, Winterthur 0-6-0   454-456 of 1887.
               4, Winterthur 0-6-0   644   of 1890.
     Serpollet Cars. - 31-33, Ex-No.7, their Nos. 2,3 and 5 in 1907.

     Names. -   1-Genève, 2-Veyrier, 3-Salève, 4-Pitons.

9.   HUTTWIL. (Huttwil-Wolhusenbahn.) Later combined with No.10.
     A light railway using one enclosed locomotive. (See page 211)
     Huttwil-Wolhusen, 26.0 km.
     S.1895, E.1946, Still Operating. Gauge. 1435.
     Locomotives. - Nos. 5, Winterthur 0-6-0   3610 of 1936.
               8, Winterthur 0-6-0   1088 of 1898. Ex-No.10.
              16, Winterthur 2-6-0   1907 of 1907.
              (Common numbering with No. 10.)

10. LANGENTHAL. (Langenthal-Huttwilbahn.)
               Later combined with No. 9 and another line as :-
               (Vereinigte Huttwilbahn.)
     A light railway with two enclosed locomotives. (See page 211)
     Langenthal-Huttwil, 15.0 km.
     S.1889 E.1946, Still Operating. Gauge. 1435.
     Locomotives. - Nos. 1-2, Winterthur 0-6-0   582-583 of 1889.
               6-7, Winterthur 0-6-0   886-887 of 1894.
               8, Winterthur 0-6-0   1088   of 1898.   "
              11-12, Winterthur 2-6-0   1904 & 1906 of 1908. "
              (II) 1-2, Winterthur 0-4-0   3522-3523 of 1931.

11. LAUZANNE. (Chemin de Fer de Lauzanne-Echallens-Bercher.)
     A light railway with some street running, one enclosed locomotive and one "Rowan"
     steam car.
     Lauzanne-Echallens-Bercher. 24.0 km.
     S.1873. E.1921. Still operating. Gauge. 1000.
     Locomotives. - No. 1, Canada Works. 0-4-0   - of 1863   ∵ ⊑⏀
                        2, Gouin   0-4-0   ? of 1865 ex-Mont Cenis Rly.   "
                   3-4, Schneider   0-4-0   1562-1563 of 1873.   "
                        5, Krauss   0-4-0   338 of 1874.   ⊑⏉
                   (II) 2, Graffenstaden 0-6-0   3857 of 1888   ⊑⏉
                   (II) 5, Graffenstaden 0-6-0   4172 of 1890.   ⊑⏀
                        6, Winterthur   0-6-0   1511 of 1903.   "
                        7, Winterthur   0-6-0   1696 of 1905.   "
                        8, Winterthur   0-6-0   2095 of 1910.   "

                      - Winterthur "Rowan" car   ? of 1876   ⊞⊞⊞

     Names. -   3-Talent, 4-Menthue, 5-Lausanne, (II)2-Echallens, (II)5-Bercher,
                 6-Gros de Vaud, 7-Talent, 8-not named.

12. LUZERN   (Lucerne).   (Kriens-Luzernbahn.)
                           Later (Trambahn der Stadt Luzern.)
     The passenger service was replaced by a parallel metre gauge electric tramway in 1900,
     which ran until 1961.
     Luzern (Schmeide)-Kriens. 3.3 km.
     S.1886. GS.1900. GE.1926. Still operating. Gauge. 1435.
     Locomotives. - Nos. 1-2. Krauss   0-4-0 1719-1720 of 1886.   (Tram.)   ⊑⏉
                        51. Winterthur 0-4-0   686 of 1891.   ∵ (Goods)   ⊑⏀
                   (II) 1. Maffei   0-6-0   2983 of 1909.   "   "
                   (II) 2. Winterthur 0-6-0   1064 of 1897. ∵   "   "

     Names. - 1-Kriens, 2-Luzern. No.1 (II) became State Rly 8651.

13. NEUCHATEL. (Compagnie du Tramway de Neuchâtel à Cortaillod-Boudry).
                 Worked by (Chemins de Fer du Jura Neuchâtelois.)
     Neuchâtel (Place Purry)-Areuse-Boudry. 9.4 km.
     Areuse-Cortaillod.   0.8 km.
     Neuchâtel (Place Purry)-Neuchâtel Station. 1.0 km. (Rack operated).
     S.1892. E.1902. Still operating. Gauge. 1000.
     Locomotives. - Nos. 1-2. Krauss   0-4-0 z 2618-2619 of 1892 (Rack tram).   ⊑⏉
                        3, Krauss   0-4-0   2556 of 1892.   ⊑⏉
                        4, Jung   0-4-0 z 203 of 1894. (Rack tram).   ⊑⏉
                        5, Krauss   0-4-0   3628 of 1898.   ⊑⏉

     Names. - 1-Neuchâtel, 2-Cortaillod, 3-Boudry, 4-Colombier, 5-Auvernier.

14. SCHAFFHAUSEN. (Georg Fischer A.G.)
     An industrial establishment using two tram locomotives for the transport of materials over
     the urban electric tramways. Later, the steam locomotives were replaced by electric and
     passenger service on the route concerned ceased in 1964.
     Schaffhausen-Birch(Mühlental), 4.0 km. (and industrial sidings.)
     GS.1913, GE.1921, Still operating for goods. Gauge. 1000.
     Locomotives. - No. 79, Winterthur 0-6-0   635 of 1890 ex-No.2 ∵   ⊑⏉
                        80, Winterthur 0-6-0   474 of 1887 ex-No.2 ∵   "
                   (Formerly Nos. 4 & 2 of the Birsigtalbahn.)

15. SENSETAL. (Sensetalbahn A.G.)
     A light railway using three enclosed locomotives. (See page 211)
     Laupen-Gummenen, 11.2 km.
     S.1904. E.1938 Still operating. Gauge. 1435.
     Locomotives. - Nos. 31-32. Winterthur 2-6-0   1537-1538 of 1903.   ⊑⏀
                        21, Krauss   0-4-0 6337 of 1910.   ⊑⏉
                        22, Krauss   0-4-0 6451 of 1911.   "
                        23, Winterthur 0-4-0   2590 of 1917.   "

                        1. Esslingen Steam car 3401 of 1907.   ⊞⊞⊞

16. SISSACH. (Sissach-Gelterkindenbahn.)
     A light railway with one enclosed locomotive, replaced by a main line railway in
     a tunnel.
     Sissach-Gelterkinden.   km.
     E.1891(Experimental),   S.1893, C.1915.   Gauge. 1000 (1435 as Railway).
     Locomotives. - Nos.G.1/3, Winterthur 2-2-2   326 of 1883 ex-Mulhouse. ∵
                            2, Heilbronn   0-4-0   305 of 1893.
                            3, Heilbronn   0-4-0   343 of 1898.   "

17. STANSSTAD. (Stansstad-Engelbergbahn.)
     An electric light railway with two enclosed steam locomotives for goods and emergency
     use. (One now preserved.)
     Stansstad-Engelberg, 23.0 km.
     E.1898, GS.1904 to 1923.   Still operating.   Gauge. 1000.
     Locomotives. - No.14, Winterthur 0-6-0   865 of 1894, ex-No.3. ∵
                       15. Winterthur 0-6-0   890 of 1894, ex-No.3. ∵   "

18. SURSEE. (Sursee-Triengenbahn.)
     A light railway with one second-hand enclosed locomotive.
     Sursee-Triengen,   9.0 km.
     S.1912, D.1965, Still operating.   Gauge. 1435.
     Locomotives. - Nos. 1-2, Henschel   0-4-0   11099-11100 of 1912.
                   (II)   1, Winterthur 0-4-0   3522 of 1931 ex-No.10. ∵
                           11, Winterthur 2-2-0   railcar 2645 of 1918. *
     Borrowed from
     State Railway -   8477, Winterthur 0-6-0   1808 of 1907.
                        8488, Winterthur 0-6-0   1968 of 1909.   "
                        8522, Winterthur 0-6-0   2345 of 1913.   "

     Note-   *See "Modern Tramway" August 1964, page 275 for article
                          and illustration - P.J. Walker.

Krauss combined rack and adhesion loco No.2, "Cortaillod" of the Neuchâtel-
Boudry tramway.
                                               Locomotive Publishing Co. Ltd.

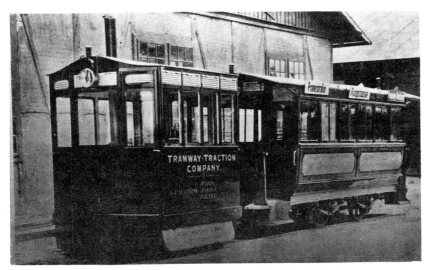

Merryweather loco undergoing trials in Vienna under the auspices of Palmer Harding.

Courtesy: Othmar Bamer 25-24.

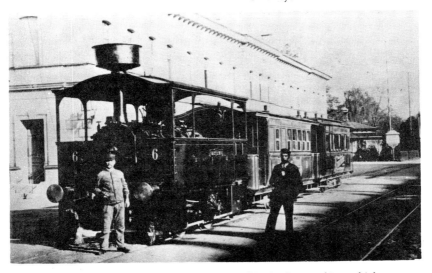

Krauss loco No. 6 "Gartenau" at Salzburg. This is the machine which now resides somewhat altered in Prague Technical Museum.

Courtesy: Othmar Bamer 17-16.

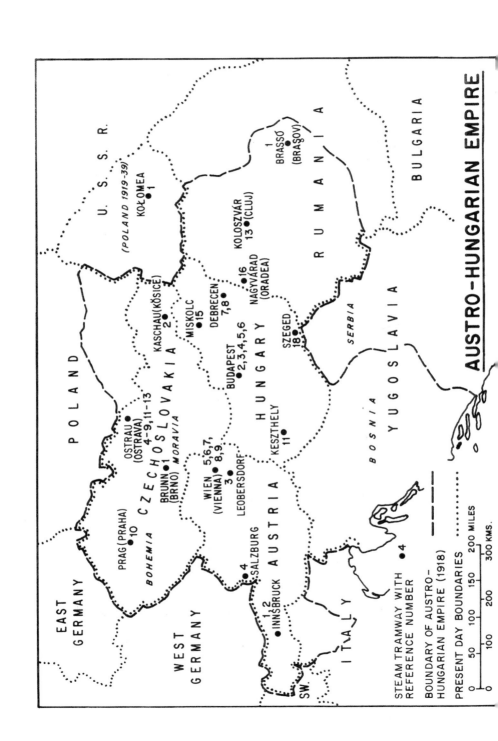

AUSTRO-HUNGARIAN EMPIRE

9. THE AUSTRO HUNGARIAN EMPIRE

During most of the period in which we are interested, the great Austro-Hungarian Empire flourished and continued to do so until broken up at the end of the 1914-1918 War. The Hapsburg monarchy then controlled the area comprising the now separate states of Austria, Hungary, Czechoslovakia, a small part of Poland, much of Jugo-Slavia and two small parts of Italy. Most of Czechoslovakia was then regarded as part of Austria and known as the Provinces of Bohemia and Moravia, while the Province of Transylvania, then in Hungary was transferred to Roumania in 1919. The parts of Poland not within the Empire, were under the control of Germany and Russia. German was the official language of the whole and titles of undertakings were often in German even where other languages were in common usage. It is hoped that the reader will excuse this brief lesson in historical geography, but it has been considered necessary in order to present the set-up in which steam trams were operated; and there were steam tramway systems in all the countries mentioned above except Jugo-Slavia and the two small parts of Italy.

AUSTRIA

There were only five steam tramway systems in Austria itself and three of these were in Vienna, a city which as capital of the whole Empire, reached a size and importance, now somewhat out of proportion to the present Republic of Austria, stripped of its former power and dependencies.

Palmer Harding of Paris fame, carried out some experiments in Vienna as early as 1876, using a small Merryweather engine (possibly that tried on Ryde Pier) and a Grantham steam car. [1] This is known to have been the subject of some previous experiments made by a Mr. Woods at Birkenhead, where the body was built. These experiments were not followed up immediately, but in 1883, the well known locomotive manufacturers, Messrs. Krauss of Munich in Germany and Linz in Austria, set up a subsidiary organization to run steam tramways in the suburbs of Vienna. Shortly afterwards. other lines were opened by the Neue Wiener Tramway Gesellschaft. One of the objectives of both companies was to reach the brickfields, so that they could both carry the inhabitants of the city and transport bricks by which the built-up area of the city could be expanded and thus widen their own market. As the Krauss lines started from several rather outlying termini, arrangements were made for their trailer cars, which were of a light design, to be hauled by horses in to the city centre. In 1888, the Neue Wiener company sold one of its lines to a new company, the A. G. der Wiener Lokalbahn, who then proceeded to extend it as a lengthy interurban route. Extensions continued until eventually, it joined up with a small urban electric tramway serving the town of Baden, on 1st January 1897. Subsequently this line was acquired and the whole converted to an electric light railway from Baden to Vienna.

After this steam was retained for goods traffic, but enjoyed a brief revival for passengers just after the 1939-1945 war, when as part of the consequent repairs, it was decided to alter the voltage of the electric supply, resulting in a temporary cessation of electric working over various sections of the line. The locomotive retained for goods work, including one of the enclosed type, were used in the meantime to provide shuttle service over the sections affected.

Apart from Vienna, Salzburg had two lengthy interurban lines, one of which was worked by enclosed locomotives and the other by unenclosed locomotives, before electrification. There were also two interurban lines at Innsbruck, that to Hall was formerly a steam tramway, using Krauss engines with enclosed wheels and motion. The other line to Igls, zigzags up a mountain-side and was officially a light railway with unenclosed 0-6-2 tank engines. The Hall line was electrified in 1909, but closed recently because of major roadworks, but the Igls line was electrified as late as 1937, with spare cars from the Hall line, and is still working.

In addition, the Nieder Österreichs Sud-Westbahn, a Standard Gauge Secondary railway at St. Polten, used a Krauss tram-engine on a branch line in the early days. The Nieder Österreichs Lokalbahn is also believed to have made limited use of Krauss tram engines.

HUNGARY

Although as mentioned overleaf, German was the official language of the Empire, the second partner, Hungary, has always enjoyed its own language and culture. It has been said that because of its flat terrain and scattered hamlets, Hungary would have been the ideal country for steam tramways. In fact however, there were fewer than one might have expected and the Hungarians tended to prefer narrow gauge light railways after the style of German Kreisbahnen.

Nevertheless, the dozen or so steam tramways which did exist, were certainly not lacking in interest. Of these, five served the City of Budapest and its suburbs. One tramway there was electrified at a very early date and was the first in Europe to use the slot conduit system and the City Council was so uncertain of its success that they insisted that the company bought a fleet of steam locomotives to stand by in case of failure.[2] When the electric system proved itself reliable, the engines were used to develop new lines in the suburbs. Another company used steam only for goods traffic, with its passenger services worked electrically, while a third was a goods only line in the industrial suburb of Kobanya, serving factories, a large brewery and pig farms: The type of conduit used in Budapest had a slide slot, with the current collector passing through an apperture between one of the running rails and a heavy check rail. A similar running rail and check rail was used on the non-conduit side, making a very wide and deep groove, which was suitable for the passage of main-line goods stock over the tram lines. Full advantage was taken of this feature by the steam tramways and the industrial establishments they served.

There were also small steam tramway systems at Debrecen, Szeged and in the aforested province of Transylvania (transferred to Roumania in 1919). These latter were to be found at, to give them their Hungarian names - Brasso, Kolozsvar and Nagyvarad. They were called Kronstadt, Klausenburg and Grosswardein in German and are now Brașov, Cluj and Oradea in Roumanian.

That at Braşov lasted with steam until 1958, Cluj closed as early as 1904, while Oradea was electrified in 1905 and is still flourishing. At Keszthely there was a railway branch line, at first worked by enclosed locomotives. Later one of these was transferred to Debrecen, where steam goods working survived until quite late. Brasov used Komarek steam railcars as well as locomotives.

BOHEMIA & MORAVIA (CZECHOSLOVAKIA)

The two provinces of Bohemia and Moravia (Böhmen und Mähren in German), plus a small part of Hungary, became an independent state in 1919 under the terms of the Versailles Treaty, having formerly been regarded as part of Austria. Although Prague in Bohemia, now the capital of Czechoslovakia, boasted a large horse tramway system, steam was proposed in 1888 but not followed up. On the other hand, Brünn (Brno), the principal city of Moravia, was served by steam tramways from an early date, using at first some Krauss locomotives which had been built for trials in several German towns, after which they were left on the hands of the makers, until taken up as a bargain by Brünn. In due course they were replaced by slightly larger machines, one of which, named "Caroline" is now preserved.

Under the same management as the Brünn system, there was the Privoz-Ostrau-Witkowitz (Sic) line in the Silesian Coalfield area. Privoz or Oderfurt were the names then in use for the area around Ostrau Station, some distance to the north of the town centre, but within the general conurbation, while Witkowitz is the site of some large steel works. In later years the Ostrau [3](Ostrava) municipality took over the above together with some electric tramways and some very narrow gauge steam lines. After the 1939-45 war, to save the cost of replacing a railway bridge, that had been destroyed, the tramways took over a branch line and the trams used the existing road bridge before running onto the railway right of way. Other extensions to the tramway system were first built as standard gauge light railways using industrial steam locomotives pulling tramway trailer cars. Some of these lines used Komarek steam railcars.

The writer has experienced some difficulty in ascertaining the facts about the steam tramway at Kaschau (Kŏsice),[4] formerly in Hungary, because of conflicting information from various sources. Steam working took over a horse tramway from the main line railway station across the town to the Baranok Restaurant in 1893 and was served by seven Wiener Neustadt locomotives. There were experiments with an early diesel loco before electrification in 1913. Both Ostrau and Kaschau use very heavy section rails with an extra deep groove, so that railway goods stock can move freely over their tramway systems and both still employ electric locomotives for this purpose.

The Krauss tram-engine now displayed in the Prague Technical Museum, does not come from any of the above-mentioned systems, but from Salzburg, having been sold to an industrial establishment in Czechoslovakia.

POLAND

Only a comparatively small part of Poland was in the Austro-Hungarian Empire. Another small part was in Germany and the rest in the Russian Empire.

In the part controlled by Austria, there is only known to have been one steam tramway, that at Kolomea, which although in Poland between the wars, is now in Russia. It was worked by the State Railways using enclosed six-coupled locomotives. (See also Chapter 12).

The part of the Silesian Coalfield based on Kattowitz, now in Poland was formerly in Germany and is described in Chapter 3.

Locomotives

There were several manufacturers within the Austro-Hungarian Empire, who built locomotives for tramways. As already mentioned there was a branch of the Krauss undertaking at Linz in Austria and this firm was the first to produce tram engines for Austrian tramways, although the former demonstration models, which had opened the system at Brünn, had been built at Munich some years earlier. Those machines produced at Linz differed from the Munich products only in minor details, i.e., most had spoked wheels instead of disc and the sides of the domes were slightly tapered instead of parallel. In all, the works at Linz turned out about 70 engines for tramways within the Austro-Hungarian Empire. The Krauss lines in Vienna had that firm's Standard enclosed Loco- motives, including two small ones which had been used for trials at Augsburg, and two railway locomotives for the Stammersdorf line.

Another firm which built tram engines from an early date was the Sigl works at Wiener Neustadt, their first being for Debrezcen in Hungary in 1884, that town taking five in all. There were two at Brünn. They also built twenty- five for two tramways in Vienna and four for Udine just over the border in Italy. These latter and those for the second system in Vienna were heavy six-coupled machines with double-opening smokebox doors in the end sheets. The State Railways' works both in Austria and in Hungary, each built a number of tram engines. The Austrian Works known as "StEG", built 16 locomotives for Vienna and two for Klausenburg (now in Roumania), while the Royal Hungarian Works at Budapest built 29 locomotives for tramways in the City and other Hungarian systems. Their earliest models were of conventional appearance, but with the roof supported only by slender rods at the corners. Conversely, later models were heavily closed in by sliding side windows and solid end sheets, with spectacle glasses and the smokebox door, after the Krauss style. They and many other Austro- Hungarian tram engines had enormous spark arrester chimneys, as a precaution against starting fires in the pine forests close to which they often ran. Many of the Hungarian engines also had enormous head-lamps.

The locomotive works at Flordisdorf in the outskirts of Vienna, built two enclosed locomotives for a tramway at Kronstadt and two more for a tramway at Grosswardein (both now in Roumania). The two latter do not appear to have reached their intended destination and finished up in the hands of the Hungarian State Railways. However, in later years the Wiener Lokalbahn [5] used several of their heavier type locomotives for its freight traffic. The tramway at Salzburg in Austria had one locomotive built by Weitzer of Arad in Hungary, but it was not of the enclosed type.

Thus, practically all the tram engines used in the Austro-Hungarian Empire were also constructed within the Empire, which was self-sufficient; the only exception being a few Henschels in Hungary and Poland. Moreover, apart from those at Udine, the Empire did not export tram engines.

Passenger & Goods Stock

The passenger carriages used on the various steam tramways in Vienna and at Salzburg were conventional multi-windowed four wheelers with open end platforms, closed by metal gates. There were some cross-bench cars at Vienna and those used by Krauss for through working over the horse tramways were necessarily of light construction, mostly built at Graz, painted dark green and had two elaborate monograms on each side. The Innsbruck-Hall tramway had some of the smallest trailer cars ever operated on a steam tramway; all had a very sharp tumble-home to the lower side panels and some had only two windows each side. In steam days they carried the title on the side in large Gothic characters. They survived as trailers to the electric cars and were in use to very recently and in fact there may still be some on the Igls line.

The cars used at Budapest were six or eight windowed four wheelers, generally similar to those in Vienna, but some had the sharply curved tumble-home like those at Innsbruck and there were matching luggage vans. Cars used at Brünn, Ostrau and Brasso were of generally similar design, with four, six or eight side windows. Cars used at Debrecen had very small windows with wide pillars between them and it has been reported that under the later Roumanian regime, all stock at Brasso (Braşov) was painted bright yellow. Much of the passenger stock for tramways in the Empire, was constructed by Ringhofer of Prague (now C.K.D.-Tatra), who included in their output, some double-deck trailer cars for Odessa in Russia. Ringhofer and Weitzer con-structed the carriages for Brünn.

Mention has already been made of Komarek steam railcars, used on several steam tramways described in this chapter. In general, their bodywork resembled the typical Austrian contemporary electric cars, being rather wide with monitor roofs, several side windows with drop sashes and curved tops. Some had matchboarded side panels, while other had the sharp-tumble-home already mentioned. One of those used at Oderburg (Bohumin) had a railway carriage type body. They were usually four wheelers, with the cylinders and motion connected to the front wheels and the boiler in a small luggage com-partment behind the driver's position.[6]

The writer has little information about goods working on tramways in the Austro-Hungarian Empire, but such traffic was evidently extensive at Budapest, Brünn, Ostrau and Kaschau, as witnessed by the use of special heavy rails, capable of accepting main-line freight stock. The Krauss tramway in Vienna carried railway wagons on standard gauge transporters, because of incompatible wheel flanges. The writer has seen some ordinary low-sided goods trucks at the two latter places and several references to the carriage of bricks at Vienna as well as beer and pigs at Budapest. The type of traffic carried at Ostrau can be well imagined from the fact that it is the centre of a large steel manufacturing and coal mining area. While there is also little information about passenger stations, the writer has seen a photo of a building like an ornate cabman's shelter at Budapest and quite simple structures in the Ostrau area.

Although we have been unable to trace the existence of any steam tramways in those territories which make up the present state of Jugo-Slavia, in the early days of the electric tramways at Sarajevo, steam locomotives from an adjoining light railway of the same gauge, used to take goods traffic over the tram lines. Eventually this traffic grew to an extent at which an electric locomotive was required.

Notes

1. See "The Engineer" 12th May 1876, page 357.

2. See "Modern Tramway" December 1966, page 424.

3. See "70 Let Mestske Dopravy na Ostravshu" by Josef Cvik, 1964.

4. See "75 Rokov Mestskej Dopravy v Kosiciach 1891 - 1966", by Kosice Municipality, 1966.

5. See "Österreichs Strassenbahnen, in Wordt und Bildt" by W. Kramer, Vienna 1951.
   "Strassenbahn in Wien" by J.O. Slezak, Vienna, 1974.
   "Dampf Tramway Krauss & Co. in Wien", by A. Laula & H. Sternhart, Vienna 1974.

6. A Komarek steam car from a railway is preserved in Prague Technical Museum.

Lokalbahn Innsbruck-Hall loco No. 2 at Berg Isel tram-station.
Courtesy: Othmar Bamer 15-14.

Table 9   AUSTRIA

1. INNSBRUCK. (Lokalbahn Innsbruck-Hall i Tirol).
    Innsbruck(Berg Isel)-Hall, 12.1 km.
    S.1891, E.1909, C.1974. Gauge. 1000.

Locomotives. -	Nos.	1-2,	Krauss	0-4-0	2362-2363 of 1890.	⊡
		3-4,	Krauss	0-4-0	2446-2447 of 1891.	"
		5-6,	Krauss	0-4-0	2608-2609 of 1891.	"
		7-8,	Krauss	0-4-0	4483-4484 of 1900.	"

2. INNSBRUCK. (Innsbrucker Mittelgebirgsbahn).
    A steam light railway electrified as a tramway using surplus stock from No.1 above.
    Innsbruck(Berg Isel)-Igls, 8.3 km.
    S.1900, E.1937, Still Operating, Gauge. 1000.

Locomotives. -	Nos.	1-2,	Krauss	0-6-2	4364-4365 of 1900.	⊡
		3,	Krauss	0-6-2	4540 of 1901.	"
		106,	Winterthur	0-6-0	584 of 1899 ex-Brunigbahn 1916.	"

3. LEOBERSDORF. (Niederösterreichische Südwestbahnen).
    A standard gauge secondary railway with a branch worked as a tramway.
    Leobersdorf(Wittmannsdorf)-Gutenstein, 33.5 km. (Tram loco also worked on other lines with
    double deck car).
    S.1879, R.1880, Still Operating, Gauge. 1435.

Locomotives. -	No.	1c,	Krauss	0-4-0	834 of 1879. (Sold 1892).	⊟
		2c-4c,	Wiener Neustadt	0-4-0	2461-2463 of 1880.	⊡
		5c-7c,	Wiener Neustadt	0-4-0	2486-2487 & 2492 of 1881.	"

    Note. -   These locomotives were renumbered 85.01 to 85.07 from 1889.

4. SALZBURG. (Salzburger Eisenbahn und Tramway Gesellschaft).
    Salzburg-St.Leonhardt-Gartenau, 13.7 km.
    Salzburg-Bergheim,   3.5 km.
    Gartenau Line - S.1886, E.1909, GS to 1921. C.1953.
    Bergheim Line - S.1895, E.1921/1950, Still Operating. Gauge. 1435.

Locomotives. -	Nos.	1-3,	StEG	0-4-0	1911-1913 of 1886.	⊟
		4-5,	StEG	0-4-0	1942-1943 of 1887.	"
		6,	Krauss	0-4-0	1879 of 1887.(Preserved at	"
		7-8,	Wiener Neustadt	0-4-0	3820-3821 of 1895.	Prague). ⊡
		9,	Krauss	0-4-0	4580 of 1901.	⊟
		10,	Weitzer	0-6-0	119 of 1901.	⊡
		11-12.	Krauss	0-4-0	4814-4815 of 1902.	⊟

    Note. -   Locomotives 1-6, 9, 11 & 12 used on Gartenau line and 7, 8 & 10 on
                      Bergheim line.

    Names. -   1-Salzburg, 2-Morzg, 3-Grodig, 4-Hellbrunn, 5-Drachenloch, 6-Gartenau,
                      7-Oberndorf, 8-Bürmoos, 9-Untersberg, 10-Weitworth, 11-Hellbrunn (II),
                      12-Fürstenbrunn.

5. STAMMERSDORF. (Stammersdorf-Auerstal Lokalbahn). Always worked by No.8.
    Stammersdorf-Auerstal, 21.8 km.
    S.1904, E.1911, C.1972 ? Gauge. 1435.

| Locomotives. - | Nos. 31-32, | Krauss | 0-6-0 | 5099-5100 of 1904 (side & centre buffers). |

    Names. -   31-Stammersdorf, 32-Auerstal. (Numbered in No.8's stock).   ⊡

6. WIEN. (Vienna). (Wiener Tramwaygesellschaft).
    Experiments with steam traction on urban horse tramway lines.
    Praterstrasse-Ringstrasse-Hietzing, 3.8 km.
    Simmering-Zentralfriedhof (Central Cemetery), 2.1 km.
    Schwartzenbergplatz-Zentralfriedhof, 7.0 km.
    H.1874, S.1876/78 only, E. Various dates, Still Operating. Gauge. 1435.

225

Locomotives. -   Merryweather 0-4-0   2 of 1874. (ex-Ryde Pier ?).
                 Grantham Car 0-2-4   - of 1876. (Starbuck body).
                 Henschel   0-4-0   974 of 1878 "Cassel".

7. WIEN. (Vienna). (Neue Wiener Tramway Gesellschaft).
    Westbahnstrasse-Breitensee-Hütteldorf, 6.1 km.
    Stermwartestrasse-Nussdorf(Zangradbahnhof), 5.0 km.
    Gaudenzdorf-Wienerneudorf, 13.0 km. (See also No.8).
    H.1873, S.1885, E.1901, Still Operating, Gauge. 1435.

Locomotives. -   Nos. 1-7,   Wiener Neustadt 0-4-0 2954-2960 of 1884.
                       8-10, Wiener Neustadt 0-4-0 2961-2963 of 1885.   "
                       11-15, Wiener Neustadt 0-4-0 3039-3043 of 1885.   "
                       20-25, StEG   0-4-0 1888-1893 of 1886.   "
                       26-31, StEG   0-4-0 1914-1919 of 1886.   "
                       32-35, StEG   0-4-0 1944-1947 of 1887.   "
                       50-53. Wiener Neustadt 0-6-0 3157-3160 of 1887. (See also No.8)."

Names. -   1-Hernals, 2-Währing, 3-Neulerchenfeld, 4-Dobling, 5-Fünfhaus,
            6-Rudolfsheim, 7-Breitensee, 8-Penzing, 9-Baumgarten, 10-Meidling,
            11-Heiligenstadt, 12-Höhe Warte, 13-Grinzing, 14-Nüssdorf, 15-Kahlenberg,
            20-Neudorf, 21-Neu Erlaa, 23-Siebenhirten, 24-Altmannsdorf,
            25-Wilhelmsdorf, 26-Guntramsdorf, 27-Vössendorf, 28-Gaudenzdorf,
            29-Vindobona, 30-Werner von Lindheim, 31-Clarisse, 32-St.Marx,
            33-Matzleinsdorf, 34-Rothneusiedl, 35-Favoriten, 50-Teufelsmühle,
            51-Schnellendorf, 52-Krottenbach, 53-Biedermannsdorf.

Note. -   No.30 later renamed "Laxenburg" and 31 renamed "Mödling".

8. WIEN. (Vienna). (Dampftramway Gesellschaft Krauss und Comp.).
    Later (Dampftramway Gesellschaft vormals Krauss und Comp.).
    Hietzing-Kettenbruke-Perchtoldsdorf-Mödling, 16.9 km.   )
    Kettenbrücke-Gaudenzdorf, 0.9 km.   ) Southern Lines
    Kettenbrücke-Ober St.Veit, 2.4 km.   )
    Stefaniebrücke-Floridsdorf-Stammersdorf, 10.7 km.) Northern Lines
    Floridsdorf-Grossenzersdorf, 14.9 km.   )
    S.1883, E.1907/1922, Still Operating. Gauge. 1435

Locomotives. -   Nos. 1-5,   Krauss 0-4-0 1360-1364 of 1883.
                       6-10, Krauss 0-6-0 1477-1481 of 1884. (No.8 preserved at St. "
                                                              Polten).
                       11,   Krauss 0-6-0 1482 of 1886. (Preserved).   "
                       12-17, Krauss 0-4-0 1602-1607 of 1886.   "
                       18-21, Krauss 0-4-0 1708-1711 of 1886.   "
                       22-24, Krauss 0-4-0 1712-1714 of 1887.   "
                       25-26, Krauss 0-4-0 1880-1881 of 1887.   "
                       27,   Krauss 0-4-0 1678 of 1885.) ex-Germany No.4. "
                       28,   Krauss 0-4-0 1800 of 1886.)   "
                       29-30, Krauss 0-4-0 4141-4142 of 1899.
                       31-32, Krauss 0-6-0 5099-5100 of 1904. (See No.5).

Note. -   Nos.31-32 later passed to the State Railways with the numbers 296.01
            and 296.02.

9. WIEN. (Vienna). (Aktiengesellschaft der Wiener Lokalbahn).
    Took over a line from No.7 and extended it in 1888, to meet existing electric
    line to Baden.
    Wien(Gaudenzdorf)-Wienerneudorf-Guntramsdorf, 17.3 km.
    S.1888, E.(GS). 1907, GD.1968, Still Operating. Gauge. 1435.

Locomotives. -	Nos. 26, 27, 28 & 33,	StEG	0-4-0	1914, 1915, 1916 & 1945 of 1886/87)
	50-53,	Wiener Neustadt	0-6-0	3157-3160 of 1887. (all ex-No. 6).
	54-55,	Wiener Neustadt	0-6-0	3628-3629 of 1892.
	56-57,	Wiener Neustadt	0-6-0	3758-3759 of 1894.
	60-61,	Floridsdorf	0-6-0	1316 & 1340 of 1899/1900.
	62 (later 64),	Wiener Neustadt	0-6-0	with tender, 1744 of 1873
	70,	Wiener Neustadt	0-8-0	5558 of 1917 ?.
	71,	Krauss	0-8-0	7104 of 1905
	72-73,	Krauss	0-8-0	7327-7328 of 1919
	74,	Floridsdorf	2-8-2	9377 of 1944 (exchanged for No. 71).

Names. -   Nos. 26-28, 33 & 50-53 retained the names they had carried when with No. 7.
No. 54-Wien, 55-Neudorf, 56-Inzersdorf, 57-Laxenburg.

Note. -   Nos. 60-74 were acquired for goods working after electrification and were not named. They and No. 55 were used for passenger service 1945/46.

Steam passenger working restored between Philadelphiabrucke & Leesdorf from 1945 to 1946.

HUNGARY

Note. -   Hungarian names and titles are given, followed in the case of places in Transylvania, by Roumanian names.

Vasut -Railway: Ut -Street: Tér -Square: Palyaudvar -Station.

1. BRASSÓ. (Braşov). (Brassó-Harmonszéki Helyi Erdekü Vasútak Rt.)
Later (Magyar Allami Vasut. i.e. Hungarian State Railways)
Ceded to Roumania in 1919.   (Câile Ferate Braşov Treiscaune).
The German name is Kronstadt.
Brasso(Franzjosef Tér)-Bertalan (Bartolomeu), 3.0 km.
Brasso(Franzjosef Tér)-Hosszúfalu, 16.0 km.
Brasso(Franzjosef Tér)-Varos,   km. (Steam railcars).
Brasso-Harmonszeki(Harman), 7.0 km. (Later R). C.1958.
S.1891, Part R. ? C.1958. Gauge. 1435.

Locomotives. -	Nos. 5091-			
	5092,	Budapest	0-4-0	362-363 of 1891.
	5093,	Budapest	0-4-0	393 of 1892.
	5101,	Floridsdorf	0-4-0	858 of 1893.
	5102,	Ganz	0-4-0	972 of 1895.
	? - ? ,	Komarek Steam railcars.		

Names. -   Brassó, Hoszúfalu, Bertalan, Honterus, Tatrang.
Note. -   These locomotives were renumbered in 1911 and those of No.10 took the numbers 5091-5093.

2. BUDAPEST. (Budapesti Villamos Varosi Vasút Rt.)
i.e. (Budapest City Electric Railway Co., Ltd.).
A conduit electric tramway opened at a very early date, with steam locomotives in reserve, later used to develop a suburban line
Egyetem Tér-Köbanyai Ut-Orczy Ter, 2.0 km. (Electric).
Egyetem Tér-Uj Kösztemeto, 7.0 km. (Suburban Steam line, E.1894).
Köbanyai Ut-Köbanya, 1.0 km.   "   "   "
E.1889 (S.1889) Still Operating. Gauge. 1435.

Locomotives. -	Nos. 1-2,	Budapest	0-4-0	301-302 of 1889.
	3-4,	Budapest	0-4-0	327-328 of 1890.
	5,	Budapest	0-4-0	553 of 1893.
	6,	Henschel	0-4-0	3802 of 1893.
	-,	Borsig "Rowan" car 4211 of 1887.		

227

3.　BUDAPEST.　(Budapesti Közuti Vaspálya Társaság).
　　Later (Budapesti Helyi Erdekü Vasútak Rt.).
　　i.e. (Budapest Local Railway Co., Ltd.).
　　Buda(Palfy Tér)-Aquincum-Fo Ter-Szt.Endré, 16.3 km.
　　Buda(Fo Tér)-O Buda, 2.0 km.
　　Budapest(Kerpesti Ut)-Rakosfalva-Cinkota, 10.0 km.
　　Budapest(Kozva Gohid)-Soroksar, 8.0 km. (Later extended as railway).
　　S.1887, E.1906/? Part D. ? Still Operating. Gauge. 1435.

Locomotives. -	No.	1,	Budapest	0-4-0	194 of 1887.
		2-4,	StEG	0-4-0	1939-1941 of 1887.
		5-8,	Budapest	0-4-0	207-210 of 1888 (type 261).
		9-16,	Budapest	0-4-0	211-218 of 1888 (type 271).

　　Names. -　　　　1-Budapest, 2-Erzsebetfalva, 3-Sokorsar, 4-Haraszti, 5-16 not named.
　　　　　　　　　　(No.4 now preserved and named "Hungaria").

4.　BUDAPEST.　(Budapest-Szent Lörinczi Helyi Érdekü Vasút Rt.).
　　Budapest(Ludoviceum)-Szent Lörincz,　km.
　　S.1887, E.1900, Still Operating. Gauge. 760 (1435 on electrification).

Locomotives. -	Nos.	1-2,	Henschel	0-6-0	2287-2288 of 1887.
		3,	Henschel	0-6-0	4593 of 1896.
		4,	Possibly Maffei	0-6-0	3594 of 1902.
		5,	Possibly Krauss	0-4-0	854 of 1880. ∵
			or Jung	0-6-0	1845 of 1912.

　　Names. -　　　　1-Budapest, 2-Kispest, 3-Szent Lörincz, 4-Ludovika, 5-Rákos.

5.　BUDAPEST.　(Budapest-Ujpest-Rakospalotai Villamos Kozuti Vasút Rt.).
　　Constructed as an electric tramway but used steam for goods in early days.
　　Budapest-Ujpest-Rakospalota, 8.0 km.
　　E.1896, GS.1896, Still Operating. (GS given up 1905). Gauge. 1435.
　　Locomotive . -　　　　　　"Ujpest", Budapest 0-4-0 683 of 1895. (Sold to No.7).

6.　BUDAPEST.　(Köbanyai Iparvasút). i.e. (Kobanya Industrial Railway).
　　An industrial tramway with enclosed locomotives, serving factories, breweries and
　　pig farms in the Kobanya suburb of Budapest.
　　Industrial sidings,　km.
　　GS.1888, D. ? Still Operating ?　Gauge. 1435.

Locomotives. -	Nos.	1,	Budapest	0-4-0	224 of 1888.
		2,	Budapest	0-4-0	329 of 1890.
		3,	Budapest	0-4-0	554 of 1893.
		4,	Floridsdorf	0-6-0	3007 of 1930 ?.

7.　DEBRECEN.　(Debreceni Helyi Vasút Rt.).
　　Palyaudvar(Station)-Nagyerdo (Great Forest) ⎫
　　Industrial Sidings,　　　　　　　　　　　　 ⎭ 6.0 km.
　　S.1884, E.1911, GS. ? Still Operating. Gauge. 1435.

Locomotives. -	Nos.	1-3,	Wiener Neustadt	0-4-0	2951-2953 of 1884.
		4,	Wiener Neustadt	0-4-0	3063 of 1885.
		5,	Wiener Neustadt	0-4-0	3288 of 1889.
		683,	Budapest	0-4-0	683 of 1895 ex-No.5 in 1895.
		5092,	Budapest	0-4-0	226 of 1888 ex-No.11 in 1911.
		(II),	2, StEG	0-4-0	2297 of 1893 ex-No.13 in 1904.
		(II),	3, StEG	0-4-0	2298 of 1893 ex-No.13 in 1904.
		10,	Budapest	0-4-0	212 of 1888 ex-No.3 in 1917.
		12,	Budapest	0-4-0	214 of 1888 ex-No.3 in ?

　　Motive Power. -　　　　1-2, Stoltz steam cars of 1905.

　　Names. -　　　　1-Debreczen, 2-Nagyerdo, 3-István malon, 4-Hortobágy, 5-Csokonai.
　　　　　　　　　　Secondhand locomotives not named.

8. DEBRECEN. (Debrecen-Hajdusámsoni Helyi Érdekü Vasut).
   from 1911 (Debrecen-Nyirbatori Helyi Erdeku Vasut).
   Debrecen(Nagyerdo)-Hajdusamson-Nyirbator, 58.0 km. (Connecting with No.7).
   S.1906, Part E. ? Still Operating. Gauge. 1435.
   Locomotives. -   Worked by No.7 above.

9. GROSSWARDEIN. German name for Nagyvárad. See No.16.

10. KASSA (Kaschau) - See BOHEMIA No.2. In Czechoslovakia from 1919.

11. KESZTHELY. (Keszthely Balatonszentgyörgyi Helyi Érdekü Vasút).
    A light railway using enclosed locomotives, later upgraded and taken over by the
    State Railways (Magyar Allami Vasút).
    Keszthely-Balaton Szent György. 9.4 km.
    S.1888. R. ? Still Operating. Gauge. 1435.
    Locomotives. -   Nos. 1-2,   Budapest 0-4-0 225-226 of 1888.
                                   3,   Budapest 0-4-0 303 of 1889.

    Names. -   1-Tassilo, 2-Gyorgy, 3-Marie.

    Note. -   The locomotives were later numbered 5091-5093 in the M.A.V.
                            series and by 1911 5092 had passed to No.7 and the others became
                            284.001-002.

12. KLAUSENBURG. German name for Koloszvar, see No.13.

13. KOLOSZVÁR. (Koloszvari Közúti Vasút).
    In area ceded to Roumania in 1919, but already closed. The German name is
    Klausenburg and the Roumanian name is Cluj.
    Koloszvár-Kolosmonastor, km.
    Koloszvár-   (Ausere Ungar Gasse),   km.
    S.1893, C.1904. Gauge. 1435.
    Locomotives. -   Nos. 1-3,   StEG,   0-4-0 2296-2298 of 1893.
                                   4,   Budapest   0-4-0 702 of 1894 (at first numbered 6). "
                                   5,   Wiener Neustadt 0-4-0 3745 of 1894.   "

    Names. -   1- ?, 2- ?, 3- ?, 4-Matyas Kiraly (King Matthew), 5- ?,

14. KRONSTADT. German name for Brasso, see No.1.

15. MISKOLC. (Miskolc-Diosgyöri Helyi Erdekü Vasut Rt.).
    An electric tramway worked at first by steam railcars.
    Miskolc-Diosgyor, 5.0 km.
    S.1906, E. Still Operating. Gauge. 1435.

    Motive Power. -   Nos. 1-3, Ganz steam cars 1906.

16. NAGYVÁRAD (Oradea). (Nagyváradi Közúti Vasut ?).
    Ceded to Roumania in 1919. (German name Grosswardein).
    Then (Câile Ferate Oradea).
    Now (Interprinderea Comunala Oradea).
    Palyaudvar(Gara Central)-Rakozci Ut(Piate Vitoriei), 5.0 km (approx).
    S.1882, E.1905, Still Operating. Gauge. 1435.
    Locomotives. -   Nos. 1-2, Krauss   0-4-0 1152-1153 of 1882.
                                   3,   Krauss   0-4-0 3390 of 1896.   "
                            -.   Floridsdorf 0-4-0 343-344 of 1881 (not delivered).
                                              (went to M.A.V. as Nos.193-194, later
                                              Nos.5171-5172, then 283.001-002).

229

17. ORADEA. Roumanian name for Nagyvárad, see No.16 above.

18. SZEGED. (Szegedi Közúti Vaspálya Rt.).
Szeged Palyaudvar(Station)-Rokus Palyaudvar, 12.0 km. ?
Steam only used for goods and continued after electrification.
H.1884, GS.1884, E.1908, Still Operating. Gauge. 1435.
<u>Locomotives.</u> -   Nos.   1-2,   Krauss   0-4-0   1432-1433 of 1883.
                      3,   Budapest 0-4-0   30 of 1878.

Names. -   1-Palfy, 2-Kallay, 3-Futar.

BOHEMIA & MORAVIA

Note. -   German names are given first as that was the official language
until 1919. They are followed by Czech names.

1. BRÜNN (Brno). (Brünner Lokal Eisenbahn Gesellschaft). See also No.8.
Now (Dopravni Podnik Mesta Brna).
Bahnhof(Hlavni Nadrazi)-Schreibwald(Pisárky), km.)
Bahnhof(Hlavní Nadrazi)-Karthaus(Kralovo Polé), km.) 7.9 km.
Ugartestrasse(Novy Sady)-Zentral Friedhof(Ustredni Hrbitov). 2.3 km.
H.1869, S.1884, E.1900 (GS to 1914), Still Operating. Gauge. 1435.

<u>Locomotives.</u> -	Nos.	1,	Krauss	0-4-0	574 of 1877.
					(ex-Charlottenburg trials).
		2,	Krauss	0-4-0	859 of 1880. (ex-various trials). "
		3,	Krauss	0-4-0	775 of 1880. (ex-Bremen trials). "
		4,	Krauss	0-4-0	778 of 1881. (ex-various trials). "
		5,	Wiener Neustadt	0-4-0	2444 of 1880. (ex-various trials). "
		-,	Wiener Neustadt	0-4-0	2451 of 1880. "
					(trials then to Kaschau).
		6,	Krauss	0-4-0	865 of 1880. (ex-Hamburg trials). "
		7-8,	Krauss	0-4-0	1304-1305 of 1883. "
		9,	Krauss	0-4-0	1632 of 1885. "
		10,	Krauss	0-6-0	2165 of 1889. (now preserved). "
		11,	Krauss	0-4-0	2514 of 1891. "
<u>Replacements</u>		(II) 1,	Krauss	0-4-0	3143 of 1894. "
		(II) 3,	Krauss	0-4-0	3245 of 1895. "
		(II) 4,	Krauss	0-4-0	3715 of 1897. "
		(II) 6,	Krauss	0-4-0	3047 of 1894. "
		(III) 6,	Krauss	0-4-0	3714 of 1897. (trials then to Ostrau). "

Names. -   Nos. 1-9 included "Grete", "Schreibwald" and "Karthaus", No.10-Caroline,
11-Clarisse, (II)1-Marietta, (II)3 or 4-Henriette, (II)6-Hedwig.

2. BOHUMIN (Oderburg). See No.4.

3. KASCHAU (Kosice). (Kassa in Hungarian). (Original owner Ing. Stefan Popper).
From 1892 (Kassai Kozuti Vasut Reszveny Tarsasag).
Later (Kassai Villamos Kozuti Vasut). From 1919 (Dopravni Podnik Mesta Kosic).
Formerly part of Hungary but ceded to Czechoslovakia in 1919.
Bahnhof(Palyaudvar)(Hlavni Nadrazi)-Baranok Restaurant(Crmel), 7.85 km.
H.1891, GS.1892, S.1893, E.1913, Still Operating. Gauge. 1435.

<u>Locomotives.</u> -	No.	1,	Wiener Neustadt	0-4-0	2451 of 1884 (ex-trials at Brünn).
		2-3,	Wiener Neustadt	0-4-0	3666-3667 of 1893. "
		4-5,	Wiener Neustadt	0-4-0	3721-3722 of 1894. "
		6-7,	Wiener Neustadt	0-4-0	3740-3741 of 1894. "

4. ODERBERG. (Bohumin). (Stadtische Dampfstrassenbahn Oderberg). Now part of No.8.
Alt Oderberg(Stary Bohumin)-Neu Oderberg (Novy Bohumin), 3.5 km.
H.1902, S.1903, E.1916. Still Operating ?. Gauge. 760.

Motive Power. - Nos. 1-2, Komarek steam railcars, 327-328 of 1903.(Boiler numbers).
                                3, Komarek steam railcar acquired 1910. 331 of 1904. '.' "
                         42-44, Komarek steam railcars 30, 32 & 31 of 1906 (works Nos.) "
                                           (Boiler numbers 357, 361 & 369). '.'

5. ODERBERG. (Bohumin). (Schlesischen Landeseisenbahn). Now part of No.8.
Neu Oderberg(Novy Bohumin)-Deutsch Leuthen(Dolny Lutyne)-Karwin(Karvina), 15.0 km.

Constructed as an electric line, but took over No.7 in 1911, whose steam locomotive
then worked goods services over both lines.

6. OSTRAU. (Ostrava). (Lokalbahn Ostrau-Karwin).
Later (Mistni Dráha Ostrava-Karviná). Now part of No.8.
Polnisch Ostrau(Ostrava)-Karwin(Karvina), 22.5 km.
S.1900, E.1909 (GS to 1919), C.1972. Gauge. 760.

Locomotives. - Two - ?
Other Motive Power. - Komarek Steam Railcars ?

7. OSTRAU. (Ostrava). (Mährisch-Schlesisch Lokalbahn A.G.).
Later (Mistni Dráha Hrušov-Polska Ostrava). Later part of No.8.
Polnisch Ostrau(Ostrava)-Hruschau(Hrušov), 3.4 km. (Passenger service over 2.5 km).
S.1904, E.1911, C.1963. Gauge. 760.
Locomotives. - Nos. 1-2, Krauss 0-8-0 5047 & 5052 of 1903.

Names. - 1-Hansel, 2-Steffel.

Other Motive Power. - 1-2, Ganz/Ringhoffer Steam Railcars, 1904.

8. OSTRAU. (Ostrava). Owned by No.1 (Brünner Lokaleisenbahn Gesellschaft). 1897-1899.
Now (Dopravni Podnik Mĕsta Ostravy). (See note - *).
Oderfurt(Privoz)-Ostrau(Ostrava)-Witkowitz(Vitkovice), 7.8 km.
Ostrau(Ostrava)-Hulwacken(Hulwaky), 2.7 km. (Part of through route to Schonbrunn).
S.1894, E.1901/1911 (GS to 1922). Still Operating. Gauge. 1435.
Locomotives. - Nos. 1-4, Krauss 0-4-0 3035-3038 of 1894.
                              5, Krauss 0-4-0 3306 of 1895. "
                              6, Krauss 0-4-0 3714 of 1898. (Tried at Brunn first). "
                              7, Budapest 0-4-0 302 of 1889.(ex Hungary No.2) "
                              8, Budapest 0-4-0 327 of 1890. " " ") "
Names. - 1- ?, 2- ?, 3-?, 4-?, 5-Brunn.
*See "70 Let Mestske Dopravy na Ostravsju" by J.Cvik, Ostrava 1964.
Also "Strassenbahn Magazin" May 1973, page 98, article by Hans Lenhardt.

9. OSTRAU. (Ostrava). (Dopravni Podnik Mĕsta Ostravy).
A steam main line railway branch line to Hultschin (Hlucin) was handed over to the Ostrava
tramways and electrified in 1946, after a bridge had been destroyed in the war. The trams
now use a parallel road bridge.

10. PRAG (Praha). (Prager Strassenbahnen ?).
Steam tramway proposed and concession granted to A.Prochazka & F.Zelenka in 1886
but never taken up.

11. SCHÖNBRUNN. (Svinov). (Mährische Landeseisenbahn Gesellschaft).
Steam light railway taken over by No.8 and eventually electrified.
Schönbrunn (Svinov)-Königsberg (Klimkovice), 7.5 km.
S.1910, E.1926. Still Operating. Gauge. 1435.
Locomotives. - Two (Possibly State Railway 493 class on loan).

12, SCHÖNBRUNN. (Svinov). (Mährische Landeseisenbahn Gesellschaft).
Steam light railway taken over by No.8 and electrified.
Schönbrunn(Svinov)-Ellgoth(Dolni Lhota)-Kiowitz Budischowitz(Kyjovice Budišcovice), 13.4 km.
S.1925/27, E.1939/48.   Still Operating.   Gauge. 1435.
Locomotives. -   Three   (possibly loaned by No.13 below).

13.   WITKOWITZ.   (Vitkovice).   (Kleinbahn Witkowitz-Zabreh).   "K.B.W.Z".
Later part of (Mistni Dráhu Mährisch Hory-Brusperk).   Now part of No.8.
Witkowitz(Vitkovice)-Heinrichsdorf(Zabreh)-Brusperk(Hrabova),   3.8 km.
S.1913/30, E.1934,   Still Operating.   Gauge. 1435.
Locomotives. -   Nos.   22,   Krauss   0-4-0   515 of 1876. "Adolf".
                                26,   Krauss   0-4-0   1205 of 1885.   "
                        27-28,   Krauss   0-6-0   2066,2065 of 1889/90.   "
                                31,   Krauss   0-6-0   3479 of 1896.   "
                                32,   Krauss   0-6-0   3563 of 1897.   "

Motive Power. -   Komarek Steam Railcar 824 of 1911.
                          Hugo Jancko Steam Railcar.   "

Note. -   The locomotives were probably borrowed from Witkowitz Industriebahn
                       and shared with No.12 above.

POLAND

Only one steam tramway subsequently in the independent state of Poland, was formerly
in the Austro-Hungarian Empire, and was in the area taken over by Russia after the 1939
war.   For others see Chapters 3 & 12.

1.   KOLOMEA.   (Kolomear Lokalbahn A.G.)   (Worked by State Railways).
Later (Polske Koleje Panstwowe) = "Polish State Railways".
Kolomea-Delatyn. 32.7 km   ?
S.1886, R.   ?   C.   ?   Gauge. 1435.
Locomotives. -   Nos.   031-
                                034,   StEG   0-6-0, 1920-1923 of 1886.

Names. -   031-Kniazdwor, 032-Peczenizyn, 033-Kolomya, 034-Słoboda.
                    They became K.K.Statsbahn Nos. 98.01-98.04.

The Krauss tram-engine in Prague Technical Museum is actually Salzburg No.6
"Gartenau" rescued from industry in Czechoslovakia.   Compare with photo on
page 217.

Photo: D.Trevor Rowe.

The second No. 6 of the Brünner Lokalbahn, "Hedwig", built by Krauss (Linz) in 1894.

Courtesy: Deutsches Museum.

Loco No. 31 and trailer from the electric tramways, on the Lokalbahn Mar. Hory-Brusperk, at Zahrady tram station, Ostrau.

Courtesy: J. H. Price.

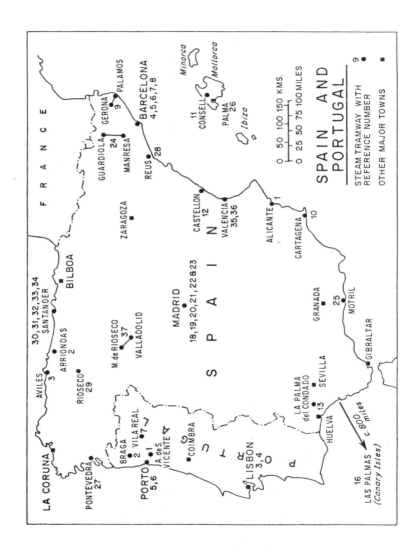

SPAIN AND PORTUGAL

STEAM TRAMWAY WITH REFERENCE NUMBER ● 9

OTHER MAJOR TOWNS ■

0 50 100 150 KMS.

0 25 50 75 100 MILES

FRANCE

PALAMOS
GERONA 9
GUARDIOLA 24
MANRESA
BARCELONA
4,5,6,7,8
REUS 28
CASTELLON 12
VALENCIA 35,36
ALICANTE 1
CARTAGENA 10

ZARAGOZA ■

BILBOA ■

30,31,32,33,34
SANTANDER
AVILES ARRIONDAS 2
3
RIOSECO 29
M.deRIOSECO 37
VALLADOLID

MADRID
18,19,20,21,22&23

S P A I N

GRANADA MOTRIL
■ 25
SEVILLA ■
LA PALMA
del CONDADO 13
HUELVA ■ GIBRALTAR ■

LA CORUNA ■
PONTEVEDRA 27
BRAGA VILA REAL 7
2 1
PORTO A.deS.
5,6 VICENTE
■ COIMBRA
LISBON
3,0
P o r t u g a l

16
LAS PALMAS c.800 miles
(Canary Isles)

Minorca
Mallorca
CONSELL 11
PALMA 26
Ibiza

10. THE IBERIAN PENINSULAR SPAIN

This chapter deals with Spain, Portugal and the dependant islands off the coasts of both. Each was served by a number of steam tramways and Spain was the only European Country where British steam tramway equipment was well represented. The two most important cities Madrid and Barcelona were each served by a number of suburban steam tramways. In fact the Barcelona-San Andrés line was opened as early as 1877 and another line opened at an early date joined Barcelona with Badalona, but this at first only used steam outside the city walls, with horse or mule traction employed between the city centre and San Martin.[1] However, steam working was gradually extended into the city between 1887 and 1893. "Trumpet Men" had to be carried on the locomotives to announce the presence of trains. Both these lines ran parallel to the coast along reasonably flat roads. In 1880 some steeply graded lines were opened from the city centre to the inland suburbs. Barcelona is the most important sea port in Spain and therefore a large and busy city, it is not surprising therefore that its tramways were all electrified soon after the turn of the century.

The steam tramways at Madrid were rather scattered round the fringe of the city and although two were opened at a very early date, 1877 and 1879 respectively, they were not quite the success of those in Barcelona and the others were much later in developing. The Compañia Madrileña de Urbanización built a large housing estate to the North of Madrid in 1903, the "Ciudad Lineal" and opened a tramway system to go with it, some parts of which were worked by steam. Another steam tramway never reached its intended destination, because a competing light railway got there first.

There were also two suburban steam tramways at Valencia, but at most other places, steam tramways were of a much more rural character, catering for the needs of small towns, farming communities and some even were linked with quarries or mines. The Tranvía de Arriondas a Covadonga deserves special mention, as it relied mainly on pilgrimage traffic. Covadonga was one of the few places in Spain not overrun by the Moors and subsequently became a centre of Christian resurgence, the tramway linked it with Arriondas, served by the north coastal railway. Although this tramway closed in 1934, its three locomotives and other items of rolling stock, still stood in a very derelict state in their yard at Arriondas until very recently.

Just as in France, many lines started life as steam tramways, some have changed their character over the years and become proper light railways, in which guise a few survive, using railway locomotives (steam, diesel or electric). Such a line, with a most complicated history, is the "Tranvía o Ferrocarril Economico de Manresa a Berga", which according to its title, right from the start, was unable to make up its mind whether it was a tramway or light railway. Although originally worked by locomotives with enclosed motion, it met the Catalan Railway from Barcelona, end on at Manresa and over the years there have been through services worked by large locomotives, even including Garratts. Part was taken over by the state and diesel railcars substituted. However there is still a certain amount of street running through intermediate towns. Another interesting example was Reus, where the line to Salou started on the street in the town centre and ran thus as far as its depot in the outskirts, whence it ran as a roadside tramway. In the 1920s it was cut back at the depot and diverted to a terminal station nearby and accessible from reserved track. Although latterly worked by diesel railcars, one of the original tram-engines, stripped of its covering was among those held in reserve in the shed, certainly until the late 1960s.

Included within the Kingdom of Spain are the Balearic and Canary Islands, which had steam tramways. On the former, Majorca (Mallorca) had a steam tramway from Palma to Puerto Pi (written Portopi in old guide books), worked by various locomotives, mainly of British origin. On the Canary Islands, there was also a steam tramway at Las Palmas, serving Puerto de la Luz, further north along the coast. Although later electrified, and closed in 1937, the line experienced a revival with steam traction during the 1939-1945 war; while the electrical equipment had been disposed of, some of the electric cars were still in the depot and the track had not yet been lifted. Consequently when petrol became scarce for the replacing buses, an 0-6-0 tank engine was borrowed from a light railway on the mainland and provided a service, pulling the electric cars made up into a train.[2]

There are no longer any tramways worked by enclosed locomotives in Spain, but until recently, it was possible to ride over some of their former routes in diesel railcars and occasionally behind a steam railway locomotive. Many light railways in Spain, including some that started life as tramways, were taken over by the state when they got into financial difficulties. The organization, known for short as "Estado" is not the same as that which manages the main line broad gauge railways.

Locomotives

The locomotives used on Spanish steam tramways were distinguished principally by the variety of their makers, design and countries of origin. As already mentioned, Spain was the only European country where British manufacturers gained a foothold. Experiments with steam are reported as having taken place as early as 1871 on a horse tramway in Santander, using a peculiar locomotive designed and built by Leonard Todd of Leith, Scotland. It was named "Prima Donna" and had single driving wheels, over five feet in diameter, with cylinders on top of the boiler, driving the wheels through gears like a traction-engine. The chimney was collapsible and 14 foot high for the smoke to clear the roof of the double deck carriage which it pulled.[3] Little has been heard of the performance of this machine, so perhaps it was as temperamental as its namesake !

The first regular steam tram service was opened in Barcelona in 1877, on the San Andrés line, using small Merryweather engines built in London. The line eventually had fifteen of these, of three different classes, each slightly larger than its predecessor. They were not fireless as sometimes described in contemporary accounts. They were followed by two more similar machines, built locally by the "Maquinista" organization and were the first two locomotives built by that firm. They appear to have been the only completely enclosed locomotives actually built in Spain. The parallel Badalona line, opened in 1884, started with four standard Krauss engines, but Mr. Albert van Capellen, formerly manager of a Dutch tramway, took over the management of this line and ordered Dutch "Breda" locomotives, of which there were eventually eight, of their standard design and the only ones exported to an European tramway.[4]

The terrain in Barcelona slopes away from the sea towards some mountains, so that the two lines already described, running parallel to the sea, had no severe gradients or curves. Not so for the German controlled "Compañía General de Tranvías" which worked a group of routes running inland and had to contend with gradients as steep as 1 in 11 and a number of sharp curves near the city centre. To work this system, the Winterthur company of Switzerland, noted for producing peculiar locomotives, excelled itself on this occasion and supplied fifteen machines, of probably the most peculiar design of all. They were long six-wheelers with more or less conventional boilers, but three cylinders were mounted well ahead of a square smokebox. They drove a stub axle connected by heavy chains to the centre axle by means of a differential (described in contemporary literature as "Jack-in-a-box" motion); other chains connected the centre axle with the leading and trailing ones, which ran in radial axleboxes, so that they could accomodate themselves to the sharp curves. Compression brakes were provided for use on the gradients and these locomotives were expected to pull two carriages.[5] It is possible that only five of these machines were actually delivered, although they were described as being very successful. By 1888, they had been replaced by Falcon locomotives of the Scott Russell design;[6] unfortunately, it is not known how many of these there were, possibly six, for although the writer has seen several photographs of them, only on one are the name and works number legible.

Two slightly smaller Falcon machines from Loughborough, and one standard machine, ran on another tramway in Barcelona, the short Sagrera-Horta branch line and others on the Reus-Salou tramway some way further down the coast and at Palma in Majorca. A Falcon loco from the latter was used in the construction of the Soller Railway and stood disused in their yard until the 1930s. Both steam tramways in Valencia favoured locomotives built by Thomas Green of Leeds and of that firm's standard design, with three drop windows each side, but the first two machines were two cylinder compounds, while the others were simple expansion. The earlier tramways opened at Madrid had an assortment of German, Belgian and Swiss machines, but the three opened after the turn of the century evidently turned to the Arthur Koppel organization for equipment, using Orenstein & Koppel and Jung locomotives supplied through him. British, German and Belgian locomotives accounted for the majority of motive power on tramways outside the major cities. Mention should be made of the Pontevedra-Marin tramway on the far west coast, which used St. Léonard machines from Belgium. The first three were fully enclosed but the fourth had only the wheels and motion enclosed and extended side tanks. The dome and chimney cap were of highly polished brass so that it looked rather like those of the Glyn Valley tramway in Wales. The Pontevedra line used Carpenter air brakes with a horizontal pump. Although foreign-built locomotives accounted for most of those used in Spain, two Spanish firms did built a few locomotives with enclosed motion; they were "La Maquinista Terrestre y Marítima" and "Nuevo Vulceno-La Navegacion e Industria S.A." both of Barcelona. Only the two built for the San Andrés tramway were fully enclosed. The latter firm built some with enclosed wheels and motion for the Manresa-Berga tramway.

The Carthagena & Herrerias Steam Tramway Co. Ltd., lived up to its English title and had a fleet of Hunslet 0-8-0 saddle tank locomotives, of surprisingly heavy and modern appearance for the 1880s and quite un tramlike. Nevertheless, in 1929, this tramway did acquire four Sentinal geared locomotives which [7] although strictly not tram engines were definitely steam and enclosed!

Like other locomotives in Spain, they remained derelict on site for many years after withdrawal.

Passenger & Goods Stock

There exists a very early photograph of a train on the Barcelona-San Andrés Tramway, showing Merryweather loco No. 2 adorned with a large coat of arms, at the head of a train of open wagons, on which are mounted back to back seats with passengers. However, a close look at this picture shows that the passengers are of distinctly British appearance, including soldiers and a policeman, part of the background, including the locomotive's condenser tank and chimney, has been touched out and no doubt it was a works photo taken before the loco left London for Spain.[8] The writer is assured that the actual passenger stock comprised small saloon and cross-bench cars and that many of them survived as trailers for the later electric cars. Most appear to have been of Belgian design and origin.

In fact, most of the passenger stock used on Spanish steam tramways, appears to have been of light construction after the style of horse cars, particularly those used at Arriondas and at Reus. As well as Belgian carriages, built mainly at Nivelles, several tramways used vehicles of British construction and the Valencia tramways were equipped with both single and double deck saloon cars, which appear to have been of Milnes design. The double deckers had covered tops and an official history of the Valencia tramways contains the following quotation "El precio del billete era de quince céntimos tanto en el interior de los coches como en el imperial", which freely translated means "the price of tickets was 15 céntimos for either inside or on the upper deck of the car. " One of the Barcelona tramways had 14 Falcon single deck cars.

To the delight of the transport photographer, the Onda-Castellon tramway ran along the main streets of Castellon until 1964 and it had some of the most modern stock on Spanish steam tramways or light railways. Smart centre entrance bogie cars were built in the late 1920s as trailers for two Simplex bogie railcars, which themselves finished up as trailer cars in steam hauled trains. They were painted in two shades of green and the locomotives were bright green, with red or yellow lining and polished brass work. Apart from these, little is known about the liveries of Spanish steam tramways except that the manufacturer of the two locomotives for Aviles (spelt Avilles by them) was instructed to paint them "Midland Colour", presumably a dark red.[9] The stock of the "Urbanizacion" tramway was white, as was that at Reus at first (later dark green). When the writer visited there in 1967, the remaining locomotives were black with blue lining. Probably grained teak or dark green predominated among the other tramways. The "Urbanizacion" system and some others had a number of cross-bench cars.

Many of the Spanish tramways carried freight and there exists an early Works picture of Falcon loco No. 2 of the Reus tramway, hauling an open goods truck, a closed van and two passenger carriages. The trucks are of typical British appearance and the coaches have turtle back roofs and open end platforms. That nearest to the viewer, appears to have a luggage compartment.[10] The Madrid-El Pardo tramway (which served the location of General Franco's Palace), had some covered baggage vans with sliding doors, which were shown in a photograph in the Arthur Koppel catalogue. He appears to have supplied both the locomotives and passenger carriages for this line. Some of the latter had open side corridors and others on bogies had sliding doors.

PORTUGAL

Only six steam tramways are known to have existed in Portugal, and of these, two although very interesting and curious, seem to have amounted to nothing but brief experiments.

The most conventional and an early starter, was that which served Oporto, the second city of Portugal and the centre of the port wine industry. Here a standard gauge horse tramway commenced operation in 1870. One line ran from below the great suspension bridge spanning the gorge between Oporto and Vila Nova de Gaya,[11] along the bank of the river Douro to its mouth (Foz de Douro) and beyond to the sardine fishing village of Matosinhos. It was soon further extended to the newly opened deep water harbour at Leixões (pronounced "Leshoins"). In 1872, another company built a second tramway across the city centre on higher ground, from Campanha to Boa Vista. This too was extended down to the coast to meet the original line near Foz. Very soon a joint through service was provided by both companies and steam operated from 1878, between Boa Vista and Leixões, each company supplying three Henschel locomotives, which were subsequently supplemented by a single Merryweather machine. Needless to say, before long the two companies amalgamated. Tram trains from Leixões were broken up at Boa Vista and the cars pursued their separate ways, drawn by mules to three separate terminals in the city centre. When electrified in stages between 1901 and 1912, the upper line followed a more direct course between Boa Vista and Matosinhos.

Like that at Covadonga in Spain, the tramway at Braga to the north, was built principally in connection with pilgrimage traffic. It linked the railway station with the foot of a hill, on top of which was situated an important church. The hill was served by a funicular and the Swiss firm at Winterthur had the contract to construct both the funicular and the tramway in 1881, (the funicular was one of their first). It has not been possible to trace any locomotives for this tram line in the Winterthur works list, but it would appear that they were Winterthur machines as one would expect, possibly the two used on the short lived tramway at Regua, to be described in a later paragraph.

The next two tramways to be described, cannot have enjoyed more than a brief and experimental existence from such information as has come to hand, they were little more than costly experiments, made with foreign capital. Powers were obtained through a concession granted to Messrs. Edwin Clark, Punchard & Co. in 1873,[12] to construct two lengthy tramways through the hilly countryside around Lisbon to Torres Vedras (33 miles) and to Pero Pinhero (28 miles), but permission was refused to link them through the narrow streets of the city. The first line was expected to carry very heavy goods and wine traffic and the other which was to run through the seaside resort of Cascaes to Cintra with its famous castle, was to carry mainly passenger traffic. However, it appears that work was only carried out on part of a line from Lisbon to Torres Vedras and the line to Cintra (now spelt Sintra) was not constructed. Both lines were to have been constructed to the Larmanjat system, which had been the subject of some experiments in Paris in 1868. With this, a single pair of large flangeless driving wheels of the engine ran directly on the paved roadway or on a prepared surface consisting of nine inch wide oak beams, laid in the road surface. There was a single guiding rail between them, on which double flanged wheels bogies ran at the front and rear of the engine. The rail projected a few inches above the road surface and the carriages were equipped similarly to the locomotives.[13]

A contemporary account states that the ruling gradient was 1 in 18, the sharpest curve was 39 feet 4 inches and that speeds of 15 miles per hour were to be attained. Some sort of service between Lisbon and Lumiar, appears to have been provided from 1873 to 1877, following trails in 1870.

Another line in Portugal must have been equally extraordinary in a different way. It was located inland between Regua and Vila Real, in one of the wine growing valleys. The line was steeply graded with gradients of 1 in 12, but evidently a weak bridge accounted for the peculiar way of working this line, which used two Winterthur 0-6-0 Locomotives permanently coupled together with a long girder (See Locomotive section). However, the line appears to have enjoyed a very short life in the form described and now forms part of a lengthy metre gauge branch line of the Portuguese State Railways.

There was a conventional steam tramway with ordinary enclosed locomotives in the Belem district of Lisbon, which ran from 1889 to 1896, having replaced a horse tram service and itself replaced by narrow gauge electric trams in 1902.

There appears also to have been a steam tramway at Aguas de Sao Vicente, in the north of Portugal. However, the existence of this line was only brought to the writer's attention through commercial past cards and so far no information has come to hand concerning the locomotives (they appear to be of German design possibly 6 Henschels), nor details of the route served.

Locomotives

Locomotives Nos. 1 and 2 were completed for the Lisbon-Torres Vedras line and after extended trials at Buckhurst Hill near London, they were despatched to Lisbon. They were saddle tank machines of typical British appearance, apart from the large unflanged driving wheels and the peculiar bogies front and rear. These two must have provided the service in Portugal, such as it was. Fourteen more engines were evidently built and their dismantled parts crated for the journey to Lisbon; it appears from recent research by K. P. Plant, that these parts never left London and were sold at a fraction of their cost price to Merryweather who used them in the construction of some industrial 0-6-0 tank engines.

The two locomotives constructed for the Regua line, were Winterthur 0-6-0s with Brown's patent boilers and that firm's characteristic rocking shaft drive. The main peculiarity of these engines is that they were permanently coupled face to face, but kept some distance apart by a long double girder, turned up at the ends and pivoted onto the frames of the engine. The whole thing resembled a bogie well wagon, with the frames of the two locomotives acting as bogies. Evidently, the load, whether human or merchandise, was carried on a six foot wide platform laid on the girders.[14] Locomotives for the tramway at Braga cannot be traced in the Winterthur works list, in spite of that firm's close connection with the line. However, from the photograph in the manager's office, the works number could be "112", that of one of the Regua locomotives, so it would appear that after brief experiments there, the Siamese twins were successfully separated and sent to work at Braga.

The first two Henschel locomotives built for Oporto, one for each tramway, were the first two tramway locomotives to be built by that firm, so it seems from their later successes elsewhere, that they got the design right the first time.

The Merryweather locomotive at Oporto was also of that firm's standard design and one account says that it was superior to the Henschel machines, nevertheless they did not buy any more. Details of the locomotives on the Belem tramway at Lisbon, are not known, but from the only photo seen by the writer, a rather distant one, they could be British machines.[15]

Passenger Stock

In view of Portugal's strong links with Great Britain, it is not surprising that the ten original cars at Oporto were built by Starbuck at Birkenhead. One was a double decker and the others, single deckers of two sizes, the smaller ones being intended for the routes with steep gradients. Each was painted in a different colour, as the present mustard coloured livery was not adopted until after electrification. The starbuck single deck cars remained in use as workmen's trailers to the electric cars, on the Matosinhos route for sardine fishermen, until 1959. One was rebuilt as an electric car, but No. 9, a large car, was brought back to England for the Tramway Museum at Crich, where it was repainted primrose yellow. No. 8, a smaller car, was repainted green and retained at Oporto, as a museum piece.

When steam operation had commenced, individual cars were pulled by horses or mules from Campanhã, Carmo and Praca de Dom Pedro to Boa Vista at the end of a long wide avenue,[16] where they were made up into trains to be hauled for the rest of the journey by steam engines. After a time the Starbuck carriages were supplemented by some French built cars and some baggage vans, to carry passengers luggage from the liners that docked at Leixões.

The Braga tramway opened with eight two axle cross-bench cars and two postal vans, all supplied by Winterthur. In 1890 one more cross-bench car and three saloons were added, but they were still of very early design with turtle-back roofs. However, they survived as trailers to the electric cars, until the latter were in turn replaced by second-hand German trolleybuses in 1963.

It is probable that Regua tramway never got as far as acquiring any passenger stock, but an account of the trial at Buckhurst Hill, with the Larmanjat locomotive for Lisbon, states that a second class carriage, a third class carriage and a van, all built by Brown, Marshall & Co., were tried with it. Like the locomotive, these had large flangeless wheels at the sides and bogies with central double flanged wheels under the ends. Presumably these were shipped to Portugal with the locomotives. *

241

Notes

1. See "Tramways, Their Construction and Working" by D. Kinnear Clark, London 1878, page 391, and "Iron" Vol. 21 for 2nd February 1883 for articles on Barcelona Steam Tramways.

2. See "Modern Tramway" for July 1968, page 167 and "Railway Magazine" 1961, page 57.

3. See "Engineer" for July 1874, page 70. (Also Kinnear Clark).

4. See "Locomotives built by Machinefabriek 'Breda'" by Prof. A. D. de Pater, Leiden 1970.

5. See "Engineering" for December 1880, page 566 and drawing.

6. See Whitcombe. The Falcon Works was owned by Henry Hughes until 1883, then by Norman Scott-Russell, who produced an improved type of tram engine. The works was taken over by the Brush Electrical Engineering Co. in 1899 and they did build a few more steam locomotives. Their agent in Spain was Julius Neville of Liverpool, whose works plate some carried.

7. See "The Locomotive" magazine for September 1930, page 291.

8. A recent comparison of photographs, suggest from the background and type of car, that this locomotive might have been tried on the National Rifle Association's temporary line on Wimbledon Common, which already had one Merryweather engine.

9. Later green, when seen by Señor Reder in the 1920s.

10. See "Tren Miniatura" for January 1959, page 3.

11. There was a broad gauge industrial rack railway laid on the streets of Vila Nova de Gaya using 4 Esslingen locomotives. (Some track still in position 1973)

12. See "Tramways, Their Construction and Working" by D. Kinnear Clark, London, 1878.

13. See "Railway Magazine" for November 1942, page 326, and "Railway Gazette" for 24th July 1942, page 81.

14. See "Locomotive Magazine" for 15th May 1941.

15. See "As Rodas da Capital" by Vasco Callixto, lisbon 1967.

16. See "The Engineer" for 10th January 1873, et seq., and "Iron" Vol. 23 for 4th April 1884.

Merryweather loco No. 2 for the Barcelona-San Andrés tramway, undergoing trials. It has been suggested that these took place on the Wimbledon Common Rifle Range line. Compare with photo on page 251.
Photo: Science Museum London - Whitcombe Collection 9170.

Table 10 - SPAIN & its DEPENDENCIES

1. ALICANTE. (Compañía General de Ferrocarriles de España).
   Later (Compañía General de Tranvías y Ferrocarriles de España).
   From 1903, (Tranvías y Ferrocarriles Vecinales de España) Belgian owned.
   Alicante-Muchamiel, 9.0 km.
   Alicante-Elche,   20.5 km.
   S. 1906, C.1910. Gauge. 1000.
   Locomotives. -   Nos.   1-4,   Tubize 0-6-0   1416-1419 of 1905.

2. ARRIONDAS. (Compañía del Tranvia de Arriondas a Covadonga).
   Arriondas-Covadonga, 17.0 km.
   S.1908, C.1934. Gauge. 1000.
   Locomotives. -   Nos.   1-3,   Borsig 0-6-0   6497-6499 of 1907.

3. AVILES. (Avilles Steam Tramways Co..) (Sic).
   Later (Tranvía a Vapor del Litoral Asturiana).
   Aviles-Salinas, 4.7 km.
   S.1892, C 1930 ? Gauge. 1000.
   Locomotives. -   Nos.   1-2,   Kerr Stuart 0-4-0   569-570 of 1892.

   Names. -   1-Avilles. 2-Salinas.

4. BARCELONA. (La Sociedad Anónima del Tranvía de Barcelona al Clot y San Andrés).
   In 1881 (Compañía de Tranvías y Ferrocarriles Económicos).
   From 1900 (Sociedad Anónima de Tranvías de Barcelona a San Andrés y Extensiones).
   Belgian owned and subsequently acquired Nos. 5 & 6.
   Barcelona(Trafalgar)-Clot-Sagrera-San Andrés, 4.5 km.
   S.1877, E.1901, Trolleybus 1941. Gauge. 1000.
   Locomotives. -   Nos.   1-5,   Merryweather 0-4-0   46-50 of 1877.
                              6-10,   Merryweather 0-4-0   69-73 of 1873.
                             11-14,   Merryweather 0-4-0   134-137 of 1882.
                               15,   Merryweather 0-4-0   ?   of 1882.
                             16-17,   Maquinista   0-4-0   1-2 of 1883.

   Note. - These locomotives are described in Spanish literature as "Fireless". This is not
           confirmed in drawing in Kinnear Clark's book, but they did have roof condensers,
           which partly concealed the chimneys.

5. BARCELONA. (Tranvía de San Juan de Horta a la Sagrera). Later taken over by No. 4.
   Sagrera-Horta, 2.8 km. (Connecting with No. 4).
   S.1883, E.1901, C.1946. Gauge. 1000 (partly replaced by a standard gauge electric
   tramway line direct from Barcelona).
   Locomotives. -   Nos.   1-2,   Falcon 0-4-0   57-58 ? of 1883. (Small type).
                                3,   Falcon 0-4-0   65 of 1885. (Standard type).

6. BARCELONA. (Compañía Anónima de los Tranvías de Vapor de Barcelona y el Litoral).
   Barcelona(Calle de Comercio)-San Martín-Badalona, 9.5 km.
   S.1881, (Part H.1884-1887), E.1903, C.1967. Gauge. 1000.
   Note. - Possibly hired locomotives from No. 4 at first, for use from San Martin to Badalona,
           and extended into Barcelona with mule traction in 1884. Whole line steam by 1887
   Locomotives. -   Nos.   1-4,   Krauss 0-4-0 1559-1562 of 1885.
                              5-9,   Dutch Breda 0-4-0 46-50 of 1888.
                             10-12, Dutch Breda 0-4-0 75-77 of 1891.

7. BARCELONA. (Sociedad Anónima - Tranvía de Barcelona, Ensanche y Gracia).
   Ensanche-Gracia,   km.
   H.1880, S.1887, E.   C.   Gauge. 1435 ?
   Motive Power. -   No.   21.   Prototype "Purrey Car" (single deck). 1887.

8. BARCELONA. (Compañía General de Tranvías). German owned.
Barcelona(Plaza Cataluña)-San Gervasio(Bonanova), 7.0 km.
Barcelona(Diagonal)-Sarría, 5.5 km.
San Gervasio-Sarría, 1.5 km.
Diagonal-Las Corts, 1.0 km.
S.1881, E.1903, C.1967. Gauge. 1422 (1435 on electrification).

Locomotives. -	No.	1,	Winterthur	0-6-0	179 of 1880. (Chain drive)
		2-5,	Winterthur	0-6-0	216-219 of 1881. " "
		6-15,	Winterthur	0-6-0	259-268 of 1882.* " "
	? (II)	1-6,	Falcon	0-4-0	158 & ?
					(possibly 154-159 of 1888 ?).

° Delivered ?

Names. -   1-Barcelona, Falcon 158-Bonanova, (II) 6-Putxet.

Note. - *A fenced street railway direct from Barcelona to Sarria crossed this tramway on the level at rightangles. Later it became an electric tramway and is now part of the underground railway.

9. BAJO AMPURDÁN. (Tranvía del Bajo Ampurdán a Palamós).
Later (Ferrocarril de Flassa a Palamos, Gerona y Banolas).
A light railway with street running in towns. Finally "Estado".
Gerona-Puente Mayor-Palamós-Flassá, 48.9 km.
Puente Mayor-Banolas, 13.9 km.
S.1887, Part D.1936, C.1955. Gauge. 750.

Locomotives. -	Nos.	1-3,	Not known	?	?	?	1887.
		4-6,	Krauss	0-6-0	1746-1748 of 1887.
		7-8,	Hohenzollern	0-6-0	2315-2316 of 1907.
		9-10,	Franco Belge	0-6-0	2021-2022 of 1912.
		11-15,	Orenstein & Koppel	0-4-0	? ? of 1910.
		16,	Not known		
		17,	Jung	0-8-0	3504 of 1929.
		18-19,	Euskalduna	0-6-0	163-164 of 1928.

Names. -   7-Palamos.

10. CARTAGENA. (The Carthagena and Herrerias Steam Tramways Co. Ltd.). British owned.
The El Descargador-Los Blancos section was owned by a Belgian Company and leased to the above. - See No. 15.
In 1913, (Tranvía a Vapor de Cartagena a la Unión y explotación de Ferrocarriles a los Blancos).
Finally (Ferrocarril de Cartagena a la Unión y los Blancos).
Cartagena-El Descargador-La Unión-Los Blancos, 15.1 km.
La Unión-Santa Lucia, 1.4 km.
S.1874, D.1959, C. ? Gauge. 1067.

Locomotives. -	Un-numbered		Fox Walker	2-4-0	186 of 1873.
	Nos.	1-2,	Hunslet	0-8-0	253-254 of 1880.
		3,	Hunslet	0-8-0	296 of 1882.
		4-5,	Hunslet	0-8-0	324,323 of 1883.
		6-7,	Hunslet	0-8-0	399,398 of 1886.
		8-9,	Hunslet	0-8-0	417-418 of 1887.
		10-11,	Hunslet	0-8-0	943-944 of 1907.
		12,	Manning Wardle	0-6-0	544 of 1875.
		13,	Manning Wardle	0-6-0	1007 of 1887.
		14,	Manning Wardle	0-6-0	1206 of 1890.
		15,	Manning Wardle	0-6-0	1720 of 1907.
		16-17,	Manning Wardle	0-6-0	1396-1397 of 1898.
		18-19,	Manning Wardle	0-6-0	1510-1511 of 1901.
		20-23,	Sentinel six wheeled		8168-8171 of 1929.

Names. -   Fox Walker-San Gines, 1-Escombreras, 2-Alumbres, 3-La Esperanza,
4-Titan, 5-Hercules, 6-Ciclope, 7-Vulcano, 8-Jupiter, 9-Marte,
10-Eolo, 11-Urano, 12-Santa Lucia, 13-Nueva Lucia, 14-Descargador,
15-Diana, 16-Apolo, 17-Mercurio, 18-Neptuno, 19-Saturno.
Sentinel locos not named.

244

11. CONSELL(Mallorca).   (Majorca Railway Co. Ltd.,).
     Later (Compañía de los Ferrocarriles de Mallorca).
     A roadside tramway owned and worked by the Majorca Railway as a feeder.
     Consell-Alaró,   3.4 km.
     S.1881, C.1935. Gauge. 915.
     Locomotives. -   Worked by Majorca Railway's general stock.   ⊔⅃

12. CASTELLÓN. (Compañía del Tranvía de Vapor de Onda al Grao de Castellón de la Plana).
     Later worked by "Estado" organization. On street in Castellon.
     Grao-Castellón-Villareal-Onda,   28.5 km.
     Villareal-Burriana-Grao de Burriana   10.5 km.   (Closed in 1934).
     Burriana-Puerto de Burriana,   2.6 km.   (Opened in 1948).
     S.1888, P (intermittently) 1926, C.1963. Gauge. 750.
     Locomotives. -   Nos.   1-3, Krauss   0-6-0   1984-1986 of 1888.
                                4,   Krauss   0-6-0   2198 of 1889.
                              5-6,   Krauss   0-6-2   2343-2344 of 1890 (Compound).
                              7-8,   Krauss   0-6-2   2392-2393 of 1890 (Compound).
                                9,   Hohenzollern 0-6-0   1890 of 1905.   "
                       (II)   7-8, Hohenzollern 0-6-0   2315-2316 of 1907 ex-No.9.   ⁝ "
                              18-19. Euskalduna   0-6-0   163-164 of 1929 ex-No.9.   ⁝ "

13. CONDADO. (Ferrocarril del Condado).
     A light railway running on the street, equipped entirely with ex-1914-1918 war military
     stock.
     Palma de Condado-Bollullos de Condado (Huelva), 8.0 km.
     S.1921, C.1931. Gauge. 600.   ⁝ ⊔⅃
     Locomotives. -   Nos.   1-2, Hunslet 4-6-0   1320-1321 of 1918. ex-British Army.

14. GERONA. See No. 9, Bajo Ampurdán.

15. HERRERIAS. - Old name for La Unión, see No. 10.
     La Sierra - (Compagnie du Chemin de Fer de la Sierra de Cartagène).
     The Belgian company which owned part of No. 10. El Descargador to Los Blancos, 4.3 km.

16. LAS PALMAS (Canary Islands). (J.Antunez - "Tranvía de las Palmas").
     Las Palmas-Puerto de la Luz, 6.7 km.
     S.1890. E.1908, C.1937. (S again 1940, C.1941.) Gauge. 1000.
     Locomotives. -   Nos.   1-2, Krauss 0-4-0   2243-2244 of 1890.
                                3,   Krauss 0-4-0   2364 of 1891.   "
                                4? Falcon 0-4-0   185 of 1890.   "

                           In 1940 - Sharp Stewart 0-6-0   one of 3339-3341 of 1885 ⁝   ⊔⅃
                                                              or 3350-3351 of 1886 ⁝   hired ?

     Name. -   Sharp Stewart - "La Pepa".

17. LITORAL ASTURIANA. - See AVILES, No. 3.

18. MADRID. (Sociedad Anónima Tranvía de Madrid a Carabanchel).
     Later (Compañía General Española de Tranvías).
     Madrid(Puente Toledo)-Carabanchel Bajo-Carabanchel Alto-Leganes, 12.2 km.
     Trials 1877, S.1979, H.1900, E.1903, C.1965. Gauge. 1435.
     Locomotives. -   No.   1, Winterthur   0-4-0   120 of 1877.
                                -, American Bronx 0-4-0   ? of 1878.   "
                                2, Winterthur   0-4-0   160 of 1879.   "
                                3, Winterthur   0-4-0   153 of 1879 ? (Intended for
                                                                           Strassburg ?).

19. MADRID. (Compañía del Tranvía de Madrid a Arganda por Vallecas).
     Later (Tranvía de Vapor de Madrid a Vallecas y Canteras).
     This tramway was never completed to Arganda, presumably because of the opening of a
     competing light railway which went beyond Arganda, in 1886. The broad gauge tramway
     closed after a short life, but was reopened under a new concession to metre gauge, in
     1891. This went bankrupt and was bought out by No. 23 in 1908.
     Madrid(Puente de Vallecas)-Vallecas-Canteras, 10.1 km.
     S.1879, C.1886 ? S again 1891, C.1931. Gauge. 1460 (from 1891-1000).
     Locomotives (Broad gauge). -
                          No.   1, Krauss 0-4-0   777 of 1879.
                              59-?, Hagans 0-4-0   90-94 of 1879.

     Locomotives (Metre gauge). -
                          No. 10-11, Corpet Louvet   0-4-0   - - of ?
                              12-13, St. Léonard   0-4-0   901-902 of 1891.
                                 14, Orenstein & Koppel 0-6-0   5489 of 1912.
                                 15, Krauss   0-4-0   1497 of 1884, ex-No.22.

20. MADRID. (Compañía del Ferrocarril Metropolitano de Madrid). Before Metro opened.
     Madrid(Atocha)-O'Donnel(Loreto),   4.0 km. (Not completed to Necropolis).
     S.1903, C.1907, Gauge. 1000.
     Locomotives. -   Nos.   1-2, Jung 0-4-0, 619-620 of 1903 (Arthur Koppel order).

     Names. -   1-Abrogadiz, 2- ?. (No. 1 sold to Minas del Castillo, with name).

21. MADRID. (Sociedad del Tranvía de Vapor de Madrid a el Pardo).
     Madrid(La Florida)-El Pardo, 12.0 km.
     S.1902, C.1918. Gauge. 1000.
     Locomotives. -   Nos.   1-2, Jung 0-4-0 587-588 of 1902. (Arthur Koppel order).
                                    3, Jung 0-4-0   591 of 1902.   "   "   "
                                    4, Jung 0-4-0   669 of 1903.   "   "   "

     Names. -   1-Madrid, 2-El Pardo, 3-Viveros, 4- ?.

     Note. - No. 21 not to be confused with a light railway to Villa del Prado.

22. MADRID. (Sociedad Anónima del Tranvía a Vapor de Madrid a Colmenar Viejo y Ramal
     a Chamartin de la Rosa).   Taken over by No. 23 in 1909.
     Madrid(Tetuan)-Fuencarral-Colmenar Viejo, 26.0 km. (Connecting with No. 23).
     S.1884, Part E.1915, Rest R.1943, C.1955. Gauge. 1000 (later 1460).
     Locomotive. -   Krauss 0-4-0 1497 of 1884.

23. MADRID. (Compañía Madrileña de Urbanizacion).   Took over No. 22 in 1909 & 19 in 1908
     Madrid(Cuarto Caminos)-Ciudad Lineal-Fuencarral, 5.8 km. (Connecting with No. 22).
     Ciudad Lineal-Chamartin,   1.0 km.
     Madrid(Ventas)-Barrio de Concepcion,   5.2 km. (With connecting line).
     Barrio de Concepción-Cantillejas,   2.7 km. (not completed).
     Barrio de Concepción-Vicalvaro-Vallecas,   -   (not completed).
     Vallecas-Canteras,   10.1 km. (ex - No. 19).
     Madrid(Tetuan)-Fuencarral-Colmenar Viejo,   26.0 km. (ex - No. 22).
     H.1898, S.1906. E.1909/1912, C.1965. Gauge. 1435.

     Locomotives. -   No.   1, ?
                               2-3, Orenstein & Koppel 0-4-0   1171-1172 of 1903.
                               4-5, Orenstein & Koppel 0-4-0   1394-1395 of 1904.
                               6-7, Orenstein & Koppel 0-4-0   1526-1527 of 1905.
                               8-9,   ?   ?   (16 locos by 1908).
                             10-15,   Those of No.19.
                                16. ?

     Motive Power. -   Nos.   1-3, ?   "Rowan" Cars.

24. MANRESA. (Tranvía o Ferrocarril Económico de Manresa a Berga).
Later (Ferrocarril de Manresa a Olván-Berga). Bankrupt in 1932.
This line was physically an extension of the Catalan Railway, by whom it was worked
after 1932. Taken over by the "Estado" organization in 1950. In spite of much
street running, when the Catalan Railway took over they used heavy railway type
locomotives, including Garratts, some of which were handed over to the Estado in 1950.
Manresa-Olván-Berga-Guardiola, 70.8 km.
S.1885, R.1932, D1961, Still operating ?. Gauge. 1000.

Locomotives. -	Nos.	1-2,	Krauss	0-6-0	1308-1309 of 1884.	⊟
		3-4,	Krauss	0-6-0	1473-1474 of 1885.	"
		5,	Krauss	0-6-0	1888 of 1888.	"
		6-7,	Krauss	0-6-0	1890-1891 of 1890.	"
		9-10,	Nuevo Vulcano	0-6-0	57 & 367 of 1901.	"
		11-14,	Maquinista	0-6-0	33-36 of 1902.	"
		15-18,	Maquinista	0-6-0	42-45 of 1904.	"
		19-22,	Maquinista	0-6-0	47-50 of 1911.	"
		23-28,	?	?		?
		29-42,	Nos. 9-22 renumbered in the Catalan Railway series.			
		-	Krauss	0-6-0	2309 of 1895.	⊟
			(intended for Roumania)			

Names. -   1-Sallent, 2-Sampedor, 3-Manresa, 4-Berga, 5-Puigreig, 6-Olván,
7-Gironella, 8- ? 9-Pedret, 10-15-not known, 16-Llobregat,
17-22-not known.

25. MOTRIL. (Title ?)
Motril-Puerto de Calahonda,   10.0 km.
Motril-Motril Puerto,   2.3 km.
H.1896, S. ? C. ? Gauge. 410.?

Locomotives. -	No.	1,	Couillet	0-4-0	685 of 1883.	"	⊟
	(II)	1,	Orenstein & Koppel	0-4-0	?	?	"
		2,	Orenstein & Koppel	0-6-0	?	?	"

26. PALMA (Mallorca). (Tranvías de Palma ?).
Later (Sociedad General de Tranvías Electricos Interurbanos de Palma de Mallorca S.A.).
Palma-Puerto Pi,   3.0 km.
S.1880, E.1915 ? C.1958. Gauge.- 914.

Locomotives. -	No.	1,	R.W. Hawthorn	0-4-0	1836 of 1880. (Brown's type)	⊟
		2,	Falcon	0-4-0	198 of 1891.	⊟
		3-5,	Falcon ?	0-4-0	199-201 of 1891 ?	"
		6,	Nasmyth Wilson	0-4-0	389 of 1899.	*
		7,	Orenstein & Koppel	0-4-0	8076 of 1921.	⊟

Note. - *   Nos. 6 & 7 may have been intended for use on Palma Docks.

27. PONTEVEDRA. (Sociedad Anónima de Tranvía de Pontevedra a Marin).
Pontevedra-Marin,   8.4 km.
S.1888, E.1922, Trolleybus 1944. C.1966. Gauge. 762.

Locomotives. -	Nos.	1-2,	St.Léonard	0-4-0	779-780 of 1888.	⊟
		3,	St.Léonard	0-6-0	851 of 1890.	"
		4,	St.Léonard	0-6-0	1404 of 1904.	⊟

Names. -   Nos. 1-2, not named individually but had plates "Pontevedra-
Marin". 3-Pontevedra, 4-Estribela.

28. REUS. (Compañía Reusense de Tranvías). Later part of "Estado" organization.
Reus(Arrabel)-Reus(Mercancias)-Salou, 8.2 km.

Note.- The street tramway from Arrabel to Mercancias was closed and diverted
to a new terminus off the road, near Mercancias, in 1921. Rest roadside.
S.1887, D.1958, C.1976. Gauge. 1000.
Locomotives.-   Nos.   1-3, Falcon 0-4-0   116-118 of 1886. (Julius Neville order)
                               4, Falcon 0-4-0   ?   of   ?   (possibly not delivered) "
                             5-6, Falcon 0-4-0   152-153 of 1888. (Julius Neville order)
                       (II)   4, Brush   0-6-2   281 of 1889. "   "

Names.-   1-Reus, 2-Fortuny, 3-Prim, 4- ?, 5-Salou, 6-Mas Calbo.
                       (II)4-not named.

Note.- No. 3 was stripped of its enclosure in 1916 and exchanged works plates
        with 5.

29. RIOSECO. (Cementos Fradera Sociedad Anónima).
Roadside industrial tramway, with unadvertised passenger service.
Rioseco-Laviana,   12.0 km.   (approx.).
S.1920, C.1969. Gauge. 650.
Locomotives.-   Nos.   1-2, Linke Hofmann   0-4-0   1909 & 1908 of 1920.
                               3, Unknown   0-4-0   (possibly made up from
                                                              parts of Others).
                               4, Orenstein & Koppel 0-4-0   5973 of 1911.
                       (II)   1-2, Decauville   0-4-0' 1070 & 1107 of ?   "   "
                               4, Maquinista   0-4-0   15 of 1897 "   "

Names.-   1-Laviana, 2-Rioseco, 3- ?, 4-Berango. (II)1-Vallcarca No.1,
                       (II)2-Vallcarca No.2.

Note.- Covering on Nos. 1-2 later removed.

30. SANTANDER. (Tram-Via de Santander).
Trials on horse tramway with a locomotive and double deck car.
S.1871 only. Gauge. 1435.
Locomotive.-   Leonard Todd 0-2-4   of 1871.

Name.-   "Prima Donna".

31. SANTANDER. (Sociedad el Sardinero). Later as No. 32.
Santander(Pl.Hernán Cortés)-Sardinero(Alameda de la Cañiza). 2.5 km.
S.1891 ?, E.1917 ?, Trolleybus ?. Gauge. 1030.   ?
Locomotives.-   Nos. 1-4, ?   ?

32. SANTANDER. (Tranvía de Vapor de Santander al Sardinero).
Later (Tranvías de Santander y del Sardinero - Belgian owned).
From 1903 (Red Santanderina de Tranvias).
Santander(Pl.Hernan Cortés)-Barrio San Martin-Sardinero. 3.7 km.
S.1877, E.1917 ?, Trolleybus ?. Gauge. 1346.
Locomotives.-   Nos.   1-2, Schneider 0-4-0   1889-1890 of 1877.
                               3-4, Schneider 0-4-0   1967-1968 of 1879.   "
                               5,   ?   ?   ?   ?   "

Names.-   1- ?, 2- ?, 3- ?, 4-Magdalena, 5- ?.

33. SANTANDER. (Tranvía de Vapor de Cuatro Caminos a Peña Castillo).
Owned by (Sociedad Nueva Montaña).
Santander(Cuatro Caminos)-Peña Castillo. 1.8 km.
S. ?, E.1910, C. ?, Gauge. 1030.   ?
<u>Locomotives</u>. -   ?

34. SANTANDER. (Tranvia Urbano de Santander a Peñacastillo).
Santander(Estacion)-Miranda   ? 5.5 km ?
S.1896, E. ?, C. ?, Gauge. 800.   ?
<u>Locomotives</u>. -   Nos.   1-2, ?

35. VALENCIA. (La Compañía General de Tranvías).
From 1898 (Compagnie Générale des Tramways Electriques de Valence) French.
Valencia(Puente del Real)-Grao-Cabañal,   6.0 km.
Grao-Playa de Levante.   1.0 km.
S.1892, E,1900, Still operating ?, Gauge. 1000.
<u>Locomotives</u>. -   Nos.   1-8, Thomas Green   0-4-0   171-178 of 1892. (Simple
                                                                          Expansion).
                            9-10, Thomas Green   0-4-0   189-190 of 1893. (Simple   "
                                                                          Expansion).

36. VALENCIA. (Compañía de Tranvías del Norte de Valencia).
Later acquired by No. 35 above. Now "Estado" organization.
Valencia(Torres de Serranos)-Puebla de Farnals, 12.0 km.
S.1892, E.1903, C.1957. Gauge. 1000.
<u>Locomotives</u>. -   Nos.   1-2, Thomas Green   0-4-0   166-167 of 1891. (Compound
                                                                          expansion).
                            3, Thomas Green   0-4-0   191 of 1893. (Simple   "
                                                                          expansion).

37. VALLADOLID. (Ferrocarril Económico de Valladolid a Medina de Rioseco).
From 1930, worked by (Sociedad Espanola de Ferrocarriles de Castilla).
From 1932 (Compañía de Ferrocarriles de Castilla y Española de Ferrocarriles Secundarios).
A light railway with street running in Valladolid and locomotives with enclosed motion.
Extensions in 1930s were definitely railways and are not listed below.
Valladolid(Campo de Bejar)-Medina de Rioseco, 44.0 km.
S.1884, R.1930, Still operating ?. Gauge. 1000.
<u>Locomotives</u>. -   Nos.   1-2, Sharp Stewart   0-4-0   3094 & 3093 of 1883.
                            3-4, Sharp Stewart   0-4-0   3231-3232 of 1884.   "
                            5-6, Sharp Stewart   0-4-0   3250-3251 of 1885.   "
                            7-8, St.Léonard   0-6-0   1680-1681 of 1909.
                     (II)   1-7, Maquinista   2-6-0   51-57 of 1911.   "
                            8-13, Maquinista   2-6-0   66-71 of 1913.   "

Names. -   1-Valladolid. 2- ?, 3- ?, 4- ?, 5-Valverde, 6-Rioseco.

Notes. -   1. Industrial roadside light railways at Mazarron and at Santullano are believed to
               have provided unadvertised passenger services on their lines.
            2. The "Castro-Urdiales a Traslavina" Railway had two enclosed locomotives
               secondhand from the Belgian SNCV (of their unsuccessful Class 13).
               They were:-
               No.6, Tubize 0-6-0 830 of 1891 (ex SNCV No. 422) named "Mioño".
                  7, Tubize 0-6-0 1207 of 1891 ("   No. 437)   "   "Muñecas".   "

TWIN LOCOMOTIVE, VILLA REAL AND VILLA REGOA TRAMWAY, PORTUGAL.

PORTUGAL

1. AGUAS DE SAO VICENTE. (Companhia do Carris do Ferro da Penafiel a Lixa.)
   Penafiel-S.Vincente-Entre os Rios) 49.0 km.
   Penafiel-Lixa)
   S.1912, C.1925. Gauge. 1000.
   Locomotives. -   Possibly 1-2.   Henschel 0-4-0   11339-11340 of 1912.
                              3-4,   Henschel 0-4-0   12180-12181 of 1913.
                              5-6,   Henschel 0-4-0   12982-12983 of 1914.

2. BRAGA. (Title not known).
   Later (Servicos Municipales de Braga).
   Estacão-Campo de Santa Anna-Bom Jesus,   3.0 km.
   S.1881, E.1914, Trolleybus 1963. Gauge. 900.
   Locomotives. -   Nos.   1-2,   Winterthur 0-6-0   (possibly 112-113 of 1887 ex-No.7).*
                              *Confirmed by photographs, unfortunately unsuitable for reproduction.

3. LISBOA. (Lisbon Steam Tramways Co. Ltd.) or (Companhia dos Tramways a Vapor).
   Experimental line worked on the Larmanjat single rail system.
   Lisboa(Arreios)-Lumiar-Torres Vedras, 52.0 km. (only completed to Lumiar).
   Lisboa(Arreios)-Cacem-Cintra,   27.0 km. (not completed).
   Trials 1870, S.1873, C.1877.   Gauge.   Single Rail.
   Locomotives. -   Nos.   1-2,   Sharp Stewart (special type)   2254-2255 of 1873.
                              3-8,   Sharp Stewart (special type)   2270-2275 not delivered.
                              9-16, Sharp Stewart (special type)   2286-2293 not delivered.

   Names. -   1-Lisboa, 2-Cintra.

4. LISBOA. (Companhia do Carris de Ferro do Lisboa).
   Caes do Sodre-Belem-Alges,   km.
   H.1887, S.1889, C.1896. E.1902 Still operating. Gauge. 1435 (900 on E.).
   Locomotives. -   Nos.   1-2, Possibly St.Léonard   0-4-0   892 of 1891. & ?

5. PORTO. (Oporto). (Companhia Carril Americano de Porto a Foz e Matosinhos).
   Acquired by No.6 in 1893, but joint through service from outset. (See No.6).
   Foz del Douro-Matosinhos-Leixões,   ? km.
   H.1870. S.1878, E.1901, Still operating. Gauge. 1435.
   Locomotives. -   Nos.   1-3,   Henschel   0-4-0   972, 986 & 994 of 1878.

6. PORTO. (Oporto). (Companhia Carris de Ferro do Porto).
   Porto(Boa Vista)-Fonte da Moura-Sao Joao da Foz,   ?   km. (Nos. 5 & 6 together 9.2 km)
   H.1873, S.1878, E.1912. Still operating (different routing). Gauge. 1435.
   Locomotives. -   Nos.   1-2,   Henschel   0-4-0   964 & 995 of 1878.
                              3,   Merryweather   0-4-0   95 of 1880.
                              4-5,   Henschel   0-4-0   1383-1384 of 1882.

7. VILA REAL. (Title not known).
   Possibly only trials. Later replaced by metre gauge railway.
   Vila Real-Vila Regua, 26.0 km.
   S.1877, C. ?, R.1905. Still operating as Railway. Gauge. 900 (1000 as railway).
   Locomotives. -   Nos.   1-2,   Winterthur   0-6-0   112-113 of 1877.
                              (permanently coupled together by a long girder framework).

Merryweather loco No.5, with large coat of arms and typical trailers on the San Andrés tramway, Barcelona.

Photo: Science Museum London - Whitcombe Collection 9624.

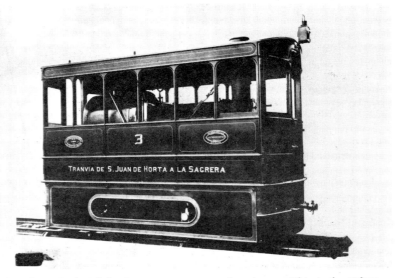

Falcon loco No.3, of the Sagrera tramway at Barcelona. This is the Falcon standard model, but Nos.1 & 2 were smaller with only five windows each side. Note both "Falcon" and "Julius Neville" works plates on the side.

Courtesy: J.H.Price.

No.1 "Abrogadiz" for the "Metropolitano de Madrid" built by Jung against an Arthur Koppel order. Perhaps this line was to be the forerunner of the Madrid Underground railway.
Arthur Koppel Catalogue.

One of the peculiar Winterthur six-wheeled chain drive locos with vertical cylinders in front of the smoke box.
Winterthur Catalogue.   Courtesy: late Dr. G. Masino.

Standard Falcon loco No.6 "Putxet" of the "Compañía General de Tranvías" at Barcelona.

Courtesy: Jordi Ibanez.

The only known photo of a Dutch "Breda" loco in Barcelona on the Badalona tramway.

Courtesy: Jordi Ibanez.

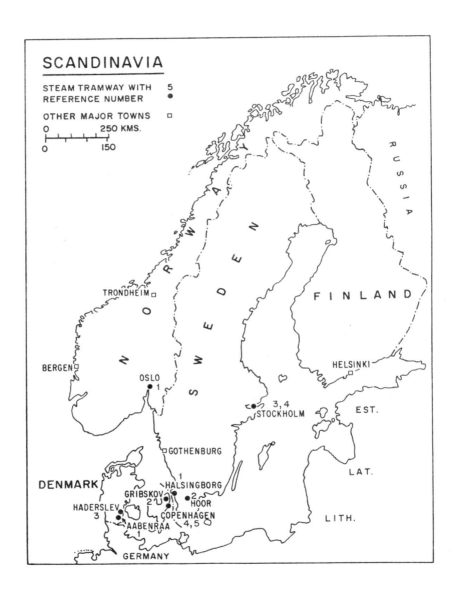

SCANDINAVIA

STEAM TRAMWAY WITH   5
REFERENCE NUMBER   ●

OTHER MAJOR TOWNS   ▫

0   250 KMS.

0   150

11. SCANDINAVIA

After the detailed descriptions of tramways in individual countries given so far, it may seem strange that these last two chapters cover a very wide field in a short space. The fact is that we have now covered all the countries of Western Europe which were industrially developed in the late 19th century and where one would expect to find the greatest number of steam tramways, which in their turn helped to spread the area of industrialization, by carrying the products of the industry to the railways and by bringing peasants from the villages to work in the factories in the towns. In those European countries which now remain, there were few steam tramways and for convenience, they are grouped together in these two short chapters. It might be mentioned in passing, that the writer has only been able to trace brief experiments in Norway.

Although highly developed in a social sense, the Scandinavian countries, with the exception of Denmark, were still decidedly thinly populated in the 19th Century, largely for geographic and climatic reasons, both of which conspired to make them relatively unsuitable for steam tramways, although their major cities enjoyed extensive horse and electric tramways networks. Owing to the abundance of timber available in these countries, a large proportion of the houses were made of that material and the fire risk that this involved, constituted a strong objection to the use of steam tramways.

There were early experiments with steam, mainly in the form of self-propelled cars in Denmark and Sweden, but little of lasting success. In fact Copenhagen (København), was one of the first cities in Europe to experiment with steam traction on urban lines and used some locally produced motive power; there were experiments on the urban tramways in 1873 with a Kohl's locomotive, followed by a Smith & Mygind's machine in 1875. Contemporary illustrations show both of these to be enclosed in bodies closely resembling the Starbuck trailers that they hauled. The Kohl's engine is said to have been capable of pulling two trailers and worked on a tramway managed by the "American Omnibus Company". In 1876, Mr. W. R. Rowan, who in spite of his Celtic name, lived in Copenhagen, designed one of the few successful types of self propelled steam passenger cars. The first few to his design were built in Great Britain, by Kitson of Leeds and ran on two bogies. The driving bogie is described in contemporary journals as "mounted on a hollow pin, several feet in diameter and within this pin is fitted the engine".[1] In other words, although enclosed within the body of the car, the boiler, cylinders and motion were integral with the front bogie and rotated with it. This eliminated one of the weaknesses of other early designs, namely, flexible pipes which invariably leaked, between a fixed boiler and movable bogie. The whole of the machinery was just behind the driver's platform and in fact the boiler took the place of an over large bogie pin. The cars were 32 feet long and were single ended, having to be turned at each end of the route on a turntable or triangular track layout. The original vehicles built at Leeds, underwent trials at Oslo (Then called Kristiania) after which they were used in public service in Denmark at Copenhagen and Gribskov. The latter is a roadside railway, originally laid with very light track and worked as a tramway, under the title "Gribskovens Dampsporvej" (The Gribskov Steam Tramway). There were also experiments with a French built double deck Bollée steam car in Copenhagen.

In 1884, a lengthy suburban steam tramway was opened to the north of Copenhagen. It started at Trianglen depot (now a museum store for trams and buses) and ran to Hellerup, thence along the coast to Klampenborg. It was worked at first by "Rowan" cars, but later with locomotives of a peculiar design and it is said that these were rebuilt from the motor bogies of the Rowan cars. At all events, the bodies were rebuilt as double deck trailers. The line closed in 1892, owing it is said to lack of patronage and accidents, but it reopened later as an electric tramway. It is also reported that the Gribskov Rowan cars were rebuilt as locomotives.[2]

In Sweden, the only real steam tramway was a short line in Stockholm from the river bridge at Slussen to the suburb of Hornstull. It used only "Rowan" cars of German and Swedish manufacture. There was also a roadside light railway at Hoor, similar to the Gribskov line and although not strictly within the scope of this book, passing mention should be made of Halsingborg, where a Decauville 600 mm. gauge light railway to Ramlosa and along the coast to Raa, was converted to a standard gauge electric railway and subsequently taken over by the urban tramway system, who worked it until 1967 with ordinary electric tramcars, and electric locos for goods, to the many industrial sidings.

Locomotives &"Rowan" Cars

The few steam tramways in Scandinavia showed a definite preference for self-propelled steam cars, particularly those designed by Mr. W. Rowan. Although the original cars were built in Great Britain by Kitson, those on the Copenhagen-Klampenborg line and the first two at Stockholm had at least the mechanical parts built by Borsig of Berlin-Tegel, who built 50 "Rowan" cars in all, mainly for the Berlin tramways. The remainder at Stockholm were built by "Atlas", a local firm, who may also have built the bodies for the first two.

Only artist's drawings of the Kohl's and Smith & Mygind's locomotives remain and they are shown as enclosed in saloon-like bodies rather like the early Starbuck passenger carriages. The locomotives which replaced the Rowan cars on the Klampenborg line, also had saloon bodies and were driven from open end platforms. They had roof condensers and inside cylinders. The wheels were not enclosed. They are said to have been built by Burmeister & Wain of Copenhagen (see note about rebuilds of Rowan cars above). The earlier "Rowan" cars were mounted on two bogies, but the later ones had a single axle with some radial action, at the rear.

Although both Sweden and Denmark did have large locomotive building establishments of their own, on the whole they left the construction of tramway engines to the smaller firms, such as Riedel & Lindegaard, Smith & Myginds and Burmeister & Wain in Denmark, with Atlas and Motala in Sweden. However, a few locomotives built by the large firm Nyqvist & Holm did find their way onto tramways. Motala built ten 0-4-0 enclosed tram engines for St. Petersburg in Russia; they had their works plates inscribed in the Russian alphabet.

It should be mentioned in passing that Kitson numbered their tram engines and Rowan cars in a separate series of works numbers from their railway locomotives, prefixed with a "T", but the first few carried numbers in both series.

Notes

1. See "Tramways, Their Construction and Working" by D. Kinnear Clark, London 1878.

2. In his notes on the Kitson Works List, deposited in the Science Museum, Dr. Whitcombe appears to assume the Gribskov and Pontilov (sic) were both in Moscow. Gribskov is definitely in Denmark and the latter is no doubt intended for Poutilov in St. Petersburg, which according to "Aperçu de Chemins de Fer Russes" had Kitson double deck cars.

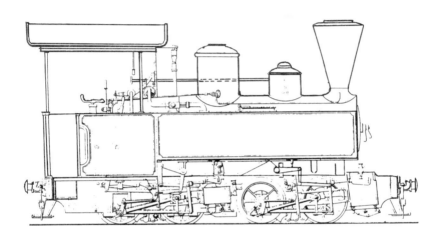

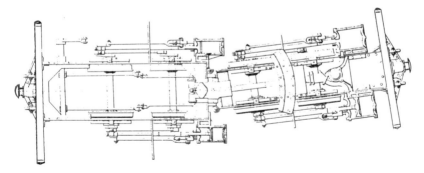

Decauville-Mallet loco used on 60cm gauge railways including the line at Halsingborg

Table 11- DENMARK

1. AABENRAA. Formerly in Germany, see Germany No. 5.

2. GRIBSKOV. (Graested Dampsporvogn). ("Gribskovens Dampsporvej").
    A roadside light railway worked by (Gribskov Driftselskab).
    Hillerød-Gribskov-Graested, 20.0 km (approx.). (extended 6.2 km to Gilleleje in 1896).
    S.1879, R.1896, D.1947, Still operating ? Gauge. 1435.
    <u>Motive Power.</u> -   Nos. I, II,   Kitson "Rowan" cars, T.13-14 of 1879.
                                  III,   Winterthur 0-4-0   156 of 1879.
                                  IV,   Hanomag 0-4-0   2154 of 1890.

    Note. - The power bogies of the Rowan cars were converted in 1892/93 to locomotives
             and other locomotives acquired when the line became a proper railway.

3. HADERSLEV. Formerly in Germany, see Germany No. 49.

4. KØBENHAVN. (Copenhagen). (Copenhagen Railway Company).
    Later (Kjobenhavns Sporvei Selskab).
    Experimental running on the Gothersgade route.   ? km.
    H.1863, S.1873 to 1879 only. E.1901 C.   Gauge. 1435.
    <u>Motive Power.</u> -   One Riedel & Lingaard "Kohl's" 0-4-0 1873.
                         One Smith & Myginds 0-4-0, 1875 (Compound).
                         Two Kitson "Rowan" cars. T.1 (2375) and T.5 of 1879.
                         One Bollée double-deck steam car, 1879.

5. KØBENHAVN. (Copenhagen). Strandvejens Dampsporvejs Selskab).
    København(Trianglen)-Hellerup-Klampenborg, 9.2 km.
    S.1884, C.1892, Reopened E.1903, C.   Gauge. 1435.
    <u>Motive Power.</u> -   Nos. 1-12,   Borsig "Rowan" cars,   3965-3975 of 1884.
                            I-XII,   Burmeister & Wain 0-4-0   ?   ?   ?
                                     (possibly rebuilt from the power bogies of the Rowan cars)

NORWAY

1. KRISTIANIA. (Oslo). (Kristiania Sporvej Selskab).
    Experimental running on various routes.
    H.1875, S.1876 only. E. ? Still operating. Gauge. 1435.
    <u>Motive Power.</u> -   One Kitson "Rowan" car (Possibly borrowed from manufacturer).

SWEDEN

1. HALSINGBORG. (Helsingborg-Råå-Ramlösa Järnvägsaktiebolag).
    (A narrow gauge railway, electrified as a standard gauge railway, but
    subsequently taken over by the local tramway undertaking and worked
    by ordinary electric tramcars).
    Halsingborg-Råå,   }
                            } 8 km.
    Halsingborg-Ramlösa, -
    S.1891, ER.1906, C.1967. Gauge. 600 (1435 on electrification).
    <u>Locomotives.</u> -   Nos. 1-2,   Decauville 0-4-4-0   (Mallet), 71 & 73 of 1889.
                            3,   Decauville 0-4-2   258 of 1898.
                            4,   Decauville 0-6-2   271 of 1891.

    Names. -   1-Raa, 2-Helsingborg, 3- ?. 4- ?.

2. HÖÖR. (Höör-Hörby Järnväg).
    A roadside light railway worked at first as a tramway.
    Höör-Hörby,   25.0 km.
    S.1882, R.1915, C. ? Gauge.   1435.

Locomotives. -	No.	1,	Nyqvist & Holm	4-4-0	160 of 1882.	⊔⌐
		2,	Nyqvist & Holm	2-4-0	229 of 1886.	"
		3,	Nyqvist & Holm	4-4-0	230 of 1886.	"
		4,	Motala	2-4-0	132 of 1893.	"
	(II)	4,	Ljunggrens	2-4-0	12 of 1904.	"

Railcar. -   -   Nyqvist & Holm "Rowan" car 162 of 1882.   ᗡ

Names. -   1-Bifrost, 2- ?, 3-Horby.

3. STOCKHOLM. (Stockholms Södra Sparvägar).
    Stockholm(Slussen)-Hornstull,   2.0 km. (approx.).
    S.1887, E.1901, Underground Railway 1963, Gauge. 1435.

Motive Power. -	Nos.	1-2,	Borsig "Rowan" cars 4209 & 4213 of 1886/87.	ᗡ
		3-10,	Atlas "Rowan" cars - - of 1887/88.	"

4. STOCKHOLM. (Djursholms Aktiebolag).
    Later (Stockholm-Roslagens Järnväg).
    Built as a tramway, but soon upgraded as a railway, retaining a short section of street
    running in Stockholm.
    Stockholm(Djursholms Osby)-Framnäsviken,   3.0 km.
    S.1890, R.1892, E.1895. Still operating. Gauge. 891.

Locomotives. -	Nos.	1-2,	Nyqvist & Holm	2-4-2	of 1890.	⊔⌐

    (Ordered as enclosed but not delivered thus.)

"Rowan" car on the Slussen-Hornstull tramway, Stockholm.
Most Rowan cars were more or less alike in appearance.
                                        Unknown Photographer.

(Upper). Official sketch of Kolomna loco No.13 for Odessa.
(Lower). Kolomna loco with roof condensers for Kieff tramways.
Both from "Locomotives of the Soviet Union" by Rakov.

Courtesy: J. H. Price.

Фиг. 269. Танк-паровоз Коломенского завода с конденсацией пара

ский проспектъ.
ɔektive de Nevski.

С. Петербургъ — St. Pétersbourg

Krauss, Moscow №3

EASTERN
EUROPE
(RUSSIA, POLAND,
GREECE, &c.)

LOCATION OF
STEAM TRAMWAY ●

0 ____ 600 KMS.
0 ____ 400 MILES

BALTIC SEA

TALINN St PETERSBURG
(LENINGRAD)
ESTHONIA

MOSCOW

WABRZEZNO

R U S S I A   AKKERMAN

WARSAWA
OPALENICA
ŁÓDŹ   (U. S. S. R.)
POLAND

KIEFF
(KIEV)

KOŁOMEA ●
(To POLAND.
1919-39)   ODESSA

CASPIAN SEA

BLACK SEA

BAKU

GREECE VOLOS

ATHENS

12. EASTERN EUROPE

1.THE RUSSIAN EMPIRE

Before the 1914-1918 war, the Russian Empire included as well as Russia itself, Finland, the Baltic States (which only enjoyed independence between the two wars) and much of Poland. Finland had no steam tramways and Poland only a few, including some lines in the suburbs of Warsaw, which were really roadside light railways, but used locomotives with enclosed wheels and motion.

We have not been able to trace the existence of any steam tramways in Latvia, or Lithuania, although each had its fair share of narrow gauge light railways, but there was a line at Tallin (Reval) the capital of Esthonia, which one report says was horse operated from 1897 and was certainly worked for passenger traffic with petrol railcars from 1915, but used steam for goods traffic.

Imperial Russia itself, a country of great distances and climatic extremes would appear to be particularly unsuitable for steam tramways, but nevertheless a few did exist in its principal cities. There were early experiments with both "Rowan" cars and conventional enclosed locomotives at St.Petersburg (later Petrograd now Leningrad), followed by regular steam operation on several lines. There were also steam tramways at Moscow, Baku, Kieff and Odessa. The latter is a port and seaside town on the Black Sea coast. It is believed that the Kieff steam tramway, which was a long suburban route, was replaced in 1912 by Hurst Nelson petrol rail-buses but was later converted to broad gauge and electrified as part of the town's electric tramway system in which guise it still flourishes.

The trials at St.Petersburg took place on the route serving the island of Wassili Ostrof, using a Winterthur and a Krauss locomotive. The former was later put to work with other Winterthur machines on the Nevski Suburban Railway which started from the Znamienska Square in front of the main line railway station and ran partly in the street to Alexandrowski and Ruibatskoye. The locomotives which had enclosed wheels and motion also roof condensers pulled trains of double deck carriages.

There was a large tram station in the northern suburb of Novaya Derevnaya, from which trains pulled by the Motala locos ran to Sesttoyetsk & Oserki.

The "Rowan" cars built by Kitson and exported from Great Britain worked on the Poutilov line in the docks area and may also have been double decked.

In this chapter, the titles of undertakings are given with considerable reserve, having in nearly all cases been taken from works of reference in other languages.

Russian Locomotives

As steam tramways were comparatively few and the demand for motive power small, Russian Tramways tended to play safe and followed the example of Western Europe, using the well tried models of the larger manufacturers. Hence we see that Winterthur locomotives were used in the first instance, followed by Krauss and a few Belgian machines. However, subsequently a few came from the Swedish firm of "Motala" and the Russian works at Kolomna built some for Kieff, Odessa and St. Petersburg.

The locomotives required for the Nevski suburban railway at St. Petersburg are described as 0-4-0s with horizontal boilers, very robustly constructed for town work with frequent stops, sharp curves and dust on the roads, therefore they had to have enclosed motion. The first nine machines were supplied by Winterthur and five more came from Kolomna. Those built by the latter for Kieff were not enclosed but had condenser pipes mounted on a frame above the whole locomotive. Those at Odessa were enclosed but had open driving platforms at each end.

Officially, imported locomotives were subject to a very heavy tax, but in the early years, steam tramways were able to claim exemption, presumably because at that time, no Russian builder was producing enclosed locomotives. The following fittings were compulsory - a whistle, a bell, a works plate, enclosed motion if working on the street and a note of the weight, boiler pressure and maximum speed painted on the locomotive. The Kitson cars of the Poutilov line are described as double deck vehicles of the "Thomas" type, seating 32 second class passengers inside and 38 third class passengers outside. They cost £1,480 each.[1]

The passenger cars used on the Nevski line were also double decked seating 22 inside and 18 outside. They ran on two axles and were fitted with hand brakes. Those at Odessa, constructed by Ringhoffer of Prague, appear to have been similar.

2. ROUMANIA

There were three steam tramways in the territory which forms the present state of Roumania. They were all in the Province of Transylvania, which at the time of their inception was in Hungary; the area was ceded to Roumania in 1919. They are therefore, described in the Austro-Hungarian chapter.

3. POLAND

The present state of Poland comprises a large area which was formerly in the Russian Empire, a smaller part in the Austro-Hungarian Empire and other areas which were anexed from Germany, some after the 1914-1918 war and others after the 1939-1945 war. The most important of these was the Silesian Coalfield, whose political boundaries were moved several times as a result of these wars. The area was served by an extensive steam tramway system based on Kattowitz. By the time it came into Polish hands, it had been electrified and much converted from narrow to standard gauge, a process which was continued under the Polish administration. (See German chapter).

There was also an extensive steam tramway and light railway network, built up at the turn of the century, based on Warsaw. Although Warsaw was then in the Russian Empire, most of the locomotives were German, built by Orenstein & Koppel, with enclosed wheels and motion, but the Wilanowa line had a short rack section, on which Winterthur locomotives were used. The gauges were metre, 800 and 750 mm, but after the 1939 war, one of the 800 mm lines was converted to 750, to match other Polish light railways. Over the years the sections within Warsaw were gradually replaced by standard gauge electric tram routes and a number of new standard gauge interurban electric routes were built in the 1920s, to the west of the city. The steam lines which remain, now start from stations in the outer suburbs and have taken on the character of proper light railways. The original locomotives were removed by the Russians in 1915 and were replaced after the war by railway type locomotives built by various German manufacturers. More recently tramway type passenger stock has been replaced by comfortable railway type bogie carriages.

4.GREECE

The capital city, Athens, boasted a steam tramway for many years. It ran from the Academy in the centre of the town to Phaleron on the coast, by way of a long tree lined avenue. It was eventually taken over by the urban tramway company and electrified. Reports that there was another steam tramway to the north of the city are thought to refer to the Attic Railway, a narrow gauge line to Kifisia, which although it had some street running, used heavy railway type locomotives and was eventually replaced by an extension of the underground railway.

Far away to the north, the Thessaly Railway Company, which built a number of metre gauge lines, also laid down a 60 centimetre gauge tramway on the street from Volos to Lochonia in 1896.[2] It shared a semi-reservation in the centre of the main street of Volos on triple mixed gauge track, with a metre gauge line of the same company and a standard gauge branch of the State Railway. The Volos-Lochonia line was extended as a light railway to Mileai in 1903 and ran thus until 1971.

Locomotives

The Athens-Phaleron tramway used orthodox Winterthur and Krauss enclosed engines in both cases the standard model current at the time of purchase. Two Orenstein & Koppel machines appear to have been acquired subsequently in 1908.

On the other hand, the first generation of locomotives for the Volos-Lochonia tramway were four Weidknecht 0-8-0 tank engines with enclosed motion and the cylinders driving the axles through Hagans Patent flexible coupling arrangements, making them in effect 0-4-4-0s. When the line was extended to Mileai, they were replaced by five conventional Belgian 2-6-0 tank engines with large spark-arrester chimneys. Three of these were in use to the end, but for a time there was one of the ex-War Department Baldwin 4-6-0s and some other locomotives about which very little is known.

Passenger Stock

The Athens-Phaleron line used ordinary Belgian type open-platform four wheeled coaches, while the Volos-Lochonia-Mileai line had a fleet of small brown bogie carriages with end platforms. It also had some goods stock.

NOTE. Tramway locomotives used in Russia had works plates usually inscribed with lettering in the Cyrillic alphabet and the Volos-Mileai locomotives had name and works plates in the Greek alphabet. For convenience, they are given here in the Roman alphabet, as nearly equivalent to the original as possible.

This with the tables that follow, concludes the account of Steam Tramways in Europe, apart from Great Britain and Ireland (already covered in Dr. Whitcombe's book). The writer has been unable to trace the existence of any steam tramways in Bulgaria, Finland, Turkey, Albania, the present state of Jugo-Slavia or the islands of Malta, Crete, etc. If any reader has knowledge of steam tramways in any of these countries or elsewhere in Europe and not mentioned here, the writer would be most grateful to hear from them.

Notes

1. See "Aperçu des Chemins de Fer Russes" by A. de Gortschakov, Brussels 1897.
2. See "The Engineer" 22nd June 1894, page 543.
   For drawings of Wiedknecht patent locos, see:-
   "Encyclopedie Theoretique et Practique des Connaissances Civiles et Militaires - Vol. 10 "Traite des Chemins de Fer", G. Ostet, Paris, 1899.

Tubize loco "Tsaggarada" for the Volos-Mileai tramway, Greece.
Tubize Catalogue.   Courtesy: Prof. A. D. De Pater.

Table 12, RUSSIA

1. AKKERMAN. Now called BELGOROD-DNEST ROVSKIY.
   Route   ?
   S.1907, C.   ?   Gauge. 1000.
   Locomotives. -   Nos.   1-2,   Borsig 0-4-0   6668-6669 of 1907.
                              3-7.   Borsig 0-4-0   6879-6883 of 1908.

2. BAKU. (Pferde Eisenbahn Baku) & Russian Equivalent.
   Baku-Sabunchi, 33.0 km.
   H.   ?   S.1888, E.1921,   Still operating. Gauge. 1000.(Now 1524).
   Locomotives. -   Nos.   1-4,   Winterthur 0-4-0 549-552 of 1888.

3. KIEFF. (Worked by J. Teretschenko).
   Kieff-Puscha Vodista, 12.0 km.
   S.1881, P.1921, E.   ?   Still operating. Gauge. 915 (Now 1524).
   Locomotives. -   No.   1,   Winterthur 0-6-0   298 of 1881.
                             2,   Winterthur 0-4-0   220 of 1881.
                           3-?,   Kolomna 0-4-0   ? of ? .

4. MOSCOW. (Société Générale des Chemins de Fer Economiques, Bruxelles).
   Moscow (Butuirskaya Zastava)-Petrovsko Razumovski, (Agricultural Academy), 5.0 km.
   S.1887, E.1923 (part), Still Operating. Gauge. 1000.(Now 1524).
   Locomotives. -   Nos.   1-2,   Krauss   0-4-0 1791-1792 of 1887.
                              3,   Orenstein & Koppel 0-4-0 2900 of 1908.

5. MOSCOW (Title ?).
   Moscow(Kaluzhskaya Zastava)-Vorobevi Gori(Sparrow Hills), 7.0 km. approx.
   H.1874 ?, S.1882, E.1911?, C.   ?.   Gauge 1524.
   Motive Power. -   Two Kitson "Rowan" Cars, T.61-62 of 1882.
                       Three Borsig "Rowan" Cars, 4253-4255 of 1888.
   Locomotives. -   Nos.   1,   Krauss 0-4-0 1633 of 1886.
                              2-3, Krauss 0-4-0 1886-1887 of 1888.
                              4-6, Krauss 0-4-0 1771-1773 of 1887.

6. ODESSA. (Odessa K...... Zheleszti Dorog).
   Odessa (Kulikovo Polé)-Bolshoi Fontan (Great Fountain), 8.5 km.
   S.1880,E.1913 ? Still operating. Gauge.   1000 (Now 1524).
   Locomotives. -   Nos.   I-II,   Krauss 0-6-0   918-919 of 1880.
                              III,   Krauss 0-6-0   1143 of 1882.
                              IV,   Krauss 0-6-0   1496 of 1884.
                              V,   Krauss 0-6-0   1961 of 1888.
                              VI,   Krauss 0-6-0   2510 of 1891.
                       VII, VIII & IX,   Krauss 0-6-0   2818-2820 of 1893.
                       X, IX & XII,   Krauss 0-6-0   3578-3580 of 1895.
                              13,   Kolomna 0-4-0   ?   of 1904.

7. St. PETERSBURG. (Leningrad). (St. Petersburger Strassenbahn)   ?
   (Experimental running on existing horse tramway).
   St. Petersburg-Wassili Ostrof, 5.0 km.
   H.   ?   S.1880-1881 only, E.   ?   Still operating. Gauge. 1524.
   Locomotives. -   No.   1,   Winterthur 0-4-0 191 of 1880.
                             2,   Krauss 0-4-0 863 of 1881.

   Note. - It is reported that Krauss 864 was built to the 1524 gauge, but altered to
            standard gauge for trials at Groningen, Netherlands. Perhaps intended for
            this line   ?

8.   St. PETERSBURG. (Leningrad). (Chemin de Fer de Nevsky Banlieue).
     St. Petersburg(Pl. Znamienska)-Alexandrowski,   10.0 km (approx.).
     St. Petersburg(Pl. Znamienska)-Ruibatskoye,   13.0 km (approx.).
     S.1882, E.1914   ? Still operating. Gauge. 1524.
     Locomotives. -   Nos. 1-3,   Winterthur 0-4-0 293-295 of 1882.
                             4-8,   Winterthur 0-4-0 362-366 of 1884.
                             9,   Winterthur 0-4-0 191 of 1880 ex-No.7. ∵
                           10-12,   Kolomna   0-4-0 1355 - ? of 1892.
                           13-14,   Kolomna   0-4-0 3260-3261 of 1902.

9.   St. PETERSBURG. (Leningrad). (Compagnie des Tramways de Saint Petersbourg).
     St. Petersburg-Novaya Derevnaya, 10.0 km (approx.).
     S.1886, E.   ? Still operating. Gauge. 750. (1524 on electrification).
     Locomotives. -   Nos. 1-8,   Cockerill 0-6-0 1483-1490 of 1886.
                             9-10, Cockerill 0-6-0 1503-1504 of 1887.
                            11-12, Cockerill 0-6-0 1888-1889 of 1895.

10. St. PETERSBURG. (Leningrad). (Chemin de Fer de Poutilov.   ?)
     St. Petersburg-Poutilov, 5.0 km. (approx.).
     S.1883, R.   ? Still operating as railway. Gauge.- 1524.
     Motive Power. -   Nos. 1-2,   Kitson "Rowan" cars, T.61-62 of 1882.

11. St. PETERSBURG. (Leningrad). (Maritime St. Petersburg-Sestroyetsk ?).
     St. Petersburg(Novaya Derevnaya)-Sestroyetsk-Kurort, 25.0 km. approx.
     St. Petersburg(Novaya Derevnaya)-Oserki, *   10.0 km. approx.
     Sestroyetsk-Lisi Nos, (for ferry to Kronstadt)   5.0 km. approx.
     S.1893, R.1914, Still operating as railway. Gauge. 1524.
     Locomotives. -   Nos. 1-10, Kolomna 0-4-0 1389-1398 of 1893.
                            11-16, Motala 0-4-0 159-164 of 1896.
                        (II) 7-10, Motala 0-4-0 186-189 of 1898.

     Note.- *   Partly on the site of the present Pioneer Railway.

ESTHONIA (To Russia in 1945)

1.   TALLINN (Reval). (Tallinna Tramide Valitus). (at first worked by Shipyard company).
     Balti Jaam(Station) - Kopli, 5.0 km.
     H.1888, GS.1915, P.1915 E.1925/47, Still operating. Gauge. 1067(horse)
     750(steam).
     Locomotives. -   Nos. 1-8 ? Orenstein & Koppel 0-6-0 7191-7198 of 1914.

POLAND

1.   GROJEC   See Warszawa.   No. 8.

2.   KATOWICE (Oberschlesische Dampfstrassenbahn G.m.b.H)
     Only steam operated when in Germany. See Kattowitz, Germany No.57.

3.   KOLOMEA. (Kolomear Lokalbahn A.G.).   Worked by State Railways, later (Polskie
     Koleje Panstwowe).   Now in Russia.
     Kolomea-Delatyn   ? 32.7 km.
     S.1896, R.   ? C.   ? Gauge. 1435.
     Locomotives. -   Nos. 031-034, StE.G. 0-6-0, 1822-1825 of 1886.

     Names. -   031-Kniaszdwor, 032-Peczenizyn, 033-Kolomea, 034-Słoboda.

4. ŁÓDŹ. (Lodzer Elektrische Zufuhrbahn).
   Later (Łódźka Waskotorowa Elektriczna Kolejka Dojozdowa).
   (Proposed as steam and three locomotives acquired but opened as electric).
   Łódź (Plac Reymont -Ruda–Pabianice, 15.2 km.
   Ruda - Tuszyn,   19.5 km.
   E.1915, GS.1916, Still Operating. Gauge. 1000.

Locomotives. -	No.	1 ?	Borsig	0-6-0	8963 of 1916.	
		2-3 ?	Henschel	0-6-0	14581-14582 of 1917.	"

5 LODZ. (Lodzer Fabriksbahn).
   (Industrial line using some second-hand tram engines from Frankfurt, Germany).
   Lodz-Koluszki,   30.0 km.
   GS.1895, GD.   ? Still Operating ? Gauge. 1435.

Locomotives. -	No.	1,	Henschel	0-4-0	2510 of 1888. ex-Germany No.46.	
		3-4,	Henschel	0-4-0	2512-2513 of 1888.	"
		6,	Henschel	0-4-0	2806 of 1889.	"
		20,	Krauss	0-6-0	3493 of 1897.	
		22-23,	Krauss	0-6-0	3133-3134 of 1894.	"
		24,	Krauss	0-6-0	3494 of 1897.	"
		30,	Krauss	0-6-0	3132 of 1895 with tender.	
		31,	Krauss	0-6-0	3495 of 1897 " "	" "

6. OPALENICA. (Opalenitzaer Kleinbahn A.G.) In Germany until 1919.
   Now (Polskie Koleje Panstwowe) i.e. "Polish State Railways".
   (A roadside light railway.)
   Opalenica-Trzcianka-Lwowek,   25.0 km.
   Nowy Tomysl-Trzcianka-Duszniki, 28.0 km.
   S.1886   ? Still operating. Gauge. 750.

Locomotives. -	No.		Krauss	0-4-0	1788 of 1886. ?	
		1-2,	Krauss	0-6-2	3304-3305 of 1895.	"
		3-4,	Krauss	0-6-0	4102-4103 of 1899.	"
		5,	?	?	?	
		6,	Henschel	0-6-2	7589 of 1906.	"
		7,	Henschel	0-6-2	8131 of 1907.	"
		8,	Henschel	0-6-2	9489 of 1909.	"
	(II)	5,	Krauss.	0-6-2	6846 of 1916.	"
		9,	Krauss-Maffei	0-6-2	16161 of 1944.	"
		10,	Krauss-Maffei	0-8-2	16162 of 1944.	"

   Names. -   - Opalenica. 1-Kaiserhof, 2-Wonsowo, 3-Neutomischel, 4-Rose.
               5 - ?, 6-Kaiserhof. (II) 5-Turowo. Others not named.

7. WABRZEZNO. (Briesen). (Stadtbahn Briesen), In Germany until 1919.
   Then (Panstwowe Przedsiebiorstwo Komunikacyjne w Wabrzesnie).
   An electric tramway worked temporarily by steam during the 1939-1945 war.
   Wabrzezno Stacji (Station)-Wabrzezno Miasto (Town), 1.06 km.
   E.1898, S.1945 Now D Still operating ?. Gauge. 1435.
   Locomotives. -   Loaned from State Railway's general stock.

8. WARSZAWA. (Warsaw). (Grojec Kleinbahn A.G.) amalgamated with Nos.9 & 11 in 1911,
   then (Towarzystwo Akcynje Warszawskich Drog Zelanstwa Dojazdowych).
   Later became (Warszawskie Koleje Dojazdowe) known in German as (Warschauer Zufuhrbahn).
   From 1949 (Polskie Koleje Panstwowe).
   Warszawa(Plac U. Lubelski)-Iwiczna-Piaseczno-Grojec-Nowe Miasto, 84.0 km.
   Piaseczno-Góra Kalwaria,   17.0 km.
   Grójec-Jasieniec,   7.0 km.
   S.1898, D.1938, Part still operating. Gauge. 1000.

Locomotives. -	No.	1,	Orenstein & Koppel	0-4-0	283 of 1898.	
		2-4,	Orenstein & Koppel	0-4-0	354-356 of 1898.	"
		5-8,	Orenstein & Koppel	0-6-0	394-397 of 1899.	"
		9-10,	Orenstein & Koppel	0-6-0	402-403 of 1899.	"
		11-12,	Orenstein & Koppel	0-6-0	496-497 of 1899.	"

	? 13,	Orenstein & Koppel	0-4-4-0		6157 of 1913.	🔔
	14-15,	Orenstein & Koppel	0-6-0		7212-7213 of 1914.	"
Replacements. -	1-5,	Henschel	0-6-0		13795-13799 of 1916.	🔔
	6 ?	Hanomag	0-6-0		7602 of 1916.	"
	?	Orenstein & Koppel	0-6-0		6931 of 1915.	"
	?	Borsig	0-6-0		8960-8961 of 1916.	"
	?	Borsig	0-6-0		8964-8966 of 1916.	"
	?	Linke Hofmann	0-6-0		1498-1499 of 1917.	"
	?	Maffei	0-6-0		4037-4038 of 1920.	"

9. **WARSZAWA.** (Warsaw), (Kolejka Konna Wilanowska), known in German as (Wilanower Kleinbahn).
From 1911 as No. 8 above. Small part rack operated at first. The Warsaw-Wilanów
section was replaced by a 1435 gauge electric tramway.
Warszawa(Plac U. Lubelski)-Wilanow-Iwiczna, 16, 0 km. (Connecting with No. 8).
S.1895, Part E.1957 (See above), GS.1972, C.1973. Gauge. 800 (to 1000 in 1930s).

Locomotives. -	No. 1,	Orenstein & Koppel	0-4-0		39 of 1895.	🔔
	2,	Orenstein & Koppel	0-4-0	("Wilanow")	60 of 1894.	"
	3-6,	Orenstein & Koppel	0-4-0		89-92 of 1895.	"
	7,	Orenstein & Koppel	0-4-0		137 of 1896.	"
	8,	Orenstein & Koppel	0-4-0		188 of 1897.	"
	11-13,	Winterthur	0-6-0z	(Rack)	1136-1138 of 1898.	🔔
	14,	Winterthur	0-6-0z	"	1306 of 1900.	"
	15,	Orenstein & Koppel	0-6-0		1168 of 1903.	"
	16,	Orenstein & Koppel	0-4-4-0	(Mallet)	1393 of 1904.	"
	17,	Orenstein & Koppel	0-6-0		3735 of 1910.	"
	18,	Orenstein & Koppel	0-4-4-0		5656 of 1912.	"

10. **WARSZAWA.** (Warsaw), (Marki Kleinbahn). From 1939 as No.8.
Warszawa (Stalowa)-Marki-Radzymin, 21.0 km.
S.1900, Part.E.1957, C.1974. Gauge. 800 (to 750 in 1949).

Locomotives. -	Nos.1-2,	Orenstein & Koppel	0-4-0		119-120 of 1896/7.	🔔
	3-4,	Orenstein & Koppel	0-4-0		215-216 of 1897.	"
	5,	Orenstein & Koppel	0-4-0		219 of 1897.	"
	6,	Orenstein & Koppel	0-6-0		294 of 1898.	"
	7,	Orenstein & Koppel	0-6-0		346 of 1898.	"
	8-9,	Orenstein & Koppel	0-6-0		540-541 of 1900.	"
Replacements. -		Henschel	0-6-0		13803-13804 of 1916.	🔔
		Henschel	0-6-0		14562 of 1916.	"
		Orenstein & Koppel	0-6-0		7676-7678 of 1916.	"
		Orenstein & Koppel	0-6-0		8163-8165 of 1916.	"
		Chrzanow	0-6-0		173 of 1928.	"

11. **WARSZAWA.** (Warsaw). (Jablonnabahn) or (Kolejka Jablonna).
Nos. 8, 9 & 11 amalgamated in 1911 as (Warszawskie Koleje Dojazdowe).
Jabłonna-Zeran-Warszawa(Most)-Goclawek-Otwock-Karczew, 46.0 km.
(Replaced by Electric trams Zeran-Warszawa-Goclawek, but steam Otwock-Karczew to 1963).
S.1899, Part E. ? C.1963. Gauge. 800.

Locomotives. -	Nos. 1-6,	Orenstein & Koppel	0-6-0	465-470 of 1899.	🔔
	7,	Orenstein & Koppel	0-6-0	490 of 1900.	"
Replacements. -	? '	Orenstein & Koppel	0-6-0	7849-7850 of 1915.	🔔
	?,	Orenstein & Koppel	0-6-0	7855 of 1916.	"
	?,	Orenstein & Koppel	0-6-0	7881-7885 of 1916.	"
		Schwartzkopff	0-4-0	8461 of ? .	"
		Orenstein & Koppel	0-6-0	10896-10897 of 1925.	"

Note.- 1. Locomotives have been changed around between the above lines and with other
light railways after nationalisation in 1949, but unfortunately we do not have
details.

2. Mileages in Poland based on "Urzedowy Pociagow" timetable 1959/60.

3. During the 1914 war the Germans built a connecting line from Struga on No.10
to Wawer on No.11. It was owned by the latter and lasted until 1923.

GREECE

1. ATHENS. (Athens, Piraeus & Environs Hellenic Tramway Co.) and Greek equivalent.
Later (Elektriki Eteria Metaforon).
Athens(Academy) - Phaleron, 5.0 km. (approx.).
S.1882, E.1909, C.1959. Gauge. 1000.

Locomotives. -

	Nos.				
	1-3,	Krauss	0-4-0	990- 992 of 1882.	⊟
	4-6 ,	Krauss	0-4-0	1124-1126 of 1882.	"
	7-8,	Krauss	0-4-0	1314-1315 of 1884.	"
	9-10,	Winterthur	0-6-0	383-385 of 1884.	"
	11-12,	Krauss	0-4-0	1316-1317 of 1886.	"
	13-14,	Krauss	0-6-0	2148-2149 of 1889.	"
	15,	Krauss	0-6-0	3392 of 1896.	"
	16,	Krauss	0-6-0	3596 of 1897.	"
	17,	Krauss	0-6-0	3808 of 1898.	"
	18-19,	Krauss	0-6-0	4977-4978 of 1903.	"
?	20-21,	Orenstein & Koppel	0-4-0	2853-2854 of 1903.	"

2. VOLOS. (Eteria Sidirodromon Thessalis) i.e. "Thessaly Railway Co."
From 1955 (Sidirodromoi Hellenikou Kratous). i.e. "Greek State Railways".
Built as a tramway in 1896 from Volos to Lochonia and extended as a light railway to
Mileai in 1903. (Triple mixed gauge on the street in Volos).
Volos-Lochonia-Mileai, 28.0 km.
S.1896, R.1903, C.1971. Gauge. 600.

Locomotives. -

	Nos.				
	31-33,	Weidknecht	0-8-0	- - of 1896 (Hagans sys.)	⊟
	34,	Weidknecht	0-8-0	- of 1898 (Hagans sys.)	"
	51-52,	Tubize	2-6-0	1338-1339 of 1903	⊟
	53-55,	Haine St. Pierre	2-6-0	1139-1141 of 1911.	"
? ?		Werd....?	0-4-0	5190-5191 of 1910.	"
?		Baldwin	4-6-0	45010 of 1917. ex. "
				U.S.A. Army.	

Note.- Locomotives were numbered in the Thessaly Railway's general list.
Nos. 52, 54 & 55 eventually became Nos. 101-103 of the State Railways.

Names. -

31-34 not named.

51 - **BOΛOΣ**	52 - **MIΛEA**	53 - **TΣAΓΓAPAΔA**
Volos,	Mileai,	Tsaggarada,

54 - **IAΣOH**	55 - **ΠIΛIOH**	(Baldwin) - **EΛΛI**	5190 - **ΔEMETPIOΣ**
Jason,	Pilion	Elli,	Demetrios,

5191 - **APΓOΣ**
Argos.

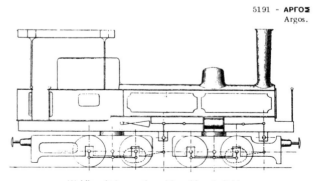

Weidknecht locomotive with rocking shaft drive

Manufacturer's photograph of Motala loco No.14 for the St.Petersburg-Sestroyetsk tramway.
Motala Catalogue.   Courtesy: U.Diehl.

The tram station at Novaya Derevnaya in the outskirts of St.Petersburg, again showing loco No.14 on the left. Note destination boards on lamp standards.
Commercial Postcard.   Courtesy: J.H.Price.

Loco No. 034 "Słoboda" for the "Kolomear Lokalbahn" Poland, with skirting
lifted to expose motion.
Stats Eisenbahn Gesellschaft Catalogue.   Courtesy: A. E. Durrant.

Orenstein & Koppel loco with enclosed wheels and motion in the outskirts of
Warsaw on the Grojec tramway.
Arthur Koppel Catalogue.   Courtesy: late F. Kemper.

APPENDIX 1

TRAMWAY LOCOMOTIVES PRESERVED

It had been my intention to write a short chapter about preserved locomotives, but there have been so many changes over the last few years, that anything would be out of date before it could appear in print. Just a few locomotives put aside for preservation some years ago, have been scrapped because of lack of storage space or funds to transport and restore them. On the other hand, a number of others have been discovered quite recently, hidden in dark corners of operators' depots or in use in some industrial undertaking's yard, perhaps with some of the covering removed, so that they may not have been immediately recognizable as ex-tram engines.

A few of those so discovered have been placed on plinths in the open in the centre of the town they served, but where they would be at the mercy of children and vandals - good hopes are not held out for their future.

The best possible solution would seem to be to restore the locomotive to working order and place it on one of the live working museum lines, where it can be seen by the public, performing the function for which it was built. Such museums do exist in several countries, where ex-tramway locomotives can be seen at weekends, pulling trains of ex-tramway stock, for the enjoyment of enthusiasts, students and the general public.

Outstanding among such musea, are the Hoorn-Medemblik railway in the Netherlands, which has one typical fully enclosed locomotive, and one partly enclosed, both in full working order, with another enclosed loco awaiting restoration. There is also an un-enclosed loco which once worked on a tramway (Westland No. 23) and several ex-tramway carriages for them to pull. Far to the south at Hellevoetsluis, a very short section of the Rotterdam Tramway line has recently reopened, with two of its former locomotives both with enclosed wheels and motion. Across the border in Belgium, there is the "Tramway Touristique de l'Aisne" which operates a weekend service over part of a former Vicinal line, with one ex-Vicinal enclosed loco and some typical ex-Vicinal four wheeled coaches. (Another loco, ex-industry, but of Vicinal design, is believed to be undergoing restoration). ∗

A formerly abandoned long branch line at Brno, Czechoslovakia has been reopened as a museum line, using the undertaking's last remaining steam tram engine, found at the back of the depot, with some appropriate passenger stock. The Chamby-Blonay Museum line in Switzerland has a Winterthur tram engine ex-Bern and one from Italy is undergoing restoration after being dumped at Rimini for many years. Another ex-Bern locomotive, almost identical to the above, is a static exhibition in the Lucerne Transport Museum.

A number of tram-locos are static exhibits in musea in various countries of Europe. For example, there are two different tram-locos in the Leonardesco Museum in Milan, (unfortunately, one is sectionalized). An ex-Grande Banlieue twin-cab loco is in store for the Saint Mandé Museum in Paris and another twin-cab loco from the Isère tramway is now working on a preserved railway in the south of France. Three Vicinal locos are exhibited at Schepdael, Brussels and an ex-Forst tramway loco is displayed in the Transport Museum at Dresden, East Germany.

Several tram-locos which have recently been discovered working in industrial yards are potential subjects for restoration. Some are not always what they purport to be; for example, that displayed in the Prague Technical Museum, does not hail from a Czechoslovakian tramway, but from Salzburg in Austria, but was sold out of service to an industrial establishment in Czechoslovakia. (Similar to those used in Brno and Ostrava).

Note. -* This is ex-Suiker Fabriek Tienen(Tirlemont Sugar-beet Factory) "Albert" Gillain 0-6-0, No. 75 of 1915 (like SNCV Class 18) and there were proposals to restore it as "S. N. C. V. No. 1000" a number which remained blank.

Standard Henschel tram-engine No. 102 of the OEG at Mannheim, now preserved in working order by the operator.

Photo: G. L. Gundry.

APPENDIX 2

BIBLIOGRAPHY

(a) BOOKS

History of the Steam Tram, (Edited by Charles E. Lee),	Dr. H. A. Whitcombe	London	1954
Tramways, their Construction & Working,	D. Kinnear Clark	London	1878
Light Railways at Home and Abroad,	W. H. Cole	London	1899
Light Railways,	W. J. K. Davies	London	1964
French Minor Railways,	W. J. K. Davies	London	1965
Les Tramways Français,	J. Arrivetz	Lyon	1956
Les Tramways Parisiens,	J. Robert	Paris	1959
Histoire des Transports Urbains en France,	J. Robert	Paris	1974
Traité des Chemins de Fer, *	A. Moreau	Paris	1899
Aperçu des Chemins de Fer Russes,	A. de Gortschakov	Brussels	1897
Les Transports en Commun à Genève,	P. Bertrand	Geneva	1963
Der Dampfbetrieb der Schweitzerischen Eisenbahnen,	A. Moser (2nd Edit).	Basel	1967
Die Entwicklung der Basler Strassen - und Uberland Bahnen,	C. Jeanmaire	Basel	1968
Nederlandsche Tramwegen met hun Autobussen,	N. V. T. A.	Amsterdam	1941
Korte Geschiedenis van een Gelders Streekvervoer Bedrijf,	Geldersche Twy.	Doetinchem	1951
Locomotiven der Nederlandsche Tramwegen,	Ir. S. Overbosch	Enschede	1946
Onze Nederlandsche Locomotiven in Word en Beeld,	H. Waldorp	Haarlem	1946
Trams en Tramlijnen, (series of paperbacks),	Prof. H. J. A. Duparc & Others	Rotterdam	1972
Beknopt overzicht van de Nederlandse Spoor en Tramwegbedrijven,	Ir. J. W. Sluiter	Leiden	1961
The Locomotives built by Machinefabriek "Breda",	Prof. A. D. de Pater	Leiden	1970
Die Dampf-Tramway, in Bau und Betrieb,	Joseph Stern	Vienna	1882
Österreichs Strassenbahnen in Wordt und Bildt,	W. Kramer	Vienna	1951
Die Lokomotivfabriken Europas (Locomotive Works of Europe),	J. O. Slezak	Vienna	1966
Strassenbahnen in Wien,	J. O. Slezak	Vienna	1972

Dampftramway Krauss & Comp. in Wien,	A. Laula & K. Sternhardt	Vienna	1974
Krauss Locomotiven, (Works List, etc). (Edited Slezak),	B. Schmeiser	Vienna	1977
Niederösterreichische Südwestbahn,	H. Sternhardt & J. O. Slezak	Vienna	1977
Dampftriebwagen und Gepäkwagen,	A. Horn	Vienna	1972
Zahnradbahnen der Welt, (World Rack Railways),	W. Hefti	Basel	1971
Deutsche Klein - und Privatbahnen, (6 vols)	G. Wolff	Gifhorn	1971
Lokalbahn A. G. München	Dr. H. Burnheim	Gifhorn	1974
Berliner Strassenbahnen	S. Hilkenbach	Berlin	1973
Hanomag Nachrichtung, (Hanomag Catalogue)		Hannover	1925
Bygone Light Railways of Europe	O. W. Laursen	Lingfield	1973
The Minor Railways and Tramways of Eastern Spain,	J. Morley & K. P. Plant	London	1972
The Tramways of Portugal,	J. H. Price	London	1964
Modern Railway Practice,	(Orenstein & Koppel sponsored ?)	Berlin	1913
Locomotives of the Railways of the Soviet Union, (in Russian)	Rakov	Moscow	1960
70 Let Městske´ Dopravy na Ostravsku,	J. Cvik	Ostrava	1964
75 Rokov Mestskej Dopravy v Košiciach,	Official Publication	Kosice	1966
La .Costruzione ed Esercizio delle Tranvie,	A. Viappiani,	Turin	1893
L'Impianto e l'Esercizio dei Tramways ñella Provincia di Milano,	G. Bianchi	Milan	1885
Storia dei Trasporti Italiani, (Series of Books)	F. Ogliari & F. Sarpi	Milan	1961
As Rodas da Capital	V. Callixto	Lisbon	1967

---

1. The full title of this work is:-
    "Encyclopedie Théoretique et Practique des Connaissances Civiles et Militaires" Volume 10 - "Traité des Chemins de Fer", by G. Ostet.

(b) MAGAZINES & PERIODICALS
(various dates for each)

The Engineer,	London
Engineering,	London
Street Railway Journal,	New York
Tramway & Railway World, (Later "Transport World").	London
Light Railway & Tramway Journal, (Later "Electric Railway & Tramway Journal" and finally "Passenger Transport")	London
Modern Tramway,	London
Railway Magazine,	London
Locomotive, Railway Carriage & Wagon Review,	London
Railway & Travel Monthly, (Vol. XVII, 1918, P. 323 "British Locomotives for Overseas Service").	London
Industrial Railway Record, (No. 8 1965, "French Vertical Boilered 0-4-0").	
Industrial Railway Record, (No. 27 1969, "Corpet Louvet locomotives" (Both by K. W. Clingan).	London
Journal of the Institution of Civil Engineers,	London
Journal of the Institution of Locomotive Engineers, (Whitcombe 1937).	London
Stephenson Locomotive Society Journal,	Birmingham
Le Vie du Rail,	Paris
Chemins de Fer Secondaires (now "Chemins de Fer Régionaux et Urbains"),	Paris
Rail et Traction,	Brussels
Rail et Route,	Paris
L'Industrie des Voies Ferrées,	Paris
Stadt Verkehr,	Dusseldorf
Deutscher Eisenbahn Freund,	Dresden
Streek en Stadsvervoer,	Den Haag
Op de Rails,	Amsterdam
Strassenbahn Magazin,	
Italiamodel,	Genoa
Illustrazione Italiana,	Milan
Tren Miniatura,	Madrid
Railway Scene, (No. 2 1968 article on Bad Doberan K. Kieper).	Malmö

(c) OFFICIAL REPORTS & PUBLICATIONS

Ispettorate Generale Ferrovie, Tranvie ed Automobilisti (Annual Reports),	Rome
Ministero dei Trasporti - Statistica (Annual Reports),	Rome
La Société Nationale des Chemins de Fer Vicinaux de Belgique, 1937.	Brussels
Les Chemins de Fer Luxembourgeois, 1950.	Luxemburg

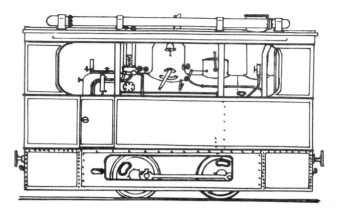

Humboldt Locomotive for uncompleted Duisburg-Meiderich Tramway.
Used at Hohenlimburg, Plettenburg & Altona-Ottensen.

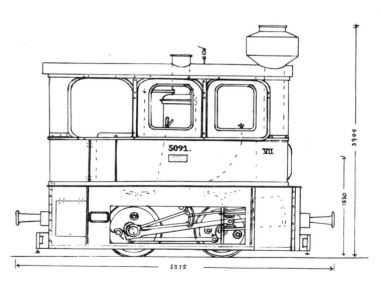

Budapest Locomotive for Brasso, Hungary.

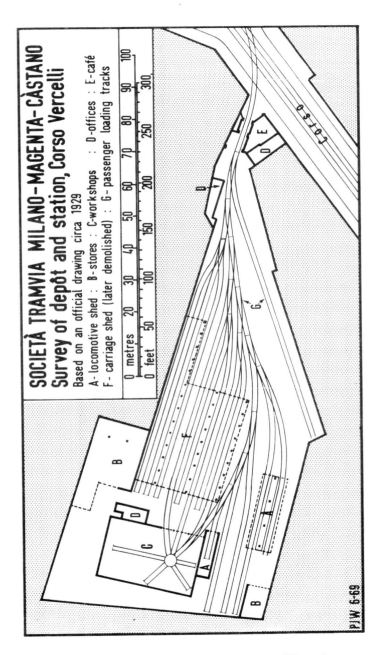

**SOCIETÀ TRAMVIA MILANO-MAGENTA-CÀSTANO
Survey of depôt and station, Corso Vercelli**

Based on an official drawing circa 1929

A- locomotive shed : B- stores : C-workshops   : D-offices : E-café
F- carriage shed (later demolished) : G- passenger loading tracks

0 metres 10   20   30   40   50   60   70   80   90   100
0 feet 50   100   150   200   250   300

PJW 6·69

Opposite: Early Charles Brown type loco built at Winterthur